Founding Republics in France and America

STUDIES IN GOVERNMENT
AND PUBLIC POLICY

Founding Republics in France and America

A Study in Constitutional Governance

John A. Rohr

 University Press of Kansas

By the same author:

Prophets Without Honor: Public Policy and the Selective Conscientious Objector (1971)
Ethics for Bureaucrats: An Essay on Law and Values (1978, 1989)
To Run a Constitution: The Legitimacy of the Administrative State (1986)
The President and the Public Administration (1989)

© 1995 by the University Press of Kansas

Published by the University Press of Kansas (Lawrence, Kansas 66049), which was organized by the Kansas Board of Regents and is operated and funded by Emporia State University, Fort Hays State University, Kansas State University, Pittsburg State University, the University of Kansas, and Wichita State University

Library of Congress Cataloging-in-Publication Data

Rohr, John A. (John Anthony), 1934–
    Founding republics in France and America : a study in constitutional governance / John A. Rohr.
        p.   cm. — (Studies in government and public policy)
    Includes bibliographical references (p.   ) and index.
    ISBN 0-7006-0733-1 (cloth). — ISBN 0-7006-0734-X
(paper)
    1. Administrative agencies—France—History.   2. Separation of powers—France—History.   3. France—Politics and government—1958–
4. France—Constitutional history.   5. Administrative agencies—United States—History.   6. Separation of powers—United States—History.   7. United States—Constitutional history.   I. Title.
II. Series.
JN2725.R65   1995
320.944—dc20   95-31166

British Library Cataloguing in Publication Data is available.

Printed in the United States of America

10 9 8 7 6 5 4 3 2 1

The paper used in this publication meets the minimum requirements of the American National Standard for Permanence of Paper for Printed Library Materials Z39.48–1984.

The vigor of government is essential to the security of liberty . . .

—Publius

The belief that the greatness and power of a nation are products of its administrative machinery alone, is, to say the least, shortsighted; however perfect that machinery, the driving force behind it is what counts.

—Alexis de Tocqueville

For my students who have explored with me
the wonderful ways of our Constitution:

"For after that faith is come,
we are no longer under a schoolmaster."
(Galatians: III, 25)

Contents

Preface

Let us look to America, not in order to make a servile copy of the institutions that she has established, but to gain a clearer view of the polity that will be best for us. . . .

— ALEXIS DE TOCQUEVILLE

Confession is good for the soul. Let me confess at the outset that I am not a comparativist and yet I have written a book in the field of comparative government. Many readers will find this revelation less than shocking, but those familiar with the stern ways of specialization in academe will surely grasp its full import. Having toiled in the fields of public law and public administration for the past quarter-century, I decided to break out of my accustomed ways and to try something different. When an academician wanders off the reservation to which his professional formation has assigned him, a word of explanation is clearly in order. This preface provides that word. It does so in two steps. First, I shall explain why I wrote this book and then why someone might want to read it.

My purpose in writing was to pursue an idea that struck me as I was finishing an earlier book—*To Run A Constitution: The Legitimacy of the Administrative State.*[1] In that book I argued that the friends of the modern administrative state would do well to ground their arguments for their favored institutions in the American constitutional tradition in general and, in particular, in the principles of government salient at the time of the founding of the Republic. Underlying my argument was the conviction that the work of the founding fathers has always held the normative high ground in American politics and government. Contemporary administrative institutions labor under a certain illegitimacy because their intellectual origins are traceable, not to the framers of the constitution, but to the anglophile civil service reformers of the late nineteenth century. These reformers—notably Woodrow Wilson and Frank Goodnow—considered the framers' principle of separation of powers a hopeless anachronism, which they rejected in favor of parliamentary principles. This, in turn, underlay their cardinal point on the distinction between politics and administration—a point that has both defined the academic field of public administration and thrown it into disarray.

Having worked through this argument, I began to wonder what might happen in a country wherein the normative foundations were the opposite of those of the United States; that is, a country in which administrative institutions embodied the abiding norms while constitutions were unstable. France, of course, is the obvious example. One of the reasons French administrative institutions are so fully developed is that there has been such instability at the top: at least thirteen constitutions since the Revolution of 1789.[2] Administration provided the stability in day-to-day French life amidst the turmoil of recurrent constitutional crises.

My musings led to earnest study of the founding of the Fifth Republic under the leadership of Charles de Gaulle in 1958. Fortunately, the publication of a massive three-volume collection of documents on the 1958 founding coincided with my new-found interest.[3] Much of the material contained in these weighty tomes had never been published before. Clearly, they are comparable to Max Farrand's monumental work on the records pertinent to the framing of the Constitution of the United States; and in reading these documents, I found some fascinating points of comparison between the two countries.

In writing this book, I had in mind an audience composed primarily of American students, practitioners. and professors of public administration—the same group of people who read *To Run a Constitution*. I hope to deepen their knowledge of the relationship between constitutionalism and administration in the United States by examining the same relationship in France. Specialists in the field of comparative politics have always said that one can learn about one's own country by studying another country. They are fond of quoting Kipling's line: "And what should they know of England who only England know?"[4] As a noncomparativist, I once viewed this claim with some skepticism. It reminded me of my high school Latin teachers who used to tell us that the study of Latin "will improve your mind." It seemed to me they were emphasizing a by-product because they doubted the inherent value of the product itself. Now I know better—both with regard to the Latin teachers and to the comparativists. By studying French constitutionalism, I have deepened my own appreciation of the American Constitution and have come to see it in a new light. In the pages that follow, I hope to share these insights with my colleagues in public administration, who received *To Run a Constitution* so generously.

It is possible that comparativists, too, will find this book of some interest precisely because I present enhanced knowledge of the United States as *the primary purpose* of my study of France. That is, such knowledge is not merely a happy by-product of my study. My choice of topics in French constitutionalism and administration was determined by what might illuminate American constitutionalism and administration, rather than by what might objectively be of the greatest importance in understanding France itself. Specialists in the comparative field would surely resist undertaking a study with such a purpose in mind, because it would necessarily present a distorted view of French politics. The French do not conduct their affairs for the edification of American observers. As a noncomparativist, however, I may perhaps claim a certain license that comparativist professionals would deny to one another.

All this exacts a price which candor compels me to acknowledge. To follow through on my approach, I have reluctantly set aside serious examination of unemployment, immigration, and a seemingly endless string of scandals in the illegal financing of political campaigns, despite the enormous importance of these matters in contemporary France. Even in the strictly administrative area, I decided to forgo a discussion of the dreadful "tainted blood" scandal wherein high-ranking medical officers in the Ministry of Health knowingly distributed blood to hemophiliacs that was HIV-infected. The marked attention this scandal has received in the American press amply testifies both to its importance and to its horror.[5] I would have devoted considerable attention to it, had my purpose been to present a comprehensive analysis of contemporary French administration. Since, however, my purpose is quite other, I have set this disgraceful incident aside, because of my conviction that French administration yields better examples than the tainted blood scandal for Americans to study France in order to reflect upon constitutionalism and administration in their own country. These "better examples" fill the pages that follow.

Constitutional studies are salient today in the field of public administration. Constance Horner, the former director of the Office of Personnel Management, has spoken of the need for "constitutional literacy" on the part of career civil servants. David Rosenbloom and James Carroll have authored a textbook on "constitutional competence" for public administrators. Phillip Cooper's textbook on administrative law raises constitutional issues in virtually every chapter. My own book on ethics in public administration argues that normative principles of public service ethics are grounded in the oath to uphold the Constitution of the United States. The May-June (1993) issue of *Public Administration Review* has a thirty-page symposium on what some authors call "the Constitutional School" of public administration. Major journals in the field regularly feature substantive articles on constitutional law and history.[6]

One principal reason for the current interest in constitutionalism in the public administration field is that the *state* has been rediscovered in the broader revival of institutional studies in political science. Because so many public administration scholars have been trained as political scientists, it is only natural that the trend in one field should influence the other. Moreover, students of public administration are often practitioners. Consequently, they bring to the study of institutions not only the intellectual enthusiasm of the political scientist but an emotional commitment as well. I say this based on over twenty-five years of teaching public administration and on hundreds of hours dedicated to public management training. I share this emotional commitment. I experience a genuine delight in observing and recounting the richly complex interaction between the elaboration of a written normative text and its external expression in governmental institutions. The delight is doubled when I study two great nations similar enough to yield comparisons that are meaningful and yet sufficiently different to make the comparisons interesting. This book is, above all, an effort to share this delight with my reader.

Although this book is intended primarily for American students of public administration, I hope many of their French counterparts will read it as well. I am deeply indebted to the many French professors, students, civil servants, and citizens who received me so graciously throughout the fourteen months I spent in a France during the past five years. Although I can never repay this personal debt, I can hope that French readers who pick up this book will learn something about their own country by seeing how an outsider analyzes what is so familiar to them. I also hope that some French students, professors, and practitioners of public administration will accept my invitation in Chapter 7 to engage in a Franco-American dialogue on professional ethics based on salient legal principles in the two countries.

OVERVIEW OF THE TEXT

The first chapter of this book introduces the American reader to the principles and practices in French public administration that he or she must understand in order to grasp the arguments presented in the subsequent chapters. It also introduces constitutional highlights from the history of the Fifth Republic that are pertinent to the discussions in the rest of the book. Neither of these introductions is comprehensive. The first does not provide a general review of French administration, nor does the second offer an overview of the constitutional history of the Fifth Republic. My limited topics were carefully selected for the purposes of this book alone. Readers interested in fuller discussions of either French administration or constitutionalism during the Fifth Republic will find an abundant literature readily available in English.[7] To refresh the reader's memory, Chapter 1 closes with a brief review of the familiar story of the founding of the American Republic in 1787.

Chapter 2, "French Constitutionalism and Administration," is essentially a second and more specialized introductory chapter. My treatment of French administration in Chapter 1 is brief because most American students of public administration already have a general knowledge of the main characteristics of the French administrative system, which is well-known throughout the world. The same is not true with regard to the text of the Constitution of the Fifth Republic and its relationship to public administration. Hence, Chapter 2 presents the specific textual information readers will need in order to follow the arguments in Chapters 3 through 7.

The next three chapters examine the work of the the framers of the French Constitution of 1958 and of the American Constitution of 1787 from the viewpoint of the classic tripartite division of executive, legislative, and judicial power. In these chapters, the American custom of listing the legislative power before that of the executive yields to the Fifth Republic's emphasis on the primacy of executive power—a matter of no small interest to students of public administration.

Chapter 3, "The Executive Power," stresses the radical difference between the offices of the prime minister and the president of the Republic as they were presented by the framers of the Constitution of 1958 and as they developed in the history of the Fifth Republic. Briefly, the office of the president of the Fifth Republic, like that of the president of the United States, developed into a far more democratic institution than the framers had originally envisioned. In France, this came about as a result of an irregular constitutional amendment mandating direct election of the president and abolishing an electoral college— a rather surprising development in view of France's unhappy experience with a popularly elected president at the time of the short-lived Second Republic (1848–1851). The American presidency was democratized by other means, including the emergence of nominating conventions and the development of a two-party system at odds with the framers' intent.

Chapter 4 addresses the legislative power. Traditionally, French republicanism had always been associated with parliamentary government. But General de Gaulle, with considerable justification, considered Parliament the chief cause of the political weakness that had brought France to the brink of civil war during the Algerian crisis of 1958. De Gaulle wanted to strengthen the executive at the expense of Parliament, but his problem was how to do this without fatally compromising the principles of French republicanism. Late-eighteenth-century Americans faced a similar problem in their efforts to establish a more powerful executive despite the widespread popular view that executive power constituted a vestige of monarchy and therefore was the mortal enemy of republicanism. The framers in both countries made similar arguments to defend their executive innovations as being consistent with the spirit of authentic republicanism. Chapter 4 also examines the constitutional constraints each country puts on legislators' accepting executive appointments, although these constraints were originally imposed for very different reasons. The chapter closes with a detailed and somewhat technical discussion of the relationship between statutory law and administrative regulation in the two countries. The American federal legislative veto, which the U.S. Supreme Court found unconstitutional in 1983, is compared in some detail with French constitutional provisions intended to enhance the government's rule-making powers.

Chapter 5, "The Judicial Power," focuses on the "Constitutional Council"—an innovation of the Fifth Republic. This council, empowered to declare acts of Parliament unconstitutional, represents a dramatic departure from the long-standing French rejection of anything suggesting "government by judges." Shortly after the death of General de Gaulle, the Constitutional Council boldly conferred powers on itself that strain the text of the Constitution and thereby invite comparison with the great decision of the Supreme Court of the United States in *Marbury v. Madison*. The final section of Chapter 5 examines the relationship between administrative law and constitutional law. In the United States, administrative law has always been in tutelage to constitutional law, but in France the experience has been just the opposite. The Constitutional Council has frequently drawn on the jurisprudence of the highest administrative court in France, the Council of State, for its major rulings. This is eloquent testimony to the power and prestige of administration in the French political culture.

Chapter 6, "Publius and the Gaullists," compares and contrasts substantive arguments and rhetorical devices used by the Gaullists and by Publius (the pseudonymous author of *The Federalist Papers*) in defending their respective constitutions. Neither, for example, disdains to use political blackmail: "the constitution or civil war" for Publius, and "me or chaos" for General de Gaulle. At a more serious level, Publius's understanding of separation of powers is contrasted with that of the Gaullists. Particular attention is given to some marked similarities in the ideas of Publius and of Michel Debré, a close associate of General de Gaulle who took the lead in drafting the text of the Constitution of the Fifth Republic.

Chapter 7, "Administrative Law and Normative Dialogue," calls for a Franco-American dialogue on administrative ethics based on the "regime values" revealed in fundamental legal principles in France and the United States.[8] The Council of State—a particularly interesting institution that serves as both an administrative body and the highest administrative court in France—receives particular attention for its truly outstanding work in protecting individual rights. Whereas the previous chapters looked back toward republican foundings, Chapter 7 looks forward to normative international discussions among public administrators.

Chapter 8 concludes the book by reviewing, highlighting, and extending its major arguments.

The four appendices are not mere decorations. Indeed, to follow the arguments in this book, the reader must refer to them frequently. This is especially true of sections that present close textual analysis of the constitutions of the two countries. I have included these appendices in the hope that the careful reader will proceed with one hand in the back of the book in order to examine the appropriate texts as the need arises. I recommend that the reader peruse the four appendices before beginning Chapter 1, in order to get a general sense of the main differences between the French and the American constitutions.

Throughout the book, I refer by name to the many participants in the drafting of the Constitution of the Fifth Republic, even though most of these names are unknown to nearly all American readers. I do this for the convenience of French readers and of Americans who specialize in French studies.

Each chapter of this book begins with a brief quotation from Alexis de Tocqueville. I rely on de Tocqueville first and foremost because he was a wise man whose writings have enriched my life. I rely on him also because he is, in a certain sense, the "patron saint" of this book. I say this because I believe that I follow his example when I write about France in order to help my fellow Americans understand their own country better. He did the same for his countrymen in writing *Democracy in America*. As he tells his French readers in the introduction to his great work, "It is not, then, merely to satisfy a curiosity, however legitimate, that I have examined America; my wish has been to find there instruction by which we may ourselves profit."[9] Whenever I wavered in my belief that one could learn about one's own country by studying a foreign one, de Tocqueville's example inspired me to carry on.

At a technical level, I must warn the reader about a troublesome expression in French law: *le commissaire du gouvernement*, which I have translated as "the representative of the government." Unfortunately, this expression is used in two very different senses. It can mean, as the term suggests, one who represents the interests of a governmental ministry in one of several types of nonjudicial proceedings, usually (but not exclusively) at the Council of State.[10] But it can also refer to an officer in a judicial proceeding before the Council of State who, despite the misleading title, does not function as an advocate on behalf of the government; this person's duty is to explain the law and the facts of a case to administrative judges and to recommend an appropriate decision.[11]

To clarify the type of "representative of the government" involved in any particular instance, I point out the inappropriateness of the title whenever it is applied to someone who is performing a neutral role in a judicial setting. If no comment is made, the "representative of the government" can be assumed to be doing what his title suggests.

Finally, let me add a word on evaluating the administrative systems in the two countries. In casual conversations in both France and the United States, persons familiar with the nature of my work often asked me which country had the better administrative organization. Their tone of voice made it unmistakably clear that they fully expected me to say that the country that was not their own had the better system. Indeed, I sometimes had the impression that many of them harbored this expectation because they could not imagine any country could be run as badly as their own. Their loaded question was, of course, only a straw in the wind—indeed, in the hurricane—of the world-wide delight in bashing bureaucrats.

When I dodged their question, as I always did, their disappointment was patent. They were not in the least appeased by my feeble protests that administrative systems were not like the Davis Cup and that since each system plays a different role in its own constitutional order, one cannot be judged simply better or worse than the other.

I mention this in the hope that the reader will forgive me for not making an overall assessment on the administrative systems in the two countries. This does not mean, however, that I have suspended my critical powers throughout this book. On the contrary, I do pass judgment on certain institutions and practices in both France and the United States, but only ad hoc and not globally. I hope the reader will find such judgments are supported by the evidence I present.

Blacksburg, Virginia
15 September 1994

Acknowledgments

Several sections of this book rely upon writings of mine that have been published elsewhere. I am grateful for the permissions I have received to make use of the following publications:

> *The President and the Public Administration* (Washington, D.C.: American Historical Association, 1989).
> "Ethical Issues in French Public Administration: A Comparative Study," *Public Administration Review* 51 (July–August, 1991): 283–297.
> "French Constitutionalism and the Administrative State," *Administration and Society* 24 (August 1994): 224–58.
> "Executive Power and Republican Principles at the Founding of the Fifth Republic," *Governance* 7 (April 1994): 113–34.

In writing a book, the most pleasant moment comes at the end, when one looks back over the years of hard work and recalls with gratitude the men and women whose generous support and cooperation made it possible.

My thanks go first and foremost to Terence Marshall of the University of Paris X–Nanterre who read the entire manuscript with painstaking care, detected more errors than I care to admit, and offered countless suggestions to strengthen my work. I am grateful to Terence and to his wife, Annie, for their gracious hospitality on so many occasions and for the evenings of enlightening conversation on French government, law, and politics in the warmth of their home.

David Rosenbloom of the American University also read the entire manuscript and strengthened it considerably with his customary constitutional insights, sound judgment, and zero tolerance for academic nonsense. My thanks to him.

Substantial portions of the manuscript were read by Phillip Cooper of the University of Kansas, William Safran of the University of Colorado, and Alain Laraby of the Paris law firm of S.C.P. Robert Collins et Associés. My thanks to these gentlemen for improving the quality of this book by their incisive criticisms. I am sure it would be a far better book had I the wit and energy to follow all their recommendations.

As a Fulbright research scholar in 1990, I received substantial financial support and professional encouragement from the *Commission franco-américaine d'échanges universitaires et culturelles*. During my Fulbright period, I had the good fortune of affiliating with the *Institut d'Etudes Politiques de Paris ("Sciences Po")* at the kind invitation of Yves Mény. That my indebtedness to Professor Mény goes far beyond his thoughtful invitation is abundantly clear from the frequency with which I cite his prolific writings throughout this book.

Additional financial support from the Lynde and Harry Bradley Foundation enabled me to return to France in 1992 and 1993 to resume my work. During these sojourns I had the privilege of residing in the community of scholars at *Les Fontaines* in Chantilly. I have fond memories of many stimulating conversations with students and scholars at that marvelous *centre culturel*. My thanks in particular to the Jesuit fathers who created and administer *Les Fontaines* and to Sister Adeline Asfour for making it possible for me to stay there.

While residing in France, I had the opportunity to interview four men who had actively participated in the establishment of the Fifth Republic in 1958: Jean Foyer, François Goguel, François Luchaire, and Georges Vedel. I am grateful to these truly venerable gentlemen for sharing with me their recollections and their profound insights into the great events in which they took part.

In trying to understand French law and administration, I received invaluable help in extended interviews with countless academicians and practitioners at all levels of French government. I cannot acknowledge all here by name because the list would be far too long. I would be remiss, however, if I failed to acknowledge explicitly the following persons whose wise comments and encouragement were indispensable: Jean-Paul Costa of the *Conseil d'Etat;* Marie-Christine Meininger, Jacques Ziller, and Alain Claisse of *Institut International d'Administration Publique;* Lucille Mariotte and Didier Bargas of the *Direction générale de l'administration et de la fonction publique;* Frédéric Périer of the *Commission des opérations de bourse;* and Gérard Conac of the faculty of law at the University of Paris I.

Since nearly all my interviews were conducted in French, I needed a great deal of help to develop my modest skills in speaking that challenging but rewarding language. Help came from many quarters. When I resided in Paris it came from Ruth Rosenblatt and during my stay in Chantilly from Jeanne-Marie Bouvier. Four present and former colleagues in the department of foreign languages at Virginia Polytechnic Institute permitted me to attend their stimulating classes in French language and literature. I thank Lloyd Bishop, Carmen Durrani, Yves Falck, and Richard Shryock for extending this professional courtesy. While residing in the United States, I sought out and found several French students—most of them engineering students at Virginia Polytechnic Institute—who were willing to help me in my French conversation. These weekly meetings were enormously helpful to me, and I remain most grateful to Hélène Lecaudey, Vincent Dieudonné, Hugues Maltère, Frédéric Giraud, Marc Tricard, Raphaël Martin, and Anne-Laure Doutriaux for teaching me so much about their language and their country.

I completed much of the work for this book in libraries and therefore wish to thank the many librarians who helped me so generously. I refer primarily to the competent and obliging librarians and staff at Virginia Polytechnic Institute and also to the librarians at the *Institut d'Etudes Politiques de Paris*, the *Institut International d'Administration Publique*, the Library of Congress, and the documentation center at the French Embassy in Washington.

My colleagues at the Center for Public Administration and Policy were unstinting with their time, their advice, and (most importantly) their encouragement throughout the long years I worked on this book. Jody Bolen and Cheryl Albig of the center's staff and Monisha Murthi, my graduate assistant, provided invaluable technical support in the preparation of the manuscript. I am particularly grateful to James F. Wolf, the center's distinguished director, who practices the sound administration the rest of us preach.

A most heartfelt word of thanks is due to my students at Virginia Tech's Center for Public Administration and Policy, where I have taught for the past fifteen years. Their dedication to public service has been a constant inspiration to me. Their hard work and intellectual curiosity make teaching them a joy. Above all, however, I thank them for the unfailing tolerance—and at times even the enthusiasm—they have shown me as I have pursued my bookish musings in their midst. Their thoughtful reflections on the Constitution of the United States make me feel I am doing something worthwhile with my life. No small gift that. As a token of my gratitude, I dedicate this book to them.

The final word is reserved for Kathy, my beloved wife of twenty-three years, and for my dear sons, Paul and Mark, who have grown tall and strong as they reach man's estate. Thank you for being who you are.

1

Introduction

Since '89 the administrative system has always stood firm amid the debacles of political systems. . . . For though in each successive revolution the administration was, so to speak, decapitated, its body survived intact and active. The same duties were performed by the same civil servants, whose practical experience kept the nation on an even keel through the worst political storms.

— ALEXIS DE TOCQUEVILLE

The purpose of this chapter, as its title suggests, is simply to introduce the reader to the principal ideas and institutions that provide the substance of this book. I shall do this in four steps: (1) a short case study presenting concretely a particularly rich interaction between constitutional principles and administrative institutions in contemporary France; (2) a brief overview of the constitutional highlights in the thirty-six-year history of the Fifth Republic; (3) a rapid survey of the salient features of the French administrative system; and (4) by way of comparison, a summary review of the main points in the familiar story of the drafting of the Constitution of the United States.

To keep this chapter within manageable bounds, I have taken "Occam's razor" to the many and varied persons, organizations, and events presenting themselves as likely candidates for inclusion. My canon of selection on what to include and what to exclude is based less on the inherent importance of certain persons, organizations, and events in France and the United States than on their importance for illuminating the specific theme of this book.

A CASE STUDY

The new school year was off to a bad start. It was only mid-September and already Ernest Chenière, the principal of Gabriel-Havez secondary school in Creil, a dreary Paris suburb, had a serious crisis on his hands. Perhaps he pondered the irony of a political crisis arising in 1989, the very year in which his countrymen were trying to overcome historic tensions by celebrating the bicentennial of the French Revolution. Ironic or not, the crisis was very real and threatened to divide the citizens of Creil into warring camps. The unlikely protagonists of the unfolding drama were three Muslim girls—two fourteen-year-olds, Samira Saidani and Leila Achaboun, and thirteen-year-old Fatima Achaboun, Leila's sister. These girls, with the obvious backing of their parents, insisted upon wearing veils to cover their heads while attending classes. The scarf or veil (a *foulard* in French and in Arabic a *hidjeb*) witnessed to their Muslim faith and their adherence to an interpretation of the Koran forbidding women to appear in public with their heads uncovered. Mindful of the French principle of separation of church and state, Ernest Chenière saw his duty and he did it. He forbade the girls to wear the veil and threatened them with expulsion if they disobeyed. For him the issue was quite simple. The secular character of the French public school system prohibited students and teachers alike from displaying their religious beliefs. Chenière believed that the traditions and laws of the Republic left no doubt in such matters. Indeed, the Constitution itself proclaimed France "a Republic, indivisible, *secular,* democratic and social." (Emphasis added.) The public school was no place to flaunt one's religious beliefs.

His prohibition had the predictable effect of causing an uproar in the school, where a majority of the students was Muslim, and in the community at large. Angry parents, unhappy students, and aggressive lawyers were frequent but unwelcome guests in Chenière's beleaguered office. He seemed particularly bothered by the lawyers who he believed were encouraging the parents and the children to make trouble for him—"ambulance chasers" intent upon "stirring up litigation"—an American in Chenière's position might have called them. Representing the Federation of Muslim Organizations in France and the Union of Islamic Organizations, these men were eyed suspiciously by Chenière and his staff. "These two guys," he remarked, "did not look at all like ayatollahs. No beard, no look of the visionary. On the contrary, they were very smartly dressed with their attaché cases and all."[1] His discomfort waxed mighty during one particular discussion in his office. As Chenière tells it, there was a long silence during which "I heard a funny noise coming from one of the attaché cases. I understood at once. It was a tape recorder rewinding. They had me on tape!" From that moment on Chenière was convinced the whole affair was being orchestrated by the lawyers to set up some sort of test case.

This impression was reinforced when a compromise he had worked out with the girls and their parents fell apart. Both sides had agreed that the girls would not wear their veils in the classroom, provided they could wear them in an open-air courtyard on the school premises. Gym classes were held out of doors, but the physical education teacher would not allow the girls to run and jump with veils on their heads. The girls maintained this prohibition broke the agreement and they resumed wearing their veils in class. This, in turn, led to their expulsion. By mid-October, *l'affaire du foulard* ("the veil affair") had won national attention. Similar incidents were reported at Marseille, Montpelier, Avignon, and Poissy. The Islamic community was not alone in defending the rights of young women to express their religious beliefs by wearing a veil in a public school. Although the Constitution of the Fifth Republic proclaimed the secular character of the French State, jurists reminded zealous school officials that the same constitution proclaimed that the Republic "shall respect all beliefs." The Jewish community watched the unfolding drama with considerable interest because of its long-standing objection to the French tradition of holding classes on Saturday mornings. Albert Cardinal Decourtray, Archbishop of Lyons, entered the fray with the sober reminder that "we must not, under the pretext of secularism, chase God out of every public expression in society."[2]

The religious issue was complicated by the feminist argument that the veil was really a symbol of the subjection of women in those quarters of the Muslim community where the right of girls to cover their heads in school was most vigorously defended. For the feminists, the real issue was not the religious liberty of the girls but their fathers' and elder brothers' desire to perpetuate their traditionally subordinate role. The Achaboun sisters indirectly supported this charge in an interview with a reporter for the popular newsweekly *Le Nouvel Observateur*. The interview revealed the girls' narrow horizons; they never went to movies, to swimming pools, or on trips sponsored by their school. They seldom watched television. When asked if they would like to marry one day, they laughed and said that in their community marriages are arranged, but then they confided to the reporter that they would like to be able to choose a husband some day.[3]

The feminist argument proved particularly divisive on the Left of the political spectrum. In the classic church-state battles that have bedeviled France since the time of the Revolution, leftists have invariably sided with the forces of secularism against the conservatives who have traditionally been more sympathetic to maintaining an important role for the Catholic church in French life. Ordinarily, this would put the Left on the side of religious liberty, but the present case had nothing to do with the Catholic church. Here the Left's customary preference for religious liberty was at war both with its secularism and with its historic commitment to the rights of women. As secularists, leftists tended to support hard-line school principals like Ernest Chenière; as feminists, they deplored the *foulard* as a symbol of male oppression. These considerations pointed toward a policy of severity toward the young girls, but how could such a policy be squared with the principle of religious liberty? Since a Socialist government was in power at this time, the divisive issue reached the highest officers of the State.

Further complicating the issue was the exceedingly troublesome problem of immigration, which ran the gamut of French opinion from the far Left, through moderates of all persuasions, to the far Right. Islam was the second largest religious community in France, far surpassing the Protestant and Jewish communities. An unpleasant but telling joke circulating in France at the time wisecracked that if Islam is the second largest religious belief in France, anti-Islamic sentiment is the largest belief.

For the most part, the remarkable surge in the Islamic population in France was due to relatively recent immigration patterns. In the postwar period, many Muslims came to France to fill a temporary need for manual laborers in positions most French nationals disdained. Although the new workers tended at first to be men who came alone, their families—often very large families—soon joined them. Unlike other immigrants to France, Muslims tended to remain aloof from French culture and society, preferring to maintain intact their own culture which centered primarily on the mosque. This tendency was reinforced by a certain discomfort many Frenchmen felt in the presence of Muslims, which at times was grounded in a high-minded concern for the distinctive cultural integrity of the nation, but, all too frequently, was nothing more than subtle racism. These circumstances contributed mightily to the importance "the veil affair" assumed. Ernest Chenière may have been correct in maintaining that it was illegal to wear religious symbols in a public school; if so, enforcement had been spotty and irregular. As a matter of fact, prior to the *foulard* crisis, Christian children had occasionally displayed crosses in school and Jewish children had done the same with the star of David.[4] Their actions passed unnoticed. Hence, more than a hint of discrimination accompanied the efforts to enforce whatever legal prohibitions there might have been against wearing religious symbols in public schools.

All these conflicting passions surfaced in what was rapidly becoming a national crisis over the headgear of the three girls from Creil and their counterparts throughout France. Clearly, the government had to act. The minister of education, Lionel Jospin, affirmed the importance of maintaining the secular character of the public schools, but muddied the waters by tempering this affirmation with the soothing assurance that if, after consultation between the school officials and the parents, the girls continued to wear the veil in the classroom, they would not be expelled. "The French public school," said the minister, "is made to educate and to integrate and not to reject."[5]

This Januslike utterance satisfied no one, least of all harried principals like Ernest Chenière, who seemed to be learning to enjoy his newfound role as champion of the secular integrity of the public schools. Meanwhile, the crisis had escalated to the point that by early November the media were reporting *foulard* incidents in as many as one-fourth of all the public schools in France.[6] With the approval of Prime Minister Michel Rocard, Jospin called upon the Council of State for legal advice on how to handle the potentially explosive situation.

The Council of State *(Conseil d'Etat)* plays a double role in French governance. On the one hand, it is the highest administrative court in the land and, on the other, it is constitutionally empowered to render advice to the government on matters that often go beyond questions of strict legality. Thus, it is at once a judicial body and an advisory council, an institutional arrangement that invites an overlap of law and policy. In response to Education Minister Jospin's questions, the Council of State, acting in its advisory capacity, maintained that Muslim girls could wear veils to school without violating the principle of secularism in public education. This finding, however, was balanced by the council's further clarification that the veils could be prohibited if they were worn in such a way as "to constitute an act of pressure, provocation, proselytizing or propaganda" that would offend either the liberty or the dignity of other members of the educational community. They also could be banned if they seriously impeded the customary routine of a public school. Finally, the council upheld the discretionary authority of principals to expel students who refused to obey directives not to wear veils in situations in which they had been found to be disruptive.

Armed with this advice, Education Minister Jospin issued an instruction to local education officers implementing the principles announced by the Council of State. The tone of the document suggested that the first task of the local principals was to meet with Muslim parents to try to persuade them not to exercise whatever right they might have to send their daughters off to school with veils on their heads. From the government's point of view, this was clearly the ideal solution to the problem and one that, for the most part, was successful. Commentators referred to the decision of the Council of State and to the education minister's subsequent instruction as meaning essentially "return to sender." That is, the ball was tossed back into the court of local principals, who now had broad discretionary powers to settle the problem as local circumstances would suggest.

The *foulard* debate has by no means disappeared from French public life; but it no longer commands the attention it had in the fall of 1989.[7] When last heard from in December 1989, the Achaboun sisters, whose family had come from Morocco, had agreed to lower their veils to their shoulders; but only after the Moroccan ambassador to France had urged them to do so. Samira Saidani held out longer, but she too had capitulated by the end of January 1990. Her father, however, was reported to have brought a defamation suit against Ernest Chenière for unflattering comments in an article the principal had submitted to a local newspaper.[8] And Ernest Chenière himself? He now holds a seat in parliament, where, as a prominent member of the conservative Rally for the Republic party, this man of color, a native of the overseas department of Guadeloupe, continues to defend the secular character of the public schools.[9]

An American following these events would surely experience a sense of déjà vu. Just as the French constitutionally affirm the secular character of their Republic, on the one hand, and its commitment to "respect all beliefs," on the other, so Americans find in the First Amendment to their Constitution a profound tension between the prohibition against establishing religion and the guarantee of its free exercise. The former suggests a certain official coolness toward or distance from religion, and the latter just the opposite. In the United States this tension has become manifest in the abiding discontent with the Supreme Court's effort of some thirty years to banish prayer and Bible reading from the public schools. Friends of the ban repair to the nonestablishment clause, while its foes invoke "free exercise" to nibble away at the ban's outer edges in order to reduce its scope.

Americans will also understand the French failure to reach closure on the *foulard* affair. There was nothing definitive in the "solution" that permitted the Muslim girls to wear the veil to school while counseling administrators to try to talk them out of doing so. No more satisfying, however, is the American resolution of the religious tension, which has led to bewildering congeries of mandates and prohibitions, defying principled analysis. In the troublesome area of public funding for parochial schools, for instance, we find that state governments may "not supply periodical magazines, maps, photographs, and charts to church schools"; but they may "give textbooks to children in religious schools" and may partially reimburse parents "for the cost of education in religious schools, through a system of tax benefits."[10]

The Supreme Court of the United States has never faced the precise issue that arose in the *foulard* affair, namely, whether a student may wear a religious symbol in a public school. Should the issue ever arise, however, one may confidently predict that federal judges would support such a right on the strength of a Vietnam era decision by the Supreme Court, overturning a school board's policy forbidding high school students to wear black armbands to protest American involvement in Southeast Asia.[11] This case dealt with free speech rather than with the free exercise of religion; but in all likelihood, a religious symbol would serve only to strengthen the students' position.

The Supreme Court did address the issue of religious garments in 1986 when it upheld an air force regulation prohibiting personnel from wearing hats indoors against a claim by a Jewish officer to wear a religious skullcap when he was in uniform. The air force countered by stressing the importance of uniformity in appearance for military discipline and morale. By the narrow margin of 5 to 4, the Supreme Court upheld the air force's position. Chief Justice Rehnquist's opinion of the Court relied heavily—indeed almost exclusively—on the explicit and extensive constitutional power of the government over its military personnel. Consequently, the decision has little relevance to public education.[12]

Thus far we have stressed the similarities in the *structure* of the arguments in both France and the United States when religious beliefs lead to behavior at odds with popular sentiment. Although the practical outcome of similar factual situations might differ in the two countries, the arguments would be formulated along the same lines. For example, the Muslim girls would probably fare better in an American public school than they did in France, but in both countries the argument would be structured in terms of balancing the constitutional concern to impose appropriate limits on the role of religion in State activities against the no less constitutional concern to protect religious practices as an important aspect of a broad national commitment to individual rights. This is what I mean by similarities in the *structure* of the argument in the two countries.

Despite these structural similarities, there are important substantive differences that introduce us to the nature of the French State and its relationship to French republicanism—two ideas we shall reexamine in the pages that follow.

In the United States, Muslim girls bedecked with *foulards* would not present a serious constitutional problem because their behavior could not possibly run afoul of the constitutional prohibition against an establishment of religion.[13] The duty not to establish a religion falls exclusively upon the state and its officers. In no sense is this a duty of the student, because a religious establishment has no meaning outside the context of state action manifested through official support or endorsement of some religious belief, symbol, or practice, for example, a crucifix on a classroom wall. In a word, establishment of religion in the United States is strictly a legal question involving a law that only the state can break.

Not so in France, where more is at stake than an American-style legalism on establishment of religion. The relationship between religion and the French State runs much deeper and broader than anything Americans have known. I use the English word *secularism* and its cognates to translate the French *laïcité*. The translation is not entirely satisfactory, but I can do no better because there has been no American experience comparable to the events in France which gave rise to *laïcité*. The word is inextricably linked with the long and unhappy struggles between the French republican tradition and the Catholic church, going back to the Revolution of 1789. Out of these bitter battles, there emerged in republican circles a strong sense of anti-clericalism that *laïcité* captures nicely. As far as schooling is concerned, it originally meant that nuns and priests have no place in the public schools of a republican State. It would be a gross understatement, however, to say that *laïcité* means merely that public school teachers should belong to the laity. This would retain the Catholic flavor of the schools and involve nothing more than a question of ecclesiastical personnel management in which laymen and laywomen would replace priests and nuns in the classroom.

Laïcité means far more than this. At the very least, it stands for State *neutrality* in matters of religion and de facto it has often meant official hostility toward religion in general and toward the Catholic church in particular. The shift from neutrality to hostility is reflected in the linguistic change from *laïcité* to *laïcisme*—the latter, like all "isms," suggesting an ideology whereas *laïcité,* at least in theory, is more readily associated with a principle.

If all this seems strange to the American reader, it is because our country has had the good fortune to avoid these great religious battles. To be sure, our church-state controversies can be quite acrimonious; but, fortunately, by French standards, they are trivial.

In France, secularism suggests a *doctrine* to be taught in the public schools and thus cuts deeper than the typically American problem of avoiding state favoritism toward religion, as when we fret over whether a clergyman may offer a prayer at a high school commencement.[14] The French doctrine of secularism traces its roots to the Enlightenment and celebrates the triumph of reason over revelation. It tries to discover universal truths and therefore must oppose religious faith, which it sees as always particularistic.

Ideally, the French republican tradition looks upon the public school as a temple of reason where teacher and students together form a community of rational inquiry for universal truths.[15] This is why religious symbols, laden with particularism, have no place in a public school. They profane the temple of reason. The secularism taught in the public schools has been called, without embarrassment, the "civil religion" of France—an expression that would amount to "fighting words" in the United States.[16]

This explains why the students as well as the teachers have a duty to respect the religious neutrality of the school. They, like their teachers, are members of the same community of rational inquiry.[17] Hence the minister of education urges local school administrators to try to persuade the Muslim girls not to wear the *foulard* and, pursuant to the opinion of the Council of State, empowers them to expel the girls if their religious garb proves disruptive.

This communitarian emphasis is quite different from the rights-driven American approach that makes it impossible for students to violate the prohibition against establishing religion on the one hand, and protects them in the free exercise of their religious beliefs on the other. It carries a salutary reminder to those Americans who call for a greater sense of community that when community arrives, authority is seldom far behind.

Jacques Minot, writing in the pages of *La Revue Administrative,* offers a telling analogy that captures the force of the idea of secularism in French public education. He notes that a visitor to a mosque will be asked to remove his shoes before entering the sacred precincts. By the same token, he argues, the religious believer should remove every sign of his faith "before entering a public school which is the sanctuary of secularism."[18] He hastens to add, however, that this does not mean the believer is asked to renounce his faith; but he is asked to keep it to himself while he is in school.[19]

This is a very different way of thinking about public education from what we observe in the United States. In our country, the state has the *negative* obligation *not* to favor religion. The French State has the same obligation but also the further *affirmative* duty to see to it that the students observe the principle of neutrality, all this to the end that the spirit of secularism will permeate the schools of the Republic. Americans worry that the state might force some religious belief upon an unsuspecting student, whereas French republicans worry that the public school's mission to preach the civil religion of France might be compromised.[20]

The significance of secularism as a positive doctrine comes into focus when one considers the relationship between the public schools and the family in France. To be sure, French teachers and educational administrators, like their American counterparts, want to please the parents of their students. In France, however, the demands of secularism at times present an interesting exception to this commonsense desire to win parental approval. This exception surfaced repeatedly in the debate over the *foulard.* For example, Guy Coq, writing in *Esprit,* argues that the principle of secularism "marks a limit to the right of families over the child in the school." Thus, the school is the place that provides "a personal right of the child to be himself away from his family."[21]

Claude Allegre, an adviser to Education Minister Jospin, hails secularism as a principle intended to "liberate the child intellectually from the exclusive influence of the family circle in order to give him autonomy in his thinking and freedom of choice."[22]

Jean Daniel, the editor of *Le Nouvel Observateur,* supports Education Minister Jospin's decision not to ban the *foulard* outright as the best way to achieve the ultimate goal of integrating Muslim children into the republican ways of France. An outright ban will drive them into Muslim schools, he argues, "with the result that these young girls will be lost to the Republic." By letting them wear their veils in school, Daniel maintains, there is a better chance "to exercise over them a greater influence than that of family discipline."[23]

Finally, philosopher Elizabeth Badinter criticizes Jospin for permitting the girls to wear the *foulard* in school because only a firm State regulation will give a Muslim girl the support she needs "to say no to her father without getting into a dreadful conflict. Without an official regulation the girl is all alone and she loses out"—a sentiment echoed pithily by another author who quips, "It is the prohibition that liberates," a contemporary feminist reprise on Rousseau's theme that at times some people must "be forced to be free."[24]

These examples will suffice to capture an element of the *foulard* controversy that one would not be likely to find in an American version of a similar problem, such as, for instance, the creation-evolution controversy. Creationist parents surely exasperate biology teachers, but prudence dissuades the latter from presenting their case as a frontal assault on parental authority.[25] In France, however, participants on either side of the *foulard* debate did not shrink from invoking the principle of secularism in order openly to undermine parental influence over a child. I believe the reason the French do this is because their strong notion of the State includes the image of the State as the teacher of republicanism and, when necessary, even as liberator of the child from a benighted family that rests content in the "shadows of integrism."[26] Those Frenchmen who link their country's strong State tradition with a profoundly secular notion of republicanism have a principled basis for challenging the intimacy of family life in a way that would be unusual and perhaps even unthinkable in the United States. We shall see more of the French State and republicanism in the remainder of this book.

CONSTITUTIONAL HIGHLIGHTS OF THE FIFTH REPUBLIC

The chapters that follow present a close textual analysis of the Constitution of 1958. To evaluate these analyses, the reader will need a general awareness of the broad constitutional background of the Fifth Republic. The present section is intended to meet this need.

Origins

The origins of the Constitution of the Fifth Republic can be traced to the unhappy consequences of "parliamentary sovereignty," a bedrock principle of French republicanism prior to 1958.

Parliamentary sovereignty dates from the Revolutionary era, which began with the storming of the Bastille in 1789 and led to the execution of King

Louis XVI three and one-half years later. The watchwords of the old order had been "throne and altar," signifying the sacral character of royal power embodied in the king, who derived his power from God and ruled in His name. The overthrow of the monarchy changed the foundation of political authority. Instead of flowing down from God to the king, it surged from below, from the people themselves, who conferred legitimate authority upon their duly elected representatives in parliament. "Law and nation" replaced "throne and altar" as the watchwords of the new order. The nation was *represented,* that is, presented a second time in the parliament of its chosen deputies who expressed the sovereign will of the people through law.[27]

This dramatic change provided a solidly democratic basis for the rule of law in France, but the law that ruled was *statutory* law, that is, laws passed by the sovereign parliament in the name of the people. Thus, the French republican principle of rule of law differed markedly from the predominant understanding of the same principle in the United States. For Americans, the Constitution of the United States, ratified by the people in 1787–1788, was deemed to be a "higher law" than statutes enacted by the people's representatives in Congress and one to which these statutes should conform. French jurists would concede a certain priority to a constitution over an Act of Parliament in the sense that elected representatives might be expected to observe their constitution. In reality, however, nothing could be done about a wayward parliament that ignored this expectation, for two reasons: (1) as a practical matter, there has been no Supreme Court in France empowered to strike down unconstitutional laws passed by Parliament; and (2) as a matter of principle, there is no logical basis to challenge a legislative enactment duly authorized by the sovereign Parliament. This is because, as noted above, the parliamentary deputies *re-present* the people and speak for them by means of law. Within the framework of democratic principle, who can challenge those who speak for the people? A constitution represents the will of the sovereign people yesterday, whereas a statute represents their will today. What democratic principle forbids the people from changing their mind?

Americans find this line of reasoning startling because we have never looked upon Congress or any other branch of government as sovereign. We shall revisit the question of sovereignty frequently in this book; but, for the present, I want only to introduce the reader to the French idea of a sovereign Parliament and to highlight its marked difference from the American constitutional tradition.

I mentioned above that the idea of parliamentary sovereignty proved to be an "unhappy" one. This is because the multiparty system in France made it difficult to form stable coalitions to support governments that could remain in office for a long time. Thus France presented the anomaly of a sovereign institution that was often too weak to govern effectively because bold and controversial actions on the part of any government were likely to bring about its fall.

This situation contributed significantly to the development of powerful administrative institutions in France that filled the political vacuum created by wavering governments and fragmented legislative coalitions. No administrative institutions, however, are equal to the task of governing a nation when it faces ultimate questions such as its own survival and identity. France faced just such questions in the late 1930s when the Parliament of the Third Republic (1870–1940) failed miserably to give the leadership that it alone could have provided. Consequently, in the spring of 1940, France fell to Hitler's armies and thereby set in motion the train of events that culminated in the Constitution of 1958.

Throughout World War II, General de Gaulle and many other Resistance leaders insisted that the true cause of the fall of France was not military but political. In Gaullist circles it became an article of faith that the divisive "regime of the political parties" throughout the 1930s rendered Parliament incapable of taking the decisive steps necessary to meet the Nazi menace. This was a major cause of France's humiliation, and de Gaulle resolved that it would never happen again.

After the liberation of France in 1944, there was a vigorous debate over the political future of the country, with General de Gaulle taking the lead in warning against a return to the parliamentary excesses of the past. After two years of provisional, makeshift governments, the French people in October 1946 approved a new constitution, which, despite General de Gaulle's strenuous objections, inaugurated the Fourth Republic (1946–1958), distressingly similar to its less-than-illustrious predecessor, especially in its adherence to the republican orthodoxy of parliamentary sovereignty.

Governmental instability reappeared in the Fourth Republic, but this structural problem was offset by the remarkable postwar economic recovery France enjoyed at that time. Under Fourth Republic governments, France took the lead in constructing new institutions for a new Europe, such as the Common Market, the forerunner of today's European Union. In foreign affairs, Fourth Republic France basked in the prestige of being one of the five permanent members of the Security Council of the United Nations.

The soft underbelly of postwar France, however, was its continuing role as a colonial power. The disastrous defeat at Dien Bien Phu in 1954 sent shock waves through the army and reignited long-smoldering resentments against unstable parliamentary governments incapable of supporting serious military endeavors. This resentment reached fever pitch during the Algerian war because for many Frenchmen, especially for those who had settled there, Algeria was no mere colony but a part of France itself. As the war dragged on from 1954 to 1958, bitter divisions arose within the nation and its Parliament. Senior army officers were increasingly exasperated by what they saw as half-hearted measures by the government to support the young men whose lives seemed to be sacrificed wantonly. In mid-May 1958, the French settlers in Algeria, fearing the government in Paris was about to enter negotiations for eventual Algerian independence, organized a mass demonstration that spilled into the government offices in Algiers, where a "self-elected revolutionary committee" seized power from the legitimate authorities.[28] The army did nothing to stop the takeover and seemed to support it. A few days later, the rebels seized control of Corsica and politicians in Paris began to ponder seriously the possibility of a military coup and even of civil war. In this charged atmosphere, René Coty, the President of the Republic, called upon General de Gaulle, who had been a private citizen since 1946, to form a government. De Gaulle was, once again, to save his country.

Drafting the Constitution

When de Gaulle accepted President Coty's call to form a government, he looked beyond the Algerian war, which was the immediate cause of Coty's appeal. He made it clear that he would accept the post of "President of the Council"—the Fourth Republic's title for the prime minister—only on condition that he could rule by decree for six months, during which time he would have a new constitution prepared for the approval of his countrymen. Thus, de Gaulle would use the Algerian crisis to promote the long-range constitutional reforms he knew were necessary if France was ever to overcome its tragic republican flaw of unstable governments.

The outcome of the Algerian war is well known. Just four years after de Gaulle had answered Coty's call, Algeria became a fully independent nation, much to the chagrin of many of the conservatives who had most enthusiastically supported his return to power. Some army officers and many French citizens residing in Algeria considered de Gaulle a traitor for failing to prosecute the war against the Algerian rebels with sufficient vigor to assure victory for France. This resentment led to several attempts on de Gaulle's life; even today one encounters disillusioned Frenchmen who detest de Gaulle for his "stab in the back" of those who wanted to hold on to Algeria at all costs.

Interesting as these events are, they are marginal to our constitutional inquiry. I mention the Algerian war only to explain how de Gaulle came to power in 1958 and how the work of drafting a new constitution got under way. To understand the context of the constitutional arguments we shall examine in the chapters that follow, the reader will find helpful a brief overview of the drafting process adopted by General de Gaulle's government from June to September of 1958.

Unfortunately for the careful reader, the Gaullists did not follow the tidy example of the American framers of 1787 who did historians the favor of completing their work in one convention, which met in one building, and for the most part followed one set of procedural rules. On the contrary, the text of the Constitution of the Fifth Republic was developed in several discrete stages with significant input from very different deliberative bodies, operating under very different procedural rules. Consequently, it is important to note the various steps of the procedure followed by the French framers of 1958. There follows a brief summary of this procedure.

After General de Gaulle had accepted President Coty's request to form a government, he sought from the National Assembly a change in the procedure for amending the Constitution of the Fourth Republic which, in effect, authorized his government to draft a new constitution pursuant to general guidelines spelled out in what became known as the Constitutional Law of 3 June 1958. Shortly thereafter, a working group *(groupe de travail)* led by Michel Debré, the minister of justice in de Gaulle's government, began drafting the text. This group worked closely with an interministerial council *(conseil interministériel)* which included de Gaulle himself and four powerful ministers of state. Pursuant to the law of 3 June, the government submitted a draft text to an Advisory Committee on the Constitution, *(Comité Consultatif Constitutionnel)* a body composed mainly of members of Parliament who were authorized to suggest revisions to the government's text. The Advisory Committee examined the text from 29 July until 14 August. Its suggested revisions were examined by the working group and the interministerial council before a new text was prepared for submission to the Council of State, again pursuant to the law of 3 June. On 25–26 August, the Constitutional Committee *(Commission constitutionnel)* of the Council of State examined the revised text and on the next two days the Council's General Assembly did the same. In each case, further revisions were suggested. The final text was presented to the people at *la Place de la République* in Paris on 4 September, the anniversary of the proclamation of the Third Republic. The time and place were selected as symbolic replies to the critics of the Constitution who challenged the document's republican integrity. On 28 September, the French people overwhelmingly approved the new Constitution, which was duly promulgated on 4 October.[29]

Of all these groups, councils, and committees, the working group under the direction of Justice Minister Debré played the most important role in drafting the text. Although many of the revisions from both the Advisory Committee on the Constitution and from the Council of State were of the highest importance, the texts they revised came from Debré's working group.

In this sense, the working group controlled the agenda. Students of public administration will be particularly interested to know that all the members of the working group, including Debré, were members of the Council of State and, as such, were career civil servants.[30] The working group interacted frequently with a group of experts *(groupe des experts)* which drew from outside the ranks of the Council of State as well as from within it.[31] Many of these experts, however, were professors of law and therefore civil servants of the State in their own right. Thus, the civil service played an absolutely crucial role in drafting the text of the Constitution for what some critics have called the regime of the bureaucrats *(le régime des fonctionnaires.)*

Throughout this book, I shall examine the various constitutional arguments thematically rather than chronologically. That is, instead of following the framers day by day, we shall move from a consideration of one constitutional theme to another, for example, from the executive powers of the prime minister to the power of the president of the Republic to remove him. Consequently, it is important for the reader to pay careful attention to the context in which an argument is presented. For example, the debate over the Constitutional Law of 3 June took place in Parliament where de Gaulle had many enemies, and where consequently the challenges to the general tended to be more strident than in other settings.

De Gaulle's purpose in getting Parliament's approval to change the procedure to amend the Constitution was intended to enable him to present his new Constitution, technically an amendment to the Constitution of the Fourth Republic, directly to the people without letting Parliament change it. He knew Parliament would be most unlikely to approve the Constitutional reforms he envisioned, which would considerably weaken that body. De Gaulle skillfully used the crisis atmosphere of the Algerian war to wring from Parliament a law taking itself out of the constitutional amending process. His foes in Parliament, notably the Communists and those Socialists who doubted de Gaulle's commitment to republican government, realized, of course, what the general was up to and therefore vigorously opposed adoption of the Constitutional Law of 3 June 1958. This explains the particularly bitter tone of the debates over that proposed legislation, which we shall consider in the chapters that follow. De Gaulle did not succeed in removing Parliament entirely from the constitution-writing process. As previously noted, he agreed to the appointment of an Advisory Committee on the Constitution, which, recruited for the most part from Parliament, would review the text prepared by Debré's working group and suggest revisions. These debates in the Advisory Committee were spirited but not as bitter as those in Parliament itself—in no small part because no Communists were included on the Advisory Committee. Although the powers of the Advisory Committee were just that—advisory—the Gaullists did not want to stir up needless trouble by rejecting too many of the committee's suggested revisions. Hence, the general tone of these debates was conciliatory and at times even soothing, as the Gaullists offered interpretations of their texts designed—sometimes disingenuously—to assuage the fears of the parliamentarians whose support they would need when the final version would be presented to the people in a referendum.

When the debate shifted to the Council of State, the tone was much more technical and legalistic, as befitted that body's role as the highest administrative court in France. This was true both of the plenary sessions of the council's General Assembly and of the sessions before its Constitutional Committee. Finally, the public debate over the finished document prior to the referendum of 28 September was popular and freewheeling, with scant attention given to close textual analysis.

The French Community

Throughout the constitutional debates of 1958, considerable attention was lavished upon the French empire which, in recognition of the anti-imperialist spirit of the postwar world, had been prudently renamed the "French Union" under the 1946 Constitution of the Fourth Republic. The framers of the Constitution of the Fifth Republic changed "French Union" to "French Community" in a further effort to accommodate the growing spirit of nationalism in the colonies.

The new community figured prominently in the constitutional text, appearing in both the preamble and the first article, where it is heralded as being "based on the equality and the solidarity of the peoples composing it." Indeed, two of the fifteen titles of the Constitution of 1958 are dedicated to the French Community.

Despite this textual prominence, the French Community envisioned by the framers of the 1958 Constitution quickly came to naught. Although all but one of the colonies ratified the new Constitution, thereby signifying their willingness to remain in the empire-turned-community, within a few short years the rising tide of nationalist sentiment sweeping Africa at that time rendered the new arrangements untenable. By 1962, the Community as envisioned in the constitutional text had ceased to exist.

Today, France continues to exert considerable influence throughout Africa by means of a loose union of francophone countries; but this, of course, is a pale shadow of the far grander plans of the Gaullists of 1958. In examining the debates of that year, the reader will come upon many references to the proposed community. To understand the constitutional principles at issue in the arguments, the reader must be aware of the ambitious but abortive community, which today is only of historical interest.[32]

The President of the Republic

The Fifth Republic is often described as a "presidentialist" or "semi-presidentialist" regime. The qualification "semi" is due to the regime's parliamentary aspects, which include a prime minister who, in constitutional theory, is accountable to Parliament. In practice, Fifth Republic prime ministers have served at the pleasure of the president of the Republic with the exception of two brief periods of "cohabitation," a term that will be explained shortly. Thus, cohabitation periods aside, the president of the Republic has been without question the dominant figure in France for the past thirty-six years, and, consequently, the Fifth Republic is often looked upon as simply a presidentialist regime.[33]

As we shall see in chapter three, the authors of the constitutional text envisioned a far more sophisticated constitutional arrangement than the description of the regime as simply presidentialist would suggest. The de facto ascendancy of the president of the Republic is due primarily to the towering presence of General de Gaulle, who, as the Fifth Republic's first president, established patterns and precedents of presidential power that have strengthened immeasurably the office he handed on to his successors.

Today, the president of the Republic is chosen by direct universal suffrage, but this was not always the case. The original text of the Constitution provided for an electoral college of some eighty thousand elected officials who would select the president of the Republic.[34] In chapter three we shall examine in some detail the reasons why the framers of the Constitution denied the president the advantage of direct popular election. For the present, it will suffice to note that the only constitutional precedent for electing a president directly by the people came from the ill-starred Second Republic (1848–1851) in which the popularly-elected president, Louis Napoléon Bonaparte, led a coup d'état that put an end to the Republic and ushered in the Second Empire, with the former republican president assuming the title of Emperor Napoléon III. These changes were ratified by popular plebiscites, which left French republicans profoundly suspicious of both plebiscites and directly elected presidents.

In 1962, President de Gaulle initiated a constitutional reform that brought about the direct election of the president. This move created a tremendous controversy not only because of the inherently controversial character of a directly elected republican president in France, but also, and even more importantly, by the flagrantly irregular manner in which de Gaulle brought it about.

Article 89 of the Constitution states the procedures for amending it. One way is by popular referendum on a text submitted to Parliament by the president on the recommendation of the prime minister and approved by both chambers of that body. The second way replaces the referendum with an approval by an extraordinary majority in a joint session of Parliament. Under this procedure, the president convenes the joint session, called a Congress *(Congrès)* to approve by a three-fifths vote a text already approved separately and in identical terms by each parliamentary chamber. In either case, it would seem that article 89 clearly prohibits amendments to the Constitution without the approval of Parliament.

Knowing that Parliament would never approve a constitutional amendment leading to the direct election of the president by universal suffrage, de Gaulle invoked article 11 of the Constitution, which empowers the president to submit several types of proposed laws directly to popular referendum without first getting the approval of Parliament. These types of proposed laws included "any bill dealing with the organization of the governmental authorities." De Gaulle argued that the manner of electing a president dealt with the "organization of governmental authorities" and therefore the proposed change could be made by referendum without parliamentary approval. An outraged National Assembly, the parliamentary chamber directly elected by the people, voted to censure the government headed by de Gaulle's staunch ally, Prime Minister Georges Pompidou. Instead of accepting Pompidou's resignation and appointing a new prime minister, de Gaulle used his constitutional powers under article 12 to dissolve Parliament. The Gaullists won both the referendum and the legislative election necessitated by de Gaulle's dissolution order. When the newly elected Parliament assembled, de Gaulle coolly reappointed Georges Pompidou prime minister. Parliament's humiliation was complete.

Despite the obvious irregularity in the constitutional procedure transforming the presidency into a directly elected office, the reform has been a tremendous success. Today, no one seriously disputes the substantive merits of the reform, despite its patently flawed origins. One cannot improve on the incisive remark by Georges Vedel, the distinguished French jurist, that "the Constitution of 1958 was a mediocre text but one that has been considerably improved by the violations it has endured."[35]

The Fifth Republic has seen four elected presidents: de Gaulle (1958–1969), Georges Pompidou (1969–1974), Valéry Giscard d'Estaing (1974–1981), and François Mitterrand, who was first elected in 1981. His second seven-year term ends in 1995. De Gaulle's first term ended in 1965 when, pursuant to the controversial amendment of 1962, he was reelected to a second seven-year term, which he did not finish. In May 1968, student unrest prompted a violent uprising that began in Paris and soon spread to other major French cities, involving workers from virtually every sector of the economy. These "Events of 1968" climaxed in a series of general strikes that "paralyzed France for several days, and threatened to bring down the government."[36]

Although de Gaulle weathered this storm and even saw his party prevail in legislative elections held shortly after order had been restored, the old charisma eventually began to fade. To rally the nation to his side again, he had recourse in 1969 to his favorite political device—the popular referendum. This time the issues concerned reducing the power of the Senate and introducing regional governments in France. Well in advance of the referendum, de Gaulle, following his familiar script of "me or chaos," warned the people that if they failed to approve his proposals, something they had never done before, he would resign immediately. The referendum was defeated and, true to his word, the general resigned the day after the results were known, even though his term of office had three years remaining. For de Gaulle, it was impossible to govern knowing he had lost the support of the people. The seven-year constitutional term of office to which he had been elected was for him a thin legalism compared to the rich personal interaction between himself and the French people that had sustained him throughout his political life. The general's view of political legitimacy was more attuned to a plebiscitary democracy than to a constitutional republic.

Since there is no provision for a vice president in the Constitution of the Fifth Republic, the president of the Senate serves as interim head of State when the presidency is vacant. Accordingly, Senate president Alain Poher filled this role until presidential elections were held, which brought Georges Pompidou to the Elysée palace, as the presidential residence is called. Pompidou died in April 1974, two years before the end of his seven-year term. Once again, a special election was organized. This time, Valéry Giscard d'Estaing, who had been de Gaulle's finance minister for six years, narrowly defeated the Socialist candidate, François Mitterrand.

Giscard d'Estaing served a full term, but lost his bid for reelection in 1981 to Mitterrand, who was reelected in 1988. Unlike his three predecessors, who were all conservatives, Mitterrand was a man of the Left who burst into office committed to a robust policy of nationalizing banking and other key sectors of the French economy, expanding social benefits, reducing the workweek, and extending annual vacations to five weeks for all. He even included four Communists among the ministers in the first government formed under his presidency. Although the ensuing economic decline cooled Mitterrand's Socialist fervor, he has remained a man of the Left throughout his long reign. As such, he made a significant contribution to the development of the Constitution of the Fifth Republic. His skillful use of his constitutional powers demonstrated conclusively that de Gaulle's Constitution provided a suitable framework of governance for those whose political convictions were very different from those of Charles de Gaulle.

If one looks for a parallel in American constitutional history, the election of Thomas Jefferson to the presidency in 1800 comes readily to mind. After the conservative administrations of Presidents Washington and Adams, Jefferson's agrarian democracy signaled a dramatic change in the new nation's political direction. Fortunately, the changes took place within the framework of the same constitution that Jefferson's Federalist predecessors had used to very different ends, thereby establishing it as a document transcending partisan interests and accelerating its progress toward its exalted role as the unifying symbol for all Americans.

Cohabitation

As noted above, the Fifth Republic is sometimes characterized as a "semi-presidentialist" regime because of the presence of a prime minister as well as of a president. Although, as we shall see in chapters two and three, the prime minister enjoys considerable constitutional powers, the president of the Republic has ordinarily dominated the political life of the Fifth Republic. I say "ordinarily" because there have been two brief periods in which this was not the case: the years 1986 to 1988 and 1993 to 1995. In both of these periods, the National Assembly was under the control of conservative coalitions that forced President Mitterrand to appoint prime ministers acceptable to the prevailing majority. This came about because legislative elections are held every five years (unless the dissolution of Parliament leads to an earlier election), whereas presidential elections occur only once every seven years. Thus, the terms of the president and the deputies in the National Assembly do not coincide. When President Mitterrand was elected in 1981, he promptly dissolved the centrist Parliament, then in its fourth year, and the electorate responded by giving the new president a leftist Parliament to his liking. Five years later, in 1986, the political mood had shifted to the Right and the conservatives emerged from the parliamentary elections with a narrow majority in the National Assembly. President Mitterrand appointed the conservative mayor of Paris, Jacques Chirac, prime minister and Chirac, in turn, formed a conservative government. Although tensions between previous presidents and their prime ministers had not been unknown in the Fifth Republic, the differences had usually been settled within the friendly confines of the various shades of French conservatism. With the appointment of Jacques Chirac, however, there was, for the first time under the Fifth Republic, a sharp Left-Right split at the summit of the State. Many political commentators called for President Mitterrand's resignation but, in marked contrast to de Gaulle's behavior in 1969, he remained steadfast in his determination to complete his seven-year term of office. This was known as the period of cohabitation.

Prime Minister Chirac's decision to challenge Mitterrand in the presidential election of 1988 only intensified the already volatile political situation. When Mitterrand defeated Chirac, he once again dissolved Parliament and was rewarded with a very narrow legislative victory for the Left. This enabled him to appoint a moderate Socialist, Michel Rocard, as prime minister, and the Fifth Republic returned to its normal pattern of the president and prime minister sharing the same political orientation, with the president clearly in the ascendant. The Fifth Republic had survived its first cohabitation period. It had been an exceedingly difficult time, but the country avoided the disaster many skeptics had predicted.

The legislative elections of March 1993 once again went against President Mitterrand and his leftist coalition, but this time the conservatives won an overwhelming victory, bringing them over 80 percent of the seats in the National Assembly. Mitterrand appointed Edouard Balladur prime minister and a new cohabitation was under way. By summer 1994, the second cohabitation was going much more smoothly than the first. There were several reasons for this. Perhaps the most important was that Mitterrand would not be a candidate for president of the Republic in 1995, thereby precluding any direct rivalry between himself and Balladur, who was expected to run for that office. Secondly, the massive repudiation of the Socialists in the 1993 elections made it extremely difficult for Mitterrand to offer serious leadership from the Left. He seemed content to conclude his term by trying to protect the accomplishments of his presidency from the conservative juggernaut and by fulfilling his ceremonial obligations as head of State in a restrained and dignified manner. Finally, Edouard Balladur has a more relaxed and less combative political style than the feisty partisan, Jacques Chirac.

The Constitutional Council

In our study of the *foulard* affair, we noted that one of the duties of the Council of State is to serve as the highest administrative court in France. The highest court in ordinary civil and criminal matters is the *Cour de Cassation* (literally, the "breaking" or "quashing court," because on appeal it can reverse decisions of lower courts). Each is supreme in its own sphere with no "supreme court" to review the decisions of either body.

Diverse as these two jurisdictions are, they share a common limitation in that neither of them has the authority to declare a law, that is, an Act of Parliament, unconstitutional. In terms of simple logic, one might look upon this limitation as a mere corollary of the doctrine of parliamentary sovereignty. Parliament would not be sovereign if a court could void its laws. However, there is more behind the common limitation than logic alone. Justice Holmes is reported to have once said that a page of history is worth a volume of logic. The aphorism applies to the incapacity of French courts to strike down Acts of Parliament. Throughout the eighteenth century, the power of French courts grew by leaps and bounds. By the time of the Revolution, activist judges, despite their frequent quarrels with the king, had become irrevocably identified with the *ancien régime*. Consequently, the French revolutionaries soon denounced *le gouvernement des juges* (government by judges) as a singularly antirepublican phenomenon. This tradition took deep root in French republican soil and, even today, the cry of *gouvernement des juges* is the constant companion of unhappy Frenchmen who believe some judge has overstepped his or her rather narrowly defined role in French public life.[37]

One of the most striking innovations of the Constitution of the Fifth Republic is its dramatic rejection of the republican tradition of parliamentary sovereignty. Although the Constitution does not state in terms that Parliament is no longer sovereign, this is the unmistakable implication of two crucial articles in the text. Article 34 enumerates the powers of Parliament not unlike the way in which the eighth section of the first article in the American Constitution enumerates the powers of Congress. Just as Congress has the power to "lay and collect Taxes . . . ," "to borrow Money . . . ," "to declare War," and so forth, so the French Parliament is empowered to legislate in a broad range of activities that include taxes, nationality, marriage, inheritance, education, national defense, and so forth. In both constitutions, the enumeration of certain powers implies the exclusion of the legislature from all areas not enumerated. This implication becomes explicit in article 37 of the Constitution of the Fifth Republic, which declares that "matters other than those that fall within the domain of law shall be of a regulatory character." "Regulations" are actions taken by the government, that is, by the executive. The clear meaning of article 37 is that whatever activities do not fall under the legislative powers granted to Parliament are reserved to the administrative powers of the government. Students of public administration will grasp at once the enormous importance of such a constitutional provision for establishing a modern administrative state, and we shall dwell on this remarkable provision at some length in chapters two and four. For the present, however, we need only note its incompatibility with parliamentary sovereignty. If there are any areas in which Parliament may not legislate, then Parliament, by definition, is not sovereign. No institution can be both sovereign and limited at the same time. The two ideas are mutually exclusive.

To reinforce the constitutional distinction between matters consigned to law, i.e., to Parliament, and those consigned to administrative regulation, i.e., to the government, the framers of the Constitution created a new jurisdiction called the Constitutional Council, *(Conseil constitutionnel)* charged with policing the border between law and regulation in order to keep Parliament within its constitutionally appointed limits.

This new institution was not a court. Although its decisions followed a judicial format, no litigants appeared before it. It had no general jurisdiction over certain "cases or controversies," as is true of the courts created under article 3 of the Constitution of the United States.[38] It was a *council,* not a court, and as such could be convened to examine the constitutionality of an Act of Parliament by any one of four constitutional officers—the president of the Republic, the prime minister, the president of the National Assembly, or the president of the Senate—but by no one else.

Thus, as originally conceived, the innovative Constitutional Council had a narrow jurisdiction that could be invoked only by the highest officers of the State. Narrow as its jurisdiction was, however, its mere existence represented a breakthrough in the long history of French constitutionalism. Articles 34 and 37 presented *textual* limitations on the sovereignty of Parliament, while the Constitutional Council embodied an *institutional* presence to make these parchment limitations real.

From this tiny acorn grew the mighty oak of today's Constitutional Council, an institution that plays a profoundly important role in contemporary France. We shall examine its remarkable growth in chapter five; but, for now, it will suffice to mention two significant steps in its development.

The first was a decision rendered in 1971 in which the Constitutional Council voided an Act of Parliament on constitutional grounds unrelated to the law/regulation boundary of articles 34 and 37. Since that time, the council, relying on a sort of bootstrap jurisprudence, has escalated its mission from one of acting on behalf of the government to enforce articles 34 and 37 against what the Gaullists of 1958 feared might become an overbearing Parliament, to one of enforcing any aspect of the Constitution against Parliament and the government acting in concert.

Secondly, in 1974 the Constitution was amended to add to the four officers that the original Constitution empowered to convene the Constitutional Council a clause permitting sixty deputies (as members of the National Assembly are called) or sixty senators to do the same. This provision has meant that today nearly every significant legislative enactment is brought before the Constitutional Council by sixty unhappy senators or deputies from the Parliamentary opposition. So powerful has the council become that some go so far as to call it a third legislative chamber because very few laws go into effect without its approval.[39] The 1974 amendment has brought the Constitutional Council out of the institutional shadows to the front and center of French politics today.

FRENCH ADMINISTRATION

Since this book highlights the connection between constitutional principles and public administration, a brief discussion of French administration is in order. Most students of public administration are already familiar with the broad outlines of French administration because of its profound impact throughout the world.[40] A fair reading of the history of administration clearly reveals the primacy of France in this field. For our purposes, it will suffice merely to recall those salient aspects of French administration which we shall encounter in the chapters that lie ahead.

The State

Perhaps nothing differentiates administration in France and in the United States more clearly than the strong-state tradition of the former and the latter's weak-state tradition. In French, the word for *state, l'Etat,* has a strongly normative force one seldom finds in its English equivalent.[41] The fact that the word is always capitalized in French suggests its importance in that language and, therefore, in that political culture.[42] The writings and speeches of General de Gaulle bring out the normative force of *l'Etat* most convincingly. Consider, for example, the very first paragraph in de Gaulle's memoir where he eloquently links the State to the nation and its destiny.

> France has emerged from the depths of the past. She is a living entity. She responds to the call of the centuries. Yet she remains herself through time. Her boundaries may alter, but not the contours, the climate, the rivers and seas that are her eternal imprint. Her land is inhabited by people who, in the course of history, have undergone the most diverse experiences, but whom destiny and circumstance, exploited by politics, have unceasingly molded into a single nation. This nation has embraced countless generations. At this moment it contains several. It will give birth to many more. But by reason of its geography, of the genius of the races which compose it, and of its position in relation to its neighbors, it has taken on an enduring character which makes each generation of Frenchmen dependent on their forefathers and pledged to their descendants. Unless it falls apart, therefore, this human amalgam, on this territory, at the heart of this world, comprises a past, a present and a future that are indissoluble. Thus the State, which is answerable for France, is in charge, at one and the same time of yesterday's heritage, today's interests, and tomorrow's hopes.[43]

I apologize to the reader for inserting such a lengthy quotation, but I believe it is essential for our purposes to let General de Gaulle speak for himself if we are to grasp his exalted vision of the State. Recall that this is the opening paragraph of the memoir, and as such sets a tone for all that follows. For de Gaulle, the State is charged with nothing less than answering for the France he loves so dearly, and this for "yesterday's heritage, today's interests, and tomorrow's hopes." We Americans may have our heritage, our interests, and our hopes in mind when we speak of the "common good" or the "public interest," but we have no *institution* that is answerable for it. In de Gaulle's vision of France, the State is such an institution.

In his earlier memoir from World War II, the general had singled out "the feebleness of the State" during the years between the two world wars as a major cause for the humiliating defeat France had suffered in 1940. The State was enfeebled because it had been captured by various political parties, each of which necessarily had a limited view of the good of France as a whole. Hence, in writing about the liberation of Paris in 1944, de Gaulle says of that most solemn moment: "I myself had already determined what I must do in the liberated capital. I would mold all minds into a single national impulse, but also cause the figure and the authority of the State to appear at once."[44] Before talking about constitutions, elections, and political parties, the State must first be restored. Significantly, at the time of his triumphal entry into Paris, de Gaulle first visited the prefecture of police before going to the *Hôtel de Ville* (City Hall) where the people awaited him. The purpose of this meaningful detour was to symbolize his control over the police as a crucial element of the apparatus of the State.[45]

During his self-imposed retirement from public life from 1946 to 1958, de Gaulle continued to speak out against the weak governing structures of the Fourth Republic. His grand notion of the State held center stage in his arguments. Thus, in an important speech at Strasbourg in 1947, he urged his followers to work for "reform of the State" and three years later he told them to "hasten to establish the State" even though the busy men and women at the helm of the Fourth Republic would surely be forgiven for thinking that a State was already in place.[46] When he returned to power in 1958, de Gaulle, not surprisingly, "pointed to the degradation of the State as the cause of the threatening calamity."[47]

Even after the Fifth Republic had been established under de Gaulle's leadership in 1958, the general continued to emphasize the central role of the State. For example, in November 1962 he urged his followers to support a reform he had in mind for "the good of the State, the fate of the Republic, and the future of France"—thereby linking the State to the Republic and to France itself.[48]

In a particularly telling comment, de Gaulle revealed to his friend André Malraux his feelings when he assumed power in 1958:

> When I saw the politicians gathered together again for the first time, I felt at once, no mistaking it, their hostility to everyone. They did not believe

in the slightest that I was a dictator, but they understood I represented the State. That was just as bad; the State is the devil, and if it exists, then they do not. They lose what they value most, and that is not money but the exercise of their vanity. They all loathe the State.[49]

This comment goes to the heart of de Gaulle's notion of the State. Politicians represent particular interests—farmers, unions, business enterprises, and so forth, and therefore they fear de Gaulle, the man of the State, who sees in himself one who speaks for all of France. There can be no doubt that de Gaulle did see himself in this way. Speaking by radio from London in the darkest days of 1940, he gave hope to his dispirited countrymen by proclaiming, "I, General de Gaulle, French soldier and leader, am aware that I speak in the name of France."[50]

At the end of the war, he referred to "exceptional powers I have exercised since June 18, 1940, in the name of the Republic."[51] In 1960, after he had become president of the Fifth Republic, he referred to "the national legitimacy that I have embodied for twenty years." In the same year, speaking of national unity, he did not shrink from saying: "I have no other *raison d'être,* as you know than this unity. I am in a sense its symbol and its guarantee."[52]

Such statements surely strike the American reader as startling and perhaps even as preposterous, but not so for de Gaulle's close associates. Witness François Mauriac's account of the origins of his allegiance to the general: "I was sitting opposite someone who did not distinguish himself from France, who said, openly, 'I am France' without anyone in the world saying he was mad."[53]

This is heady wine. An American statesman saying "I am America" would surely be mad. I believe the strong-state tradition goes a long way toward explaining why a statement that would be sheer madness in the United States could be taken as authentic patriotism in France. De Gaulle claimed to speak for France as a whole, and most of his countrymen believed him. No American statesman can speak for the United States "as a whole" because our institutions and traditions render meaningless any notion of "a whole" for our amazingly diversified nation. Indeed, the very grammar of the name of our country—a *plural* noun modified by an adjective—mocks the idea of a comprehensive whole. We have never had a Charles de Gaulle because, happily, we have never needed one.

One need not soar to the heights of Gaullist rhetoric to grasp the significance of the State in the French political tradition. At the mundane level of everyday politics and government in today's less stressful times, French politicians and administrators regularly pay homage to its centrality. Thus, a governmental decree of March 1990 permits the preservation in official files of highly personal information concerning those who are likely to present a threat "to the security of the State or to the public safety."[54] The text makes an interesting distinction between public safety on the one hand and the security of the State on the other. This implies that there is a State interest in its own security that is something other than the more general public safety, an implication quite consistent with the legal doctrine of the State as a moral person with its own rights and duties. A comparable American regulation would probably mention "national security" or possibly "public safety," but it would be a rare American text that would *add* a concern for the security of the state itself as an independent entity.

Every New Year's eve, President Mitterrand customarily offers his best wishes to his countrymen in a televised address. In the course of his remarks on the last day of 1990, the president rehearsed a list of things badly needed in France. They included such high priority items as "a healthy moral climate to mobilize our collective energy," "a greater equality in the sharing of the benefits derived from the labor of everyone," and "education of our youth for careers in order to diminish the curse of unemployment." Heading the president's list, however, was the assertion that "we have need of the State and of its authority in order to control private interests."[55] It is simply unthinkable that a president of the United States would speak of the state in such a way in such a context.

In an address to the students at the prestigious *Ecole Nationale d'Administration* (ENA) in 1991, Socialist prime minister Michel Rocard assured the aspiring high-level civil servants that their careers in public service would soon regain the esteem in public opinion they once had enjoyed. Conceding that during the 1980s "business careers rediscovered a legitimacy in the eyes of the French people," he confidently predicted that "the '90s will be the years of the rehabilitation of the public service." The reason for this confidence, Rocard tells his listeners, is his firm belief that "the State is back." *(L'Etat est de retour).*[56] Presumably, Rocard's glad tidings found a warm reception at ENA because, according to Michel Debré, the school's founder, its purpose was to instill in the students "a sense of the State."

Jacques Chirac, a former prime minister and prominent conservative leader, took advantage of a televised interview in 1990 to criticize his Socialist opponents for using their official positions to partisan advantage—hardly a novel complaint from the opposition in any democratic country. Chirac, however, in typically French fashion accused the government of using major powers of the State—its fiscal powers, its police powers, and its administration of justice—to serve its own interests. An American might see in this unremarkable charge nothing more than another case of "corruption in government" or an "abuse of power," but Chirac phrased it as "a crisis of the State."[57]

In presenting these examples, I must not overstate my case. The French are by no means impervious to the danger of excessive regulation by the State—especially in economic affairs. Indeed, they have a clearly pejorative word for it—*étatisme* (statism). For example, the recent failure of the proposed merger between Renault (a State-owned enterprise in France) and the Swedish company Volvo was blamed on the bad reputation of the French State as a major shareholder.[58]

Although the French State, despite recent decentralization reforms, remains highly centralized, one must not yield to the common tendency to exaggerate French centralization. Centrifugal forces play a key role in contemporary French administration. For example, there are several important "independent administrative authorities"[59] exercising powers that, at least in principle, are not unlike those of independent regulatory commissions in the United States. I say "at least in principle," because these authorities are relative newcomers to the French administrative scene and seem to be struggling to define their proper role. Nevertheless, the *Commission des opérations de bourse* (COB), which performs functions roughly equivalent to those of the American Securities and Exchange Commission (SEC), showed some independence in investigating, along with the SEC, the well-publicized Péchiney Affair, an international stockmarket scandal involving French and American companies.[60] The COB found itself in an awkward position because close personal friends of President Mitterrand figured prominently in the scandal. Further, the *Conseil supérieur de l'audiovisuel,* the French approximation to the Federal Communications Commission (FCC), struck an independent note in a recent report reprimanding two television channels for giving too much broadcast time to the government.[61]

The past decade has seen several reform efforts aimed at making a broad range of public services "user centered,"[62] in order to counter the image of French administration as aloof and arrogant toward the citizenry. Although laws regulating the civil service clearly reinforce the well-known hierarchical structure of French public administration, these same laws no less clearly affirm the rights of civil servants vis-à-vis their hierarchical superiors. Yves Mény, a leading French political scientist, has aptly characterized this curious blend as one of both "subordination of the administration to the government" and "paradoxically, the independence of public officials from political power."[63] To avoid the error of seeing the power of the French State as monolithic, one need only examine Ezra Suleiman's study of the French notaries *(les notaires),* a remarkable group of distinctively French officeholders who combine public and private power to a degree guaranteed to confound simplistic generalities about a French State that is unified and omnipresent.[64]

I mention these matters to put my remarks on the French State in perspective. They are intended as correctives to an exaggerated view of the practical effects of the strong-state tradition in France. Despite these correctives, the French State—centralized, consolidated, and steeped in tradition—remains an "awesome entity."[65] As such, it provides the normative foundation for public administration in France.

Les Grands Corps

The French civil service is among the most powerful in the world. Indeed, knowledgeable commentators have described it as "one of the main driving forces, if not *the* driving force, in French life."[66] High-ranking civil servants—*hauts fonctionnaires*—enjoy a social prestige comparable to that of federal judges in the United States. No study of elites in French society would be complete without careful attention to high-ranking civil servants.[67]

The prestige of the high civil service is due in no small part to the structure of the French personnel system that places every civil servant of the State, that is, of the central government, in a corps. The most prestigious of these corps are called *les grands corps de l'Etat* (the great corps of the State). There is some dispute among personnel experts about just which corps merit the rank of *grands,* but there are some one finds on everyone's list:

- *Conseil d'Etat* (Council of State): specializes in administrative law but covers a remarkably broad range of administrative activities beyond questions of law; it has been aptly called "the great administrative corps *par excellence.*"[68]
- *Inspection des Finances* (Financial Investigators) and *La Cour des Comptes* (Court of Audits): both of these corps monitor the regularity of the financial transactions of the State and its officers.
- *Corps des Ponts et Chaussées* (Corps for bridges and roads) and *Corps des Mines* (Mining Corps): technical corps staffed by engineers who deal with questions far beyond the narrow confines of roads, bridges, and mines.

In addition to these five corps, one often finds the *corps préfectoral* (prefects' corps) and the *corps diplomatique* (diplomatic corps) included among the *grands corps.*[69]

What these *grands corps* have in common is that most of their members are graduates of elite professional schools called, appropriately enough, *les grandes écoles* (the great schools). In the field of public administration, the best known of the *grandes écoles* are *Ecole Polytechnique* for engineers and ENA for the other *grands corps*. Admission to these schools is determined by rigorous examinations so that there is no doubt that the civil service ends up with its fair share of "the best and the brightest" young men and women in France.

This recruitment system has been justly criticized as elitist, but repeated efforts to change it significantly have been to no avail. A prominent French executive put it well when he said, "Ninety percent of the population want to abolish the *Ecole Polytechnique,* but they all also want their sons to go there."[70] As for ENA, an article in a Socialist journal marking that school's thirtieth anniversary in 1975 rehearsed the familiar and thoroughly justified attacks on its elitist character but dutifully acknowledged the brilliant performance of its graduates. With refreshing candor, the author asked, "Must we abolish a professional school because its alumni are too good at what they do?"[71]

The elitism in the French civil service is nothing new nor did it come about by accident. J.-L. Bodiguel tells of an official report from the era of the restoration of the Bourbon monarchy in the early nineteenth century in which the authors argued that the great task at hand was to "justify rank by merit and wealth by talent and virtue." That is, if the privileged classes were to maintain their positions in society in the face of the rising tide of democracy, they would have to show that they earned it. Emile Boutmy, the founder of a school that trained many of the high-ranking civil servants during the Third Republic (1870–1940), justified the establishment of his school on the grounds that "the upper classes can only maintain their hegemony by invoking the rights of the most capable." Boutmy, like many serious Frenchmen before and after him, adopted a strategy intended to ensure that the upper classes, whose talents were believed to be so badly needed in public life, would achieve high position on merit, since they could no longer count on privileged birth or wealth.[72]

The prestige of the civil service is due not only to its elite character, but also to its effective performance. It has often been observed that a strong civil service was necessary to bring stability to France because the political character of the country was notoriously unstable. As France lurched from one revolution to another, monarchies, empires, and republics—to say nothing of foreign armies—came and went with distressing regularity. Depending on how one defines the word *constitution,* France has had from thirteen to fifteen of them since the Revolution of 1789. That France has survived and flourished under such circumstances as one of the world's great nations is owing in considerable part to its elite civil service. An eloquent testimony to its importance is the legal requirement imposed upon civil servants to obtain permission to leave their jobs.[73]

The substantive contributions of the civil service have been many and varied. The Council of State, for example, which was created by Napoleon in 1799, provided an extremely useful integrating mechanism by bringing together in one deliberative body representatives of the prerevolutionary aristocracy and the newly created imperial aristocrats who owed their rank to the emperor.

One need not reach back to the Napoleonic era for examples of great statesmen relying on the civil service. Throughout World War II and its immediate aftermath, General de Gaulle frequently charged civil servants with serious responsibilities in organizing the activities of the Resistance movement. Jean Moulin, the best known of these organizers, had been a prefect before the war. When the Nazis executed him, de Gaulle turned to another civil servant, Alexandre Parodi, who was to represent de Gaulle at the meetings of the Resistance Council.[74] The darker side of this story is, of course, the important role played by collaborationist civil servants in supporting Maréchel Pétain's Vichy regime.[75]

De Gaulle's reliance upon the civil service as one of the major institutions in French public life was evident throughout his career. Shortly after the Allied landing in North Africa, the general used the BBC to urge his countrymen to give what support they could: "French leaders, soldiers, sailors, airmen, *civil servants,* French settlers in North Africa, arise. Help our allies." (Emphasis added.) Typical is the record of one of many important meetings during and after the liberation in which the future of France was planned. Present at a meeting with de Gaulle at the Palais Chaillot on 12 September 1944 were representatives of "the unions, industry, commerce, the universities, the bar associations, *the civil service,* and, of course, the Resistance."[76] (Emphasis added.)

Not surprisingly, when de Gaulle returned to power in 1958 and needed a new Constitution to rechart the course of the nation, he turned to the Council of State, the *grands corps* with special expertise in administrative law. As noted above, de Gaulle's justice minister, Michel Debré, himself a councillor of State, formed a small working group of young councillors who drafted the text that eventually became the Constitution of the Fifth Republic.

In governing the Fifth Republic as its first president, de Gaulle relied heavily upon civil servants, appointing a substantial number of them to ministerial posts. He tended to prefer civil servants to the experienced politicians from the parties because the former were more likely to share his vision of the good of France as a whole, a characteristic de Gaulle looked for in men imbued with a "sense of State." In a word, de Gaulle "brought the administration to prominence as never before."[77]

Reliance upon civil servants to govern the Fifth Republic did not end with General de Gaulle. A study published in 1987 showed that throughout the Fifth Republic all the prime ministers (ten at that time) had at one time or another been civil servants. Eighty percent of the finance ministers and 54 percent of all other ministers had also begun their careers in the civil service, as had 42 percent of the deputies elected to the National Assembly, the more powerful chamber of the bicameral French legislature.[78] Further, senior civil servants sometimes double as mayor of the town wherein they reside, thereby supplementing high administrative office with a local power base. These developments help to explain why, as noted above, the Fifth Republic is often called *la République des Fonctionnaires* (the Republic of the bureaucrats).[79]

In addition to civil servants' holding political office at all levels, there is a marked tendency to turn to civil servants to head special investigatory or problem-solving bodies—as President Mitterrand did in the scandal involving the environmental group Greenpeace and the destruction of its ship *Rainbow Warrior*, which was monitoring French nuclear testing in the Pacific Ocean.[80]

The political role of civil servants is encouraged by a constitutional prohibition against ministers, that is, members of the government, holding seats in Parliament. A parliamentarian who accepts a minister's portfolio must resign his legislative seat—a practice much closer to an American-style presidential system than to a conventional parliamentary regime. Should his government fall, the parliamentarian-turned-minister could be out of a job, although, as a matter of fact, erstwhile parliamentarians have shown considerable ingenuity in circumventing this regulation.

Unlike parliamentarians, civil servants who accept a minister's portfolio can always return to their corps when they leave their high office. A particularly dramatic example of a *grand corps* providing a safe haven for a cashiered minister concerned Prime Minister Michel Rocard. When President Mitterrand asked for his resignation in the spring of 1991, he returned to his corps, the Financial Inspectors, where he prepared a serious but ultimately unsuccessful campaign to become the Socialist candidate for president of the Republic in 1995.[81]

To conclude this review of the importance of the civil service, let us consider two remarkable statements which confirm the point I have been making. The first came from Jacques Delors, a Frenchman who serves in the highly visible position of president of the Commission of the European Union in Brussels. In a lengthy interview on French television, Delors responded to the fears of a substantial portion of the French electorate that the country's interests would be ignored in the larger European community. Delors said this would not happen. France would always be able to hold its own in European affairs. The first reason he gave for his confident prediction was "the quality of our public service and of our bureaucrats. . . . There is no other administration which operates as well as the French administration."[82] Instead of bashing bureaucrats, French statesmen salute them.

The second statement came from President Mitterrand at the customary ceremony in which he exchanges greetings with representatives from the major organizations in French society at the beginning of a new year. On 3 January 1992, he received the representatives of the civil service. After cautioning against yielding to a certain "caste spirit" that would offend democratic values, he assured the civil servants of his full support. He went on to complain that there are too many people who "for too long a time have wanted to destroy not only the State but also the public service, *which is the same thing.*"[83] (Emphasis added.) In view of the exalted French notion of the State, the president intoned a remarkable paean to the prestige of the civil service in general and to the *grands corps* at its apex.

The Council of State and Administrative Law

The principles of administrative law developed by the Council of State provide a striking example of the importance of administrative action in French governance. The council's strength lies in the fact that it is both the highest administrative court in France and the government's highest official advisory body. That is, it adjudicates cases brought against officers of the State and advises the government of the day on the suitability of proposed legislation. A British commentary on the council captures nicely the essence of this dual role by describing the daily routine of a councillor of State:

> In the same afternoon, one person may act as a member of a judicial panel on tax cases and then come down the lift to advise on the drafting of a new law on privatizing a television channel. Far from creating a conflict of interests, the dual function is seen as enriching administrative adjudication.[84]

In addition to their twofold role as judges and advisers, councillors of State are routinely "seconded" to various ministries where they serve as line administrators or as members of a minister's *cabinet*. Thus French administrative judges enjoy a well-deserved reputation of being practical men and women who understand the problems and pressures of everyday public administration. This reputation is crucial for the morale of both public administrators and aggrieved citizens because there is no appeal from a decision of the Council of State. As noted above, France, unlike the United States, has no Supreme Court where administrative decisions can be reviewed.

Throughout its long history, the Council of State has developed a reputation for independence and integrity that ranks it among the most respected institutions in France. On one occasion the council defied even General de Gaulle by setting aside the conviction and capital sentence of a dissident French army officer in Algeria. The council found legal flaws in the decree that the general, as president of the Fifth Republic, had relied upon to establish the military tribunal which tried and convicted the officer.[85]

Perhaps the most striking example of the council's importance appears in its relation with the Constitutional Council, a major Fifth Republic innovation we have already described. In formulating the constitutional jurisprudence it relies upon to void Acts of Parliament, the Constitutional Council followed closely the principles of *administrative law* developed by the Council of State.[86] Thus, the constitutional principles that safeguard individual liberties in contemporary France have been developed by an institution in tutelage to administrative law. As noted above, prior to the establishment of the Fifth Republic, laws passed by Parliament could not be declared unconstitutional. However, administrative decrees could be and were overturned by the Council of State if they were found to violate either a law or the Constitution. Thus, prior to the blossoming of the Constitutional Council, there was a well-established jurisprudence in administrative law aimed at controlling *governmental* (as opposed to parliamentary) action, that is, a jurisprudence aimed at decrees rather than at laws. The Constitutional Council mined this jurisprudence to discover legal principles which it applied against laws voted by Parliament. This is a complete reversal of the American legal experience, wherein administrative law is thoroughly dominated by the constitutional law developed in the ordinary federal courts and, indeed, in the long history of the common law.

I believe the important role of the Council of State in safeguarding civil liberties through its administrative jurisprudence challenges the facile assumption that a powerful administrative state necessarily jeopardizes individual rights. I shall develop this point more fully in chapters five and seven.

The Prefect and Decentralization

The role of the prefect is still another highlight of French administration. Since the Revolution, France has been divided into departments *(départements)* which are supervised by a prefect. Today there are ninety-six departments in metropolitan France. Prior to a decentralization reform in 1982, the prefect was in the difficult position of being the executive officer of the local (departmental) government even though he was appointed by the national government in Paris. Thus, his role required considerable political skills. As a representative of the State, he had to see to it that national programs and standards were enforced in his department, but as the department's executive officer, he was expected to alert the central government in

Paris to local needs and desires. Thus, traditionally the prefect was called upon to exercise considerable bureaucratic statesmanship. When this complicated system was at its best, it gave a good example of what F. F. Ridley has called "integrated administrative decentralization."[87]

Needless to say, the system was not always at its best, and consequently the Socialist government that came to power in 1981 introduced reforms intended to be far-reaching.[88] Just how far-reaching they have been in fact is a matter of some dispute. At first, it seemed the prefect would be a casualty of the reform because the president of the locally elected departmental council *(conseil général)* replaced the prefect as executive officer of the department. As if to add insult to injury, the prefect lost his venerable title as well. Henceforward, he was to be known as the *commissaire de la République* (superintendent of the Republic), but a few years later his familiar title was restored, thereby confirming the stability of administrative traditions in France.

In recent years, there has been a marked growth of "regionalism" in France that has divided the country into twenty-two regions, each of which includes several departments. Each region has its own prefect who doubles as prefect of one of the departments in the region. The regions, like the departments, have their own elected councils whose presidents serve as executive officers. The prefects are tasked with monitoring the legality, that is, the conformity with the national law, of actions taken by the regional and departmental councils. At times this duty creates tense relations between a prefect and a council president. Since neither officer is the hierarchical superior of the other, personal relationships and political skills assume considerable importance in the mutual effort to avoid serious public embarrassment. Although the formal powers of the prefect have been diminished by the decentralization reform of 1982, he or she retains considerable informal influence both as a monitor of the workings of local governments and, perhaps more importantly, as an advocate for local causes with officers of the central government in Paris.

The resilience of the prefect's office was cleverly summarized by a civil servant in an article written for *Le Monde* at the time of the decentralization reform. Noting that the "prefect" would disappear only to be reincarnated as "superintendent of the Republic" and that his diminished duties would require each department to replace him with a new "head of departmental services" *(chef des services départementaux),* the author formulated the *théorème de Deferre* (Deferre's theorem)—so named after Gaston Deferre, the minister of the interior who championed the decentralization reform. The theorem was *moins un égale deux* (minus one equals two: $-1 = 2$). That is, the loss of one prefect leads to the creation of two officers in his stead.[89]

Consulting the Public

French administrators today, like their American counterparts, are expected to be attentive to the needs and wants of the public. Consequently, administrators in both countries encourage private associations to participate in the policy-making process, but they do so in very different ways. In the United States, the Administrative Procedure Act requires that notice of proposed rules appear in the *Federal Register* along with an address to which all interested parties might send their comments. In France, policy making includes a procedure called *concertation* (dialogue or consultation) in which high-ranking ministry officials contact certain groups they think might be interested in a forthcoming policy initiative. Civil servants and representatives of these associations then discuss the proposed policy and how it might be strengthened. The difference between the two countries is that in France the State selects the private groups to which it will listen. The idea behind *concertation* is that the State and private groups embark together on a quest for the common good with the very important proviso that only those groups invited by the party in power may participate. The French procedure has the decided advantage of expediting the rule-making process, which in the United States has been known to drag on for years. The price the French pay, however, is that excluded groups challenge the legitimacy of the outcome and readily take to the streets to register their displeasure in ways that are never pleasant and sometimes become violent. There seems to be a direct relationship between the exclusionary character of *concertation* and the readiness of Frenchmen to resort to "direct action" to manifest their displeasure.[90]

THE AMERICAN FOUNDING

The broad outlines of the founding of the American Republic are well known. When the Revolutionary War had been brought to a successful conclusion, the newly independent states came together in a loose alliance under the Articles of Confederation. The unhappy nature of this union is clear enough from the name historians have visited upon the years it covered: "the Critical Period." Nationalist-minded statesmen saw the need for closer cooperation among the thirteen states if they were to maintain their independence from potentially hostile foreign powers and to achieve the prosperity their rich and diverse land seemed to promise. To this end, fifty-five prominent Americans assembled in Philadelphia in 1787 pursuant to a directive from the Congress of the Confederation of 21 February of that year. The text provided that the delegates should meet for the sole and express purpose of revising the Articles of Confederation and reporting to Congress and the several legislatures such alterations and provisions therein as shall when agreed to in Congress and confirmed by the states render the federal Constitution adequate to the exigencies of Government and the preservation of the Union.[91]

Going far beyond their legal charge from Congress, the delegates transformed themselves into "founding fathers" by drafting an entirely new constitution that was to go into effect when ratified by popularly elected conventions in at least nine states. After a protracted debate during the fall of 1787 and the first half of 1788, the new constitution was approved and the new Republic, graced with George Washington as its first president, came into being in March 1789.

During the ratification debate, the friends of the proposed constitution were hard-pressed to justify the flagrant violation of the mandate the Congress of the Confederation had given to the delegates at Philadelphia. Called into convention for the "sole and express purpose of revising the Articles of Confederation," they had scrapped the text they were to revise. What is more, by deciding that the approval of the people in only nine of the thirteen states would suffice to replace the Articles of Confederation with the new constitution, they ignored the provision in the articles specifying that amendments required unanimous consent. Although ingenious arguments were offered to justify the legality of the framers' handiwork—and are still being offered today—it is hard to resist the conclusion that, despite the glorious history of the constitution they wrote, their work was "plainly illegal."[92]

The Gaullists faced a similar problem in 1958 as they puzzled over how to get out of the Fourth Republic and into the Fifth without giving Parliament a chance to seriously weaken the new constitution which was designed to ensure executive supremacy over the legislature. Their solution was to employ the legal fiction that the Constitution of 1958 simply amended the Constitution of 1946, but even this was not enough to circumvent the clear provisions in the 1946 document requiring parliamentary approval of constitutional amendments.[93] They solved this problem by relying on the crisis atmosphere of early June 1958 to persuade a nervous Parliament to approve a dispensation *(dérogation)* from the ordinary procedure of amending the Constitution of the Fourth Republic.[94]

Throughout this book we shall give considerable attention to the Federalists and the Anti-Federalists, as the friends and enemies of the proposed constitution were called. Following eighteenth-century custom, the authors of pamphlets on both sides of the great debate masked their identity behind pseudonyms that were often borrowed from classical antiquity. We shall respect their desire for anonymity: in some cases out of necessity when the true identity of an author is unknown—e.g., the brilliant Anti-Federalist Brutus[95]—and at other times simply in order to read their works as they presented them.

This second consideration is particularly important in the case of Publius, the author of the famous *Federalist Papers,* whose identity is well known. James Madison, Alexander Hamilton, and John Jay collaborated in writing this political science classic, with the most important essays coming from the pens of Madison and Hamilton. In discussing *The Federalist,* I ordinarily refer to Publius as the author because the real authors saw their serial essays in support of the constitution as a unified whole embodying a consistent interpretation—indeed, a philosophy—of politics. Because the political careers of Hamilton and Madison followed very different and antagonistic paths after their joint literary effort of 1787–1788, I believe it is distracting and perhaps even misleading to identify the author of a particular essay in *The Federalist* as anyone other than Publius. I do not want to burden the text of *The Federalist* with what we know of the subsequent careers of its two principal authors. The text should speak for itself.

Today, *The Federalist* is best known as an authoritative commentary on the Constitution. Pity the poor lawyer whose brief in a constitutional case is not embellished with a suitable "proof text" (no matter how irrelevant) from this venerable classic. So successful was Publius that we tend to lose sight of his original rhetorical and polemical purposes. His Anti-Federalist opponents had been all but forgotten until they were rediscovered during the 1980s, when American scholars celebrated the bicentennial of the Constitution by probing both sides of the argument surrounding its ratification.[96] Having been saddled with the unfortunate name of "Anti-Federalist," it is no wonder that these authors rode off into the historical oblivion pitilessly reserved for those who back losing causes. Fortunately, Herbert Storing's splendid book *What the Anti-Federalists Were FOR* has rehabilitated them and shown that their principled opposition to the constitution was based on positive ideas of governance which they correctly found wanting in the constitution they opposed. The rediscovery of the Anti-Federalists has had the salutary effect of liberating Americans from a demeaning ancestor worship that came to regard the Constitution as a sacred text handed down from on high. It has reminded them that their constitution emerged from the profoundly human and ennobling work of dialogue, argument, and debate, as befits a document that has contributed so significantly to the development of a free society.

Certainly the most important contribution of the Anti-Federalists was their crucial role in getting the Bill of Rights added to the Constitution. This is somewhat ironic, because today the Anti-Federalists give aid and comfort to those Americans who deplore the anemic sense of community in our country, which they trace to our excessive preoccupation with individual rights. Although sweeping generalizations demand many qualifications, I believe I can confidently assert that there is more emphasis on community and similar values in the Anti-Federalist corpus than in *The Federalist*. Hence, the irony that the Bill of Rights—that mighty bastion of American individualism—comes from those of our eighteenth-century ancestors who worried the most about our life together as a people.

Interestingly for our comparative purposes, the Anti-Federalists were profoundly influenced by the great French philosopher Montesquieu who had noted the importance of civic virtue for a solidly republican regime. Following their French mentor, the Anti-Federalists argued vigorously that republics could exist only over a relatively small territory wherein the people had similar interests and backgrounds. They dismissed as a contradiction in terms the Federalist idea of a "federal republic" over a vast territory reaching from the forests of Maine to the swamps of Georgia.

As for the Federalists, they proposed to marry this vast empire to republican principle by refining the nature of representation and by relying on the enlightened self-interest of the great constitutional officers—ideas the Anti-Federalists dismissed as chimerical. We shall return to these matters when we examine the Anti-Federalists' "small republic" argument in chapter four.

Before concluding this section, we must say a word about the all-important principle of separation of powers, which will form a recurring theme throughout this book. As we shall see in the chapters that follow, both the French and the American constitutional traditions take the principle of separation of powers with the utmost seriousness, but they understand it very differently.[97] The powerful idea of a sovereign Parliament, which underlay French republican orthodoxy prior to 1958, is utterly at odds with the American version of separation of powers. For Americans, neither Congress, nor the president, nor the judiciary is sovereign. Each of these institutions is a "branch" of the government, as we say today, or a "department," as they said in the late eighteenth century. Regardless of the word one prefers, the key point—then as now—is that each great institution of the state exercises only *partial,* not plenary power. Plenary power is found only in the Constitution itself, which was ratified by the sovereign people. In ratifying their constitution, the people approved the distribution of powers contained therein, that is, certain enumerated legislative powers to Congress, the executive power to the president, and the judicial power to the courts. In American constitutional theory, no specific institution of government *re-presents* the people, that is, presents them a second time as though it were a microcosm of the people themselves. This *is* how French republicans, at least prior to 1958, saw their popularly elected Parliament, and this explains why laws passed by Parliament could not be declared unconstitutional. At the risk of wearying the reader, I must repeat a question that is absolutely fundamental to the inquiry that lies ahead. What democratic principle could possibly justify a French judge in overruling the will of the French people themselves as expressed by a sovereign assembly that *re-presents* them?

For Publius, the power of judicial review of Acts of Congress involved nothing more than a simple application of the separation-of-powers principle. Far from seeing in Congress a microcosm of the people, Publius stresses the *delegated* nature of congressional authority and invokes the familiar legal principle that "every act of a delegated authority contrary to the tenor of the commission under which it is exercised is void."[98] The "delegated authority" in question is Congress' power to legislate and the "commission" is, of course, the Constitution itself which is the fundamental law of the land and, as such, must be interpreted by judges. For Publius, it is obvious that judges should prevent congressmen from violating the terms of the commission that empowers them to legislate in the first place. Does this mean that unelected judges are the constitutional superiors of directly elected congressmen? Is this the American version of what the French would decry as *gouvernement des juges?* Not at all, says Publius:

> Nor does this conclusion by any means suppose a superiority of the judicial to the legislative power. It only supposes that the power of the people is superior to both; and that where the will of the legislature declared in its statutes, stands in opposition to that of the people declared in the constitution, the judges ought to be governed by the latter, rather than the former. They ought to regulate their decisions by the fundamental laws, rather than by those that are not fundamental.[99]

Publius's cool assurance makes sense only if we demystify the role of the elected official and recall that judges have no less constitutional legitimacy than members of the House of Representatives, even though the latter are directly elected and the former are not. Each holds his office in the manner specified by the Constitution that the people have ratified. It has pleased the people to choose one set of officers themselves while permitting others to be selected in other ways. The American people have distributed their sovereign powers among many constitutional officers chosen in many different ways—direct election, indirect election, appointment by the president with the advice and consent of the Senate, appointment by the president alone, appointment by judges, appointment by the heads of executive departments, and so forth. In all, there are at least twenty-two ways in which one may hold office under the Constitution of the United States, and direct popular election is but one of them. Each officer plays a legitimate role in governing the Republic, provided he stays within his appointed sphere. Popular election has absolutely nothing to do with constitutional legitimacy.[100]

2

French Constitutionalism and Administration

Napoleon fell but the more solid parts of his achievement lasted on; his government died, but his administration survived.

— ALEXIS DE TOCQUEVILLE

The previous chapter provided a brief review of the constitutional highlights of the Fifth Republic. This chapter examines more closely the text of the Constitution of the Fifth Republic and, in particular, those textual provisions that influence the French administrative State. By marrying constitutionalism to the administrative state, I suggest that the offspring of this union is a regime anchored in the principle of the rule of law in a way that safeguards liberal and democratic principles within the context of the statist exigencies of a modern industrial society.

Before plunging into the substance of our inquiry, a few preliminary observations on French constitutionalism are in order. The French constitutional tradition might best be described as one of continuity amidst change.[1] Americans will be forgiven if, in reading French history, they see more of the latter than of the former. Constitutional changes scandalize us—not amendments, of course, but the overthrow of one constitution in favor of another. We have had but one constitution and it has defined us as a people. The very name of our country, the United States of America, is juridical nomenclature, unlike the names of countries like France, Belgium, and Germany, whose ancient origins are not juridical but tribal. Our "states" are "united" only because and only to the extent that our Constitution says they should be. The idea of a new constitution for the United States strikes us as shocking and perhaps even as subversive. Our identity as a people, a nation, and a country is inextricably woven into the fabric of our two-hundred-year-old Constitution.

Not so with France. By French standards, the Constitution of the Fifth Republic has proved remarkably stable, and yet from time to time serious political problems prompt patriotic Frenchmen to suggest with perfect equanimity that it may be time to establish a Sixth Republic.[2] Frenchmen can do this so easily because the identity of France is not tied to a particular constitutional text. No small part of General de Gaulle's forcefulness was his utterly convincing appeal to an "eternal France," and the French knew what he meant. An appeal from an American statesman to an "eternal United States" would be absurd and preposterous. There is nothing eternal about our country. It does not trace its origins to some distant, dim, and misty past. We know *exactly* when and how it came into being as a product of deliberation and choice. Its origins are juridical, not mystical.

With these differences between France and the United States in mind, we can readily grasp why American constitutionalism is so tightly connected to a specific document whereas French constitutionalism is seen as a tradition rather than a text. The various French constitutional texts are concrete manifestations of this constitutional tradition but the tradition itself is more fundamental than any of them. It is this tradition that provides constitutional continuity amid the dramatic changes of regime that have marked French history over the past two centuries.

A good example of this constitutional continuity appears in the preamble to the Constitution of the Fifth Republic:

> The French people hereby solemnly proclaims its attachment to the Rights of Man and the principles of national sovereignty as defined by the Declaration of 1789, reaffirmed and complemented by the preamble of the Constitution of 1946.

Thus the preamble to the 1958 Constitution embraces and ensures the vitality of the principles of the Revolution of 1789. Further, the reference to the preamble of the Constitution of 1946, which had created the Fourth Republic, makes explicit the link between the 1958 Constitution and the *republican* aspect of the French constitutional tradition. The preamble to the 1946 Constitution "solemnly reaffirms," in addition to the Declaration of the Rights of Man and of the Citizen of 1789, "the fundamental principles recognized by the laws of the Republic." The specific republican reference is important because not all of the French constitutional tradition is republican. There have been royal, imperial, and other types of constitutions as well. In mentioning "the laws of the Republic," the authors of the 1946 Constitution had in mind the Third Republic, which came to a disastrous end with the collapse of French arms and political institutions in 1940. They were determined to reinstate French republicanism after the authoritarian hiatus of the Vichy years. The preamble to the Constitution of the Fifth Republic mentions the Fourth Republic in order to stress the continuity of the new regime with its immediate predecessor and to underscore the republican character of both.

These historical connections were not merely antiquarian musings by the founding fathers of the Fourth and Fifth Republics. They were intended to ground their handiwork within a specific aspect of the French constitutional tradition. The Constitutional Council created by the founders of the Fifth Republic to interpret the Constitution authoritatively has held that the preamble is a legally enforceable part of the Constitution itself.[3] Thus the connection between the present republic, its two immediate republican predecessors, and the Declaration of 1789 is no museum piece. On the contrary, it states the relevance and vitality of the French constitutional tradition for France today.

Our examination of French constitutionalism and administration will center on the bifurcated nature of executive power under the Fifth Republic. First we shall examine the powers of the president of the Republic, then the powers of the government, which is headed by the prime minister, and finally the complex relationship between the president and the government. In each case we shall see how the Constitution readies the State for action, a hallmark of vigorous administration. Throughout we shall emphasize the *text* of the Constitution rather than the history of the Fifth Republic. Historical examples will be used only to illuminate the meaning of the text.

THE PRESIDENT OF THE REPUBLIC

Many of the constitutional powers of the French president resemble those of his American counterpart. He is elected for a fixed term of office and is re-eligible (article 6).[4] He appoints many high-ranking officers (articles 8, 13, 56, and 65), promulgates the laws (article 10), receives ambassadors (article 14), negotiates treaties (article 52), exercises the pardoning power (article 17), and is constitutionally empowered to send messages to Parliament (article 18).

A major difference between the constitutional descriptions of the two presidential offices is that the French Constitution, like many other postwar constitutions, describes the executive power and the head of State in relation to a host of administrative institutions that the text of the Constitution presumes to be already in place. For example, article 13 details certain presidential powers in relation to such institutions as the Council of Ministers, the Council of State, the Audit Office *(La Cour des Comptes),* prefects, and so forth. Article 15 places him in charge of the armed forces and then adds that he "shall preside over the higher councils and committees of national defense." Nowhere is the constitutional foundation of these institutions explained. They are simply *there.* The Constitution of the Fifth Republic presupposes an elaborate administrative structure that is already in place, awaiting the arrival of its newly created head of State.

This contrasts sharply with the wording of the American Constitution, which provides that offices shall be created "by law" (II,2).[5] At the national level, there are no prejacent institutions. Whatever administrative organizations may eventually emerge will do so as and when Congress sees fit. The American Constitution does provide an administrative *structure;* there will be executive departments but the names and functions of these departments will be determined by Congress. Each of these executive departments will be headed by a single "principal officer" and staffed with an undetermined number of "inferior officers" (II,2). Thus it would be wrong to say that the framers of the American Constitution simply ignored administrative questions, but their textual expression of administrative interest was purely formal. The framers of the Fifth Republic were much more concrete. Not only were the institutions named but their natures and functions were well known. No Frenchman in 1958 had to be told about the Council of State, or prefects, or the Audit Office. These administrative officers and institutions were household words with historic tasks that were certainly familiar, and in some cases distinguished and venerable as well.

As noted above, the French president, like his American counterpart, promulgates the laws. He possesses as well the additional constitutional power to "sign the ordinances and decrees decided upon in the Council of Ministers" (article 13). Ordinances and decrees are among the trappings of the administrative state. They have a long history replete with royal as well as republican connotations. They need no explanation or legitimation in the constitutional text of the Fifth Republic.[6]

The Constitution of the United States recognizes no such power in the American president, although the long-standing presidential practice of issuing certain types of "executive orders" might bear a faint resemblance.[7] But the case for the American president's authority to issue executive orders cannot lay claim to a simple given of American history. Some executive orders are grounded in implicit or explicit congressional authorizations. Others derive from explicit constitutional powers of the president, such as his authority to "receive ambassadors and other public ministers." Still others come from a tortured logic that purports to discover all sorts of strange and wonderful powers in the teeming womb of the clause that vests "the executive power" in the president.[8] In both countries, executive authorities have governing powers that parade under a variety of legal banners—ordinances, decrees, executive orders, rules, regulations, directives, and so forth. The imperatives of a modern industrial state will settle for no less. Nevertheless, in the United States, the very nature of such powers invites attacks on their constitutional legitimacy, but in the French administrative state, despite debates over the constitutionality of specific ordinances and decrees, the constitutional legitimacy of such powers is sure and unimpeachable.

At several points in the Constitution of the Fifth Republic, the American reader will come across passages he will find truly remarkable. For example, article 5 states:

> The President of the Republic shall see that the Constitution is respected. He shall ensure, by his arbitration, the regular functioning of the governmental authorities, as well as the continuance of the State.

This language confers on the French president a much grander and more statesmanlike task than the American president's lawyerly duty to "take care that the laws be faithfully executed" (II,3). The American president's duty to care for the faithful execution of the laws states accurately enough his primary responsibility as the chief executive officer of the Republic. The French president's duty to ensure respect for the Constitution suggests that in some sense he stands *outside* the Constitution as its champion rather than within it as simply its creature.[9] The American president is clearly a creature of the Constitution and nothing but its creature. There is nothing in the *text* of the American Constitution that remotely resembles the high language imposing upon the French president the duty to ensure the continuance of the State. The truly exceptional presidency of Abraham Lincoln provides the noblest example of high statesmanship by an American president, but Lincoln's efforts, for all their nobility, were never intended to do more than preserve the very constitution of which he was an officer. The thrust of article 5 is quite different, because it obliges the French president to preserve the continuance of the State; but the French State is not created by the Constitution. Like the Council of State, prefects, decrees, and ordinances, it is simply *there* and it is the president's duty to assure its survival.

The American Constitution imposes upon the president the duty to swear to "preserve, protect and defend the Constitution of the United States" and thus casts him in the role of constitutional protector like his French colleague. But the same one-sentence oath requires him to swear that he "will faithfully execute the office of President of the United States" (II,1). This language clearly reinforces his role as a constitutional officer and nothing but a constitutional officer. The French president's duty to the State, which is not a creature of the Constitution, suggests that he is more than a constitutional officer.

Another hint of an extra-constitutional role for the French president appears in Title VIII of the Constitution of the Fifth Republic, which addresses the judiciary. Article 64, which is part of Title VIII, provides in part: "The President of the Republic shall be the guarantor of the independence of the judicial authority." This presidential prerogative raises an interesting question on the principle of separation of powers. The French constitutional tradition, like our own, is grounded in this principle. Indeed, *The Federalist Papers* give abundant evidence of our founding fathers' debt to the French philosopher Baron de Montesquieu on separation of powers. The Declaration of the Rights of Man and of the Citizen of 1789 goes so far as to say that "a society . . . in which there is no separation of powers has no constitution" (article 16). There is no doubt that the French constitutional tradition is as firmly committed to the principle of separation of powers as our own, even though this principle is interpreted quite differently in the two countries.[10]

The French president's constitutional duty to guarantee the independence of the judiciary illuminates this difference. An American reading the present French Constitution might see in this presidential duty an invitation to a fox-and-chicken-coop problem. When Americans proclaim the principle of judicial independence, they mean independence from Congress and from the president. To an American, it makes no sense to announce that the president must guarantee the independence of the judiciary. This is because Americans see their president as a constitutional officer who is himself subject to the principle of separation of powers both to protect his own independence and to keep him from compromising the independence of his separate but constitutionally equal competitors in Congress and in the courts. The word "competitors" is used designedly. According to *Federalist* 51, the system of separation of powers will be preserved by a vigorous but wholesome competition among the constitutional officers who head each of the great departments of government. "Ambition must be made to counteract ambition. The interest of the man must be connected with the constitutional rights of the place." This model of separation of powers is at war with the idea of an officer tasked with preserving the independence of a branch of government which is not his own. The French president's duty to guarantee the independence of the courts appeals to his sense of responsibility and of patriotism but not to his self-interest and ambition. The American view of separation of powers looks to self-interest to do the work of virtue, to serve as virtue's surrogate. The French president's duty to guarantee the independence of the courts suggests that he is above the battle rather than a participant in it. But to be above the constitutional battle that is fought on the field of separation of powers is to be above the Constitution itself. This reinforces the lofty image of the French president we saw in article 5, where he is expected to maintain respect for the Constitution and to ensure the continuance of the State.

The most dramatic constitutional statement reinforcing the image of the French president as a man above the battle appears in the famous article 16, wherein the president is authorized to assume emergency powers in times of national peril. Whatever ambiguity might surround the term "administrative state," it is absolutely certain that at the very least it means a state that can act when action is called for. At the time of the drafting of the Constitution of the Fifth Republic, General de Gaulle took a personal interest in the wording of this article.[11] As we saw in the previous chapter, de Gaulle came to power in 1958 in the midst of a crisis in the Algerian war that had immobilized the government he replaced. He was determined that France would never again suffer the humiliation of inaction in the face of impending national disaster, as it had in the dark days of 1940. Fortunately, article 16 has been invoked only once throughout the thirty-five years of the Fifth Republic. This was in 1961, when dissident generals led a rebellion in Algeria, which belonged to France at that time. President de Gaulle relied on article 16 to crush the short-lived rebellion but, in doing so, raised a host of questions on the perennial problem of the relationship between exceptional powers and the rule of law. These questions are of particular interest to Americans because our Constitution has no special provision for emergencies, though we are no more immune from them than the French. Throughout our history we have handled them on an ad hoc basis with widely varying degrees of success and failure. Rather than "muddle through" in the American fashion, the founders of the Fifth Republic adopted the opposing strategy of formally anticipating emergencies in advance and setting up rules to deal with them. To understand how this strategy worked in practice, we must first examine the text of article 16:

> When the institutions of the Republic, the independence of the nation, the integrity of its territory or the fulfillment of its international commitments are threatened in a grave and immediate manner and when the regular functioning of the constitutional governmental authorities is interrupted, the president of the Republic shall take the measures commanded by these circumstances, after official consultation with the Premier, the presidents of the assemblies and the Constitutional Council.
>
> He shall inform the nation of these measures in a message.
>
> These measures must be prompted by the desire to ensure the constitutional governmental authorities, in the shortest possible time, the means of fulfilling their assigned functions. The Constitutional Council shall be consulted with regard to such measures.
>
> Parliament shall meet by right.
>
> The National Assembly may not be dissolved during the exercise of emergency powers (by the president).

The most important question on the sole use of article 16 was whether the putsch of the generals in Algeria was of sufficient gravity to trigger the invocation of the emergency powers. The rebellion took place during the night between 21 and 22 April 1961. On 22 April, President de Gaulle, pursuant to the first paragraph of article 16, undertook the "official consultation" required before the president can take any specific measures to deal with the emergency. His consultation with the Constitutional Council was particularly interesting. As noted in the introductory chapter, this council is tasked with deciding certain questions of constitutionality that may be raised by various governmental officers. Its most important task is to respond to challenges to the constitutionality of laws passed by Parliament before such laws go into effect. President de Gaulle advised the Constitutional Council by letter of the deteriorating Algerian situation. The council met the next day, 23 April, and issued an opinion affirming that the necessary conditions for exercising emergency powers had been met. That evening, President de Gaulle informed the nation by radio in accordance with the second paragraph of article 16 and on 24 April his remarks appeared in the *Journal Officiel*. By dawn of 26 April the rebellion had been crushed but the state of emergency remained in effect until 30 September 1961.

These dramatic events triggered a host of questions, both practical and doctrinal. For example, what would happen if the nature of the emergency were such that the Constitutional Council could not assemble because the councillors were being held hostage by terrorists?[12] Or if the situation were so desperate that the president could not wait a full day—or even a few hours—to permit the council to gather a quorum? The text of article 16 is categorical; the president must consult the Constitutional Council before he can act. But what if he simply cannot do so? Learned commentators maintain that in such circumstances the principle of *force majeure* would exempt the president from his explicit constitutional duty to consult the council.[13] This is surely a sensible reply but it tends to undermine the value of having a set of rules laid out in advance to handle emergencies if the rules yield when an uncooperative emergency fails to follow the tidy a priori provisions of the Constitution. The reliance on *force majeure* is not a notable improvement over the admittedly messy American practice of "muddling through."

Less speculative and more serious was the problem of duration. The crisis was over in four days but the emergency period dragged on for over five months. The third paragraph of article 16 suggests that normal constitutional government should be resumed "in the shortest possible time" but there is no legal mechanism to enforce this standard.

Still another problem concerned the substance of the opinion rendered by the Constitutional Council. The first paragraph of article 16 states two independent conditions that must be met before emergency powers can be invoked. The first is vague and would seem to present but a minor obstacle to a president bent upon declaring an emergency. All that is required is a finding of "threats" that are "grave and immediate" to any *one* (not all) of the following: the institutions of the Republic, the independence of the nation, the integrity of its territory, or the fulfillment of its international commitments. Given that the world is a dangerous place, it would seem that on almost any given day a president with a little imagination and a mildly suspicious temperament could find ample justification to meet the first condition for invoking emergency powers.

The second condition that must be met before article 16 can go into effect is far more specific and stringent: "the regular functioning of the constitutional governmental authorities [must be] interrupted." The Constitutional Council found this condition was met by the fact that the rebellious generals had issued orders that usurped the legitimate authority of Parliament and of the government over Algeria and had deposed and forcibly detained legally constituted civilian and military officers.[14] Significantly, however, the council failed to explain how the constitutional criterion of the *interruption* of the regular functioning of the constitutional governmental authorities had been met. Throughout the brief crisis, the president, the Parliament, and the government continued to function without any notable interruption.

Commentators have supported the opinion of the Constitutional Council by arguing that it would be absurd to require the president to wait until the government, Parliament, or his own office simply could not function before invoking the emergency powers. The constitutional criterion of "interruption" can be considered fulfilled by the relaxed standard that the great institutions of the State cannot carry out their functions in a "regular" and "normal" way.[15] This is certainly a sensible interpretation but, precisely because it is so sensible, it diminishes the likelihood that the conditions for invoking the emergency powers of article 16 could ever be tamed by the rule of law in any real sense. This problem is underscored by the fact that article 16 requires only that the president *consult* the Constitutional Council. He does not need the council's permission in order to act. The council, of course, was quite aware of its limited role under article 16. In supporting the president's decision to invoke this article, the council abandoned its usual formula in which it says that the council "decides" thus-and-so in favor of the more modest claim that the council is "of the opinion that the required constitutional conditions have been met."[16]

Paragraph 4 of article 16 states that Parliament shall meet during the emergency period and paragraph 5 forbids the president to use his ordinary powers to dissolve the National Assembly. The intent of these wise provisions was surely to safeguard against an executive dictatorship.[17] Under the French Constitution, Parliament is limited to two annual sessions, neither of which is to exceed three months (article 28 as amended). Under article 16, the Parliament is to remain in session for the duration of the emergency, even though it might thereby exceed its normal constitutional maximum of six months per year. It so happened that in 1961 Parliament was scheduled to convene on 25 April, two days after President de Gaulle announced the invocation of article 16. This ordinary session adjourned in early July and then reassembled shortly thereafter in accordance with article 16. During this "article 16 session," the parliamentarians planned to initiate a legislative debate on a proposed agricultural bill that had nothing to do with the Algerian crisis that had triggered the invocation of the emergency powers.

President de Gaulle advised the prime minister that Parliament could not exercise its legislative powers during an article 16 session. According to the president, Parliament could meet and could discuss agricultural matters but it could not pass any laws. Understandably, the parliamentarians objected strenuously and some of them started proceedings to file a motion to censure the government, only to be told by the president of the National Assembly, a staunch Gaullist, that such a motion was itself out of order in an article 16 parliamentary session. This was because the Parliament's power to censure, that is, to bring down the government, balanced the president's power to dissolve Parliament. As long as article 16 is in effect, however, the president cannot dissolve Parliament. Therefore, it was argued, to maintain a proper balance of constitutional powers, the Parliament should not be allowed to censure the government during an article 16 session.

These examples will suffice to bring out some of the difficulties inherent in the French effort to provide for emergencies in advance. Clearly the founding fathers of the Fifth Republic were determined to spare their country any danger of repeating the disastrous course of inaction that cost France so dearly in 1940. The regime they envisioned would never be incapacitated. At the same time they wanted to safeguard against the likely abuses inherent in any reliance on extraordinary constitutional powers—a lesson learned the hard way by Americans during the Civil War and during both world wars.[18] Hence the prophylactic measures of article 16, which bring in their wake a new set of problems that serve only to restate the conundrum of how to reconcile emergency powers and the rule of law. Fortunately for France, this troublesome article has been invoked only once and, even more fortunately, the invocation came during the presidency of a man whose selfless dedication to his country was beyond any doubt.

THE GOVERNMENT VERSUS PARLIAMENT

Despite the importance of the French presidency, the most distinctive feature of the Constitution of the Fifth Republic is the division of executive power between the president and the government headed by the prime minister; a division remarkable by any standard but bizarre and heretical to the public administration faithful for whom unity in the executive is the law and the prophets. In the final section of this chapter we shall consider the administrative implications of this strange constitutional "hybrid" or "dyarchy."[19]

The present section examines this second executive, the government and its prime minister, in its relation to Parliament. Our emphasis will be on the *textual* (as opposed to the historical) relationship between the second executive and the Parliament.

The founding fathers of the Fifth Republic insisted upon the parliamentary character of their handiwork,[20] but they made no secret of their determination to check the abuses of parliamentary democracy which had cursed republican France with chronic governmental instability. Gaullist political analysis attributed this institutional defect to the fact that political parties held sway in Parliament and by their very nature represented particular interests rather than the general interest of France itself and its people as a whole. In the parliamentary tradition, governments are necessarily responsible to Parliament. England, with its two-party system, was able to marry governmental stability to parliamentary responsibility, but in France the multiparty tradition made such a happy union all but impossible. French governments had been overthrown with distressing regularity because they were responsible to a fickle Parliament.

The Constitution of the Fifth Republic adhered faithfully to the tradition of governmental responsibility to Parliament (articles 20, 49, and 50); this is, of course, an irreducible minimum of the modern parliamentary tradition. This formal responsibility, however, was carefully hedged with a number of constitutional provisions intended to protect governmental stability and thereby to ensure the capacity of the government to act when action—especially unpopular action—is called for. These provisions are many and varied. The prime minister, for example, is appointed by the president of the Republic (article 8) and, interestingly, members of the government cannot be members of Parliament (article 23), even though they may address Parliament and be questioned by the parliamentarians (article 48). For our purposes, however, the most important constitutional provisions are (1) those that distinguish between the legislative power of Parliament and the regulatory power *(pouvoir réglementaire)* of the government and (2) those that assure the government a dominant role in the legislative process. We will examine these two types of constitutional provisions in the order indicated. Our purpose is to show how the constitutional text supports the political objective of creating an indispensable element of the administrative state—a government that can act.

The Law/Rule Dichotomy

The relationship between laws and rules in the French legal tradition opens a broad vista of exceedingly complicated questions that far exceed the modest scope of this chapter.[21] Our comparative purposes will be met by a simple analysis of some of the language in the constitutions of the Fifth Republic and of the United States.

As we saw in the previous chapter, the Constitution of the Fifth Republic, like that of the United States, has an important section that explicitly enumerates the powers of the national legislature. Article I, section 8, of the American Constitution empowers Congress to legislate in many areas of our national life: taxes, commerce, bankruptcy, naturalization, post offices, military affairs, and so forth. The same is true of article 34 of the French Constitution, which enables Parliament to pass laws concerning fundamental rights, national defense, citizenship, elections, marriage, crimes and their corresponding punishments, the armed forces, the civil service, taxes, schools, labor relations, the nationalization of industries, and so forth.[22]

Article 37, however, brings an abrupt halt to this Franco-American similarity. There we read: "Matters other than those that fall within the domain of law shall be of a regulatory character." The regulatory power is vested in the prime minister who is the head of the government (article 21). Thus whatever areas of French life are beyond the reach of Parliament fall squarely under the regulatory power of the prime minister and the government he (or she) heads.[23] The contrast with the American Constitution could hardly be greater. Pursuant to the logic of American federalism and our Lockean traditions, our national government is quite literally a government of limited powers. Even today, despite two centuries of expansive interpretation of national power, many aspects of American life are simply off-limits to the national government because they fall neither under the enumerated legislative powers of Congress nor under any other governing power the Constitution grants either to the president or to the courts. This point is reenforced in the Bill of Rights where national governmental power in such important matters as speech, press, and religion is explicitly withheld in the most uncompromising language.

The French approach is quite different. There is abundant freedom of speech, press, and religion in France but it is not based on State *incompetence* in these matters as Americans would have it. Quite the contrary, these fundamental liberties in France are explicitly *affirmed* in the Declaration of the Rights of Man and of the Citizen of 1789, which is part of the Constitution of the Fifth Republic. The American Constitution simply expels state power from these fundamental areas of human affairs: "Congress shall make no law. . . ." In France, these guaranteed liberties are assured, provided that the protected rights are exercised in such a way as not to "endanger public order established by law."[24] Thus the French constitutional tradition treats law as the handmaid, not the enemy of liberty, even in matters as important as speech, press, and religion. The salience of statutory law in French constitutionalism underscores the remarkable innovation in article

37 where the regulatory power of the government appears on an equal constitutional footing with law and reaches all matters in French life that are outside the domain of law as provided by article 34.[25]

The importance of all this for public administration is that under the Fifth Republic the government may exercise rule-making power that is based directly on the Constitution. It may also, of course, exercise the rule-making power to implement laws in those areas committed to law by article 34. But it is the rule-making power that can be exercised independently of statute that will interest American students of public administration. Such power, of course, would be unthinkable in the United States where administrative rule making, a stranger to the constitutional text, always rests on *derivative* power and the derivation is almost always from a statute.[26] Because of article 37, French legal commentators often speak of an "autonomous rule" *(régle-ment autonome)* by which they mean a rule promulgated "spontaneously" by the government without benefit of a supporting statute.[27] This is an extremely important attribute of the administrative state under the Fifth Republic. In matters other than the broad range of activities explicitly committed to the domain of law by article 34, the government can act *sua sponte*. There are no such "self-starters" in American administrative law.

The relationship between articles 34 and 37 introduced a profound change in the understanding of sovereignty in the French republican tradition. As noted in the introductory chapter, Parliament, prior to 1958, had been looked upon as sovereign because there and only there the elected representatives of the people gathered to address the great issues of the day. Because Parliament was sovereign it could legislate in any domain it pleased. By limiting the legislative sphere to those areas mentioned explicitly in article 34, the founders of the Fifth Republic clearly undermined the sovereignty of Parliament. In doing this, however, they did not confer sovereignty upon the government. The autonomous rule-making power of the government, like the legislative power of Parliament, is itself limited because it can be exercised only in those areas that are not committed to law by article 34.[28]

Neither the Parliament nor the government is sovereign because each limits the sphere of the other's activities and the very notion of a limited sphere is at war with the meaning of sovereignty. To support this division of power, the Constitution of the Fifth Republic created the Constitutional Council and, as noted above, tasked it with policing the borders between Parliament and the government to be sure that Parliament does not legislate beyond its appointed sphere (article 61).

Americans will find nothing startling in this arrangement. To us it sounds like separation of powers with judicial review of acts of Congress. Of course, it is not that simple but the comparison is not altogether misleading. For Americans, neither Congress, nor the president, nor the judiciary is sovereign because only the people are sovereign and this sovereignty is expressed in their constitution, which distributes some powers to one institution and other powers to another. Thus Americans intuitively approve of the notion of judicial review of Acts of Congress, even though there is no explicit constitutional language to support this venerable tradition. Surely Chief Justice Marshall had it right when he argued that the logic of the Constitution required such a power, if the various branches of government were to stay in their constitutionally appointed places.

In looking at the Constitutional Council, Americans are likely to see a striking parallel to their own Supreme Court. This, however, is where the analogy breaks down. The Constitutional Council is not a court even though it has the power to declare legislative enactments unconstitutional, a power that in the United States would be clearly judicial.[29] The awesome power to declare a law unconstitutional is withheld from French judges because of long-standing fears of judicial usurpation *(gouvernement des juges)* that antedate the Revolution.[30] This traditional fear was closely linked with the republican principle of sovereignty in Parliament wherein each member represents not just his own constituency, but all of France.[31] Consequently, French republicanism has traditionally resisted principled limitations on parliamentary power, such as subjecting the laws of Parliament to judicial review for constitutionality, because such limitations would seem to compromise the sovereignty of Parliament and therefore would compromise the very foundation of republicanism itself.

The interaction between articles 34 and 37 clearly signals a departure from this tradition and therefore breaks new ground in French constitutionalism and in French republican doctrine. And all this to emancipate the autonomous rule-making power of the government from the heavy hand of parliamentary control! One can hardly imagine a more profound example of administrative imperatives transforming constitutional principles.

Article 37 has two paragraphs. Thus far we have examined only the first which, as we have seen, consists of a single sentence stating that all matters not subject to law are subject to the regulatory power. The second paragraph underscores the seriousness of the founders of the Fifth Republic in emancipating governmental rule-making power from parliamentary control. This paragraph begins by providing that legislation in effect prior to the adoption of the Constitution can be modified by a governmental decree if the legislation in question deals with a subject that is not included on the list of those matters assigned to Parliament by article 34.[32] To do this, the government need only consult the Council of State. Thus, the government can change previous *legislation* without the approval of Parliament. This gives a powerful retroactive force to the autonomous rule-making authority of the government.

The same paragraph, (article 37, paragraph 2) also addresses the situation in which the government might discover that Parliament has legislated in a domain reserved to the regulatory power of the government *after* the 1958 Constitution is in effect. Presumably, such a situation would be unusual because the Constitutional Council is charged with preventing such an abuse. It could come to pass, however, because the Constitutional Council's jurisdiction in such matters is not automatic. As mentioned above, prior to a constitutional amendment adopted in 1974, only four officers could convene the Constitutional Council to examine the constitutionality of a law passed by Parliament: the president of the Republic, the prime minister, and the presidents of the National Assembly and of the Senate, the two legislative chambers that together constitute the Parliament.[33] If none of these officers should convene the Constitutional Council to challenge the constitutionality of a law passed by Parliament, the law would go into effect and could not be challenged afterward on constitutional grounds by citizens or commercial enterprises adversely affected by the suspect law.[34] Hence, the importance of the second paragraph of article 37, which permits the government to change such legislation by decree, provided it can get the Constitutional Council to agree that the law in question really does involve a matter subject no longer to law but to the regulatory power of the government.

As a final example of how the text of the Constitution manipulates the law/rule dichotomy to the advantage of the government, we should note that article 38 empowers the government to ask Parliament for approval to act by ordinance in a matter explicitly assigned by article 34 to the domain of law. In itself, there is nothing remarkable about this power; it can be looked upon as merely a governmental request for a delegation of legislative power. What makes it noteworthy, however, is that it undercuts the law/rule dichotomy and does so to the advantage of the government, since it allows an administrative act to become effective in a matter explicitly reserved to the lawmaking powers of Parliament. Precisely because it is such a far-reaching governmental power, it can be exercised only for a fixed period of time and requires prior consultation with the Council of State and the approval of Parliament, the Council of Ministers, and the president of the Republic.[35]

The Government's Role in the Legislative Process

The law/rule dichotomy gives the government a constitutionally approved basis for using the expeditious means of rule making (e.g., decrees and ordinances) to short-circuit the legislative process, which is always cumbersome and often ineffective. In the Fifth Republic, however, the constitutional support for the government's needs is not confined to means; it reaches ends as well. Often the government will want Parliament to pass certain laws in order to implement its program. When such matters fall within the domain of law, the government, pursuant to article 38, can rely on ordinances approved by the Council of Ministers as a temporary expedient. Eventually, however, such matters must be subjected to the vagaries of the legislative process. When this happens, the government is by no means without resources. We will now examine the important, indeed the dominant, role the Constitution envisions for the government within the legislative process itself.

At the outset we should note that there is nothing particularly startling in the observation that in a parliamentary system the government should play an important and perhaps even a dominant role in the legislative process. In the French National Assembly, as in the British House of Commons, the government owes its position to the support it enjoys among the members of the legislative body and therefore it is only natural that it should play a significant role in enacting legislation. Because of the multiparty system in France, however, this support has been less stable historically than the support ordinarily enjoyed by a British government. French governments, especially before the Fifth Republic, tended to rest more on the shifting sands of ad hoc coalitions than on the solid rock of one majority party. This was one reason why French governments under the Third and Fourth Republics were so short-lived. The founders of the Fifth Republic set out to change this by writing into their constitution detailed rules of legislative procedure that would enhance the chances for future governments to survive and to enact their legislative programs, even if their parliamentary support was somewhat shaky.

These pro-government rules of procedure appear in articles 39 to 49 of the Constitution of the Fifth Republic. Article 39, starts out gently enough by noting in an even-handed manner that the law-making initiative belongs both to the prime minister, who acts on behalf of the government, and to individual members of Parliament. The plot thickens, however, in the second paragraph of article 39, which begins with the words *projets de loi,* an expression that might best be translated as "government bills." The French legislative process draws a sharp distinction between *projets de loi,* bills introduced by the government, and *propositions de loi,* bills introduced by individual parliamentarians and best translated as "members' bills." These two types of bills follow very different legislative tracks. Before a government bill can be debated in Parliament, it must first be reviewed both by the Council of State and by the Council of Ministers. With this distinguished lineage, government bills enjoy much greater prestige than members' bills.

Article 40 severely restricts the scope of members' bills by stating flatly that they are inadmissible "when their adoption would have as a consequence either a diminution of public financial resources, or the creation or increase of public expenditures." Thus, significant areas of public policy are simply off-limits to members' bills.

Article 41 revisits the law/rule dichotomy by providing that members' bills can be declared inadmissible if the government finds they trespass upon the government's rule-making preserve by dealing with matters not specifically designated as legislative in article 34. To exercise this power to stop debate on a member's bill, the government needs only the concurrence of the president of the chamber (National Assembly or Senate) that is considering the bill in question. If the president of the chamber concerned disagrees with the government, either party may convene the Constitutional Council, which is required to decide within eight days whether the member's bill goes beyond the sphere that is properly legislative.

We have already noted above that the government, through its prime minister, can invoke article 61 to convene the Constitutional Council in order to challenge the constitutionality of a law after it has been passed by Parliament and before it goes into effect. We have also seen that the second paragraph of article 37 permits the government to challenge the constitutionality of a law *after* it is in effect, provided that the Constitutional Council had not already approved it before it went into effect. Thus the Constitution treats legislation that is suspected of violating the law/rule boundary as a moving target and gives the government three shots at it: (1) during parliamentary debate, under article 41; (2) after the parliamentary vote but before the law takes effect, under article 61; (3) after the law has been in effect, under article 37, paragraph 2.

Articles 42, 43, and 44 address questions of amendments and parliamentary committees in such a way as to continue the constitutional theme of ensuring governmental domination of the legislative process. Under the Third and Fourth Republics, the government did not have a right to amend texts it had submitted to Parliament.[36] This governmental weakness was corrected by the constitutional provision that "the [m]embers of Parliament and the Government shall have the right of amendment" (article 44). This provision put the government on an equal footing with parliamentarians but the relationship between amendments and parliamentary committees worked to the advantage of the government.

Prior to the Fifth Republic, French parliamentary practice required that amendments adopted by parliamentary committees, whose meetings then as now were closed to the public, would be included in the texts formally debated in public sessions of the two legislative chambers. That is, the public debate would center on the *amended* text—namely, the text that emerged from committee. This was true both for government bills and members' bills. The Constitution of the Fifth Republic changed this by providing that

the public discussion of government bills would be based on the text originally submitted by the government and not on amendments approved by a
parliamentary committee. This change applied only to government bills, not
to members' bills. The latter would continue to include amendments approved in committee as the text considered in public debate. In practice this
meant that amendments to government bills approved by parliamentary
committees were not really amendments at all. They were simply recommendations that the committee members would have to submit, one by one, as
proposed amendments to the original government text which, regardless of
committee action, remained the basis of the formal debate in public session.[37]

Parliamentary committees and amendments were a favorite target of the
Gaullist reformers of 1958. In 1955 Michel Debré had complained that one
of the problems with parliamentarianism under the Fourth Republic was
that these committees were too powerful and there were too many of them.[38]
The ease with which amendments could be added to government bills led
critics to complain that French laws lacked coherence; indeed, they were not
laws at all but "merely a series of amendments" which yielded texts that
were rendered "complicated and obscure, if not contradictory."[39]

Not surprisingly, therefore, the Constitution limits the number of permanent committees to six in each house of Parliament (article 43). However,
a further provision permits the government to require that special committees be created to examine specific bills when the government so desires (article 43). Thus the government gets the best of both worlds—fewer permanent
committees and as many special committees as it wishes. By giving the government the right to require the creation of a special committee, the Constitution clearly enables the government to structure the legislative process to
its liking, even though members of the government cannot be members of
Parliament (article 23). This would seem to constitute a rather severe limitation on the principle of separation of powers.

Before concluding our discussion of amendments, we must examine the
provision in article 44 for a combined vote *(vote bloquée)*. This provision
permits the government to require either house of Parliament to cast but one
vote on a legislative package that contains a text under debate and whatever
amendments the government wishes to include. The package is then voted
up or down as a whole. This enables the government to restore as much of
its original text as it finds desirable, if, in the opinion of the government, too
many extraneous or unacceptable amendments have been added during the
course of the debate. The government need not reject *all* amendments but
only those it does not approve. Needless to say, critics of the Constitution of
the Fifth Republic have singled out the combined vote as a particularly offensive aspect of what they call "rationalized parliamentarianism."[40]

Articles 45, 47, and 48 further enhance the role of the government in the legislative process by putting the parliamentary agenda under its control (article 48), by permitting the government to promulgate its appropriation bills by ordinance if Parliament fails to act on such bills within seventy days (article 47), and by expediting the inevitable delays in a bicameral legislature through its power to dispense with customary readings of bills as well as through its power to demand the creation of a joint committee to resolve differences between the two assemblies (article 45). Further, once such a committee has agreed upon a common text, it cannot be amended without the government's approval (article 45).

Article 49 describes in some detail the procedures intended to ensure government accountability to Parliament. The first paragraph explains how the prime minister may pledge the responsibility of his government to the National Assembly and the second explains the difficult procedure that body must follow if it wishes to challenge the responsibility of the government through a motion of censure. Somewhat ironically, the third paragraph of this article, which taken as a whole is dedicated to ensuring the responsibility of the government to Parliament, contains a provision that has probably evoked more criticism of government domination of Parliament than any other part of the Constitution. Under article 49, paragraph 3, the prime minister, after consulting with the Council of Ministers, may pledge his government's responsibility before the National Assembly on a specific government bill. When he does this, "the text shall be considered as adopted, unless a motion of censure, filed in the succeeding twenty-four hours, is voted under conditions laid down in the previous paragraph" (article 49, paragraph 3).

What this means is that when the prime minister invokes "49, 3," a bill can be considered as adopted by the National Assembly—i.e., it can become law—*without a vote*. The only option available to the National Assembly is to file a motion of censure which, if successful, would bring down the government and could lead to new elections. Obviously, this is a prospect the members of the majority coalition would find distasteful. The more prudent course for the majority is to do nothing and to let the government prevail.

This remarkable provision pushes up against the outer limits of legitimate parliamentary procedure. It was included in the Constitution to encourage stable governments and it has contributed to this end but, obviously, it has done so at a price.[41]

To conclude our discussion of the relationship between the government and Parliament and to put the relationship in proper perspective as well, we might recall what Mark Twain is reported to have said after listening to one of Wagner's overtures: "This music is better than it sounds." Our focus has been almost exclusively on the text of the Constitution of the Fifth Republic to the virtual neglect of the history of the Fifth Republic itself. Clearly the text stacks the deck in favor of the government to the point that one might worry about the vitality of Parliament in French politics. The history of the Fifth Republic allays such fears. As a matter of fact, French governments of both the Right and the Left, with encouragement from the jurisprudence of the Constitutional Council, have exercised their powers over Parliament with considerable restraint.[42]

For example, governments have been quite sparing in their use of their power under article 43 to require the creation of ad hoc committees rather than rely upon the six permanent committees the Constitution permits in each assembly.[43] The text itself, unsullied by empirical evidence, might suggest that special committees would be the rule and permanent committees the exception. This would have undermined the importance of the committee system as a parliamentary institution, but this did not happen. Similarly, the government's power under article 41 to declare a member's bill inadmissible has been used infrequently, especially in the last decade.[44] Even more importantly, the jurisprudence of the Constitutional Council has transformed the harsh textual dichotomy between law and rule into a supple "moving boundary."[45]

These examples offer specific illustrations of a broader point: the parliamentary heritage is too deeply ingrained in French political culture to consider abject surrender as a serious option for parliamentarians. To be sure, the role of the minority opposition is very weak when compared with American congressional practice, but so is the opposition in the British Parliament. The crucial point is that within the confines of an unfriendly text, French parliamentarians have worked out a modus vivendi for a reduced but by no means negligible role for Parliament in a new version of French republicanism. Members of the government have been willing conspirators in the plot to accommodate new constitutional rules to traditional political norms. If it had not been committees, amendments, and the jurisprudence of the Constitutional Council, it would have been something else. Tradition tames text.[46]

PRIME MINISTER VERSUS PRESIDENT

In examining the powers of the president and of the government headed by the prime minister, we have seen how the text of the Constitution of the Fifth Republic ensures that both executives will have the capacity to act, a capacity that is the hallmark of an effective administrative state. Impressive as these executive powers are, however, the very fact that there are *two* executives does not seem conducive to sound administration. Not surprisingly, the explanation of the dual executive is political, not administrative.

At the time of the founding of the Fifth Republic, there was solid agreement between the Left and the Right that France needed a strong executive, but there was considerable disagreement on how to bring this about. On the Right, a powerful head of State elected independently of Parliament was the executive of choice.[47] This view prevailed in the president, whose office and powers we examined in the first part of this chapter. The Left looked to a powerful chief of government responsible to Parliament, to be sure, but protected against the parliamentary whims that had wantonly overthrown so many governments under the Third and Fourth Republics. This view prevailed in the generous executive powers conferred upon the government, which is headed by the prime minister.[48] Thus a bifurcated executive emerged as a distinctive feature of the Fifth Republic; a feature which, we might note for comparative purposes, is, in principle, at odds with the insistence in *The Federalist Papers* upon "unity in the executive" as a cardinal principle of good government (*Federalist* 70).

The constitutional text underscores the bifurcated nature of executive power under the Fifth Republic. For example, the president is the "commander of the armed forces" (article 15) but the prime minister is "responsible for national defense" (article 21), and the government he heads "shall have at its disposal the administration and the armed forces" (article 20). Further, article 13 confers on the president the power to "make appointments to the civil and military posts of the State," even though article 21 grants virtually the same power to the prime minister, namely, to "make appointments to the civil and military posts." At a higher level of statecraft, the prime minister is charged with directing "the operations of the Government" (article 21) which, in turn, is itself empowered to "determine and direct the policy of the nation" (article 20). And yet article 5 tasks the president with (1) seeing to it that "the Constitution is respected," (2) ensuring "the continuance of the State," and (3) serving as "the guarantor of national independence."

The textual ambivalence on executive power could have been an invitation to anarchy, but the fact that General de Gaulle was the first president of the Fifth Republic dispelled any doubts as to where the supreme executive power lay. The pattern established by de Gaulle was so deeply ingrained in the institutional life of the Fifth Republic that his three successors, Georges Pompidou, Valéry Giscard d'Estaing, and François Mitterrand, had little trouble in maintaining de facto presidential supremacy over their prime ministers until 1986. Prior to 1986, the president and the prime minister had always shared similar political beliefs and belonged to political parties with the same orientation. Hence, it was relatively easy for them to work closely together and, because of the precedents set by General de Gaulle, this meant in practice the subordination of the prime minister to the president.

Thus the political practices of the Fifth Republic have belied the constitutional text. At least until 1986, de facto executive unity prevailed over the apparent executive dualism in the Constitution. If one compares the text of the Constitution of the United States with American political practice, the result is just the opposite. A literal reading of article 2 suggests a unified executive establishment headed by the president of the United States, whose immediate subordinates are the heads of the executive departments, who, in turn, are assisted by "inferior officers." But American administrative practice, driven by our national penchant to diversify power, has buried this tidy primitive scheme beneath an avalanche of such strangers to the constitutional text as the president's cabinet, permanent presidential councils, independent regulatory commissions, government corporations, advisory committees, administrative law judges, special prosecutors, and the mighty array of administrative organizations under the control of Congress.[49]

In both France and the United States, deeply rooted political traditions have shaped administrative structures in such a way as to confound simplistic constitutional pieties. Americans have moved from textual unity to de facto diversity, whereas Fifth Republic France has moved in the opposite direction—from textual diversity to de facto unity. In both countries the movements, though in opposite directions, followed profound imperatives of the respective national cultures.

In noting the presidential domination over the prime minister throughout most of the thirty-five years of the Fifth Republic, we have qualified this tendency with the caveat—"at least until 1986." That was the year in which the Right won the parliamentary elections, even though President Mitterrand, a Socialist, still had two years of his seven-year term remaining. Article 8 empowers the president to appoint the prime minister, but since the prime minister is responsible to Parliament (articles 20, 49, and 50) President Mitterrand, as a practical matter, had to choose someone who would be acceptable to the newly elected conservative majority. As noted in the previous chapter, he chose Jacques Chirac, the leader of the most powerful party in the conservative coalition, the RPR *(Rassemblement pour la République)*. Thus began the first "cohabitation," wherein a Socialist president and a conservative prime minister shared the executive power under the Constitution of the Fifth Republic. A second cohabitation began in March 1993, when the conservatives once again controlled Parliament and, as noted above, President Mitterrand chose Edouard Balladur as prime minister.

The story of the first cohabitation is already an oft-told tale.[50] It lasted twenty-five months and during this period the executive dualism of the constitutional text was tested severely. Prime Minister Chirac emerged as President Mitterrand's opponent in the presidential elections of 1988 and, consequently, the textual tensions in the Constitution were exacerbated by the partisan fury of two ambitious men competing for the nation's highest office. Despite the fierce partisan struggles between the president and the prime minister, the overall assessment of the first cohabitation period is rather favorable.[51] Happily, the anticipated disasters of the doomsayers failed to materialize. The administrative state did not grind to a halt, despite the partisan division at the apex of executive power. The upshot of the first cohabitation was a renewed confidence in the vigor of the Constitution. It proved it could guide the ship of state through not only the smooth seas of partisan harmony between presidents and prime ministers but through the tempests of partisan strife as well.

It is no exaggeration to say that the real "winner" of the cohabitation era was the Constitution itself. The two great protagonists, President Mitterrand and Prime Minister Chirac, were both losers: Mitterrand because for two years he presided over a diminished presidency and Chirac because he lost his presidential bid in 1988 and his post as prime minister when his coalition lost the legislative election in the same year. It was only fitting that the Constitution should emerge victorious because at the very outset of the cohabitation era President Mitterrand reminded a hostile National Assembly that there can be only one answer to the question of how the power of the State will be exercised under the new and challenging circumstances: "the Constitution, nothing but the Constitution, the entire Constitution."[52]

There is more than a little irony in Mitterrand's fervent invocation of the Constitution, for the Constitution itself was one of the main reasons why the prime minister's executive authority eclipsed that of the president during both cohabitation periods. The Constitution of the Fifth Republic does not provide the president with a veto power over legislation. Hence, the government's extraordinary influence in the legislative process, which we previously examined in this chapter, favored the prime minister, whom the Constitution places at the head of the government.

Americans might be somewhat puzzled at the profound constitutional misgivings with which the French entered the first cohabitation period. To an American, it all looks like business as usual—the national legislature controlled by one party and the presidency by another. To be sure, Americans complain about "gridlock" and "deadlock" when things do not go well[53]—as they surely did not during the disgraceful budget crisis in the fall of 1990.[54] But when things do go well—as they did so splendidly in the Persian Gulf War—we celebrate our pluralism and rejoice to see confirmed once again the wisdom of our founding fathers who so wisely divided power to preserve liberty. In a word, divided power has its ups and downs, but for Americans it is utterly routine.

Not so in France. When the Right won the legislative elections in 1986, many serious and informed Frenchmen thought President Mitterrand should resign, even though two years of his seven-year term remained.[55] They reasoned that a national legislative election represents the expression of the will of the French people, just as had been true of the presidential election of 1981. The Socialist president should yield to the conservative National Assembly because the people had changed their preference from Left to Right. That is, the will of the people is supreme and its more recent manifestation should prevail over an earlier one.

There is a certain logic in this position, but the logic rests on the metaphysical assumption of *one national will*. Such an assumption would seem to be more compatible with the exigencies of a plebiscitary democracy than a constitutional republic. For the president to resign simply because of an adverse outcome in a national legislative election would set at naught the constitutional provision for a seven-year presidential term.[56] This, of course, makes eminently good sense to Americans, who would never dream of suggesting that a president should resign simply because the "off-year" congressional elections did not go his way. They hardly ever go his way. Sometimes such elections are called "repudiations" of the president and perhaps rightly so; but no one suggests the repudiated president should resign.

Why not? Why would the question of a presidential resignation pursuant to an adverse legislative election be unthinkable in the United States, whereas it was taken so seriously in France, even though the French president, like his American counterpart, is elected entirely independently of the legislature? In answering this question, we find, as is so often the case in comparative studies, that in studying other countries we learn more about our own.

Americans do not look upon an election—congressional or presidential—as *simply* an expression of the will of the people. Elections do, of course, express the will of the people but they do so in fulfilling the design of our Constitution, which is the object of the primordial expression of the will of the people. Elections express our will only because our Constitution tells us when and where and how we should do so. The very Congress we elect is itself a creature of the Constitution and has no meaning whatsoever outside the constitution. That same Constitution provides that our president shall serve for four years and no congressional election can shorten that fixed term. Therefore we do not even think about it because our most fundamental political belief is constitutional supremacy, not electoral supremacy.

This is a salutary reflection because at times some Americans, including, alas, some American presidents, become so preoccupied with presidential "mandates" that they seem to forget about the supremacy of the Constitution. Indeed, during the 1930s, the great constitutional scholar Edward S. Corwin had to remind President Roosevelt that, despite his overwhelming electoral popularity, his powers did *not* come from the people but from the Constitution.[57] It is only the Constitution itself that comes directly from the people. All other powers are mediated through the Constitution. In American constitutional theory, elections do not confer power on anyone. They merely determine who will occupy a particular office that the Constitution has already endowed with certain powers. This is why Americans, for the most part, acquiesce so cheerfully in the power of unelected federal judges to void on constitutional grounds acts taken by elected congressmen and an elected president—precisely the sort of power the French would eye suspiciously as *gouvernement des juges*.[58] It also explains our habitual failure to abolish the electoral college, and its alternative method of selecting the president in the House of Representatives with each state getting one vote. Majoritarian-minded reformers correctly point out that under the present system we have elected—and surely could again elect—a president who receives far fewer popular votes than his principal rival. Such an event, we are solemnly assured, would precipitate a great legitimacy crisis; but thoughtful Americans scoff at this constitutional scarecrow, secure in their belief that their countrymen would accept a minority president as long as he were chosen by the duly authorized constitutional procedures.

Public administration follows this pattern. It is *constitutional* supremacy, as opposed to the supremacy of elected officials, that offers the best hope of grounding the administrative state in our American constitutional tradition. When elected officials grow weary of the powers of the bureaucracy, they rail about "who elected Paul Volcker"—as though popular election were the sole constitutionally legitimate entitlement to govern. Clearly it is not. The Constitution is no less explicit in stating how "inferior officers" are to be appointed than it is in detailing the procedures for electing members of Congress.[59]

And French constitutionalism? The emergence of the Constitution of the Fifth Republic as the big winner of the first cohabitation suggests that France is well on its way toward a regime of constitutional supremacy. But the happy outcome of cohabitation reinforces the pluralistic thrust of the explicit constitutional provisions for (1) autonomous rule-making powers for the government, (2) the power of the Constitutional Council to void acts of Parliament, and (3) an executive power divided between president and prime minister. Together, constitutional text and constitutional practice support the proposition that the old French constitutional tradition of a sovereign Parliament has yielded to a new constitutional order that distributes power among diverse institutions. This, in turn, suggests at the very least a considerably expanded agenda for a Franco-American constitutional dialogue. Public Administration should claim its rightful place in this dialogue.

3

The Executive Power

Though it is no longer a question whether we shall have a monarchy or a republic in France, we are yet to learn whether we shall have a convulsed or a tranquil republic, whether it shall be regular or irregular, pacific or warlike, liberal or oppressive, a republic that menaces the sacred rights of property and family, or one that honors and protects them both.
— ALEXIS DE TOCQUEVILLE

The previous chapter examined certain *textual* questions on executive power in the Constitution of the Fifth Republic. The present chapter looks behind the text to the arguments that shaped it and compares these arguments with those that shaped the textual provisions on executive power in the Constitution of the United States. I begin with executive, rather than legislative or judicial power because it presents a stark contrast between the American founders of 1787 and their French counterparts of 1958. For Publius, executive power presented a problem for republican government; for General de Gaulle, it was the solution.[1]

THE PRIME MINISTER AS CHIEF EXECUTIVE OFFICER

As we saw in chapter two, one of the most notable features of the Constitution of the Fifth Republic is that it divides the executive power between the president of the Republic and a government headed by the prime minister. Though not entirely without precedent in French constitutional history, this arrangement is sufficiently unorthodox to merit such descriptions as "dual executive," "dyarchy," "copilotage" and, of course, as "cohabitation" during the two periods when the president and the prime minister were from opposing political orientations.[2] For the most part, the French executive has been far more unified in practice than the unadorned constitutional text suggests. Nevertheless, the parchment division of executive power intrigues American observers of French politics because it seems to be so utterly at odds with the administrative orthodoxy of Publius's stern imperative on "unity in the executive."[3] The founders of the Fifth Republic seem to be closer in spirit to such Anti-Federalists as George Mason, who favored an executive council that would at once assist and check the president, than to Publius.[4]

A careful examination of the debates of the 1787 Constitutional Convention in Philadelphia, however, reveals that many of the framers of the American Constitution were not nearly as fastidious about executive unity as Publius. For example, early drafts of the document would have given the Senate the exclusive power to make treaties and to appoint ambassadors and judges. Thus instead of considering these powers as inherently presidential powers shared by the Senate, Americans interested in discerning "the intent of the framers" might do well to look upon them as inherently executive powers that belonged at first to the Senate and only later were awarded in part to the president. This puts the senate-presidential relationship in a very different light. It suggests that the framers may have looked upon the Senate, which after all comprised only twenty-six men, as something akin to the formal executive council George Mason sought in vain. This view is reinforced by the fact that supporters of the Constitution answered Mason's complaint about the absence of an executive council by saying that, as a practical matter, the Senate filled this purpose nicely.[5]

Similarly, a review of the debates on the Constitution of the Fifth Republic reveals a strikingly different interpretation of the French executive than what we might expect from considering the history of the Fifth Republic alone. Specifically, the debates suggest that the founders of the Fifth Republic envisioned a unified executive but, surprisingly, the executive unity was to come not from the president, who was seen as something other than an executive officer, but from the prime minister.

Remarkably clear statements to this effect were made on 31 July before the Advisory Committee on the Constitution by Raymond Janot, the government's representative *(commissaire du gouvernement),* and, as such, a major player in the preparation of the constitutional text (see chapter one). In the context of an extended discussion on the relationship between the president and the prime minister, Janot repeatedly affirmed the role of the latter as "head of the executive."[6] Paul Reynaud, the distinguished president of the Advisory Committee on the Constitution, thanked Janot for expressing his views so forcefully in this important matter and summarized his position as stating that "there will be only one head of the executive and that is the prime minister."[7]

This theme was echoed by various speakers in different ways throughout the course of the debates. Pierre-Henri Teitgen, for example, told the Advisory Committee that although the Constitution granted the president certain exceptional powers, it conferred authority on the prime minister for whatever concerned "the life of the State."[8]

In the debate before the General Assembly of the Council of State on 27 August, Guy Perier de Feral sought from Janot an explanation of why some, but not all, presidential acts had to be countersigned by the prime minister. In the course of his explanation, Janot stated once again that "the prime minister is the head of the executive power" and Perier de Feral immediately interrupted him to say approvingly, "That is what I wanted to have you say."[9]

No less a figure than René Cassin, vice president of the Council of State, assured that body's constitutional committee on 25 August that the president would be merely the nominal head of the armed forces, "whereas the real power would belong to the government," which, of course, is headed by the prime minister.[10]

Janot, who was the government's leading spokesman before the several deliberative bodies that examined the developing constitution, never missed an opportunity to correct anyone who might have underestimated the role of the prime minister as head of the executive. During the 31 July debate before the Advisory Committee on the Constitution, for example, he replied to a criticism from Edmond Barrachin that the proposed text created a "bicephalous" government by first conceding that the draft before the committee might have some technical flaws but then insisting that "there is no doubt in the minds of the authors of the document that the prime minister is indeed the head of the executive power."[11]

Before the same body one week later, Janot again corrected what he considered an erroneous interpretation of the prime minister's power. The context involved the thirty-second article of the draft submitted to the Advisory Committee, which provided in part that both the prime minister and the members of Parliament could initiate legislation.[12] Paul Coste-Floret, citing a constitutional law of 3 February 1875, maintained that the president, not the prime minister, should share this power with members of Parliament because everything in the proposed constitution "makes the president of the Republic the true head of the executive power."[13] Janot immediately rejected this interpretation by arguing that if the president were the head of the executive, the position of the prime minister would be meaningless. He then explained that the president is an "arbitrator" rather than an executive and concluded with his now familiar refrain that the prime minister heads the executive power.[14]

Ever vigilant against deviations from executive orthodoxy, Janot had to correct a wayward Roland Maspétiol during a debate on the Constitutional Council before the General Assembly of the Council of State on the evening of 27 August. Maspétiol had objected to a provision that enabled the president of the Republic and the presidents of the two parliamentary assemblies to each appoint three members of the Constitutional Council. He found this objectionable in view of the council's projected role as referee between the executive and the legislative powers. It was not fair, he maintained, to grant the legislative power six appointments while the executive in the person of the president of the Republic has only three. Before addressing the substance of Maspétiol's argument, Janot matter-of-factly reminded him that "one must not say that the members named by the president of the Republic represent the executive, because the head of the executive is the prime minister."[15]

Because of Janot's position as representative of General de Gaulle's government, his unrelenting insistence on the executive supremacy of the prime minister can fairly be taken as the official position on this matter, just as his need to repeat himself so often can be taken as a sign of unofficial skepticism. The dominant executive role of the prime minister has deep roots in Gaullist orthodoxy, reaching back at least as far as the famous Bayeux address of 16 June 1946, wherein the general distinguished the duties of the head of State from those of the premier which came to nothing less than "directing the policy and the work of the government."[16] During his dramatic appearance before the National Assembly on 2 June 1958, de Gaulle echoed this aspect of the Bayeux address when he remarked that in the constitution he envisioned the president of the Republic, who would be the head of State, could not also be head of the government because "the latter would be responsible to Parliament"—a form of accountability that would be utterly inappropriate for a French republican president.[17] Thus at the very outset of the constitution-making process, de Gaulle and his followers, faithful to the spirit of Bayeux, envisioned a prime minister who is no mere subordinate of the president of the Republic and who, as the debate unfolds, grows in stature into the role of chief executive officer, as Janot would have it. In a word, Janot's vision of a powerful and independent prime minister is consistent with previous Gaullist doctrine if not with subsequent Gaullist practice.

If the founders of the Fifth Republic saw the prime minister as the head of the executive, what role did they envision for the president as head of State? Arbitrator *(arbitre)* is the word used most commonly to describe the president in those functions that are uniquely his own. Commenting on a text that would eventually find its way into article 5 of the Constitution, René Cassin explained to the General Assembly of the Council of State the meaning of the following sentence: "He [the president] shall ensure, by his arbitration, the regular functioning of the governmental authorities, as well as the continuance of the State." According to Cassin, this provision underscores the president's role as a "conciliator," a role that was apparently closely akin to that of arbitrator. He then offers two examples of presidential arbitration: appointing a prime minister and dissolving Parliament. In each case there will be competing interests and conflicting points of view. After hearing all sides, the president will make a final decision.[18]

Somewhat characteristically, Janot offers a fuller explanation of "arbitration" than Cassin's. On 25 August he explained to the Council of State's Constitutional Committee that the president would arbitrate in three ways. First, by virtue of his moral authority he would see to it that the institutions of the State functioned properly. Secondly, he could take certain actions on his own initiative which do not require the signature of the prime minister or any other minister. Thirdly, in particularly grave crises, he could exercise the emergency powers provided in what would eventually become the famous article 16 of the present Constitution, which we have already examined in some detail.[19]

The next day Janot repeated the same points before the General Assembly of the Council of State with the significant addition of the president's role as presiding officer of several councils—notably, of course, the Council of Ministers. Clearly, Janot had a very broad understanding of the president's role as arbitrator. This is particularly clear if one looks closely at the range of presidential actions that need not be countersigned by any minister. These include, in addition to Cassin's examples of appointing the prime minister and dissolving Parliament, the power to promulgate the results of referenda approved by the people, to send messages to Parliament, to convene the Constitutional Council in order to examine the constitutionality of laws voted by Parliament, to convene the same body to settle constitutional difficulties that may arise from international agreements, and to appoint three members of the Constitutional Council as well as its president.

This is a rather impressive array of powers for any president. Because the prime minister is the head of the executive, it is logically imperative that all these arbitration powers of the president be considered nonexecutive in order to avoid the constitutional embarrassment of subordinating the president to the prime minister. Thus one must conclude that the logical result of Janot's position on executive supremacy for the prime minister, on the one hand, and broad arbitration powers for the president, on the other, is a rather narrow view of executive power—an ironic conclusion in view of the patent need for a strong executive that brought de Gaulle to power in 1958.

"Arbitrator" was the most common presidential image throughout the constitutional debates but it was not the only one. For René de Jean, the president of the Republic, along with the Constitutional Council, is the "guardian of the Constitution,"[20] whereas André Deschamps, the general reporter of the Council of State, portrays him as the source of the State's legitimacy.[21] Raymond Triboulet, disregarding Janot's strictures, views the president as partially an executive officer, that is, "to the extent that he is not acting as supreme arbitrator."[22]

The most creative analysis of the president's role appears in Michel De-bré's famous address to the Council of State just before that august body examined the developing constitution as it approached its final form. Debré's words take on added meaning because of his widely acknowledged role as the most important contributor to the Constitution of the Fifth Republic.[23] Noting the president's exceptional emergency powers and his powers as head of the (now defunct) Community, Debré highlights his powers as "the higher judge of the national interest." From this lofty perch, the president does not exercise power himself but solicits appropriate action from others who hold power. Thus the president can: (1) ask Parliament to reconsider a law it has passed; (2) ask the Constitutional Council to determine the constitutionality of a law voted by Parliament; and (3) ask the people to approve a proposal by referendum or to elect a new parliament after the president has dissolved its predecessor. Thus, for Debré, the president of the Republic should be the "keystone of our parliamentary regime." Dire emergencies aside, his role is not to act on his own but to get others to act in the best interests of the nation.[24]

Throughout the debates, the proponents of the constitution defended the executive supremacy of the prime minister while presenting the president in a variety of non-executive roles such as arbitrator, conciliator, guardian of the Constitution, font of legitimacy, and so forth. Thus it would seem to be incorrect to say that the framers of the Constitution of the Fifth Republic intended to create a dual executive. As Janot, the government's representative, said so often: There is but one head of the executive and that is the prime minister. And yet it is not quite so simple. We have already noted Raymond Triboulet's position on the president as at least partially an executive officer. René Cassin was quite troubled by a confusing text that conferred the regulatory power upon the prime minister even though another text preserved the president's traditional regulatory power to sign ordinances and decrees debated by the Council of Ministers. He found the efforts to reconcile these texts unconvincing. In fact, he was so disturbed that he used his position as president of the General Assembly of the Council of State to object three times within a matter of minutes.[25] A similar complaint on an earlier draft came from René Coty, the lame-duck president of the moribund Fourth Republic.[26] These provisions and the bewildering division of the appointing authority between the president and the prime minister raise serious doubts about the persuasiveness of Janot's insistence upon the prime minister as the head of the executive.[27] An early draft of the constitutional text confirms these doubts. This version, commonly known as the Red Book, was submitted to the Advisory Committee on the Constitution on 29 July. It was on the basis of this text that Janot assured that body that despite some possible technical flaws in draftsmanship, the intent of the document was to affirm the role of the prime minister as head of the executive.[28] However, a brief commentary on this text, approved by the minister of justice, Michel Debré, suggests a somewhat different interpretation. To be sure, Debré states that the government, which even in this early version was headed by the prime minister, "has the responsibility of executive power"—a position perfectly consistent with that of Janot. Where they part company, however, is in Debré's statement that the president *"shares* in the exercise of the executive power by signing the most important acts in the life of the State and by presiding over the Council of Ministers."[29] (Emphasis added.) We noted above that Janot had mentioned the president's constitutional power to preside over councils as an example of his role as arbitrator, but Debré sees it as a way of sharing executive power. These two statements cannot be reconciled logically because there is a complete disjunction between executive power and the power of arbitration. The precise purpose of creating the notion of the president's powers as "arbitrator" was to distinguish his powers from the executive powers of the prime minister. Further, if the president shares *any* executive power, the prime minister cannot be head of the executive without also being in charge of the president himself, which would clearly be a constitutional absurdity.

So where does all this leave us? With what I hope is a deeper, albeit perplexed, understanding of what the founders of the Fifth Republic meant by executive power. If one looks simply at the constitutional text and the history of the Fifth Republic, one might well say that the founders intended to establish a dual executive, but the dominant role of General de Gaulle in the early years created a pattern of de facto executive unity in which the prime minister was almost always subordinate to the president except for the two cohabitation periods. An examination of the debates reveals a more complicated undertaking. *De Gaulle's government, as officially represented by Raymond Janot, frequently, explicitly, and unmistakably rejected the idea of a dual executive.* Instead, they presented a thesis of executive power unified under the prime minister with the president playing a nonexecutive role; but throughout the course of the long debates it became clear that, despite the insistence on the executive supremacy of the prime minister, the thesis labored under serious logical inconsistencies.

The muddled nature of executive power in the Constitution of the Fifth Republic suggests an interesting comparative reflection. Despite Publius's celebrated call for "unity in the executive," the American understanding of executive power is not without its ambiguities. Indeed, the expression "unity in the executive" itself has two very different meanings in Publius's treatise on administration in *Federalists* 68–77. Primarily, he has in mind a defense of the framers' decision to put one person, as opposed to some sort of commission or council, at the head of the executive. His secondary concern, which is the focus of our inquiry, addresses the president's control over the branch he heads. Here Publius's subtle doctrine should not be confused with the management textbook notion of "unity of command."

The complexity in Publius's writings on executive power tracks the complexities of the Constitution itself. The best known of these, of course, are the explicit constitutional grants of executive authority to the Senate in matters concerning appointments and treaties. There are, however, others as well: e.g., Congress' authority to declare war, to make rules for the armed forces, to create offices "by law," and to vest the power to appoint inferior officers in the president alone, the heads of executive departments, and the courts of law. These congressional powers could properly be considered executive rather than legislative.

These specific constitutional provisions do not defeat Publius's call for unity in the executive. They are simply examples of the American understanding of the principle of separation of powers in which each branch is given a "check" (that is, a power ordinarily associated with another branch) in order to maintain the "balance" necessary to sustain the principle of separation itself. Thus the Senate exercises judicial authority when it tries officers impeached by the House of Representatives, the president participates in the law-making process when he recommends or vetoes legislation, and the courts exercise executive power when they appoint officers as provided by law.

More interesting than the explicit constitutional exceptions to the norm of unity in the executive are the implicit conclusions one might draw from a careful reading of article 2, where one would expect to find the full flowering of Publius's doctrine of unity. The first sentence of article 2 vests *the* executive power in the president of the United States. Presumably this means all of it is his. This presumption is reinforced by examining the opening sentence of article 1, which states that all legislative power *herein granted* is given to Congress. That is, all the legislative power granted by the Constitution belongs to Congress, but Congress is not given all conceivable legislative powers. It is given only those legislative powers that are *herein granted*. Thus, in many countries, the national legislature regulates marriage, but Congress may not do so because marriage does not fall within its enumerated powers nor is the regulation of marriage "necessary and proper" for the exercise of any other power of the national government.[30] Article 2 has no "herein granted" limitation; *the* executive power belongs to the president. The contrast between the opening sentences of articles 1 and 2 has always given aid and comfort to the champions of presidential power.[31]

As article 2 unfolds, however, the plot thickens. Section 2 mentions "executive departments" each of which has its own "principal officer." They are subordinate to the president since he can require their opinions in writing on matters pertinent to their tasks, but do they possess any constitutional authority of their own? Their offices are created "by law" and when Congress by law directs them to perform certain duties, it would seem to be their constitutional duty to execute the will of Congress regardless of what the president might want.[32] If this is the case, it would seem they do have some executive authority of their own; but if they have *some* executive authority, it follows that the president cannot have *all* of it. What, then, are we to make of the first sentence of article 2, which, as we have just seen, vests *the* executive power in the president?

The president's claim to a monopoly of executive power is further weakened by the famous provision in the third section of article 2 that "he shall take care that the laws be faithfully executed, and shall Commission all the Officers of the United States." The close connection between the "take care" clause and the commissioning clause suggests that his power to commission officers exists in order that the laws might be executed. It is textually explicit that the president is not expected to execute the laws himself, but to see to it that others do so. It would seem, therefore, that the officers so tasked would have executive authority from the Constitution to carry out the laws and that the president has the constitutional duty to be certain they do so faithfully. Again, if these officers have *any* executive authority, the president cannot have *all* of it.

All this is reinforced by the legal accountability in the impeachment provisions of section 4, which reach not only the president but the officers he appoints as well. What begins to emerge from an examination of the text of article 2 is something quite different from the "managerial presidency" we have known throughout most of the present century. The constitutional text suggests an image of the president as a magistrate who *presides* (as becomes a *president*) over a legal establishment charged with carrying out the laws voted by the Congress. Indeed, "magistrate" is precisely the word used most frequently at the time of the founding to describe the president. His magisterial role runs counter to the contemporary image of the president as a great national leader and helps to explain Publius's enthusiasm for the electoral college—as opposed to direct popular election—as the most appropriate way to choose a president. The electors deliberating in each of the several states are more likely to escape the "heats and ferments" associated with other forms of choosing officers. In startling contrast to our experience, Publius hopes that presidential elections will not "convulse the community."[33]

Publius's eagerness to avoid heat, ferment, and convulsion is consistent with his magisterial view of the presidency. This view is reinforced by his belief that the president will use his veto power sparingly and only in two types of situations: "that of an immediate attack upon the constitutional rights of the executive, or in a case in which the public good was evidently and palpably sacrificed."[34] Indeed, the fact that the Constitution requires the president publicly to state his reasons for vetoing proposed legislation underscores the legal character of his office and invites further speculation that the framers may have intended this power to be exercised on constitutional grounds alone—a practice followed by our first six presidents. As a practical matter, this brief textual exegesis must yield to the imperatives derived from American history, which presents a very different image of the president. History's presidency, however, reveals its own complexities on the meaning of executive power, with the accountability of presidential subordinates running to all three branches of government. Not the least of these complexities has emerged in the era from Watergate to Whitewater, which has seen a plethora of court-appointed special prosecutors, utterly independent of Justice Department discipline, seeking indictments against executive branch officials for lying to Congress and other irregularities.[35] These recent examples of constitutional ambiguity are simply contemporary expressions of abiding tensions in American constitutional history traceable to the founding of the Republic and, indeed, to the constitutional text itself. Publius, like Raymond Janot, announced a doctrine on executive power he thought was clear and comprehensible but constitutional texts and constitutional history have conspired against both of them.

THE INDEPENDENCE OF THE PRIME MINISTER

To those more familiar with the history of the Fifth Republic than with its Constitution, the notion that the prime minister should be independent of the president must seem strange indeed. Cohabitation aside, prime ministers have served de facto at the pleasure of the president. Thus, when Pierre Bérégovoy replaced Edith Cresson as prime minister in April 1992, there was no doubt whatsoever that the decision was made by President Mitterrand.[36] This well-established practice belies the constitutional text whose strict interpretation, as William Safran notes, provides that "only the Assembly, and not the president, can get rid of the premier."[37] The relevant constitutional texts are clear enough in this matter:

> Article 50. When the National Assembly adopts a motion of censure, or when it disapproves the program or a declaration of general policy of the Government, the Prime Minister must submit the resignation of the Government to the president of the Republic.

> Article 8, paragraph 1. The President of the Republic shall appoint the Prime Minister. He shall terminate the functions of the Prime Minister when the latter presents the resignation of the Government.

Throughout the constitutional debates, the president's inability to remove the prime minister received considerable attention. It was looked upon as an indispensable support for the prime minister's role as head of the executive. Nowhere was this seen more clearly than in the debates before the Advisory Committee on the Constitution, a deliberative body dominated by parliamentarians who, understandably, had more than a passing interest in hearing that the prime minister was responsible to Parliament and not to the president. And this is precisely what they heard.

Reviewing a long list of questions about the proposed constitution, Raymond Janot gave careful consideration to the problem of "how the president of the Republic would be able to get rid of a prime minister whose policies were not in conformity with the president's views."[38] Janot began by replying that his response in this matter is "very firm." The president may not remove the prime minister because:

> the management of the executive power is not divided between two persons; the president of the Republic names the prime minister and, on the proposal of the prime minister, he names the other ministers of the Government. The Government which is responsible before Parliament governs with Parliament's approval. There is no two-fold responsibility of the Government before Parliament and before the president of the Republic. The Government is responsible before Parliament. This is precisely what the text means.[39]

Paul Reynaud, the president of the Advisory Committee, interrupted only to add with warm approval, "That is very important." Janot continued by showing how the wording of the text supported his interpretation[40] and concluded by repeating his point that the prime minister is responsible to Parliament and that there is no twofold responsibility.[41]

The importance of this matter can be seen from the careful attention given to it by participants from very different political persuasions. Thus on 7 August, the managerial committee of the Socialist party instructed their members on the Advisory Committee to be sure it is clear that the "President of the Republic cannot dismiss the prime minister" and went on to propose a revised text stating explicitly that the prime minister would remain in office "as long as he enjoyed the confidence of the National Assembly."[42] On the same day, de Gaulle's advisers briefed him for his appearance before the Advisory Committee. Among the points mentioned was the reminder that "it appears evident" from the text submitted to the Advisory Committee that the president may not dismiss the prime minister.[43]

The general did not disappoint his briefers. When questioned on this point on 8 August, his response was unequivocal. The president cannot dismiss the prime minister because, if he could, the latter would be unable to govern freely. "The person who heads the Government," the general continued, "must be free to govern as he sees fit. The Government is responsible to Parliament and not to the head of State."[44] De Gaulle repeated this point twice in completing his answer to this question. He simply could not have been more emphatic in denying to the president any power to remove the prime minister.

When de Gaulle had finished his reply, Paul Reynaud underscored the importance of this matter and assured the general that his answer would allay the fears of those who had questioned the authentic parliamentary character of the proposed constitution. Later the same day, after de Gaulle had departed, Reynaud relied upon his assurances to oppose the Socialist amendment noted above, which would have stated explicitly that the prime minister should remain in office as long as he had the support of the National Assembly. Reynaud argued that there was no need for such specific language in view of the general's "categorical declaration."[45]

De Gaulle's solemn assurances that the president could not dismiss the prime minister made a profound impression. Three weeks later, they were recalled by André Deschamps, the general reporter for the Council of State, when he introduced the proposed constitution for that body's consideration. Indeed, it seemed there was simply no controversy about this matter because on 19 August a group of Gaullist advisers amended the text that had been reviewed by the Advisory Committee in order to strengthen the language affirming the immunity of the prime minister from presidential removal.[46]

In view of these strong statements from the friends of the constitution and from the general himself, it is remarkable that the constitutional practice of the Fifth Republic has been so different. In no sense has this practice been the result of subterfuge; it has been entirely aboveboard and without apology. At his famous press conference of 31 January 1964, President de Gaulle stated flatly that the prime minister served at the pleasure of the president, a sentiment echoed over the years by such diverse statesmen as Georges Pompidou, Jacques Chaban-Delmas, François Mitterrand, and Pierre Mauroy.[47] Indeed, as one commentator has remarked, the subordination of the prime minister to the president has become "one of the principal *constitutional conventions* on which the operation of the Fifth Republic depends."[48]

To understand this striking difference between constitutional word and deed, it is helpful to note that, despite de Gaulle's assurances, there was throughout the constitution-drafting process an abiding undercurrent of doubt about the proper relationship between the president and the prime minister. Chief among these doubters was Michel Debré, the principal architect of the constitution. According to François Luchaire's notes from a 19 June meeting of the working group on the constitution, Debré thought that the power to appoint an officer carried with it the power to remove him and that therefore the silence of an early outline of the constitution on the removal question implied that the president, who was empowered to appoint the prime minister, had the power to remove him as well.[49] Luchaire, who believed that occasions might arise in which the president should have the power to remove the prime minister, seems to have been dissatisfied with Debré's reliance on constitutional silence and notes that Debré promised to give more thought to the question of whether this matter required an explicit affirmation.[50]

Apparently, little changed during the next ten days, for in a memorandum prepared on 30 June for Louis Jacquinot, a minister of State in de Gaulle's government, Luchaire once again noted Debré's position that the power to appoint implies the power to remove. This time he added his own opinion that Debré's interpretation applied in administrative law for the appointment of high-ranking civil servants, but not in constitutional law where the position of prime minister was at stake. Luchaire thought this point required clarification.[51]

The text that emerged from the interministerial meeting of 30 June made some progress, but not in the direction that both Debré and Luchaire had in mind. It seemed to deny the president the power to remove the prime minister: "The president of the Republic shall appoint the prime minister and, on the proposal of the latter, shall appoint the other members of the Government and terminate their functions."[52] This text closely resembled the version that would go to the Advisory Committee on 29 July, but Luchaire remained unsatisfied. In an extensive and penetrating set of "observations" for the Advisory Committee, he put the question directly as to whether the president can dismiss the prime minister and advised the committee to give a straight answer. "It is better to answer this question clearly than to leave it up in the air," he wrote.[53] At this point in the constitution-making process, Luchaire dropped the preference he had indicated earlier for some sort of presidential authority to remove the prime minister and settled for clarity alone.

Throughout the constitution-making process, many voices were raised in defense of some sort of presidential power to remove the prime minister and not all were as circumspect as Debré and Luchaire. During the Advisory Council debate, for example, Albert de Bailliencourt proposed an unsuccessful amendment that would have given the president unequivocally the power to dismiss the prime minister and all other ministers.[54] Pierre Seligman argued before the Council of State that it would be very dangerous to withhold from the president the power to remove the prime minister if he so desired. This would enable the prime minister to challenge the president directly. Anticipating that General de Gaulle would be the Republic's first president, Seligman readily conceded that this would be unthinkable as long as he was in office, but urged his fellow councillors to look beyond the first president. He continued, "And if you want to have a really strong executive power, you must not contemplate permitting the prime minister to cling to his office against the winds and the tides when the president of the Republic has valid reasons to ask for his resignation."[55]

Two particularly interesting comments on the president's removal power came at the very end of the process. President René Coty initiated a last-minute effort to permit the president to terminate the prime minister provided he convene Parliament immediately.[56] Coty based his position on the admittedly unlikely event that the prime minister should plot a coup or should betray his trust in some other outrageous manner. The requirement for a parliamentary session would provide an adequate check against presidential abuse of this power.

Maurice Thorez, speaking on behalf of the Communist party in a radio address on 22 September, urged his listeners to reject the proposed constitution, which was at that time being debated by the French people in anticipation of the 28 September referendum. Among the reasons he gave for this advice was "that the President of the Republic would have more power than the last kings of France. He appoints the ministers and dismisses them at his pleasure."[57] Clearly, Thorez's comments seriously distorted the language of the proposed constitution; but, if his talents as an exegete were wanting, one might essay a more generous judgment on his abilities as a seer.

Most important of all, however, was the position of General de Gaulle himself on the president's power to remove the prime minister. We have already seen the unequivocal language he used before the Advisory Council in assuring that body that the president had no such power under the proposed constitution, but there is reason to suspect that de Gaulle harbored some serious doubts in this crucial matter. At a meeting of the interministerial committee on 23 June, the general stated his belief that the president should have the power to "dissolve" both the National Assembly and the government if either should exceed its constitutional powers. Although technically governments are not "dissolved," the context makes it clear that the general meant putting an end to a government and, therefore, presumably dismissing the prime minister. Guy Mollet and Pierre Pflimlin opposed this idea, arguing that it would draw the president too closely into routine political affairs that would undermine his role as arbitrator. De Gaulle seemed to meet them halfway, agreeing that ordinarily the president should not have this power but that he should have it in exceptional circumstances. Debré added, perhaps significantly, that the ordinary times of the twentieth century are no longer what they were in the nineteenth century.[58]

A second indication of some backsliding on de Gaulle's part emerges from the way in which he edited the summary of his remarks to the Advisory Committee on the Constitution before they were released for publication.[59] This editing, which took place the year after the Constitution had been approved, appears in the general's (now the president's) own hand and strongly suggests some second thoughts on his part on the question of the president's removal powers. The summary presented to de Gaulle reported as follows his response to the question of whether the president can remove the prime minister:

> No! For if it were so, he [the prime minister] would not be able to govern. The prime minister is responsible before Parliament and not before the head of State, an impartial figure who must not get involved in political situations but whose essential role is to look to the smooth functioning of the duly constituted Authorities.[60]

This is an accurate summary of de Gaulle's complete statement before the Advisory Committee on 8 August.[61] Nevertheless, he introduced the following changes (indicated in italics) for the text he approved for release to the public:

> No! For if it were so, he [the prime minister] would not be able to govern *effectively.* The prime minister is responsible before Parliament and not before the head of State *in that which concerns* political situations. *The essential role of the head of State is to assure* the smooth functioning of the duly constituted *public* Authorities.[62]

By saying that the prime minister is not responsible to the president "in that which concerns political situations," de Gaulle clearly implies that he *is* responsible in nonpolitical situations and this, in turn, recalls the distinction he had made between ordinary and extraordinary situations in his colloquy with Pflimlin, Mollet, and Debré on 23 June 1958. Perhaps this is what de Gaulle had in mind all along and he did not shrink from rewriting a little history to get there.

A final example of de Gaulle's ambivalence in this matter appeared in a change he introduced to the text approved by the Council of State on 28 August. That text provided: "The president of the Republic shall appoint the prime minister. He may terminate the latter's functions only upon the presentation by the prime minister of the resignation of the Government." Pierre Avril, citing Guy Mollet, maintains that de Gaulle himself made the change to what became the final version of the present Constitution: "The president of the Republic shall appoint the Prime Minister. He shall terminate the functions of the Prime Minister when the latter presents the resignation of the Government." It would seem that the change from the negative to the positive proposition (that is, deleting the forceful word *only*) weakens the prime minister's exemption from presidential discipline, but de Gaulle claimed otherwise by explaining that "the affirmative excludes every other possibility," apparently meaning that the revised text would serve to strengthen the independence of the prime minister.[63] Avril remarks wryly that "it is not certain that the grammatical explanation is as innocent as it appears."[64]

The discussion of the president's power to remove the prime minister was but part of a much larger debate on the distribution of the appointing and removal powers in general. The final version of the Constitution divides the appointing power between the president and the prime minister in a bewildering way that has generated extensive commentary and not a little confusion.[65] Unlike the debate over the president's power to remove the prime minister, the broader questions of appointment have less to do with great constitutional principles than with the complexities of the modern administrative state. For example, the division of the appointing power between president and prime minister was necessary because of technical questions of administrative law on delegated and subdelegated power and on legal protections for civil servants.[66]

All this contrasts markedly with the founding of the American Republic in 1787. The text of the American Constitution says nothing about removal from office save for the impeachment clause, which is restricted to convictions for "Treason, Bribery, or other high Crimes and Misdemeanors."[67] The provision in article 2 for appointing officers other than with the advice and consent of the Senate was an afterthought on the part of the framers, added at the very end of the convention. This relative neglect reflects the simple administrative structure envisioned by the framers. Although the problem of delegated power can be traced back at least as far as John Locke, it did not assume its technical character until the present century and especially during the New Deal era, wherein one finds debates similar to those that engaged the founders of the Fifth Republic in 1958.

Although the American Constitution says nothing about removal from office other than through impeachment, this difficult issue could not be long avoided. The first Congress addressed it squarely in the famous "decision of 1789," which gave the president unfettered discretion to remove the heads of the executive departments. Here the American debate, like the French debate over the removal of the prime minister, transcended technical administrative questions and reached broad constitutional principles of accountability and the nature of republican government.[68]

Anticipating the removal problem, Alexander Hamilton, writing as Publius, had argued that the president would need the advice and consent of the Senate to remove officers he had appointed with the Senate's approval.

His reason was that "the consent of that body [the Senate] would be necessary to displace as well as to appoint."[69] Interestingly, this is the same line of reasoning Luchaire attributes to Michel Debré to support the latter's position in the early stages of the drafting process, to the effect that the president has the power to remove the prime minister because he has the power to appoint him. In both cases, the underlying principle seems to be that the procedure to remove a high officer should be no more complicated than the procedure to appoint him.

Neither Publius nor Debré prevailed and in neither case was the rejection of their common position long in coming. Debré's interpretation was rejected in the text of the Constitution itself and the first Congress lost no time in rejecting Publius's gloss.[70]

In defending the Senate's right to share in the removal power, Publius had in mind a broader plan for administrative stability in the executive branch of government. He rejected the Anti-Federalist argument that the Constitution should have limited the number of terms a president could serve. The absence of such a limitation, Publius argued, enables the people to keep a successful president in office for a long time "in order to prolong the utility of his talents and virtues, and to secure to the government, *the advantages of permanency in a wise system of administration.*" (Emphasis added.) If the president were limited to one or two terms in office, presidential turnovers would obviously take place more frequently than if the president were indefinitely re-eligible. This, in turn,

> would be likely to induce every new president to promote a change of men to fill the subordinate stations; and these causes together could not fail to occasion *a disgraceful and ruinous mutability in the administration of the government.* [Emphasis added.]

This quotation, linking administrative stability to the indefinite re-eligibility of the president, is taken from *Federalist* 72. Publius revisits the question of administrative stability in *Federalist* 77, but this time in the context of how to preserve it once the new president comes into office, regardless of how many terms his predecessor has served. This is where Publius turns to the Senate, maintaining that its role in consenting to the removal of officers will "contribute to the stability of the administration."

> A change of the chief magistrate therefore would not occasion so violent or so general a revolution in the officers of the government, as might be expected if he were the sole disposer of offices. Where a man in any station had given satisfactory evidence of his fitness for it, a new president would be restrained from attempting a change, in favor of a person more agreeable to him, by the apprehension that the discountenance of the Senate might frustrate the attempt, and bring some degree of discredit upon himself.

Thus, a newly elected president would be very careful about trying to remove competent officers who had served his predecessor well because, if the Senate refused to go along, the president would be permanently burdened with a high-ranking subordinate whom he had unsuccessfully tried to remove. This is a powerful statement by Publius, calculated to reassure "those who can best estimate the value of a steady administration." It shows how seriously he took the need to protect competent public servants filling the highest offices in the Republic from a newly elected president.

Today, of course, we take it for granted that an incoming president should have virtually unfettered discretion to pick his own "team." Despite his call for unity in the executive, Publius would be profoundly suspicious of such a practice. Pulling no punches, he says an executive "prostitutes" his authority when he appoints men "whose chief merit is their implicit devotion to his will." Our willingness to give the president a free hand in these matters can be traced to the congressional "decision of 1789," which rejected Publius's interpretation of the Senate's role in removals. Surely there are sound democratic principles to support our relaxed attitude. Nevertheless, it may be salutary to recall Publius's plan for administrative stability the next time we read about the average tenure of politically appointed executives being less than two years and then complain about the amateurish way our government is run. On the other hand, the speedy congressional rejection of Publius's plan in 1789, combined with the fact that in 1793 Hamilton himself rejected the plan he had proposed as Publius, suggests that, whatever its merits, it was doomed from the outset.

UNIVERSAL SUFFRAGE LEGITIMATING PRESIDENTIAL HEGEMONY

Perhaps the remarkable disparity, between the executive of the founding debates and the real executive of the Fifth Republic can be explained in part by the personal stature of General de Gaulle and what may have been his hidden agenda, but a more principled explanation is required to explain the *permanence* of this disparity, which has grown into a constitutional convention.[71] The election of the president by universal suffrage offers at least a partial explanation based on principle.

The 1958 Constitution provided for the indirect election of the president by an "electoral college" composed of a broad range of some 80,000 officeholders. In 1962, pursuant to the dubious constitutional procedure described in chapter one, President de Gaulle had the Constitution amended by referendum so that henceforth the president would be selected by universal suffrage. Throughout the constitutional debates of 1958 this reform had been the missing link between the powerful presidential role envisioned by the founders and the exigencies of republican government. Thus, on 27 August Edouard Delvolvé admitted to his fellow councillors of State that he would feel much better about the extraordinary emergency powers of the president under article 16 "if the president were elected by a majority of the French people."[72]

Referring likewise to the "truly exceptional powers" of article 16 as well as to other presidential powers in general, Paul Coste-Floret argued before the Advisory Committee that the presidential electoral scheme was "one of the weaknesses" of the Constitution which he characterized—no doubt much to the chagrin of Debré and Janot—"as a true compromise between a presidential regime and a parliamentary regime."[73] Specifically, he scored the provision that would permit the president to be elected on a second round by a mere relative majority. His quarrel was not with the relative majority provision as such but with a relative majority *of an electoral college*. This was too narrow a political base to support such weighty presidential powers. Coste-Floret added: "If you [the government] had gone all the way to election by universal suffrage—something that was entirely plausible—we could then understand an election by relative majority."[74]

President Coty approached the question of universal suffrage from a different angle when he criticized an early draft of the constitution that provided the president would use his arbitration powers to assure the proper functioning of the institutions of the State.[75]

Coty questioned the propriety of "proclaiming that the president of the Republic is the arbitrator who assures the proper functioning of the duly constituted public authorities whereas in the final analysis this functioning will depend on Parliament or on universal suffrage."[76] Coty does not say that the president should be chosen by universal suffrage, but he does question the legitimacy of his role as arbitrator precisely because, unlike the parliamentarians, he is *not* chosen in this way. The normative link between arbitration powers and universal suffrage is unmistakably clear in Coty's comment, even though the link would not be forged until the constitutional amendment of 1962.

Coming at the same problem somewhat differently, François Valentin criticized the draft presented to the Advisory Committee because it left the precise rules for electing the president to an organic law to be passed at some future time. Valentin found this intolerable because "in reality the president of the Republic is the sovereign."[77] The rules for his election should be firmly embedded in the Constitution and not be subject to change with every new presidential term. To change the *corps électoral* with each president would be analogous to a hereditary regime changing the royal family with each new king.[78]

Like Coty, Valentin does not mention universal suffrage explicitly but his reference to the president as the "sovereign" is striking nonetheless.[79] The French republican tradition ordinarily looks upon Parliament as sovereign precisely because its members are directly elected by the people. To stay within the bounds of republican orthodoxy, Valentin's sovereign would have to be chosen by the people.

Pierre-Henri Teitgen offers still another example of the link between presidential powers and universal suffrage. In a radio address on 25 September, Teitgen explained why his political party, the "Popular Republican Movement," would support the proposed constitution. One reason he gave is that, by selecting its officers through popular election, the constitution preserves both "democracy and the Republic."[80] He then notes that while universal suffrage will determine the membership of the National Assembly, the president, who draws his powers of arbitration from election, will be selected indirectly: that is, he will be "chosen by those who have been chosen by the rest of the nation."[81]

Teitgen's statement was intended to affirm the republican character of the proposed constitution, but by emphasizing election as the legitimating source of power and then contrasting the directly elected assembly with the indirectly elected president, he suggests a hierarchy of legitimacy that favors the Parliament at the president's expense. This point of view is at odds with General de Gaulle's expansive view of the president's role as arbitrator in the new regime. Thus the implication of Teitgen's remarks, like those of Delvolvé, Coste-Floret, Coty, and Valentin, points to the inconsistency between the grand Gaullist vision of the president as arbitrator, on the one hand, and the failure to elect him by universal suffrage on the other. The logic of the presidency of the Fifth Republic demands universal suffrage. It is the missing piece in the puzzle.

No one stated the republican imperative for popular election of the president more clearly than François Luchaire. In a note of 30 June 1958 to Minister of State Louis Jacquinot, he argued that if the president is to play an effective role vis-à-vis the members of Parliament, he must be elected directly by the people as they are. "Any other solution deprives him of the base of *legitimacy* which he must have in order to balance the legislative power."[82] (Emphasis in original.) Luchaire dismissed the proposed electoral college as inadequate because it would give disproportionate weight to rural areas and could end up with a head of State being chosen by a mere 20 percent of the French voters.

The notion of legitimacy through popular election is, of course, bedrock French republican principle. De Gaulle and his advisers heard it time and again during the stormy sessions of the National Assembly on 1-2 June. From these sessions there emerged the crucial Constitutional Law of 3 June 1958 that set the stage for the new constitution. Many of de Gaulle's critics in the assembly thought the proposed legislation gave his government far too much power. A major theme in this attack was the reluctance of members of the National Assembly to part with the sovereign power that was theirs through election by universal suffrage. The following remarks capture the gist of the argument:

> Ladies and gentlemen, despite the drama in which our country is engaged and its will to bring about its own resurrection, I cannot delegate to General de Gaulle that part of the sovereignty of the people which I still hold from my mandate.[83]

> As a trustee of a part of the national sovereignty, I do not feel I have the right to ratify, to legalize this violence which is being perpetrated against us.[84]

> It will be impossible for me to vote to delegate some part of the law-making power which has been delegated to me through universal suffrage.[85]

During the same debate, Pierre-Henri Teitgen spoke in support of de Gaulle's government, stating his belief that the constitution, which was about to be drafted, would respect "the two fundamental principles of democracy, i.e., that the executive power as well as the deliberative power flow from the national sovereignty and that the Government should be responsible before the Assembly elected by universal suffrage."[86]

Although, as noted above, Teitgen eventually supported the Gaullist constitution in September, it did not meet the first of the two criteria he had announced for a democratic regime before the National Assembly in early June. In the unamended Constitution of the Fifth Republic, the executive, that is, the government headed by the prime minister, does not flow from the "national sovereignty" but from the appointing power of the president who is not elected by universal suffrage.

Legitimacy through universal suffrage was at the heart of Felix Gaillard's criticism of the constitution in a 24 September radio address in which he explained the position of his Radical Republican and Radical-Socialist party. Although the party urged a "yes" vote in the referendum, Gaillard voiced serious reservations. He did not say that the president should be elected by universal suffrage but he felt that those who were so elected—the members of the National Assembly—were too weak in comparison with the president. His demanding criterion for a democratic regime was that it be based "on the election by direct universal suffrage of a National Assembly which has the last word."[87] Clearly, no serious Gaullist would accept such a standard; there would certainly be times when the "last word" should be uttered by the president as "arbitrator." Nevertheless, a popularly elected Gaullist president would meet Gaillard halfway. Parliament would not always have the last word but, when the last word was the president's, it would at least be spoken in a voice strengthened by the legitimating force of universal suffrage.

Michel Debré and Raymond Janot joined forces in opposing a president elected by universal suffrage because, according to Debré, it would transform the parliamentary regime the Gaullists envisioned into a presidential regime which would be incompatible with French republicanism. A president so elected, said Debré, would be drawn excessively into the day-to-day affairs of the government.[88] Janot was more blunt. He maintained universal suffrage would strengthen the president's hand to the point where the regime might collapse into a dictatorship.[89] The same dark thoughts may have been troubling Debré when he reacted to a modest proposal for a plan to elect the president by nothing more than an *indirect* universal suffrage with a curt and enigmatic rejection on the grounds that "it's very dangerous."[90] Perhaps Debré had in mind the unfortunate result of the only French experience with a directly elected president, which took place under the Second Republic (1848–1851). As noted in chapter one, the popularly elected president, Louis Napoléon Bonaparte, led a *coup d'état* that transformed the Second Republic into the Second Empire and had himself proclaimed Emperor Napoléon III.

To one looking back at 1958 today, the fears of Debré and Janot seem exaggerated and perhaps even somewhat contrived. Debré had little trouble setting his scruples aside just four years later when President de Gaulle told him of his plan to amend the Constitution in order to have the president elected by universal suffrage.[91] Indeed, he looked upon the idea most favorably. Echoing the critics of 1958 and forgetting his earlier misgivings, Debré celebrated universal suffrage: "In our times, direct universal suffrage alone confers a legitimacy which corresponds to the highest political responsibilities."[92]

He gave two reasons for his remarkable conversion. The first arose from the emergence of France as a nuclear power. Because of the serious consequences of the use of such power, the president needs a new source of legitimacy. The legitimacy that comes from universal suffrage will increase the credibility of the *force de frappe*.[93]

The second reason came from the collapse of the French Empire which, as we have seen, had been redesigned as a "Community" under the Constitution of the Fifth Republic. In Debré's words, "As long as the Community was made up of French citizens, as long as Algeria was a land under French sovereignty, the election of the president of the Republic by universal suffrage was out of the question: the electors in France would have been very much in the minority."[94]

Debré adds that even before the Bayeux address in 1946, de Gaulle had always wanted the president elected by universal suffrage but the idea "had been set aside because of the need to have the empire participate in designating the president."[95]

Thus the failure to endow the Constitution of the Fifth Republic with a popularly elected president was due more to pragmatic calculations than to principle. The principled objections to this regrettable but prudent constitutional flaw were not refuted in 1958 but merely set aside. When the Empire-turned-community disappeared, the difficulties with universal suffrage disappeared with it and de Gaulle and Debré set out to heal the glaring defect in their Constitution. With a popularly elected president in place, the strained, scholastic arguments over the nature of executive power vis-à-vis "arbitration" quickly lost their relevance. So did the hand-wringing over the president's power to remove the prime minister. Although the constitutional text still makes the prime minister responsible to Parliament alone, the spirit of the document has been changed significantly. The republican imperative of universal suffrage was one of the main reasons why the prime minister was responsible to the popularly-elected Parliament and not to the president. The universal suffrage reform of 1962 offers the president a principled argument to defend his de facto power to dismiss the prime minister, despite constitutional language to the contrary.[96] It also goes a long way toward explaining and justifying the de facto approximation to a unified executive under the leadership of the president. The same principle explains and justifies the exceptional cohabitation arrangement, wherein political authority is divided because the will of the people is itself divided.

The president of the United States, unlike his French counterpart, is still chosen by an electoral college. Every presidential campaign yields a predictable crop of quadrennial newspaper articles calling for the abolition of this "undemocratic anachronism." Undemocratic and anachronistic it well may be, but there is no doubt the framers of the American Constitution took it very seriously. Indeed, the manner in which the president was to be selected was one of the most extensively debated topics during the entire Philadelphia Convention. Because the United States is a much more democratic society today than it was two hundred years ago, many contemporary Americans are shocked at the prospect of a candidate who loses the popular vote becoming president nonetheless because of the vagaries of the electoral college.

This is no place to review the case for electoral reform in the United States, but the French experience under the Constitution of the Fifth Republic suggests some reflections on what Americans might learn from examining the thoughts of the framers of their own Constitution on how the president should be elected.

The most obvious fact that emerges from such an examination is that the democratic character of the presidency was not a matter of the highest importance for the framers. The French argument about legitimacy from universal suffrage alone is much more likely to appeal to contemporary Americans than to their venerable ancestors. The framers of the Constitution were profoundly committed to the principle of government "by consent of the governed"—"popular government" as they often put it—but not necessarily to universal suffrage as the sole norm for legitimacy. Popular consent to a constitutional order was of enormous importance to them, but the manner in which officers were selected within that order was an entirely different matter. Senators, for example, were originally selected by the state legislatures, but they were no less legitimate than the popularly elected members of the House of Representatives. Their legitimacy came from the Constitution that was duly ratified by the people and detailed the manner in which they were to be selected.

As far as the president was concerned, the notion of popular election made little headway at the Philadelphia Convention. Indeed, one of the reasons for rejecting direct popular election of the president was that it might encourage demagogues—a point that recalls Janot's fear that a French president chosen by universal suffrage might soon become a dictator, a fear buttressed by the unhappy precedent of Napoléon III.

The text of the American Constitution itself further supports the argument that the president envisioned by the framers would not necessarily be a democratically elected officer. Ross Perot's presidential campaign in 1992 put the spotlight on the framers' alternative to the electoral college—the House of Representatives selecting the president with each state getting one vote. As a horde of journalists pointed out during that election campaign, this would mean that sparsely settled Wyoming would have as many votes as teeming California. Further, there is evidence to suggest that the framers thought the selection of the president by the House of Representatives would be the rule and not the exception.[97] What is less well known is that the Constitution does not require that the members of the electoral college be chosen by popular vote. The first section of article 2 provides that "each State shall appoint, *in such Manner as the Legislature thereof may direct,* a Number of Electors, equal to the whole Number of Senators and Representatives to which the State may be entitled in the Congress." (Emphasis added.) Thus, even today, a literal reading of the Constitution would permit a state to have its legislators pick the presidential electors, although it would be unthinkable that any state would do so. Like a French prime minister meekly submitting to presidential removal, American legislators understand the force of conventional practices that have assumed a constitutional life of their own.

Both the French and American Constitutions began with electoral colleges to select the presidents of their respective countries. The French system was not fully democratic and the American system was even less so. Both countries dramatically democratized their presidential selection procedures: the French through an irregular constitutional amendment that abolished the college and the Americans by informally making the college more democratic than it was originally intended to be and by developing such robustly democratic extraconstitutional practices as nominating conventions and primary elections. In both countries the result has been to increase the legitimacy of presidential executive leadership and thereby to draw closer to conformity with the elusive administrative orthodoxy of unity in the executive.

4

The Legislative Power

To concentrate the whole social force in the hands of the legislative body is the natural tendency of democracies; for as this is the power that emanates the most directly from the people, it has the greater share of the people's overwhelming power, and it is naturally led to monopolize every species of influence. This concentration of power is at once very prejudicial to a well-conducted administration and favorable to the despotism of the majority.

— ALEXIS DE TOCQUEVILLE

The careful reader is no stranger to the legislative power under the Constitution of the Fifth Republic. In the previous chapter we documented the Gaullist insistence in 1958 upon the principle that the prime minister and his government were responsible, not to the president, but to the parliamentary legislature, a pledge belied by subsequent events. In chapter two we saw the diminished role of the "rationalized" Parliament and its virtual impotence in 1961 when President de Gaulle invoked the emergency powers of article 16.

The present chapter begins where its predecessor left off by examining the question of republican legitimacy, but this time the issue of universal suffrage yields to the normative demands of an authentically parliamentary regime. The chapter then addresses the Fifth Republic's dramatic departure from parliamentary tradition by the constitutional ban on members of the government (the executive) serving as members of Parliament (the legislature). This provision has considerably enhanced the political role of civil servants in the Fifth Republic. The chapter concludes with a detailed examination of how the Constitution severely curtailed the law-making powers of Parliament by creating a zone of administrative rule making that is off-limits to the legislature and thereby severs the traditional link between French republicanism and a sovereign Parliament.

REPUBLICAN LEGITIMACY AND THE PARLIAMENTARY REGIME

French Republicanism

Parliamentary government has been a traditional hallmark of French republicanism; one necessarily implies the other.[1] This is why the architects of the

93

Fifth Republic insisted upon the responsibility of the prime minister and his government to Parliament and not to the president. Any other arrangement would have conceded the constitutional high ground to de Gaulle's critics who questioned his commitment to republican principles. In a symbolic response to these charges, de Gaulle presented the new constitution to the French people at a time and place inextricably linked with French republicanism: *la Place de la République* in Paris on 4 September, the anniversary of the events that led to the creation of the Third Republic which, having survived for some seventy years, had proved to be the most durable of French republics.

Even before the constitutional drafting process was under way, de Gaulle's republican credentials had become a favorite target of his opponents. Thus during the 1 June debate over the general's investiture by the National Assembly as president of the Council (the Fourth Republic title given to the officer the Fifth Republic would designate as prime minister), a Socialist deputy, referring to the Algerian crisis that prompted President Coty to ask de Gaulle to head the government, maintained that his "republican conscience" would never permit him to support the investiture of a man who "has been called to this post by seditious factions and by an army that is in open rebellion and out of control."[2]

Offering a variation on this theme of military coercion replacing republican legitimacy, another deputy acknowledged that there was a time when de Gaulle could have rallied men around him to save France "without separating the nation from the Republic," but now he would come to power by confronting the National Assembly with the threat of a military coup.[3]

Other critics mounted broad, unfocused attacks on de Gaulle's republicanism in general by asserting that no deputy could support the general's investiture without betraying his duty of "fidelity to republican institutions."[4]

Immediately after de Gaulle's investiture as president of the Council, his critics resumed the antirepublican theme, but shifted its focus to the procedure for drafting the new constitution. As we saw in chapter one, de Gaulle proposed to rely primarily on a working group *(groupe de travail)* of civil servants from the Council of State under the supervision of Michel Debré, the minister of justice. This group would report to de Gaulle and to an "Interministerial Council" which included the most important ministers of the government, each of whom would be advised by a team of technical and legal experts—civil servants for the most part—who would, in turn, interact with the working group. Thus the drafting process was to be dominated by civil servants and government ministers whose work would be reviewed by the Council of State, an administrative body, before being submitted to the people for their definitive approval or rejection.

Conspicuous by their absence in this proposed procedure were members of Parliament, who were not bashful in expressing dismay at their exclusion. The drafting procedure was amended to mollify them by introducing an Advisory Committee on the Constitution *(Comité Consultatif Constitutionnel)* to be composed mainly of parliamentarians but, as the group's title indicated, with nothing but *advisory* power. This group would have a chance to evaluate and comment upon the labors of the working group and the Interministerial Council before the proposed constitution would go to the Council of State.[5] Parliamentary committees in each chamber selected the Advisory Committee's members, who represented a broad range of political parties, although no Communists were included.

Many parliamentarians were unhappy with this arrangement, seeing the whole process as a violation of republican traditions dating back to the time of the Revolution. On 3 June, for example, a disgruntled parliamentarian reminded the Council of the Republic (the Fourth Republic name for what had been the Senate in the Third Republic and would once again become the Senate in the Fifth Republic):

> In France, the cradle of modern democracy, the first republican constitution which has served as a model for the others in our country and throughout the world was the work of the Constitutant Assembly appointed by the Estates General of 1789.[6]

The broad charge of antirepublicanism announced by de Gaulle's opponents during the National Assembly debates was muted during the long process of drafting the constitution because the critics tended to concentrate on specific constitutional provisions rather than on the global question of the republican character of the emerging regime. In September, however, when the proposed constitution came before the people for ratification, the antirepublican theme resurfaced. Claude Bourdet, speaking on behalf of the Union of the Socialist Left, captured the spirit of the attack. De Gaulle's constitution, he asserted, "usurps the name of the Republic" but falls short of the real thing because of the president's power over the ministers of government, who, as nonparliamentarians, will be out of touch with ordinary citizens. Furthermore, General de Gaulle, as president, will have a variety of constitutional weapons at his disposal to reduce the role of Parliament below minimal republican standards. These include his power to dissolve Parliament, to circumvent it by proposing legislation to the people directly through the referendum procedure, and to displace the legislature by invoking his emergency powers under article 16. Finally, if the people fail to support the general, "he will threaten you once again with the paratroopers."[7]

In responding to attacks of this nature, de Gaulle and his supporters adopted a twofold strategy. First, they defended specific constitutional provisions with specific arguments. For example, as we shall see below, they contended that the ban on parliamentarians serving as ministers would strengthen parliamentary government by making it more stable and therefore correct a perennial defect in French republicanism. Or, as we saw in the previous chapter, they defended the innovation of having the president appoint the prime minister by arguing that republican principles required only that the Parliament be able to remove the prime minister, regardless of who appoints him.

Secondly, they parried the general charge of antirepublicanism by reciting the fundamental tenets of the French republican creed with particular emphasis on the principle that the government must be responsible to the Parliament. Thus during the investiture debate on 1 June, General de Gaulle as president of the Council designate assured the National Assembly that any constitutional revisions proposed by his government would state clearly and adhere faithfully to the three principles which, in France, must be the foundation of a republican regime: (1) universal suffrage as the source of all power; (2) the effective separation of the legislative and executive powers; and (3) the responsibility of the government before the Parliament.[8]

Immediately after de Gaulle's investiture as president of the Council on 1 June, the Parliament debated what came to be known as the Constitutional Law of 3 June, a text we have mentioned in each of the preceding chapters. It will be recalled that this extremely important document authorized a departure from the ordinary procedure for amending the Constitution of the Fourth Republic and thereby opened the way for de Gaulle's government to present a new constitution under the technical guise of an elaborate amendment to the existing constitution. More importantly for the purposes of our present discussion, the law spelled out the principles that were to guide those who drafted the constitution. They included the three principles de Gaulle had announced during the investiture debate.[9] During the debate on the Constitutional Law of 3 June, he identified these principles as "the foundations of the democratic and republican institutions of our country."[10]

Following the general's lead, Michel Debré turned aside challenges to Gaullist republicanism by assuring his listeners that the new government's constitutional plans had nothing to do with changing the country's republican character. Rather, the task was simply "to assure the effective functioning" of French republicanism in practice.[11]

Throughout the long drafting procedure and the ratification debate in September, the friends of the new constitution followed the pattern of pointing to its parliamentary provisions to support its republican character.[12] The most elaborate statement to this effect came from Michel Debré in a famous address to the Council of State, wherein he drew a sharp distinction between the authentic parliamentary regime of the new constitution and its counterfeit, the regime of the assembly *(le régime d'assemblée)* of the Third and Fourth Republics, which had brought so much political misery to France.

In an incisive attack on previous parliamentary practices, Debré described the regime of the assembly as one that monopolizes all governing powers to such an extent that the executive exists merely at its whim. Indeed, there is no recourse against the regime of the assembly even when it violates the constitution. The proposed constitution, according to Debré, by redesigning parliamentary powers and procedures, will correct these excesses and restore an authentic parliamentary regime to France.

In an exceedingly bold rhetorical move, Debré corrects himself and says that instead of talking about reforming the parliamentary regime, he is tempted to say that the new constitution will "establish it," because the Republic has never succeeded in instituting an authentic parliamentary regime. He does not reveal whether he has yielded to this temptation, but his point is clear enough. The traditional powers of Parliament are to be curbed in order to save parliamentary government from its own excesses.

American Republicanism

Republicanism played a central role in the American ratification debate of 1787–1788 and did so in a way that provides an interesting comparison with France in 1958. The basic strategy of the Gaullists was to collapse the question of republicanism into one of parliamentarianism and then to offer a new definition and a new theory of parliamentary government to justify the parliamentary innovations of the Fifth Republic. The friends and foes of the proposed American constitution sparred over the definition of republicanism in a way that went beyond a sterile *lis de verbis* and issued in Publius's famous defense of the "extended republic," often regarded as the most important contribution to political theory in the *Federalist Papers*.

Publius thrice defines the word *republic* and each time the definition becomes more elaborate. The first definition is utterly inadequate for late-eighteenth-century America: "a Government in which the scheme of representation takes place."[13] This definition would satisfy an aristocratic regime as long as one group of aristocrats represented the rest of them. Thus it ignores the popular aspect of late-eighteenth-century republicanism and therefore falls of its own weight. Publius did better the next time, adding the qualification that "all power should be derived from the people," that terms of office should be of "short duration," and "that the trust should be placed not in a few, but in a number of hands."[14] In his third and final definition, he allowed power to come "directly or indirectly" from the people and then restated more emphatically the link between republicanism and popular government. The republican standard that power must come directly or indirectly from the people means "from the great body of the society, not from an inconsiderable proportion, or a favored class of it."[15]

Clearly, the Constitution of the United States meets these criteria and, no less clearly, the definitions were designed precisely to meet this appointed end. Hence, the emphasis on the republican legitimacy of all officers chosen *indirectly* by the people. This includes the president, the vice president, senators, the Speaker of the House, the president pro tempore of the Senate, judges, ambassadors, consuls, the heads of the executive departments, and the "inferior officers" of article 2; that is, every officer mentioned in the Constitution, save the members of the House of Representatives.

Not to be outdone, the Anti-Federalists fashioned definitions of republicanism guaranteed to embarrass the proposed constitution. Thus Brutus, following Montesquieu, insists that a "free republic" has as an essential component, the requirement that it be confined to a small territory, and thereby rejects the republican character of Publius's continental empire.[16]

Federal Farmer defines "free government," a common synonym for a republic, as one that assures a "full and equal representation of the people in the legislature, and the jury trial of the vicinage in the administration of justice."[17] Since the proposed constitution did not guarantee jury trial in the vicinage, it was not a free government. (As an indication of the influence of the Anti-Federalists on the Bill of Rights, however, one should note the Sixth Amendment guarantee of a "speedy and public trial, by an impartial jury of the State and *district* wherein the crime shall have been committed.") (Emphasis added.)

For the visionary Centinel, "a republican or free government, can only exist where the body of the people are virtuous and where property is pretty equally divided." In addition the legislature must be unicameral.[18] Clearly, the proposed constitution would be doomed, if Centinel's norms were to prevail.

Fortunately, the Anti-Federalist argument went beyond the feckless game of defining the proposed constitution out of the realm of republican legitimacy. They gave substantive reasons to support their definitions. Thus Brutus supplemented his reliance on Montesquieu's authority with a careful argument showing why "in a republic, the manners, sentiments, and interests of the people should be similar" and that such similarity can be found only in small countries.[19] For Federal Farmer "the full and equal representation" standard of "free government" meant more than merely holding elections. It also meant that those elected should possess "the same interests, feelings, opinions, and views the people themselves would were they all assembled." Developing the same point, George Mason, perhaps the most influential of all the Anti-Federalists, insisted that representatives "ought to mix with the people, think as they think, [and] feel as they feel."[20] In a word, republican government should be close to the people. The representatives should be "perfectly amenable" to them "and thoroughly acquainted with their interest and condition." All this can take place only within a small territory where there is a reasonable expectation that the representative will really know the people and be known by them.

Centinel's argument for a unicameral legislature flowed from the common Anti-Federalist theme of a harmonious and even homogeneous republican ideal in which there would be but one social order and therefore no need for upper and lower houses to accommodate aristocrats and commoners. The British Parliament with "King, Lords, and Commons" was fine for England with its various social "orders in society" or "classes" as we would say today. Such institutions had no place in republican America where a unicameral legislature would serve as a microcosm of the people who all belong to the same social order. Although the "small republic" argument of the Anti-Federalists posed serious problems to the friends of the constitution, Publius met them head-on. Usually deferential to Montesquieu, Publius defies his mentor in *Federalist* 9 and flatly rejects his requirement of a "small extent for republics." If Americans follow Montesquieu in this matter, they would have to subdivide the existing thirteen states and they would end up splitting themselves "into an infinity of little jealous, clashing, tumultuous commonwealths, the wretched nurseries of unceasing discord and the miserable objects of universal pity or contempt."

Having rejected the small republic argument, Publius offers a new theory of republicanism. He will present "a Republican remedy for the diseases most incident to Republican Government."[21] Michel Debré could have used similar language to justify the changes he proposed as parliamentary remedies for the great French parliamentary disease of unstable government. Like the Gaullists, Publius sees instability as one of several republican diseases, but in *Federalist* 10 his attention is riveted on the dangerous tendency of republican governments to trample individual rights. Precisely because republicanism necessarily implies popular government, great issues are "too often decided, not according to the rules of justice, and the rights of the minor party; but by the superior force of an interested and over-bearing majority." Publius's republican remedy for this republican disease is to "extend the sphere" of the Republic. That is, let one large republic replace several small ones and "you make it less probable that a majority of the whole will have a common motive to invade the rights of the other citizens." Thus, a large republic assures a greater diversity of interests—especially economic interests—and therefore makes it less likely that a permanent majority of farmers, for example, will continually oppress a permanent minority of merchants. In the extended republic, there will never be one stable majority that always gets its way. Laws will be passed by unstable and shifting coalitions that represent the broad diversity of interests in the large republic.

Publius acknowledges the force of the Anti-Federalist argument that the elected representatives should resemble their electors, but boldly raises his readers' sights to consider the likelihood that the large republic will present "men who possess the most attractive merit and the most diffusive and established characters." Blessed with this abundant pool of talent, the citizens of the extended republic have a better chance to find representatives who will "refine and enlarge the public views." Should this happen, then "the public voice pronounced by the representatives of the people, will be more consonant to the public good, than if pronounced by the people themselves convened for the purpose."

Publius's grand vision of the extended republic offers a vision of a legislature that goes beyond the Anti-Federalist idea of a microcosm of society. Representation in the large republic offers the hope of producing a legislature that is *better* than the people themselves.

This breathtaking view of the possibilities of republican government marks Publius as a bold innovator, just as Michel Debré was similarly marked by his "temptation" to say that the Fifth Republic offered France its first authentically parliamentary regime. Both men challenged common understandings of politically important ideas: the small republic for Publius and a sovereign parliament (i.e., the "regime of the assembly") for Debré. Both men offered new definitions of republicanism and of such related ideas as "free" or "popular government" for Publius and "parliamentary regime" for Debré. Both men used their new definitions to the same end—to save republicanism from itself or, as Publius would say, to provide republican remedies for republican diseases.

Before leaving the question of republicanism, there is one final point of considerable interest in comparing our two foundings. By an odd coincidence, the expression "federal republic" appears in the debates over the two constitutions. James Wilson used the expression to describe rather accurately the character of the new American government. Strictly speaking, "federal republic" was an oxymoron because republics, by definition, were supposed to be consolidated and therefore not federated *qua* republics. This was an important point for the Anti-Federalists, who had argued that the new government was a senseless compromise between a consolidated nation on the one hand and a treaty among sovereign states on the other. Consequently, the Anti-Federalists denounced the constitution as a "spurious brat," a "13 horned monster" and a "heterogeneous phantom." To defend the elusive middle ground between a treaty among sovereign states and a consolidated nation, James Wilson had hit upon the attractive expression "federal republic." This annoyed Patrick Henry, the most colorful of the

Anti-Federalist orators, who railed that the "favored bantling" would have been nameless had not James Wilson, "in the fertility of his genius suggested the happy epithet of a *Federal Republic.*"[22]

République Fédéral entered the 1958 French debate in a letter from two Senegalese deputies to Michel Debré in which they proposed it as the most suitable term to characterize the relationship between France and its former empire, which had been called the "French Union" under the Fourth Republic. The deputies held no illusions about the language they suggested. They knew the relationship would be neither federal nor republican in any real sense. Nevertheless they stated: "In Africa, certain words have a force that is quasi-magical and 'federal republic' is one of them."[23]

When the working group took up this question, there was considerable uneasiness about just how to describe France's relationship to its former colonies, some of which were now called "associated states." The classic question of federation versus confederation arose, but, despite some rumors about African interest in a *"fédération à l'américaine,"*[24] it was abundantly clear that no one cared to pursue seriously the idea of a real federation, much less a real republic. Nevertheless, the intriguing "federal republic" language found its way into a draft text presented by the minister of foreign affairs to the working group before eventually disappearing without a trace.[25]

Reading between the lines, it seems that all concerned found the discussion unsettling and embarrassing. François Luchaire seemed to capture the mood of the working group when he remarked, perhaps somewhat wearily, that "in view of the present condition . . . , it is necessary to establish a confederation but to call it a federation in the hope that the magic of the words will win the support of the Africans."[26]

This curious episode points to the fundamental incompatibility of imperialism (however well-intentioned) and republicanism (however broadly defined). Republican institutions pull in the direction of equality whereas imperialism pulls in the opposite direction. Even the most enlightened statesmen will have trouble rigging up a republican facade to cover a receding empire. The American founders had the similar but far more profound problem of trying to talk seriously about republicanism despite the gaping wound of slavery on the body politic. Perhaps wisely or perhaps cynically, they wrote their constitution without ever mentioning the offending word. There are but three indirect references to slavery in the unamended Constitution and they are so deftly concealed that most Americans today read their constitution without the slightest awareness of what the oblique references really mean. Fortunately, republican principles eventually gained the upper hand in both countries, permitting Americans to exorcise the demon of slavery and the French to repent of their imperialist ways.

INELIGIBILITY AND INCOMPATIBILITY

The previous section stressed the Gaullists' parliamentary innovations, some of which we had already seen. Chapter two, for example, touched upon the diminished roles of legislative committees, the constitutional constraints upon amendments to government bills and the notorious "49, 3," which permits laws to be passed without a vote. In the remainder of this chapter, we shall examine in some detail two of the most important parliamentary innovations: the ban on ministers serving in Parliament and the crucial constitutional distinction between matters subject to law and those subject to administrative regulation.

Ministers Barred from Parliamentary Service

Article 23 states that membership in the government "shall be incompatible with the exercise of any Parliamentary mandate, with the holding of any office at the national level in business, professional, or labor organizations, and with any public employment or professional activity."

The exclusion of members of Parliament from the government is the most important and the most onerous of these incompatibilities. The most important, because it represents a sharp break with traditional parliamentary practice. The most onerous because the parliamentarian who resigns his legislative mandate to join the government will encounter some difficulties in returning to Parliament at the end of his ministerial service. At times, he or she will have to wait until the next parliamentary election and that could be a matter of years, since such elections are regularly scheduled at five-year intervals. The five-year interval could be shortened by a special election if the president should dissolve Parliament or if Parliament itself should cause a government to fall and this, in turn, should precipitate an election; but no one can count on such unforeseen events. Since no Fifth Republic government has ever survived a full five-year Parliament, the problem of the former minister is by no means merely speculative.

Often enough, parliamentarians-turned-ministers have had the good fortune to be replaced by obliging supporters who resign from Parliament when the minister leaves the government. In this case, a special election is held in which the former minister will have a chance to regain his seat in Parliament shortly after his resignation.[27]

These complicated maneuvers contrast with the relatively simple procedures by which others whose work is incompatible with a position in government can resume their previous careers. Thus civil servants who join the government are considered to be temporarily "detached" from their corps, which they rejoin when they leave the government.[28] The restoration of business and labor leaders to their previous callings is regulated by the associations that employed them before their stints as ministers. Professional men and women, like lawyers, simply resume their normal practice when their ministerial days are over.[29]

Parliamentary incompatibility for ministers was a cardinal tenet of Gaullist orthodoxy. François Luchaire lists it first among several ideas General de Gaulle discussed with him on 6 June, just before the serious work of drafting the constitution got under way. The general told him that the parliamentary and ministerial functions were to be "absolutely distinguished" and that a deputy should become a minister only "by exception" and with the clear understanding that "he abandons his parliamentary career."[30]

The summary notes from a 13 June meeting of de Gaulle and his closest advisers link the innovative idea of incompatibility to the traditional French principle of separation of powers. The heart of the matter was the tendency of the French political culture to form a multiparty system. If ministers remain members of Parliament, they will bring their partisan divisions into government with them, thereby rendering the government weak and unstable—a situation that Publius, the champion of executive unity, would surely deplore. According to the notes of this meeting, deputies and senators who join the government would be considered *ineligible* for Parliament in the future. This standard would have been far more severe than the *incompatibility* between governmental and parliamentary roles that eventually emerged in article 23. That is, under article 23 one cannot be parliamentarian and minister simultaneously, but a former minister is not precluded from future parliamentary service. The notion of ministerial *ineligibility* for a return to Parliament is consistent with de Gaulle's comment to Luchaire on 6 June to the effect that parliamentarians joining the government should *abandon* their parliamentary careers.

All this flows logically from the general's long-standing fear of and contempt for political parties as representing only partial views of what is best for France, whereas the government should look to the general interest of the nation. The Gaullist hostility to political parties was particularly clear in a decision taken at the 13 June meeting that members of the government should retain no partisan affiliations. Thus the Gaullist vision of public service might best be described as a "Hatch Act in reverse," with nonpartisan neutrality expected of the *highest* officers of the state. This explains in part why de Gaulle so often appointed civil servants to ministerial posts.

The draft of the constitution that the government presented to the Advisory Committee on the Constitution at the end of July reduced the ineligibility requirement to incompatibility, but this retreat was not enough to save the proposed text from a withering attack by this body, composed primarily of unhappy parliamentarians. In defending the incompatibility clause before the Advisory Committee, de Gaulle said nothing about his earlier belief that parliamentarians should become ministers only by way of exception. Quite the contrary, he assured the Advisory Committee that there would be no problem whatsoever with parliamentarians joining the government, provided they resign their seats as deputy or senator, a point repeated emphatically by Raymond Janot, the government's representative.[31] Nor is there a trace of the earlier idea that ministerial service would create a permanent ban on future parliamentary service. The general makes it clear that the proposed text would permit a former minister to run for Parliament at the election following his departure from the government.

In this same address, de Gaulle acknowledged that his concern for governmental stability was an important reason for the incompatibility clause; but even more important, he insisted, was the principle of separation of powers which the Constitutional Law of 3 June obliged the government to follow. His explanation of the principle was disarmingly (and probably disingenuously) simple: the legislative power (Parliament) should control the executive (the government); but the same person cannot be simultaneously both controller and controlled. Therefore the same person cannot be at once parliamentarian and minister. Q.E.D.

Michel Debré was more candid in explaining the incompatibility clause to the Council of State on 27 August. He admitted the practice violated customary parliamentary norms and was more consistent with a presidential regime. This must have been a difficult admission for Debré to make because the dominant theme of his address to the Council of State was his impassioned defense of the authentically parliamentary character of the proposed constitution. The justification for the departure from parliamentary tradition was the desperate instability that had plagued the Fourth Republic. Deputies would lightheartedly vote to overthrow a government in the hope of winning a minister's portfolio for themselves in the new government. They knew they would not be in office long before their government would, in turn, be overthrown; but they could always resume their seat in the National Assembly with the advantage of the impressive title of former minister and the career-enhancing experience of having held high office. Debré complained that under this system ministers no longer sought power for its own sake. Ministerial office was like a soldier's campaign medal that the seasoned politician could proudly display. All this Debré denounced as an unseemly " 'race for portfolios,' a deadly game for the state."[32]

As noted above, the Advisory Committee on the Constitution, primarily a body of parliamentarians, did not look kindly upon the incompatibility clause. It recommended a compromise that would have put parliamentarians-turned-ministers on a leave of absence *(mis en congé)* from their respective assemblies and would have curtailed their partisan activities as well. A host of arguments was launched against incompatibility, ranging from complaints that it treated deputies and senators like criminals to arcane scrutiny into just how the "substitutes" *(suppléants)* might be chosen to replace parliamentarians who resign in order to enter the government.[33]

Within this wide range of arguments, there were two themes directly relevant to our inquiry: (1) the effect of the incompatibility clause on the civil service, and (2) the government's misguided reliance on the excesses of the American interpretation of the principle of separation of powers.

Paul Reynaud, the distinguished president of the Advisory Committee, warned that the proposed reform would put an end to Parliament's role as a "school for statesmen."[34] He agreed with Pierre-Henri Teitgen's prediction that the incompatibility clause would discourage parliamentarians from entering the government; and that, therefore, future ministers would come from the civil service. Even the prime minister, Reynaud mused, may be an obscure prefect unknown at home and abroad. Assuming General de Gaulle would be the first president of the Republic, this would not be a serious problem as long as he remained in office. A constitution, however, cannot be "custom-tailored" to fit just one man as president. It must be written so that it is "ready-to-wear" by whoever might be president. France would be ill-served by an unlucky combination of a weak president and a politically untested prime minister.[35]

In a remarkably prescient statement, Edmond Barrachin warned the friends of the constitution that their opponents would skillfully exploit the incompatibility clause by arguing that ministers will be cut off from the people and fall under the exclusive influence of the president. This, they will say, "points the way to a technocracy dependent on purely personal power."[36]

Throughout the debate there was considerable resentment toward civil servants who could become ministers without resigning their positions. The following comments typify this "bureaucrat bashing" *à la française:*

... there is nothing shameful about being a member of Parliament and it would be strange if a prefect can be a minister and then return to his prefecture, a councillor of State can return to the Council . . .[37]

... I don't see why it [the incompatibility clause] cannot be extended to the civil service . . .[38]

... One need only read the *Journal Officiel* to know that the high-ranking civil servants who were just recently appointed as ministers, took all the customary precautions in case there should be a change in government. Consequently, it is somewhat strange on the one hand to see civil servants taking all these precautions with the approval of the government and on the other hand—excuse me for speaking so frankly . . .[39]

As a variation on this theme, the Advisory Committee, proclaiming its protective concern for career public servants, frequently warned that the incompatibility clause would lead to resentment on the part of the parliamentarians toward the civil service ministers *(fonctionnaires ministres)*. As elected officials, the parliamentarians will see the minister as being out of touch with the real needs of the people. Eventually, this could lead to demagogic attacks on the civil service from parliamentarians, who will have no possibility of exercising authority themselves.[40]

To underscore the threat to sound administration in the likely hostility between elected parliamentarians and civil service ministers, the critics of the incompatibility clause point to the presidential regime in the United States as a particularly unfortunate example. François Valentin says that those who are at all familiar with American government "cannot but be profoundly struck by the mindset of the members of Congress toward the members of the Administration." He goes on to say that in his opinion there is "no word to express this attitude other than the word scorn." The congressmen base their sense of superiority on the fact that they are elected by the people.[41]

Paul Coste-Floret echoes Valentin's assessment of American administration as he explains his opposition to the incompatibility clause: "You need only look at what is going on in America and at the scorn of the American parliamentarians for the ministers associated with the Administration."[42]

Pierre-Henri Teitgen captured the gist of many of those who saw in the incompatibility clause a misguided and excessively rigid application of the separation-of-powers doctrine that was in danger of pushing France toward an American-style presidential regime alien to its traditions. Teitgen maintained that the proposed text "proceeds from an abstract and theoretical logic, from an abstract and theoretical conception of the principle of separation of powers."[43]

Congressmen as Officeholders

These references to the United States suggest that a close look at the incompatibility clause in the American Constitution might be in order. It appears in article 1, section 6:

> No Senator or Representative shall, during the Time for which he was elected, be appointed to any civil Office under the Authority of the United States, which shall have been created, or the Emoluments whereof shall

have been increased during such time; and no Person holding any Office under the United States, shall be a member of either House during his Continuance in Office.

The most obvious difference between the American and French provisions is that the former reaches *ineligibility* as well as incompatibility. The words preceding the semicolon make members of Congress *ineligible* for *certain* federal offices for a *fixed period* of time. The words following the semicolon declare membership in Congress to be *incompatible* with *any* federal office.

The incompatibility clause resembles article 23 in the French Constitution in that an American legislator, like his French counterpart, can escape the burden of incompatibility simply by resigning. The American incompatibility provision is much broader, however, extending as it does to "any Office under the United States"; whereas the French ban goes no further than the very high and very few offices held by members of the government. Thus French civil servants, unlike their American colleagues, can and do become members of Parliament without being required to resign from the civil service. As long as they are in Parliament, they do not draw their civil service salary nor can they be promoted. Significantly, however, they retain the right to return to the civil service when their parliamentary careers come to an end, a fringe benefit that would be unthinkable for an American congressman who had once been a civil servant.

The incompatibility clause of the American Constitution concerns *federal* office alone. An early draft of the constitution would have banned congressmen from state offices as well, but this provision was deleted, mainly because of the states' rights argument that the people should not be kept from conferring high state office on a worthy citizen simply because he already held federal office.[44] Despite the permissive language of the Constitution, as a matter of fact congressmen do not hold state offices. This restraint is due for the most part to restrictions in state law on holding offices simultaneously at both the national and state levels. Thus, in a roundabout way, the states' rights position has prevailed but not in the way the framers of the Constitution had envisioned.[45] They refused to prohibit the states from sending their officers to Congress but the states have refused to avail themselves of this opportunity.

As far as subnational government is concerned, the French incompatibility clause is no less permissive than the American, but in France the constitutional permissiveness has a tremendously important practical effect. Through a remarkable arrangement known as plurality of mandates *(cumul des mandats),* French parliamentarians and members of the government frequently hold local government offices. This has been a long-standing, distinctive, and controversial trait of French politics which is usually defended on the grounds that a local official (e.g., mayor of a city) makes a more effective parliamentary representative. Not surprisingly, this system has been severely criticized over the years and has undergone a mild reform in the 1980s with promises of more reforms to come.[46]

As noted above, the American Constitution addresses the question of ineligibility as well as of incompatibility. For the duration of the term for which they have been elected, members of Congress are ineligible to hold federal offices, "which shall have been created, or the Emoluments whereof shall have been increased during such time." This constitutional ineligibility is rather mild because it affects relatively few offices and, at least for members of the House of Representatives, is of a relatively short duration, that is, two years minus the time that will have elapsed before the disqualifying legislation is passed in a given term.

We saw above that some former ministers under the Fifth Republic have managed to regain their parliamentary seats by getting their substitutes to resign, thereby creating the need for a new election, which often turns out favorably for a popular minister who has recently resigned from the government. Americans have been no less clever in avoiding the full force of the categorical language of their ineligibility clause. For example, in 1909 President Taft wanted to nominate Senator Philander Knox as secretary of state but the salary for that office had been raised during Knox's term, and therefore he was ineligible for the appointment. An obliging Congress rescinded the pay raise for the office of the secretary of state, thereby easing the Senate's conscience in approving the nomination as being in conformity with the spirit of the ineligibility clause. Clearly, it violated the letter of the Constitution because the ineligibility attaches to any office "the Emoluments whereof shall have been increased." The fact that the emoluments were later decreased has, strictly speaking, no bearing on the fact that they had been increased.[47] Therefore a literal reading of article 1, section 6, would clearly have disqualified Senator Knox. In general, Congress, presidents, and attorneys general have followed a relaxed interpretation of this stringent provision and the courts have gone along by denying standing to anyone inclined to raise a legal challenge.[48] President Clinton's nomination of Senator Bentsen as secretary of the treasury is but the latest example of this relaxation. Bentsen's situation was similar to that of Senator Knox and was resolved in a similarly favorable manner.[49]

The relaxed interpretation seems consistent with the goals of the framers of the Constitution, if not with their language. Both the ineligibility and incompatibility clauses were inserted in the Constitution to avoid the corruption Americans saw in Great Britain, where the king was accused of getting members of Parliament to do his bidding by "bribing" them with the prospect of high office. Clearly, there was no question of President Taft trying to bribe Senator Knox, nor of President Clinton bribing Senator Bentsen. Congress' willingness to rescind the pay raises of Knox, Bentsen, and others similarly situated was a sensible accommodation to the president's need to have a free hand in choosing his highest officers.

The Anti-Federalists dismissed the ineligibility clause as an utterly inadequate safeguard against future executive efforts to corrupt Congress. During the Virginia ratification debate, William Grayson joined Patrick Henry in arguing that to be truly effective the ban must not be confined to newly-created offices and to those whose emoluments had recently been increased. The constitution should be amended to prohibit "any Senator or Representative from being appointed to any office during the time for which he was elected."[50] Thus, Grayson and Henry would have escalated the Constitution's *incompatibility* clause to one of *ineligibility* for the duration of one's term in Congress.

Federal Farmer went even further, arguing that members of Congress should be ineligible "to any offices whatever during the period for which they shall be elected to serve, and *even for sometime afterward.*"[51] (Emphasis added.) He asserted that by limiting ineligibility to so few offices, the Constitution invites the risk that "a majority of the legislators . . . will be mere expectants for public office."[52]

Luther Martin, a Maryland Anti-Federalist who had been a delegate to the Philadelphia Convention, correctly pointed out that the ineligibility clause had been considerably watered down in the convention's closing days.[53] An earlier version would have forbidden the appointment of members of the legislature to "any office" under the authority of the United States and the ban would have lasted not only during the term of service, but "for the space of one year after its expiration."[54]

This stringent measure seems more consistent with the rhetoric of the framers of the Constitution throughout the Philadelphia Convention. They took seriously the notion that legislators could be corrupted by the offices within the gift of the executive. Thus, Hugh Williamson acknowledged that he "had scarcely seen a single corrupt measure in the Legislature of N-Carolina, which could not be traced up to office hunting."[55] George Mason bristled at what he saw as the delegates' shameful timidity in addressing directly the problem of the executive corrupting the legislature. Masking his disgust with humor, Mason "ironically proposed to strike out the whole section [on ineligibility], as a more efficient expedient for encouraging that exotic corruption which might not otherwise thrive so well in the American Soil."[56]

The targets of Mason's irony were many and varied. Although few delegates would dismiss out of hand the likely corruption of legislators, several of them reminded the reformers that severe prophylactic measures against such corruption exacted a high price.

Charles Pinkney, for example, expressed his concern in a metaphor strikingly similar to Paul Reynaud's reference to the French Parliament as a "school for statesmen" in 1958. Pinkney hoped to see the Senate "become a School of Public Ministers, a nursery of Statesmen," but feared that stringent ineligibility rules would discourage men of "the first talents and ambitions" from entering the Senate.[57]

James Wilson, whose own state of Pennsylvania "had gone as far as any State into the policy of fettering power," remarked that even that state had the good sense to stop short of rendering "the members of the Legislative ineligible to offices of Government." The problem with excessive strictness in this matter is that it demeans the legislature and deprives it of "its power of attracting those talents which were necessary to give weight to the Governt. and to render it useful to the people." Anticipating a common theme in the Federalists' defense of the Constitution, Wilson candidly acknowledged that he "was far from thinking the ambition which inspired to Offices of dignity and trust, an ignoble or a culpable one."[58]

In arguing against a measure to prevent senators from holding federal office, Gouverneur Morris offered an example of the sort of thinking that won for the Federalists the accolade (or the opprobrium) of being "hard-headed realists." The ban was a "dangerous expedient," because the Senate would be the institution wherein the rich would be represented. Such persons

> ought to have every inducement to be interested in your government. Deprive them of this right, and they will become inattentive to your welfare. The wealthy will ever exist; and you never can be safe unless you gratify them as a body, in the pursuit of honor and profit. Prevent them by positive institutions, and they will proceed in some left-handed way . . . It is good policy that men of property be collected in one body, to give them one common influence in your government. Let vacancies be filled up as they happen by the executive.[59]

Morris had voiced these sentiments on 2 July 1787. A slightly revised version of the ineligibility clause was before the delegates once again on 14 August. Ever faithful to his political realism, Morris this time sounds an ominous note on the danger of excluding military officers from both houses of Congress:

> Exclude the officers of the army and navy, and you form a band having a different interest from and opposed to the civil power: you stimulate them to despise and reproach those "talking Lords who dare not face the foe." Let this spirit be roused at the end of a war, before your troops shall have

laid down their arms, and though the Civil authority be "entrenched in parchment to the teeth," they will cut their way through to it.[60]

Thus Gouverneur Morris ties the rather technical questions of incapacity and ineligibility to such grand questions of high politics as the place for the wealthy in a republican regime and the relationship between the military and the civil powers.

Before concluding this section, let us briefly consider the commentary of the distinguished jurist Joseph Story on the ineligibility and incompatibility clauses. Story was appointed to the Supreme Court by President Madison in 1811 and served there until his death in 1845. His famous *Commentaries on the Constitution* were published in 1833. Story's treatment is particularly important for our purposes because he recommends a relaxation of the incompatibility clause, which, had it been adopted, would have made the American Congress of the 1830s strikingly similar to the Parliament of the Fifth Republic.

Having acknowledged the incompatibility clause as an appropriate expression of American political principles, Story cautiously observes that nevertheless the exclusion from Congress of all persons holding federal office is "attended with some inconveniences." His argument deals only with the heads of executive departments—that is, officers known as *secretaries* in the United States and as *ministers* in France. Because of the incompatibility clause, these officers are "precluded from proposing or vindicating their own measures in the face of the nation in the course of debate." Consequently, their legislative plans are submitted by "other men," that is, members of Congress, "who are either imperfectly acquainted with the measure or are indifferent to their success or failure." Thus, Story concludes "that open public responsibility for measures, which properly belongs to the executive in all governments, and especially in a republican government, as its greatest security and strength, is completely done away."[61]

To remedy this defect, Story suggests that the heads of the executive departments be given a seat, "like territorial delegates, in the house of representatives where they might freely debate without a title to vote."[62] This is a reasonably accurate description of the role of a French minister in the Parliament of the Fifth Republic. Excluded from membership in Parliament by the incompatibility clause of article 23, French ministers are compensated by article 31, which guarantees them access to both legislative chambers, gives them a right to be heard in each of them, and, underscoring the importance of administration in French constitutionalism, permits them to bring their administrative assistants along. Although they do not vote, they play an extremely important role in the French legislative process—a role the learned Story would have approved for their nineteenth-century American counterparts.

Story's proposal echoes in constitutional theory some of the curious constitutional practices of Alexander Hamilton as the nation's first secretary of the treasury. Although ordinarily a champion of presidential leadership and of a unified executive, Hamilton's behavior as treasury secretary at times had pronounced parliamentary overtones, which suggested for himself a role somewhat akin to that of a prime minister. This could be seen in the extraordinary emphasis he placed upon the fact that the first Congress had designated the Departments of State and War as *executive* departments, while withholding this adjective from Hamilton's Treasury Department. The significance was underscored by the fact that Hamilton, knowing Washington intended to appoint him secretary of the treasury, played an active role in drafting the statute that created the department he would head. Further, Hamilton skillfully exploited statutory language requiring him to report on certain matters to Congress in order to establish close and direct ties between that body and his office. When his relations with Congress became tense, as they often did, he would hastily retreat to the friendly confines of executive power to avert unwelcome congressional attention. All this led an exasperated Jefferson to complain that his wily archrival "endeavored to place himself subject to the House [of Representatives] when the executive should propose what he did not like, and subject to the executive when the House shall propose anything disagreeable."[63]

These sketchy references to the constitutional theory of Joseph Story and the constitutional practice of Alexander Hamilton have been presented to offset the somewhat exaggerated views on American separation of powers that characterized the French constitutional debates of 1958. To be sure, by European parliamentary standards, separation of powers in the United States is "abstract," "theoretical," "rigid," and so forth. A close look at the specifics of the American tradition, however, reveals a complexity that resists facile generalization.

Let us close our comparative discussion of incompatibility and ineligibility on the happy note that in both countries the constitutional provisions have contributed to achieving their appointed ends. The French provision aimed at securing stable government and such stability has been a hallmark of the Fifth Republic. The Americans intended to keep their president from corrupting members of Congress with bribes of high office. Corruption of this sort has never been a problem in the United States.

THE DOMAINS OF LAW AND REGULATION

In chapter two we examined the crucial constitutional distinction that created separate domains for law and regulation in articles 34 and 37. This distinction is perhaps the most important innovation in the Constitution of the

Fifth Republic because it limited the subject areas in which Parliament could legislate, and therefore, put an end to the French republican tradition of parliamentary sovereignty. Like the Congress of the United States, the Parliament of the Fifth Republic is a legislature of limited competence.

As far as the administrative focus of this book is concerned, the limitation on parliamentary sovereignty shows only one side of the coin. No less important is the flip side, which affirms that all subject matters not in the domain of law fall under the jurisdiction of the regulatory power of the government. As one participant in the drafting process remarked, "The Constitution makes the Government the legislator of common law and the Parliament the legislator by exception."[64] This change amounted to a Copernican revolution in French constitutional law, inverting the traditional relationship between Parliament and the government. French parliaments, relying on broad delegations of legislative authority, enabling acts *(lois d'habilitation)*, outline laws *(lois cadres)*, and other self-denying legislative measures, had often reinforced the strong administrative traditions of France; but they always did so in such a way as to ensure, at least in principle, the subordination of the government to Parliament.[65] The Constitution of the Fifth Republic changed all this. The logic, if not the precise language, of the *text* makes the regulatory power of the government the fundamental power of the State and permits Parliament to legislate only in specifically named areas.[66]

Not surprisingly, this remarkable innovation triggered stiff resistance throughout the constitutional drafting process. We shall examine the powerful jurisprudential arguments for and against the creation of separate domains of law and regulation, but first let us follow the evolution of the text, and then let us look at the administrative origins of the law/regulation distinction. Only then shall we be able to grasp the full significance of the jurisprudential argument which we shall consider in some detail in the final pages of this chapter.

Evolution of the Text

Long before the creation of the Fifth Republic, thoughtful French jurists had seen the need to increase the regulatory powers of the government. Even during the desperate Resistance period, Michel Debré found time to address this issue as optimistic Frenchmen looked forward to happier times. Throughout the era of the Fourth Republic, several serious reform efforts were undertaken, but without notable success. Even at the height of the Algerian crisis that brought him to power in May 1958, General de Gaulle endured technical briefings on constitutional law from Raymond Janot, who convinced him of the need for some sort of constitutional provision for a "regulatory domain."[67]

Although these ideas were in the air when the working group and the interministerial committee began drafting the Constitution in mid-June, it was only in early July that a vague outline began to emerge of what would eventually become articles 34 and 37.[68] Michel Debré, clearly the dominant figure throughout the entire drafting process, at first favored a system whereby the government would enjoy certain legislative powers when Parliament was not in session.[69] His initial reaction to the idea of two constitutionally distinct domains was rather cool.[70]

By mid-July, however, the two-domain approach was in the ascendant.[71] From then until the final version was completed, the textual changes of practical significance centered on precisely what substantive matters would be subject to law. The mid-July texts were rather stingy in this matter, granting to the sphere of law, that is, to Parliament, only such absolutely fundamental matters as the organization of public institutions, the safety of individuals, crimes and their corresponding punishments, the fiscal resources of the State, the ratification of treaties, the declaration of war, and the guarantees of such basic public liberties as freedom of speech and religion.[72] By the end of July, the list had grown to include the relationship between the State and local governments, public establishments, nationalized industries, nationality, the family, military service, education, health care, and the right to work. This expanded list appeared in the "Red Book," the familiar name of the text submitted by the government to the Advisory Committee on the Constitution on 29 July.[73]

Since parliamentarians composed two-thirds of the Advisory Committee, their displeasure at the limitations imposed upon their institutional home came as no surprise. The main thrust of their attack was to expand the domain of law, but, remarkably, they showed little interest in challenging the boldly innovative principle that limited the scope of parliamentary authority. As the Advisory Committee went about the self-serving business of augmenting the domain of law, Raymond Janot, the government's representative, leveled the very telling charge that the committee *"without challenging the general principle"* of the reform was defeating it in practice by so increasing the jurisdiction of Parliament that, as a practical matter, "you end up with a solution which is nothing other than what we have at present." (Emphasis added.)[74] Janot's concern was understandable. As we shall see below, the Advisory Committee overlooked few significant areas of human activity as it embellished the parliamentary sphere of competence and correspondingly impoverished the autonomous sphere of governmental regulation.[75] With the wisdom of hindsight, however, it is clear that Janot saw the cup as half empty rather than as half full. The Advisory Committee's acceptance in principle of the two-domain reform loomed large when the principle itself would be challenged before the Council of State, the next major hurdle the proposed constitution had to clear before being submitted to the people. It was no small advantage for the government to be able to remind that council, an administrative body, that the Advisory Committee, a group composed primarily of parliamentarians, had accepted the principle of a limited domain of law, disputing with the government only over how to apply the principle in practice.

The Advisory Committee finished its work on 14 August, submitting to the government an extensively revised draft constitution. Significant changes were proposed in such important areas as individual rights, the role of the Constitutional Council, parliamentary procedure, presidential emergency powers, political parties, and, as we saw in the previous section, the right of parliamentarians to serve as ministers. Since the committee's role was merely advisory, the government was free to reject whatever changes it found unacceptable. Because the committee's report was made public, however, the government could not risk a wholesale rejection of its recommendations without raising a storm of political protest. Consequently, the Interministerial Council, in preparing a revised text to be submitted to the Council of State, accepted as many of the Advisory Committee's recommendations as it could without compromising the essential aspects of the Gaullist reform. The two-domain proposal of law and regulation presented a particularly acute problem. The Advisory Committee had so expanded the domain of law (and therefore the jurisdiction of Parliament) that the Interministerial Council, like Janot, believed that the practical effects of these changes would bring the reform to naught. Despairing of a compromise between the Red Book and the Advisory Committee's extensive additions, the Interministerial Council submitted both versions to the Council of State in the hope that an acceptable compromise might emerge from that august body.

Before examining the efforts of the Council of State, let us consider briefly some of the salient differences between the two texts submitted for its consideration. Both had the same introduction: "Laws shall be passed by Parliament. Questions relevant to the following matters shall be controlled by law." Both texts then listed these matters—differing substantially, of course, in what appeared on the respective lists—and then in a subsequent article used identical language to state that "subject matters other than those mentioned in article 31 [the article of the *draft* text which enumerated the matters subject to law] shall be of a regulatory character." Thus, the Advisory Committee and the government agreed on the grand principle that there should be a constitutional distinction between the domains of law and regulation and that everything that is not a matter of law is subject to the regulatory power of the government. The only disagreement concerned the extent of the subject matter amenable to law. We have already noted above the areas the government was willing to subject to law—taxes, crime, war, treaties, nationality, education, and so forth. To these the Advisory Committee added a breathtakingly broad range of activities that included such matters as elections to local government offices, civil capacity status, rules for property, marriage, civil responsibility, the rights of labor unions, family allotments, supervision of public finance, the management of nationalized enterprises, the national economic plan, the fiscal accounts of the State, and so forth.

On 25 August the Council of State received the government's proposed text with the two versions of the law/regulation distinction. The document went first to the Council of State's Constitutional Committee and then to its General Assembly. The Council came to the government's aid in several ways. First, it used its technical legal skills to tilt the text in favor of the government. For example, the Red Book had assigned to the domain of law those questions pertaining to "personal duties imposed by the demands of national defense."[76] The Advisory Committee had altered the reference to national defense obligations so that the text assigned to the domain of law questions relative "to personal duties, notably those which are imposed by the demands of national defense." This none-too-subtle change dramatically expanded the scope of Parliament's power, for, under the Advisory Committee's version, the domain of law covered *all* personal duties, not just those related to national defense, as the government text would have had it. The clever addition of the word *notably* merely highlighted national defense without in any way limiting personal duties to this one area.

As seasoned administrative law experts, the councillors of State could play this game with the best of them. Hence, they recommended changing the text to provide that the domain of law would encompass questions relative "to national defense and to the duties imposed by it upon the citizens personally and in their property." The purpose of this change was, of course, to cut back the domain of law from all personal duties to those concerning national defense alone.

The Council of State also helped the government by distinguishing two types of questions subject to law: (1) those for which "laws shall establish the regulations" on the one hand, and (2) those for which "laws shall determine the fundamental principles" on the other. This distinction, which figures prominently in the final version of article 34 of the Constitution, traces its origin to the Constitutional Committee of the Council of State.[77] It had the happy effect of establishing an acceptable middle ground between the crabbed scope of parliamentary power envisioned in the government's Red Book and the expansive revisions of the Advisory Committee. The purpose of the distinction was to give Parliament an entrée into many important areas, but to confine its role to legislating *fundamental principles* alone. Thus, Parliament is so confined in such vital areas as the powers and resources of local governments, education, property rights, civil and commercial rights and obligations, employment, unions, health insurance, and organizing the national defense forces. Since only the fundamental principles in these areas are ceded to the domain of law, it follows logically that specific (and therefore meaningful and practical) regulations are left to the government, which can act *independently* in these matters, that is, without waiting for Parliament first to pass a statute authorizing government action.

However, the government did not always find the Council of State helpful to its cause. Leading members of the council's General Assembly mounted a fierce attack on the *principle* of the two-domain proposal which was correctly perceived as sounding the knell of the sovereign Parliament. We shall examine this jurisprudential debate at the end of the chapter but, for the present, suffice it to note that this debate issued in a text approved by the Council of State which would have weakened the Gaullist insistence upon an independent sphere of governmental activity beyond parliamentary control. It would have done this by adding to the list of subjects assigned to law a final clause providing that, by an organic law, Parliament could also regulate "all subject matters recognized to be of a legislative nature."[78] Such open-textured language, had it survived, could have been a virtual invitation to Parliament to expand its own jurisdiction as it would see fit.

The government rejected the gloss proffered by the Council of State, substituting an ambiguous paragraph of its own which it added to article 34 of the final version of the Constitution. This paragraph states that "the provisions of the present article may be developed in detail and amplified by an organic law."[79] Amplified? Does this mean that Parliament can expand the domain of law and therefore its own jurisdiction as it pleases? Does it restore sovereignty to Parliament? At the end of the day, did the government surrender the high ground it had gained so laboriously throughout the long drafting process? Not at all, if the subsequent history of the Fifth Republic is a reliable guide. A leading constitutional commentary published in 1989 deemed only one decision of the Constitutional Council interpreting this paragraph worthy of comment, and this decision restricted rather than expanded Parliament's jurisdiction.[80] Thus the paragraph's lackluster legal history belies its suggestive language. Nevertheless, we should note that to accommodate weighty jurisprudential objections raised by the Council of State, the government offered a compromise text whose ambiguous language casts a shadow of doubt on the capacity of the independent regulatory sphere to withstand parliamentary incursions.

The salient point of comparison to the Constitution of the United States is the final clause of article 1, section 8, which enumerates the powers of Congress. After listing a long array of congressional powers in such matters as taxation, commerce, borrowing, bankruptcy, patents, the militia, wars, and military affairs, the framers added a clause giving Congress the power "to make all Laws which shall be necessary and proper for carrying into Execution the foregoing Powers, and all other Powers vested by this Constitution in the Government of the United States or in any Department or Officer thereof." This is the famous "elastic clause" which the Anti-Federalists charged made a mockery of the Federalists' claim that the proposed constitution would create a government of limited powers. Thus, Brutus claimed that if this clause were linked to the sweeping congressional power to "lay and collect Taxes, Duties, Imposts and Excises," the national government could so burden the wealth of the people as to leave nothing for the state governments to tax, and, therefore, that state governments would soon evanesce.[81]

The Anti-Federalists' fears were exaggerated, but their interpretation of the text was not entirely off the mark. The "elastic clause" has been the primary constitutional vehicle for the massive federal presence in the lives of twentieth-century Americans, and to those who resent this development the ghosts of the Anti-Federalists could fairly say, "We told you so." The taxing power of Congress (and, by Supreme Court interpretation, its spending power as well)[82] is limited only by the extremely broad standard that it be exercised for "the common defense and the general welfare of the United States." This loose norm combined with the necessary and proper clause provides constitutional justification for the activist administrative state Americans know today.

Thus the practical significance of ambiguous constitutional language adopted by the founders in France and in the United States has been quite different. The "necessary and proper" clause has done yeoman work for Americans of a nationalistic persuasion, assuring its rightful place among the most important clauses in the Constitution of the United States. The enticing language in the final paragraph of article 34, however, stating that "the provisions of the present article may be developed in detail and amplified by an organic law" has been of little importance in expanding the scope of parliamentary power.

Administrative Origins of the Law/Regulation Distinction

We have just examined the evolution of the texts creating the mutually independent domains of law and regulation. To put these texts in a proper political perspective, we must examine the extent to which they are grounded in the imperatives of the administrative state.

When we speak of the "administrative state," we usually refer to the long process by which modern industrial democracies came increasingly to rely upon administrative regulation and adjudication to do the work of statutes enforced in courts of law. It is an oft-told tale, usually beginning toward the end of the last century and continuing to the present day. In telling the Anglo-American version of the story, one recounts Dicey's exaggerated fears of *droit administratif,* the reports of a host of prestigious British commissions investigating changes in administrative law and practice, and, in the United States, the rise of the managerial presidency along with the remarkable growth of those American constitutional anomalies known as independent regulatory commissions. During the debate over the two domains of law and regulation, Marcel Waline, a distinguished French jurist, had occasion to comment on the fact that "in the United States they have had to get around the provisions of the Constitution in order to give regulatory powers to the president and his administrators."[83]

Waline's remark occurred in a context in which he was arguing that the notion of distinct domains for law and regulation seemed more appropriate for an American-style presidential regime than for French parliamentary democracy. Like the British and the Americans, the French, for all their administrative traditions, had difficulties of their own in reconciling venerable constitutional traditions with modern administrative imperatives. Delegations of legislative authority to the government proved to be a particularly nettlesome issue in France, especially in the interwar period when unstable parliamentary majorities, unable to rally sufficient legislative support for needed legislation, came to rely increasingly on "decree laws" which, in effect, transferred the legislative authority from Parliament to the government. This unwholesome tendency reached its zenith in the disgraceful parliamentary abdication masquerading as delegation that brought the ill-starred Vichy regime to power in 1940. In 1946, the authors of the Constitution of the Fourth Republic, seeking to redeem the parliamentary tradition, simply prohibited the delegation of legislative authority without solving the underlying problems that had led to excessive delegations under the Third Republic. Predictably, the reform failed and soon "parliament found ways to surrender its sovereign powers as the law-making authority to the executive."[84] Prominent among these was the *loi Reynaud* of 17 August 1948, which "delegalized" subject matters considered to be of an inherently regulatory nature, thereby permitting the government to amend by decree legislation already in force.[85] Not to put too fine a point on it, Parliament authorized the government to undo the work of earlier parliaments. Measures of this nature strengthened the hand of succeeding governments but, ironically, shortened their lives as well, as jealous parliamentarians were all the more willing to censure, and therefore bring down, such powerful institutions exercising authority that had once been their own.

Reflecting on this sorry state of affairs, Jérôme Solal-Céligny, a member of the working group, observed on 2 July in an exceptionally thoughtful memo that the government had to have real legislative power. "Make no mistake about it," he wrote, "this is the only road to constitutional reform."[86] For Solal-Céligny, separation of powers once meant that Parliament and the government performed different but complementary functions, but in mid-twentieth-century France this was no longer true. If a contemporary government is truly to *govern,* it must "continually adapt the structure, the institutional mechanism, and the rules of law to meet demands." Governments need the authority to fashion "measures of general import" *(dispositions de portée générale);* the authority "to legislate."[87] This is not to say the government should replace Parliament but the government should have the legislative powers necessary to carry out its mission without having to return to Parliament for continuing reauthorizations to do so. This is the problem with the various forms of delegation which can be revoked as easily as they are given. The new meaning of separation of powers, according to Solal-Céligny, is that the Constitution should confer directly upon the government the full range of powers it needs to govern effectively and Parliament should exercise control over it through its powers of censure.

Solal-Céligny's memo was written on 2 July when the working group had just begun to address in earnest the questions that would eventually issue in the two domains of law and regulation. His concern with the needs of a modern administrative state were echoed weeks later in the remarks of Raymond Janot on 31 July when he defended a well-developed two-domain proposal before the Advisory Committee on the Constitution. This continuity underscores the pervasive theme of administrative imperatives driving constitutional reforms at the founding of the Fifth Republic. Borrowing Solal-Céligny's very words, Janot stressed the need for contemporary governments to be able to take "measures of general import" *(dispositions de portée générale)* to carry out their policies. Janot repeated Solal-Céligny's new understanding of separation of powers and, like him, contrasted the France of mid-twentieth-century with earlier times when the executive power was confined primarily to applying the general language of legislation to specific situations. That day is long gone, Janot assured the Advisory Committee, and today's governments must take the initiative in defining the nation's policies without having continually to seek parliamentary approval. As for delegation of legislative authority, he reminded his listeners of both the failed efforts to rely upon it and the futility of trying to prohibit it. All this followed the gist of Solal-Céligny's memo.

Janot's only notable departure from the Solal-Céligny script is that he carefully avoided calling for legislative power for the government. That is, he avoided the word *legislation*. This, of course, is because the text Janot defends—a text that did not exist when Solal-Céligny wrote his memo—made a sharp distinction between legislative and regulatory matters. By 31 July, the government neither wanted nor needed *legislative* power as such. This would only dim the bright line dividing law from regulation. As long as regulations could be of general import and could be issued without a supporting act of Parliament, the government would be content with whatever name might be given to such a power. Solal-Céligny's explicit call for legislative power for the government is prudently given a decent burial. "[A] rose by any other name would smell as sweet."

We mentioned in the previous section of this chapter that the Advisory Committee did not challenge the two-domain proposal in principle. This may have been because, as practical politicians, they knew Janot was right when he said that the two-domain proposal was simply an effort to give constitutional legitimacy to widespread current practices that were being carried out in a haphazard and inconsistent way. The imperatives of the modern administrative state demanded vigorous governmental action, and such action was frequently forthcoming but only on the tentative, ad hoc, and somewhat uneasy basis associated with delegation and "delegalization." The two-domain proposal would regularize these episodic practices. If this is revolutionary, Janot said, it is a revolution in theory alone.

Jurist Marcel Waline was unwilling to dismiss theoretical matters in this cavalier manner. He noted that the significant innovation in the two-domain plan was not the enumeration of Parliament's power but rather the affirmation that all other powers are the government's. In the past when Parliament granted extensive powers to the government—as it often had in fact—it was always with the understanding that what Parliament had given Parliament could reclaim. The two-domain proposal changes all this and thereby undermines the traditional understanding of separation of powers. If contemporary realities have rendered this understanding out of date, there is need for a new theory of separation of powers. Waline alludes to the idea that Parliament's new role in separation of powers will be to control the government rather than to pass laws for the government to execute. He maintains that under the new Constitution Parliament will have only very limited powers to control the government. To support his point, Waline offers a case in which the government issues a rule in its own regulatory domain. If the rule offends Parliament, it can do nothing about it because article 41 permits the government to reject as inadmissible any effort of Parliament to legislate outside its appointed sphere. Hence, Waline detects a hollow ring in the new understanding of separation of powers that purports to give control of the government to Parliament.[88]

The two-domain proposal was not the only innovative approach to the problems of the administrative state. During the debate before the Council of State, Jean Burnay counseled against constitutional limitations on the scope of Parliament's legislative powers. He argued that the absence of such limitations would not necessarily exclude a broad range of governmental regulatory activities that could really be legislative in character. The government could be empowered to submit to Parliament regulations of a legislative nature and if, after a certain interval, Parliament had taken no action to block or modify them, they would become law. This plan offered the best of both worlds by encouraging vigorous governmental initiatives without depriving Parliament of the last word.[89]

Burnay's creative suggestion is of considerable comparative interest because of its striking resemblance to the American practice of the "legislative veto," an imaginative approach to the problems of the administrative state that flourished for a half-century until it came to an untimely end at the hands of the Supreme Court in 1983.[90]

The legislative veto is a statutory provision conditioning the exercise of delegated authority upon a subsequent congressional judgment. The judgment may be made by either or both houses of Congress. At times, even a congressional committee can make the judgment. The judgment itself can be one of approval or disapproval, that is, a statute may provide that proposed executive actions cannot go into effect without the approval of one or both houses of Congress. Conversely, a statute may permit executive actions to become effective within a fixed period (for example, sixty days), unless one or both houses disapproves.

The origin of the legislative veto is usually traced to the Executive Reorganization Act of 1932. This act authorized the president to reorganize the executive branch of government by submitting a reorganization plan to Congress. If neither house disapproved of the plan within sixty days, the plan would become law. This arrangement came to be known as the one-house veto, because either house of Congress could block the president's plan simply by registering its dissent. Over the next half-century, Congress passed more than two hundred laws with some form of legislative veto. These laws ran the gamut of public policy: reorganization plans, arms sales, foreign aid, federal employees' salaries, presidential impounding of appropriated funds, deployment of troops in hostilities, the governing of the District of Columbia, and rules promulgated by a host of administrative agencies.

The particular advantage of the legislative veto was that, like Jean Burnay's proposal, it brought the best of both worlds. Congress could delegate broad powers to administrative agencies without losing control over the emerging administrative state. The legislative veto became particularly attractive when it seemed clear that the judiciary had a very permissive attitude toward Congress' willingness—at times even its eagerness—to delegate its legislative authority to administrative agencies. The legislative veto came to be looked upon as a practical expression of the principle of separation of powers in the contemporary administrative state. Proponents of the veto argued that Congress lacked the technical expertise (and at times the political courage) to write detailed standards into its broad delegations of authority. It was not the part of wisdom to require Congress to do the impossible or even the impolitic. The legislative veto gave Congress an after-the-fact check on agencies prone to abuse their authority. In this way, the people's elected representatives would maintain important controls over the modern administrative state. This line of reasoning was not without its critics, notably presidents who reluctantly signed into law bills with legislative vetoes that presidents maintained threatened their constitutional powers. Presidents frequently regarded the legislative veto as impermissible congressional meddling in the execution of public law. Lacking an item veto, however, presidents usually approved bills with legislative vetoes as the lesser of two evils—better arms sales legislation with a veto than no arms sales legislation at all, for example.

In 1983 the Supreme Court declared the legislative veto unconstitutional in *Immigration and Naturalization Service v. Chadha*. Although the facts of the case did not extend beyond narrow issues of immigration law, the court's sweeping opinion clearly implied that all forms of the legislative veto were unconstitutional. As one commentator observed: "In that single decision, the Court implied the unconstitutionality of more provisions in more federal laws than in all its other decisions combined since 1789."[91]

Jagdish Rai Chadha was an alien who had been lawfully admitted to the United States on a nonimmigrant student visa. After his visa had expired, the Immigration and Naturalization Service ordered him to show cause why he should not be deported, in accordance with the Immigration and Nationality Act. The same act conferred discretion on the attorney general to suspend deportation if an alien met certain statutory criteria, for example, at least seven years' residence in the United States, good moral character, and extreme hardship. The Immigration Act also provided a one-house veto to enable either the House or the Senate to overturn a decision by the attorney general to suspend the deportation of a particular alien. In Chadha's case, the attorney general decided to suspend deportation, but the House of Representatives exercised its veto over this decision and thereby returned Chadha to the status of a deportable alien. Chadha sued, contending that the legislative veto was unconstitutional and therefore the attorney general's decision to suspend his deportation should be reinstated.

The Supreme Court agreed with Chadha in an opinion heavily laden with references to the founding fathers and their vision of the Republic that was their handiwork. Writing for a six-member majority, Chief Justice Warren Burger maintained that when the House of Representatives overturned the attorney general's decision to suspend Chadha's deportation, it performed a legislative act. Legislation was involved because Chadha's legal status had been changed; "absent the House action, Chadha would remain in the United States." The chief justice then made the textbook argument that the Constitution did not permit legislation by one house of Congress alone. Article 1, section 7, made it unmistakably clear that legislation required favorable action by both houses. Thus, the one-house veto was clearly unconstitutional. A veto requiring action by both houses was also unconstitutional because, before a bill can become law, it must be presented to the president. A two-house veto violated this "presentment" clause. A one-house veto was unconstitutional because it violated both the presentment and the bicameral clauses.

The *Chadha* case is important because it provides a remarkably clear example of the Supreme Court using the very words of the Constitution to upset a sensible accommodation of the principle of separation of powers to the contemporary exigencies of the administrative state. It is unfortunate that the Court did this because, unlike the French, Americans had found a way to adjust to the administrative state with only a mild departure from traditional constitutional practices. The Constitution of the Fifth Republic, on the other hand, was far more radical, calling for nothing less than the abandonment of the bedrock French constitutional principle of parliamentary sovereignty.

Curiously, however, during the course of the Fifth Republic, parliamentary power has expanded beyond the bounds suggested by a literal reading of the constitutional text. The Constitutional Council has played a major role in this expansion but not, as we noted above, by a broad interpretation of the permissive language inviting Parliament to "amplify" the powers it enjoys under article 34. Ironically, the power of Parliament has increased because several governments have chosen to let it do so and the Constitutional Council has gone along with the practical accommodations arranged between the legislative and executive powers. A decision of 30 July 1982 nicely illustrates the Council's accommodating spirit and contrasts sharply with the rigidity of the Supreme Court of the United States in *Chadha*.[92]

On 20 July 1982, the Socialist Parliament passed a price-fixing law which was challenged on constitutional grounds by more than sixty conservative deputies. The challengers' principal target was the fact that "infractions" were punished by fines specified in the law itself. French law distinguishes three levels of criminal wrong-doing: infractions *(contraventions),* misdemeanors *(délits),* and crimes *(crimes).* Article 34 states that laws voted by Parliament shall "make the rules concerning . . . the determination of crimes and misdemeanors as well as the punishments applicable to them."

Since infractions and their punishments were *not* included in article 34, it was clear that they fell under the regulatory power of the government as provided in article 37. Hence, Parliament's decision to include infractions and their punishments in a price-freezing *law* seemed to be an unmistakably clear example of legislative encroachment upon the regulatory domain of the government. This, in turn, seemed to be precisely what the framers of the 1958 Constitution wanted to prevent, and to prevent it is precisely why they created the Constitutional Council.

Predictably, the Constitutional Council found that the legislature had indeed intervened in the regulatory sphere but, remarkably, refused to find this intervention unconstitutional.

The council's reasoning was eminently practical. The purpose of the distinction between articles 34 and 37 was to guarantee the government its own proper regulatory sphere free from legislative interference. Article 41 gives the government authority to reject as "irreceivable" any proposed legislation or amendment that it considers beyond the legislative domain. Article 37 permits the government to modify by decree legislation already passed that it deems to have trespassed upon the regulatory sphere, provided that the Constitutional Council agrees that the legislation in question is of a regulatory character. Thus the government has constitutional means both to block legislative incursions into its domain *before* they are passed and to modify them by decree *after* they have been passed. Hence, the council stated, there is no need to strike down as unconstitutional a legislative encroachment on the regulatory domain. The fact that the government chose not to challenge the law before it was approved indicates that, as a practical matter, it has no objection to it. If it ever should have such an objection, it can always modify the legislation by decree.

This is truly an astonishing decision, given the tremendous emphasis the framers of the 1958 Constitution placed upon limiting the scope of Parliament's power—a point we have already developed at some length in this chapter and which we shall revisit in its final section. Even more astonishing is that three founding fathers with absolutely impeccable Gaullist credentials—Michel Debré, Raymond Janot, and Jean Foyer—had made statements prior to 1982 supporting the position the Constitutional Council made its own in that year. That is, these bastions of Gaullist orthodoxy viewed with equanimity parliamentary incursions into the regulatory domain of the government that they had fought so hard to establish.[93]

Michel Debré explained his position quite simply: "Parliament can make incursions into the government's domain as long as the government accepts them and even more so if the government invites them. Such is the logic of our institutions."[94]

As a practical matter, Debré's statement is quite sensible but it blunts the ideological cutting edge that drove the reform of 1958. Clearly, the times had changed between 1958 and the mid-1970s when Debré, Janot, and Foyer offered their relaxed interpretation of the relationship between the domains of law and regulation. The times had changed even more by 1982 when the Constitutional Council delivered its decision. Parliament no longer posed a serious threat to the constitutional powers of the government and had not done so for at least two decades.

Further, the important constitutional amendment of 1974 permitting sixty members of either legislative chamber to challenge the constitutionality of a law added a new dimension to the relationship between government and Parliament. The 1958 debates portrayed the relationship as predominantly adversarial, but the 1974 amendment allied the parliamentary majority and the government against a potentially disruptive parliamentary minority. Disruptive because a mere sixty deputies or senators could raise a constitutional challenge to any trivial or merely technical violation of the regulatory domain by Parliament, even though the violation in question created no serious problem for the government. Such challenges would be mere obstructions, serving only to clog the docket of the Constitutional Council. To avoid all this, the Constitutional Council simply refused to find a constitutional violation in every instance in which Parliament crossed the law/regulation frontier.

The contrast between the Constitutional Council's decision of 30 July 1982 and the United States Supreme Court's decision in *Chadha* could hardly be greater. Both jurisdictions were faced with a sensible accommodation between the legislative and executive powers in their respective countries that were at odds with the constitutional texts they were required to construe. The Supreme Court of the United States, following a literal and highly formalistic jurisprudence, struck down the legislative veto, whereas the Constitutional Council, looking more to the goals of the Constitution than to its words, permitted the literal violation.

The consequences of the Supreme Court's decision in *Chadha* have not been happy. Not surprisingly, Congress and the administrative agencies have found a host of ways to circumvent *Chadha*. Sometimes the decision is simply ignored without even the figleaf of circumvention. By 1991, just eight years after *Chadha,* Congress had enacted over two hundred new and presumably unconstitutional legislative vetoes with no end in sight.[95] Thus the rigidity of the *Chadha* court has had the ironic effect of diminishing respect for the rule of law among the nation's lawmakers themselves.

Conversely, the Constitutional Council's 1982 decision does not seem to have had any seriously adverse effects. Most assuredly, it has not unleashed an aggressive Parliament. Indeed, the need to do something about the weakness of Parliament was a major theme in a series of thoughtful constitutional reforms proposed by a blue-ribbon commission appointed by President Mitterrand in 1992.[96] Although the logic of the decision implies that Parliament may legislate on *any* subject matter,[97] it may overstep the constitutional limits of article 34 only if the government approves and, therefore, in no sense does the decision restore the sovereign Parliament of earlier republics. By relaxing somewhat the constitutional constraints on Parliament, the Constitutional Council softens the hard edge of the fiercely principled debate over the domains of law and regulation at the time of the founding in 1958. We shall examine "the high warfare of principle" in these jurisprudential debates in the next (and final) section of this chapter.

Before doing so, however, a concluding thought on the Supreme Court and the Constitutional Council may be in order. I have praised the flexibility of the Constitutional Council and criticized the formalism of the Supreme Court in *Chadha*. In fairness to the Supreme Court, however, I should acknowledge that, unlike the Constitutional Council, it is, after all, a real *court* and, therefore, its adherence to textual exegesis in *Chadha* is certainly understandable and perhaps even praiseworthy.[98] The Constitutional Council, faithful to its name, is not a court but a real *council*. It is essentially a political institution that borrows judicial trappings and rhetoric to fulfill its crucial role in the dispensation of the Fifth Republic. Thus its decision to ignore the rather clear language of the Constitution of the Fifth Republic can also be described as "certainly understandable and perhaps even praiseworthy." Thus with regard to *Chadha* and to the 30 July 1982 decision, it might be fair to argue that both institutions fulfilled the roles they were intended to play in their respective regimes. On this happy note, we may conclude this section.

The Jurisprudential Debate

Earlier in this chapter we noted that the two-domain proposal undercut the traditional principle of parliamentary sovereignty and, in so doing, launched a long series of jurisprudential debates culminating in the unsuccessful efforts of the Council of State to restore to Parliament the power to expand its own jurisdiction. The troubling character of challenges to parliamentary sovereignty can be seen in the thoughtful reaction of François Luchaire throughout the drafting process. Luchaire's reactions are particularly interesting because of his double role as constitutional scholar and as active participant in the preparation of the constitutional text.[99] His critical reflections on the progress of the text suggest that his professorial role gave him a certain distance from his busy activities in drafting the document.

For example, in commenting on an early draft apportioning a narrow range of activities to the sphere of law, Luchaire interprets the text as merely specifying "the minimal domain of the law but it is obvious that the legislature can make decisions in all other matters as well."[100] These words were written on 2 July, but by the middle of that month it was by no means obvious that the legislature of the Fifth Republic would retain its traditional sovereign power.

The reason for Parliament's sovereignty was, of course, that the members of the National Assembly were chosen by direct universal suffrage. This required clarification of the respective roles of the assembly, on the one hand, and the indirectly elected Senate, on the other. Thus Luchaire was troubled by an early text stating that "the legislative power is exercised by the two assemblies." He saw a need for clarification here because the chamber elected by universal suffrage should have "the last word" in legislation.[101]

His concern for the supremacy of the National Assembly over the Senate resurfaced in his reaction to the complicated procedure for resolving disagreements between the two chambers. An early version of what would eventually become article 45 of the Constitution provided that such a legislative impasse should be resolved by a call from the prime minister for a joint committee with equal representation from each chamber. If this fails, the government would ask the National Assembly to settle the matter.

Although this arrangement clearly favored the assembly over the senate, Luchaire still found it wanting because of the indispensable role of the government in asking the assembly to make the final decision. In effect, this meant the government and the Senate could join forces to maintain an impasse even if the National Assembly had the will to resolve it. An American might see this as an elementary application of the principle of checks and balances, but to Luchaire it was "a rather serious infringement of the principle according to which the last word ought always to go to the chamber elected by direct universal suffrage."[102] In the United States, no one gets the last word.

As late as 29 July, Luchaire still had misgivings about the two-domain proposal that was on its way to the Advisory Committee on the Constitution. Echoing the sentiments he had voiced on 2 July, he criticized the idea of limiting the sphere of law as inconsistent with no less an authority than the venerable Declaration of the Rights of Man and of the Citizen (1789), which provides that "the law is the expression of the general will."[103]

Luchaire's emphasis on the general will and universal suffrage points to the foundation of the case for parliamentary sovereignty. To understand this case fully, however, we must first grasp the meaning of the principle of separation of powers in the French constitutional tradition.

The principle of separation of powers has a long and somewhat bewildering history. At the outset, one must not confuse separation of *powers* with a mere separation of *functions*. The latter can be traced to the ancient world where political commentators frequently insisted upon the differences in various forms of governing *activities* or functions, that is, it is one thing to make a law and quite another to enforce it. Modern authors tend to go beyond distinguishing governmental functions in order to examine distinctions among constitutional powers as a means of structuring a regime in order to prevent arbitrary rule. American schoolchildren are familiar with the tripartite distinction of legislative, executive, and judicial powers they find in the first three articles of their Constitution. This does not mean merely that the government of the United States sometimes performs functions that are legislative, others that are executive, and still others that are judicial. The government does all this, of course, but more significantly, it relies upon different officers holding different constitutional powers to do it—congressmen to legislate, judges to adjudicate, and so forth. These officers are independent of one another and to preserve their independence, a system of "checks and balances" has been incorporated into the Constitution. A check is a constitutional power ordinarily associated with one branch of government that is given to another—for example, the American president, who heads the executive branch, has the power to veto legislation. He possesses this power primarily to protect himself and the branch he heads against an overreaching legislature. Congress has the traditionally executive powers to declare war, to create offices, and to make rules for the armed forces in order to safeguard against presidential excesses. Judges may be empowered by Congress to exercise the ordinarily executive power of appointing officers.

The American regime is organized around the principle of constitutional *checks*—such as the presidential veto, congressional discipline over the armed forces, and the judicial appointing power—in order to maintain the constitutional *balance* demanded by the separation of powers doctrine. Thus, a check is a means to maintain balance.

The French take separation of powers no less seriously than Americans. Indeed, as we saw in chapter one, the Declaration of the Rights of Man and of the Citizen asserts flatly that "[a] society in which rights are not guaranteed, and in which there is no separation of powers, has no constitution." Despite this unequivocal adherence to the principle of separation of powers, the French understanding of the meaning of the principle differs markedly from the American position described above. The first inkling of this difference appears in article 6 of the Declaration itself which proclaims that "law is the overt expression of the general will." This was the text Luchaire had in mind when he scored the effort to limit the sphere of law as inconsistent with the nature of law as the general will.

Surely his point is well taken. How can any area of human activity be declared off limits to the *general* will without robbing that will of its generality? More importantly, what would be the moral or political basis to justify limiting the general will which is the will of the people? By what principle of democratic government does one limit the will of the people?

This is a serious consideration, but if we return to the question of separation of powers, it seems to prove too much. What basis can there be for an independent executive in the face of a legislature which authoritatively announces the general will? The short answer would seem to be: none. The logic of the notion of law as the expression of the general will tends to preclude an independent executive and thereby tends to pressure the principle of separation of powers to collapse into a mere separation of functions wherein the executive does nothing but the bidding of its legislative master.[104]

The notion of law as the expression of the general will comes, of course, from Jean-Jacques Rousseau, whose writings profoundly influenced the French Revolution which began in 1789, the year of the Declaration of the Rights of Man and of the Citizen. Rousseau had argued that sovereignty resides in the people, an extremely attractive idea to revolutionaries who wanted to draw up a new constitution to replace the old order they had rejected. The notion of popular sovereignty offered a solid foundation for the exercise of unfettered power to begin anew.

Rousseau's teaching presented a serious problem, however, for his revolution-minded disciples, because the master's doctrine had been developed with a direct democracy in mind. Indeed, Rousseau had explicitly rejected representative institutions.[105] The Constituent Assembly that undertook the task of drafting a new constitution realized, of course, that there was no way a great nation state, like late-eighteenth-century France, could be a direct democracy. Representative institutions would have to play a central role in the constitutional monarchy they envisioned in the document they worked on so diligently from 1789 to 1791.

Two major lines of argument materialized to address the problem of how to adjust Rousseau's principle of popular sovereignty to the realities of representation. The first took seriously the possibility that the people's representatives might express their own corporate will, a particular will, rather than the general will of the people, which could be discovered with certainty only in a direct democracy. To safeguard against this possible abuse, the king should be given a "suspensive veto" over the laws passed by the National Assembly. This veto had nothing to do with an American president's veto, which has been variously described as intended to protect the president against Congress or as conferring upon him the role of legislative partner with Congress. The French king's veto was intended to enable him to appeal to the people when he had reason to believe the assembly had mistaken or ignored the general will. Hence, the veto was not absolute but merely "suspensive." It held legislative enactments in abeyance until the people had been consulted in their "primary assemblies," that is, in their electoral districts.[106]

The brilliant and mercurial Abbé Sieyès offered the second line of argument that rejected the suspensive veto, on the grounds that an appeal to the people in their electoral districts would yield nothing more than a series of particular wills, not the general will of the nation as a whole. To substitute the will of an aggregate of particular communities for the general will itself would be "nothing less than cutting up, chopping up, tearing up France into an infinity of petty democracies, which would then be united only by the bonds of general confederation."[107] He went on to argue that the unitary character of the general will could be expressed only in a unified National Assembly. "The people or nation can have only one voice, that of the national legislative. . . . The people, I repeat, in a country that is not a democracy (and France cannot possibly be one), the people can speak and act only through its representatives."[108]

Sieyès rejected the idea of representation as merely "an unavoidable alternative to democracy imposed by the imperious law of numbers in a populous state."[109] Representation in a National Assembly was not a necessary evil but a positive good. Only a unitary, that is, a unicameral, National Assembly can utter the expression of the unitary general will that is law.

The short-lived Constitution of 1791 adopted the royal suspensive veto but with disastrous consequences that led within a year to the collapse of the constitutional monarchy and to the proclamation of a republic.[110] With the suspensive veto discredited, Sieyès's notion of the National Assembly as the authentic voice of the general will moved front and center in French republican thought and remained there until 1958. This, in broad outline, is the origin of the *régime d'assemblée* which Michel Debré denounced with such vigor before the Council of State.

The *régime d'assemblée* brought in its wake a subordination of executive to legislative power on the flawlessly logical grounds that the executive has no basis to claim any authority that is independent of the general will. The meaning of separation of powers would somehow have to be adjusted accordingly. More importantly, the *régime d'assemblée* was at war with the idea of constitutional supremacy. To be sure, the legislature should abide by the Constitution; but if it does not, by what principle can it be faulted? The National Assembly expresses the general will, which is the will of the people themselves and, as such, knows no superior—not even a constitution which previously had expressed the general will differently. Today's general will trumps yesterday's.

This is why French legislatures have had powers beyond anything the American Congress could imagine—including, alas, the power to vote its own demise in 1940 and thereby to hand the country over to the "French

State" (not a Republic) headed by Maréchal Pétain. In sharp contrast, American federal judges—for weal or woe—stand ready to discipline Congress when they believe it has gone too far in surrendering its own powers, as we saw above in the *Chadha* case.[111]

To Americans, for whom the rule of law means preeminently the rule of *constitutional* law interpreted by a robustly independent judiciary, the unfettered power of French parliaments prior to 1958 is shocking. By 1958 many Frenchmen were ready to agree. For all its excesses, however, the *régime d'assemblée* offered the redeeming value of conceptual clarity as to the nation's ultimate legal authority, something that is sorely missing in the cheerfully chaotic American regime, where, President Truman notwithstanding, the buck stops nowhere. The sovereign Parliament, as the *régime d'assemblée* is known when it is on its best behavior, provides a solid foundation for the positive legal order and does so on the uncontestably democratic grounds of direct universal suffrage. This is no small advantage for democrats who have the good sense to recognize the value of order, stability, and security in human affairs. We may safely surmise that this was the aspect of parliamentary sovereignty that prompted François Luchaire's uneasiness in the face of the two-domain proposal that would drastically alter France's parliamentary ways.

Similar concerns explain the dramatic debate over the same proposal before the Council of State on 28 August. Philippe Renaudin scored the undemocratic character of the two-domain proposal, especially its corollary in article 41 authorizing the government to reject as "inadmissible" proposed legislation outside the domain reserved for law. He found it intolerable that Parliament, "the authority chosen by universal suffrage," should yield to an executive chosen by other means.[112] His sentiments were echoed by André Heilbronner and Pierre Seligman, the latter seeing the innovation "as an affront to the very principle of republicanism."[113]

Tony Sauvel based his attack squarely on the administrative grounds of the meaning of "regulation," which he defined as "a delegation which can be withdrawn by the legislator." What the proposed constitution calls regulatory power comes directly to the government without an intervening legislative act and therefore is not regulatory power at all. In effect, the new constitution creates two legislative powers and gives one of them to the nonelected government.[114]

This line of argument was developed more fully by Léon Julliot de la Morandière, dean of the faculty of law at the University of Paris and, judging by the extreme deference shown him by all concerned, a redoubtable figure. Announcing his desire to take the debate to a higher level and "to unburden the conscience of a jurist," Julliot de la Morandière based his attack on the principle of separation of powers. He reminded his listeners that the

Constitutional Law of 3 June, which authorized the government to draft a constitution, states that the "executive power and the legislative power must be effectively separated in such a way that the government and the Parliament shall assume each on its own behalf and on its responsibility the plenitude of its prerogatives."[115] He challenged the idea that certain subject matters are inherently legal, whereas others are inherently regulatory.[116] Since the time of the Revolution, he maintained, a law is simply "a general rule applicable to all citizens or to a certain category of citizens." To make a general rule is to make law, and if the general rule comes in the form of a regulation, it must be based upon law with sufficient clarity to withstand judicial scrutiny. The proposed constitution simply confers legislative power upon the executive and thereby violates the principle of separation of powers.

It fell to Roger Latournerie to rebut the argument of the formidable dean, a task undertaken with considerable delicacy. He maintained that French legal history offered examples of executive power independent of statutory authorization, citing a particular power of the highway police derived directly from the Constitution. From this mundane administrative example, he soared to the highest matters of statecraft, finding that the jurisprudence of the Council of State allows that in times of peril "the executive authority has all the powers indispensable to assure the security of the nation and the very life of the nation."[117] Here he may have proved too much. If such power is inherently executive, how can it be reconciled with article 16, which confers exceptional emergency power on the president, whom, as we saw in the previous chapter, the Gaullist faithful presented as an officer whose powers are most emphatically *not* executive?[118]

Philippe Renaudin offered the most creative amendment to the two-domain proposal when he suggested that the enumeration of legislative powers be preceded by a sentence providing that "the domain of law comprehends essentially the following subject matter."[119] The addition of the word *essentially* would, of course, nullify the entire reform because there would be nothing to prevent Parliament from legislating in areas that were not essentially legislative. That is, *any* subject matter could be legislative without being *essentially* so. This clever ruse gave Jérôme Solal-Céligny, a member of the working group who had taken a decisive role in the formulation of the two-domain proposal, an opportunity to state with unmistakable clarity just what the Gaullist framers had in mind. Renaudin's amendment, he maintained, would undermine the system the government envisioned. The government is not interested in merely expressing a wish that only certain subject matters might be treated by law. It wants to specify these as clearly as possible and to separate effectively the legislative and regulatory domains.[120]

As we saw above, the Council of State eventually adopted open-ended language that would have permitted Parliament to extend its sphere to "all matters recognized as being of a legislative nature."[121] Not surprisingly, the government rejected this language, substituting its own ambiguous text which, again as noted above, became paragraph 7 of article 34.

If one follows the ebb and flow of the Council of State's jurisprudential debate with an eye toward meaningful comparisons with American constitutionalism, the most likely candidate is Raymond Janot's response to the frequent charge that the two-domain proposal is undemocratic because it undermines the sovereignty of Parliament or, more precisely, the sovereignty of the National Assembly, whose members are chosen by direct universal suffrage. To this Janot responds:

> Personally, I do not believe this is undemocratic. If the French people adopt this constitution, it is they who are sovereign and the commands of the sovereign bind the Assembly. To say that the Assembly is sovereign is simply an abuse of language. There is but one sovereign and that is the people. The people may distribute their powers as they see fit.[122]

Janot's statement strikes a familiar chord in the American constitutional tradition. In reading it, one recalls James Wilson's famous address in support of the Constitution on 26 November 1787 before the Pennsylvania ratifying convention.

Like Janot, Wilson faced the problem of reconciling the notion of sovereignty, which implies unity, with a constitution that divided the supreme political power. Janot's constitution divided the supreme power between Parliament and the government; Wilson's divided it between the states and the national government.

Wilson begins his argument by stating the common understanding of sovereign power: "There necessarily exists in every government a power, from which there is no appeal; and which, for that reason, may be termed supreme, absolute, and uncontrollable."[123] He then asks, "Where does this power reside?" In answering his own questions, he says that "Blackstone will tell you, that in Britain, the power is lodged in the British parliament; that the parliament may alter the form of the government; and that its power is absolute and without control."[124] Thus Sieyès would play Blackstone to Janot's Wilson.

Wilson continues that Americans have improved "the science and practice of government" that they learned from their British ancestors by developing "the idea of a constitution, limiting and superintending the operations of the legislative authority." To find sovereignty in an American constitution is, for Wilson, an opinion that "approaches a step nearer to the truth, but does not reach it."[125] Wilson then states his own position unequivocally: "the truth is, that, in our governments, the supreme, absolute, and uncontrollable power remains in the people. As our constitutions are superior to our legislatures; so the people are superior to our constitutions."[126] In language remarkably similar to Janot's, he continues:

> The consequence is, that the people may change the constitutions, whenever and however they please. This is a right, of which no positive institution can ever deprive them.[127]

Wilson's speech also addressed the question of representation. Although Wilson says nothing about Rousseau's general will, his position nevertheless bears a curious resemblance to that of his transatlantic contemporary Abbé Sieyès. Like Sieyès, Wilson celebrates the growth of representative institutions as a positive good and not merely as a poor substitute for direct democracy. Representation marks a distinct advance of modern political thought over that of the ancients, who, for all their wisdom, failed to develop effective representative assemblies. Unlike Sieyès, he prudently avoids the sensitive issue of the representatives' knowing the interests of the people better than the people themselves—a point stated boldly enough by his colleague James Madison just four days earlier in *Federalist* 10.[128]

The major difference between Wilson and Sieyès is that the latter conferred the status of representative only upon officials directly elected by those qualified to vote. Wilson maintains that all officials in the proposed American constitution will be representatives. He justifies his position by this oft-quoted description of the constitution: "In its principles, it is purely democratical."[129] By this he means that all officers are chosen either directly or indirectly by the people. Members of the House of Representatives will be chosen directly by the people; senators by state legislators who are themselves chosen by the people; the president by either the democratically elected House of Representatives or by an electoral college appointed in such manner as the democratically elected state legislatures shall determine; and so forth. Hence, Wilson asserts in a speech on 4 July 1788 celebrating the adoption of the new Constitution: "All those in places of power and trust will be elected either immediately by the people, or in such a manner that their appointment will depend ultimately on such immediate election."[130] Later he will laud representation as the "chain of communication between the people, and those to whom they have committed the exercise of the powers of government."[131] No matter how many links there are in the chain, it assures a connection between the people and those who govern them. The system is "purely democratical" because "all the derivative movements of government must spring from the people at large."[132]

Wilson's argument has enormous consequences for American public administration because it justifies the status of nonelected officials as representatives of the people. Wilson drew this conclusion explicitly in a series of lectures on law which he delivered in the winter of 1790–1791. After stating that during the colonial period there was widespread mistrust of judges and executive officers because, unlike the popularly elected assemblymen, they were appointed by the crown, he continued:

> Indeed, if I mistake not, an inferiour proportion of attention, in this and in most of our sister states, has been employed about these important parts of the political system. Laws have abounded: their multiplicity has been often a grievance: but their weak and irregular execution, and the unwise and unstable administration of justice, have been subjects of general and well grounded complaint.
>
> Habits contracted before the late revolution of the United States, operate, in the same manner, since that time, though very material alterations may have taken place in the objects of their operations.
>
> Before that period, the executive and the judicial powers of government were placed neither in the people, nor in those, who professed to receive them under the authority of the people. They were derived from a different and a foreign source: they were regulated by foreign maxims: they were directed to foreign purposes. Need we be surprised, that they were objects of aversion and distrust? Need we be surprised, that every occasion was seized for lessening their influence, and weakening their energy? On the other hand, our assemblies were chosen by ourselves: they were the guardians of our rights, the objects of our confidence, and the anchor of our political hopes. Every power, which could be placed in them, was thought to be safely placed: every extension of that power was considered as an extension of our own security.
>
> At the revolution, the same fond predilection, and the same jealous dislike, existed and prevailed. The executive and the judicial as well as the legislative authority was now the child of the people; but, to the two former, the people behaved like stepmothers. The legislature was still discriminated by excessive partiality; and into its lap, every good and precious gift was profusely thrown.
>
> Even at this time, people can scarcely divest themselves of those opposite prepossessions: they still hold, when, perhaps, they perceive it not, the language, which expresses them. In observations on this subject, we hear the legislature mentioned as the *people's representatives*. The distinction, intimated by concealed implication, though probably, not avowed upon reflection, is, that the executive and judicial powers are not connected with the people by a relation so strong, or near, or dear.
>
> But it is high time that we should chastise our prejudices; and that we should look upon the different parts of government with a just and impartial eye. The executive and judicial powers are now drawn from the same source, are now animated by the same principles, and are now directed to the same ends, with the legislative authority: *They who execute, and they who administer the laws, are as much the servants, and therefore as much*

the friends of the people, as they who make them. The character, and inter-
est, and glory of the two former are as intimately and as necessarily con-
nected with the happiness and prosperity of the people, as the character,
and interest, and glory of the latter are. Besides, the execution of the law,
and the administration of justice under the law, bring it home to the for-
tunes, and farms, and houses, and business of the people. Ought the executive or the judicial magistrates, then, to be considered as foreigners? Ought
they to be treated with a chilling indifference?[133] [Emphasis added.]

I apologize to the reader for the lengthy quotation but, when read with
Wilson's position on representation in mind, it is an extremely important
statement for those who look for ways to legitimate administrative institutions in the United States.

I believe the same argument is relevant to the French legitimacy crisis
provoked by the two-domain proposal. Raymond Janot had it right when he
said it is the French people who are sovereign, not their popularly elected
National Assembly. They exercised that sovereignty in approving the Constitution of 1958, which provided for a National Assembly that was *not* sovereign even though under that same Constitution it alone was to be chosen by
direct universal suffrage. One of the reasons Parliament is not sovereign is
because its legislative domain is restricted by articles 34 and 37.[134] The sovereign people have decided that some decisions are to be made under article 34
by directly elected representatives and others under article 37 by "representatives" (in James Wilson's sense of the term) who are indirectly elected.
These "Wilsonian" representatives comprise the government whose head,
the prime minister, is appointed by an elected president—directly elected
since 1962 and indirectly elected previously. The French people in 1958, like
the American people in 1787–1788, exercised their sovereignty in approving
a new political order that distributed offices and power in a certain way. For
the Americans, it was a question of dividing power between state and national governments and then subdividing the powers of the latter among
Congress, the executive, and the courts. The constitutional powers of unelected judges are no less legitimate than those of the directly elected congressmen or the indirectly elected president. The same holds for the appointed "principal officer in each of the executive departments and their
inferior officers." *All* powers were given or withheld in that one great act of
sovereign consent which has never been revoked.

In 1958, the sovereign French people divided certain powers among the
Parliament, the government, the judiciary, the president of the Republic,
and certain administrative bodies, such as the Council of State. None of
these is sovereign because only the people are. Janot's advocacy of popular
sovereignty offers a principled solution to the problem posed by the separate
domains of law and regulation.

5

The Judicial Power

But I am at a loss how to explain the political action of the American
tribunals without entering into some technical details respecting their
constitution and their forms of proceeding; and I cannot descend to these
minutiae without wearying the reader by the natural dryness of the subject.
Yet how can I be clear and at the same time brief? I can scarcely hope to
escape these different evils. Ordinary readers will complain that I am tedious,
lawyers that I am too concise. But these are the natural disadvantages of my
subject, and especially of the point that I am now to discuss.

— ALEXIS DE TOCQUEVILLE

Article 3 of the American Constitution provides that "the judicial Power of
the United States shall be vested in one Supreme Court, and in such inferior
Courts as the Congress may from time to time ordain and establish." The
Constitution of the Fifth Republic has no statement even remotely similar,
for two reasons. First, for technical and historical considerations rooted in
the traditional French horror of *gouvernement des juges,* the judiciary is
called an "authority" rather than a power. Secondly, there is no "one Supreme Court" in France because three institutions exercising judicial authority are each supreme in its own sphere.[1] The Council of State is the supreme
judicial authority in administrative law. The Court of Cassation (or the
"Annulling Court"—*La Cour de Cassation*) is the highest court of appeals
in civil and criminal matters. Finally, questions on the constitutionality of
laws passed by Parliament fall under the exclusive jurisdiction of the Constitutional Council, which, as we have seen in previous chapters, is not really a
court at all. Not surprisingly, the daunting task of sorting out these various
jurisdictions has proved a challenge worthy of the best legal minds in
France.

The Constitution of the Fifth Republic devotes but three short articles
(64 to 66) to the ordinary courts headed by the Court of Cassation. Provisions are made therein for the selection, discipline, and independence of the
judges.[2]

An administrative jurisdiction independent of the ordinary judicial authority dates from the Napoleonic era. At the time of the Revolution, hostil-

ity to the reactionary courts of the *ancien régime* ran so high that a law passed in 1790 provided that

> judicial functions are distinct and will always remain separate from administrative functions. On pain of breach of faith, judges may not in any way at all upset the operations of administrative bodies nor summon administrators before them for reasons connected with their functions.[3]

This legislative expression, a harbinger of the abiding French mistrust of judges, created all the predictable problems of unchecked power that are found even in the best of times. To safeguard against widely reported abuses of unfettered discretion by administrative officers, Napoléon, in 1799, supplemented the 1790 law by creating the Council of State, a body he intended to be "half-administrative, half-judicial."[4] That is, it was to adjudicate complaints against administrative officers without being part of the ordinary judicial system. The Council of State took root and flourished, providing legal stability and administrative leadership as empires, monarchies, and republics came and went. By 1958, the Council of State had established a worldwide reputation for having developed an admirable body of administrative law grounded in jurisprudential principles that contributed significantly to its well-deserved prestige. The extent of its prestige is evident from what we have already seen of its central role in drafting the Constitution of the Fifth Republic.

The founders of the Fifth Republic presented their countrymen with a bold innovation in the Constitutional Council, which has been variously described as both "a masterpiece" and as "an institution altogether foreign to French political traditions, customs and ideas."[5] Its primary purpose, as we saw in chapter two, was to police the constitutional boundary erected between the spheres of law and regulation. This it did at first, but shortly after General de Gaulle's death in 1970, it developed an extraordinary life of its own, thereby confirming the wisdom of what Yves Mény calls the law of institutional life that "no creator of an institution can hope to control the future of its creature."[6] It is no exaggeration to say that the Constitutional Council has totally transformed French constitutional law and has provided France for the first time with the institutional capacity to impose constitutional discipline upon an errant Parliament. In a word, the Constitutional Council has taken a giant step toward realizing the longstanding dream of French jurists to see their country actualize its full potential as a "legal State" *(Etat de droit).*[7]

This chapter will examine the Constitutional Council in three stages. First, we shall review its development under the Fifth Republic in order to grasp fully the constitutional significance of this remarkable institution. Then we shall review the founding debates of 1958 to discover what sort of institution the framers of the Constitution had in mind when they created the council. Finally, we shall consider the important relationship between the Constitutional Council and the Council of State in order to see how a constitutional jurisdiction which is not a *supreme court* relates to a well-established and prestigious jurisdiction of administrative law.

THE DEVELOPMENT OF THE CONSTITUTIONAL COUNCIL

Chapter one introduced the reader to the Constitutional Council where we learned that it is not a court. This is because no litigants appear before it. Its nine members serve nine-year, nonrenewable terms with three councillors being replaced every third year. The president of the Republic, the president of the Senate, and the president of the National Assembly each appoints three members. The president of the Republic designates one of his appointees as president of the Constitutional Council and this officer casts a tie-breaking vote. Tie votes are possible because former presidents of the Republic are entitled to serve on the council for life, thereby creating the possibility of an even number of councillors. Following French judicial practice, the councillors issue no dissenting or concurring opinions, nor is the distribution of votes among the councillors revealed officially. Every decision is issued as though it were unanimous in order to suggest the certitude of the law. Like justices of the Supreme Court of the United States, the councillors have no constitutional qualifications they must meet to be eligible for appointment.

The Constitutional Council convenes to monitor the regularity of referenda and of presidential and parliamentary elections. It must review parliamentary rules and all organic laws to assure their conformity to the Constitution. Organic laws are parliamentary enactments of greater dignity and solemnity than ordinary legislation. As such, they require the elaborate procedure stated in article 46. The constitution itself calls for organic laws to complete the detailed development of institutions whose constitutional foundations are described only in broad outline. For example, the number of deputies and senators, their salaries, and the rules for their election are matters the Constitution assigns to the realm of organic law.

The Constitutional Council's jurisdiction is mandatory in all the situations mentioned in the previous paragraph. It is optional in the case of ordinary legislation, that is, laws that are not organic, which is the case with nearly every law passed by Parliament. The option, however, belongs not to the council but to certain officers of the State: the president of the Republic, the prime minister, and the presidents of the Senate and of the National Assembly. As noted above, these officers alone could convene the Constitutional Council prior to an important constitutional amendment in 1974. Since 1974, sixty members of either house of Parliament may convene it as well, but no one else may do so. Thus, unlike the Supreme Court of the United States, the Constitutional Council does not control its own docket.[8] It acts only at the behest of officials. More importantly, unlike any American court, the council has no jurisdiction over constitutional challenges to legislation brought by aggrieved citizens, nor does any other judicial body in France. The constitutionality of laws passed by Parliament is strictly off-limits to all ordinary and administrative courts. Therefore, if none of the officers mentioned above chooses to convene the Constitutional Council, there is no judicial forum in which a flagrantly unconstitutional law can be challenged. For decades French jurists have deplored this situation. Recently, serious efforts have been made to empower ordinary citizens to challenge the constitutionality of statutes applied against them, but to date without success.[9]

The Constitutional Council reviews a law after it has been approved by Parliament and before it is promulgated by the president. Hence, the council's reviewing power is often described as "abstract" or a priori as opposed to the "concrete" or a posteriori reviewing power of an American federal court whose jurisdiction is limited to adversarial "cases or controversies" in actual litigation. Another important difference is that the Constitution of the Fifth Republic specifies the council's timetable. Decisions on constitutionality are to be rendered in one month and, in cases of emergency, the government can shorten this period to eight days. The Supreme Court of the United States, for the most part, manages its time as it alone sees fit.[10]

From "Executive Auxiliary" to "Guardian of Liberty"

The Constitutional Council's early years gave no indication of its brilliant future. During de Gaulle's presidency from 1958 to 1969, its optional jurisdiction was invoked only seven times and each time with the same result of upholding the position of the government. Alec Stone, the leading American scholar on the Constitutional Council, maintains that an "examination of this early jurisprudence shows the extent to which the Council strained to provide maximum support for the executive against Parliament."[11] This judgment was confirmed by François Luchaire's telling metaphor of the Constitutional Council as "a cannon aimed at parliament."[12] In 1964, François Mitterrand mocked the council as a " 'Supreme Court for the *Musée Grévin,* a derisory cap of a derisory democracy' whose 'sole utility is to serve as an errand boy for General de Gaulle.' "[13]

All this changed dramatically on 16 July 1971 when the Constitutional Council handed down a decision that Didier Maus has aptly characterized as a "fundamental psychological turning point" that transformed the council from "an executive auxiliary" to the "guardian of liberty."[14] The decision involved a statute submitted to the council by Senate president Alain Poher. The challenged law would have amended a well-known 1901 law on the freedom of association for nonprofit organizations, including political parties. Specifically, it would have empowered state officials to impose certain burdens on associations suspected of supporting illegal purposes. The Senate had refused to approve the law on the grounds that it violated the freedom of political parties guaranteed by article 4 of the Constitution. The National Assembly passed it anyway pursuant to the complex procedure of article 45, which enables the assembly to override a reluctant Senate. Hence, the appeal from the president of the Senate to the Constitutional Council.[15]

Senate president Poher's appeal was in itself quite unusual because theretofore the principal activities of the Constitutional Council had been to monitor elections and to settle to the government's advantage procedural disputes between the government and the Parliament along the border that divided the realm of law from that of regulation. Poher's appeal raised a substantive question of individual liberty. Remarkably, the council voided the challenged statute.[16]

Even more remarkable than the decision itself was the council's reasoning to support it. Instead of following the Senate's lead and striking down the measure as violative of the constitutionally guaranteed freedom of political parties, the council broke new ground and based its decision on the preamble to the Constitution of 1958. Prior to 1971, it had been widely assumed that the preamble offered the nation uplifting and inspirational language that was *not* legally enforceable.[17] The dramatic change signaled by the 16 July decision was remarkable because the preamble's extremely broad language opened breathtaking vistas of constitutional powers, which the council now conferred upon itself. The first paragraph of the preamble provides:

> The French people hereby solemnly proclaims its attachment to the Rights of Man and the principles of national sovereignty as defined by the Declaration of 1789, reaffirmed and complemented by the Preamble of the Constitution of 1946.

Thus, the preamble includes the rights stated in the Declaration of the Rights of Man and of the Citizen of 1789; for example, the freedoms of speech, press, and religion to name but a few. (The full text of the Declaration appears in Appendix A.)

The preamble also proclaims the attachment of the French people to the Declaration of 1789 as it was "reaffirmed and complemented by the Preamble of the Constitution of 1946." Thus, in constitutionalizing the preamble of the 1958 Constitution, the council also constitutionalized at least part of the much longer preamble of the Constitution of 1946. This preamble, which is printed in full in Appendix B, announced adherence of the French people not only to the Declaration of the 1789 but also to "the fundamental principles recognized by the laws of the Republic." In its decision of 16 July 1971, the Constitutional Council found the freedom of association provided in the 1901 law on that topic to be one of these fundamental principles and that this freedom was violated by the statute under review.

In basing its decision on the "fundamental principles recognized by the laws of the Republic," the council chose "the least precise of possible constitutional sources"[18] and thereby served notice of its willingness to maximize its discretionary capacity to void other statutes in the future. That is, the Constitutional Council chose *not* to base its decision on specific language dealing with political parties in article 4, nor upon any of the specific rights detailed in the Declaration of 1789, but upon the vague standard of "fundamental principles" recognized by unspecified laws of the Republic. The decision of 16 July was the council's first step—and a gigantic step it was—toward the self-serving goal of what Alec Stone calls "judicial inflation," whereby the council enhances its own power by multiplying "texts, principles, and rights purported to be invested with *valeur constitutionnel* [constitutional value]."[19]

We mentioned above the constitutional amendment of 1974 that added sixty deputies or sixty senators to the four officers empowered to convene the council in order to examine the constitutionality of laws passed by Parliament. The origin of this important amendment is not entirely clear.

The year 1974 saw the arrival of a new president of the Republic, Valéry Giscard d'Estaing, and a new president of the Constitutional Council, Roger Frey. Both men were the third to hold their respective positions. Frey, like his two predecessors, was a staunch Gaullist known to have favored a more active role for the council he now headed. Loïc Philip maintains that Frey thought the Constitutional Council should have the power to convene itself when laws concerning fundamental liberties had been approved by Parliament.[20] Such a proposal would have found little support among Frey's Gaullist allies, who, in general, did not look kindly upon major changes in the Constitution their deceased leader had bequeathed them. It would have been anathema to the Left where such a proposal would have been regarded as one more humiliating attack on the diminished Parliament of the Fifth Republic.

Against the background of a possible constitutional amendment giving "self-convening" *(auto-saisine)* power to the Constitutional Council, President Giscard d'Estaing's proposal to enable sixty members of either parliamentary chamber to convene it appeared modest and reasonable.

The president's reasons for favoring the reform are probably due to the fact that, although he was a conservative, he was not a Gaullist. His support in Parliament was shaky, especially since his margin of victory over François Mitterrand in the 1974 presidential election was exceedingly thin. He set out to broaden his appeal to some elements of the parliamentary opposition and one way to do this was to permit sixty members—presumably from the opposition—of either chamber to demand a constitutional review of legislation passed by the parliamentary majority. For the most part, the Left was not impressed and dismissed the proposed amendment as a trivial "reformette."[21]

If the origin of the amendment is vague, its effect is astoundingly clear. It has transformed French politics. Since 1974, senators and deputies of both Right and Left have used their new powers to check parliamentary majorities on constitutional grounds. The Constitutional Council has obliged by implementing the logic of the decision of 16 July 1971, fashioning a grand panoply of constitutional rights and principles to channel the parliamentary enthusiasm of both conservative and Socialist majorities along constitutionally appropriate lines.

In effect, the Constitutional Council has come at times to function as a third chamber of Parliament.[22] As such, it played an extremely important role when the Socialists came to power in 1981 with an ambitious redistributive agenda. Having been out of power for over two decades, the Socialists were in no mood to squander the fruits of their electoral victories at both the parliamentary and presidential levels. Socialist deputy André Laignel set the menacing tone of the new government when he told his conservative opponents: "You are legally wrong because you are politically in the minority."[23] In such an unsettling atmosphere, so redolent of the *régime d'assemblée* of the Fourth Republic, the Right looked to the Constitutional Council for solace. They were not disappointed. In a series of controversial decisions, the council succeeded in moderating some aspects of the Socialists' reforms—most notably the amount of compensation due to owners of industries that were about to be nationalized. Needless to say, the Socialists were outraged at seeing their reform efforts weakened by a Constitutional Council staffed by holdovers appointed during the period of conservative hegemony. Knowledgeable commentators spoke of a constitutional crisis and, interestingly for our purpose, recalled Franklin Roosevelt's titanic constitutional struggles with a conservative Supreme Court of the United States in the 1930s.

Fortunately for the Socialists, council members serve only nine-year, nonrenewable terms, so eventually they were able to make some appointments of their own. This worked to their advantage in 1986 when the conservatives regained control of Parliament and thereby initiated the first cohabitation period. When the council proceeded to uphold constitutional challenges to conservative reforms brought by the Socialist minority, it was the Right's turn to howl and howl they did. "In fact, by far the most vitriolic attacks by politicians on the council ever recorded occurred during this period."[24]

The fact that the Constitutional Council succeeded in infuriating both the Right and Left may have increased its legitimacy in the eyes of all. In any event, by the end of the first cohabitation period there could be no doubt that the council had emerged as a key player in French politics regardless of who is in power.

The power exercised by the Constitutional Council in voiding in whole or in part legislation approved by parliamentary majorities is as obvious as it is impressive. Less obvious but no less impressive is the disciplinary effect the *threat* of council disapproval has had in imposing constitutional norms on parliamentary discourse and thereby disciplining legislative possibilities by constitutional constraints. This interesting and important phenomenon Alec Stone accurately, if somewhat inelegantly, characterizes as the "juridicization" of French politics.[25]

The Council of Revision and the Preamble

This brief account of the Constitutional Council suggests certain points of comparison with the American experience of judicial review. The council's bold decision of 16 July 1971 conferring extensive jurisdiction upon itself inevitably reminds the constitutional historian of Chief Justice Marshall's judicial tour de force in *Marbury v. Madison* wherein the Supreme Court, undeterred by the absence of an explicit text, nevertheless interpreted the Constitution as conferring upon the judiciary the power to declare acts of Congress unconstitutional.[26] The constitutional amendment of 1974 recalls the Fourteenth Amendment to the Constitution of the United States, which provides the textual foundation for nearly all the major cases in the twentieth century involving civil rights and civil liberties. This amendment has "nationalized" the Bill of Rights and prompted one knowledgeable commentator to go so far as to claim that it "has become the text upon which most twentieth-century constitutional law is a gloss."[27] Like the 1974 amendment to the Constitution of the Fifth Republic, the Fourteenth Amendment to the Constitution of the United States has transformed the constitutional politics of the nation.

The records of the debates at the Philadelphia Convention of 1787 reveal that the framers of the Constitution gave serious consideration to a "Council of Revision" that would have borne some similarities to the French

Constitutional Council. The early sessions of the convention were dominated by the extremely nationalistic "Virginia Plan"; so called because it
was presented by Governor Edmund Randolph of Virginia. It provided that
"the Executive and a convenient number of the National Judiciary, ought to
comprise a Council of Revision with authority to examine every act of the
National Legislature before it shall operate."[28] That is, like the French Constitutional Council, the Council of Revision would have exercised *abstract*
review over acts of Congress before they could go into effect. It would have
been a real council, that is, an overtly political institution, and not a court
with litigants and real cases before it.

Although the framers eventually rejected the Council of Revision, the
idea did not die easily. This was due primarily to the fact that two of the convention's most prominent members, James Madison and James Wilson,
were among its champions. After the proposed council had suffered an early
rejection by the delegates, Wilson moved that it be reconsidered on the
grounds that the executive's veto power would need the support of the judiciary to win popular approval. Madison seconded the motion, noting that in a
Republic, as opposed to a monarchy, the "Executive Magistrate would be
envied and assailed by disappointed competitors: His firmness therefore wd.
need support."[29]

Wilson, again seconded by Madison, raised the same issue much later in
the convention, but this time he stressed the judiciary's advantage in sharing
the president's veto power. He recognized that the judges could defend
themselves against unconstitutional laws that threatened their own powers
by simply refusing to enforce them; but "this power of the Judges did not go
far enough." They should also share with the president the power to void
laws that may be unjust, unwise, dangerous, or destructive, "and yet not be
so unconstitutional as to justify the Judges in refusing to give them effect."[30]

The most interesting point to emerge from the detailed debate on the ill-
starred Council of Revision is the apparent connection in the minds of the
framers between the presidential veto power and the power of the courts to
void legislative acts on constitutional grounds. Today we are accustomed to
presidents exercising their vetoes on policy grounds, whereas the judiciary
"vetoes" only those acts of Congress it finds unconstitutional. Clearly this
distinction between constitutional and policy issues was known to the framers, as the previous paragraph unmistakably indicates. Nevertheless,
throughout the convention the frequent linkage between the executive veto
and judicial review of unconstitutional legislation tends to blur it.

This tendency is reinforced by the fact that both powers were often discussed in the context of the executive and judiciary defending their respective constitutional positions against an overbearing legislature, as though
this were the primary and perhaps the only legitimate use of the respective

vetoes. Further, as we saw in our earlier discussion of the president as "magistrate," the textual requirement in the seventh section of article 1 that the president, like a judge, must give reasons to support his vetoes suggests that the framers looked for a certain judicial quality in the exercise of this power. Finally, the simple fact that the first six presidents exercised their vetoes only on constitutional grounds reinforces this judicial-executive axis.

The upshot of all this is that perhaps it should come as no surprise that American constitutional history reveals the Supreme Court's power of judicial review as a form of political power; judicial politics, to be sure, but politics nonetheless. The framers of the Fifth Republic clearly anticipated some sort of political role for the Constitutional Council when they conferred lifetime council membership on former presidents of the Republic. The American framers seriously considered a close judicial-executive partnership in assessing legislative acts on both constitutional and other grounds as well. The fact that they ultimately rejected this plan does not mean they removed politics from adjudication at the highest level of the state.

The preamble to the American Constitution provides a point of contrast rather than a comparison to the Fifth Republic. The preamble has never been seriously considered as legally binding. Brutus, one of the most skillful Anti-Federalists, tried to pick a fight on this issue but no one on either side of the argument seemed interested in the challenge. Considering the expansive ends for which the Constitution was "ordained and established"—a more perfect union, justice, domestic tranquillity, the common defense, the general welfare, and "the Blessings of Liberty for ourselves and our Posterity"—Brutus concluded that "it has in view every object which is embraced by any government."[31] By this he meant that the Constitution was not an appropriate document for a federal government of limited powers but for a consolidated government with plenary powers. If the preamble is an enforceable part of the Constitution, Brutus is surely correct; such a preamble would mock the detailed language of the eighth section of the first article which so carefully and so cautiously enumerates the powers of Congress.

In the very first Congress, however, two representatives—John Page of Virginia and Thomas Tucker of South Carolina—stated without raising any objection that the preamble was "no part of the constitution."[32]

Joseph Story made the same point but with greater depth and insight in the careful analysis of the preamble in his learned *Commentaries on the Constitution*. Story rejected any interpretation purporting to find in the preamble an independent source of power for the national government. "Its true nature," he wrote in 1833, "is to expound the nature and extent and application of the powers actually conferred by the Constitution, and not substantially to create them."[33] This interpretation of the preamble was upheld by the Supreme Court in 1905.[34]

Some Americans might be disappointed—perhaps even shocked—to learn that the preamble they lovingly memorized as schoolchildren is not part of the Constitution. They should recall, however, the crucial distinction between a document that is important and one that is legally enforceable. The Declaration of Independence is not legally enforceable but it has shaped our political culture and continues to do so. James Monroe grasped the real meaning of the preamble when he wrote in 1788:

> The introduction, like a preamble to a law, is the Key of the Constitution. Whenever federal power is exercised contrary to the spirit breathed by this introduction, it will be unconstitutionally exercised, and ought to be resisted by the people.[35]

The preamble is inspirational literature that informs the national political conscience and, like a sacred text, emboldens the best in us to resist injustice. It is not the basis of a lawsuit but a moral standard to which we hold ourselves and those who govern us. This is why the use of the present tense is so meaningful—"We the People of the United States . . . *do* ordain and establish this Constitution for the United States of America."[36] (Emphasis added.) The popular act of consent to the work of the framers of two centuries ago is not only a historical fact but an ongoing reenactment as well. We live under the constitutional order established by the founding fathers not because, as obedient sons and daughters, we do what we are told but because we choose to do so.

THE DEBATES ON THE CONSTITUTIONAL COUNCIL

Having reviewed the development of the Constitutional Council, we shall now examine the debates from 1958 to see the extent to which the framers of the Constitution anticipated subsequent events. A conference held at Aix-en-Provence in 1988 to commemorate the thirtieth anniversary of the Constitution provides an interesting link between the founders' view of the Constitutional Council and what its history had revealed three decades later. American scholars who immerse themselves in the founding of their own Republic will be forgiven if they are a bit envious of their French academic colleagues, because the conference participants included eight *témoins* (witnesses) who had taken an active role in the development of the 1958 text—Raymond Janot, François Luchaire, and Pierre Pflimlin among them. The American historical imagination runs wild at the prospect of a conference on the Constitution of the United States in 1817 graced by the presence of James Madison, Charles Pinckney, and Rufus King.[37]

The Aix-en-Provence conference followed the customary academic format of formal papers followed by discussions, with the striking addition of including among the discussants some of the very men whose work had been analyzed. This interaction between scholarly analysts and practical participants is most instructive for Americans who pour so much energy into discerning the elusive "intent of the framers." The most interesting exchange between an academic author of 1988 and a *témoin* of 1958 came in Raymond Janot's spirited reaction to Loïc Philip's paper on the origins of the Constitutional Council. The latter's careful examination of the texts from the founding period *(Travaux Préparatoires)* convinced him that the framers first thought of the Constitutional Council as a successor to the lackluster Constitutional Committee *(Comité Constitutionnel)*, a moribund institution of the Fourth Republic with insignificant constitutional responsibilities matched by undistinguished achievements. Only later, according to Philip, did the framers see its central role as the familiar one of policing the constitutional frontier between the domains of law and regulation. Janot rejected this interpretation, insisting that the framers had always thought of the Constitutional Council's primary task in terms of protecting the integrity of the division between the two domains. Luchaire supported Janot's recollection but Philip insisted that the texts indicated otherwise. Thus there emerged a fascinating clash between textual evidence and personal recollection—a constitutional expression of the ancient conflict between written texts and oral traditions and their competing claims for reliability.

To supplement the impressive textual evidence Philip presents to buttress his case for the salience of the obscure Fourth Republic Constitutional Committee,[38] one might add the curious fact that General de Gaulle himself mistakenly referred to the Constitutional Council as the "Constitutional Committee" on the solemn occasion of his address at the *Place de la République* on 4 September when he presented the proposed constitution to the French people for their considered and definitive judgement.[39] In all likelihood the error was simply a misstatement on the part of the general and his advisers but, in light of Philip's argument, it was a strange error to make at so auspicious an event.

Whatever the textual complexities, Janot's firmness in asserting that the origin of the Constitutional Council is the distinction between law and regulation carries the day. Perhaps the best explanation of the discrepancy between text and recollection lies in the fact that the former is incomplete. Philip notes that Janot, Luchaire, and Jean Foyer formed a subgroup of Michel Debré's working group *(groupe de travail)*. Their task was to prepare the articles for what eventually became the section of the Constitution dealing with the Constitutional Council. Their efforts were accepted "without much change by the working group"[40] and included in the Red Book that the government submitted as its draft text to the Advisory Committee on the Constitution. There is no written record of the subgroup's deliberations that may have provided the forum for Janot's vivid recollections.

If this is the case, it serves as a salutary warning to those who examine written sources in order to discern the intent of the authors of great historical documents. American constitutionalists are all too familiar with this problem. Despite James Madison's painstaking efforts to provide posterity with a contemporaneous account of what really happened at the Philadelphia Convention of 1787, his record has maddening gaps, especially in matters concerning the work of special committees appointed to draft new versions of the evolving text.

Such frustrations are, of course, endemic to the scholarly enterprise. They do not detract from its value but they teach scholars circumspection in stating their conclusions.

Anticipating the Future

The constitutional status of the preamble received considerable attention during the long debates before the Advisory Committee on the Constitution from 29 July to 14 August. The focal point was an unsuccessful amendment offered by Fernand Van Graefschepe that would have prefaced the list of subject matters under the jurisdiction of Parliament's legislative power with a reference to the "general principles and individual liberties defined by the preamble."[41] The proposed amendment was worded in such a way as to suggest that the legislative powers of Parliament would be limited by the preamble's principles and liberties. Raymond Janot, the government's representative to the Advisory Council, opposed the amendment vigorously.

The text of the preamble submitted to the Advisory Committee, like the preamble in the final version, referred to the Declaration of the Rights of Man and of the Citizen of 1789 and to the preamble of the 1946 Constitution. Janot warned the Advisory Committee that a reference to the preamble *within the text* of the Constitution would constitutionalize all the rights and principles maintained in these two documents.[42] To clarify his position, he explained that the preamble as such did not have constitutional status but it would acquire such status if a reference to it were included in the Constitution itself. This, he explained, is why language describing France as a Republic that is "indivisible, secular, democratic, and social" appears in the body of the Constitution and *not* in the preamble. The framers intended those descriptive adjectives to have constitutional status. He concluded by arguing that to constitutionalize the preamble to a document creating a

Constitutional Council would be a virtual invitation to establish the dreaded "government by judges" *(gouvernement des juges)*. Since Janot spoke as the official representative of General de Gaulle's government, it seems fair to conclude that the Constitutional Council's decision that the preamble is part of the Constitution cannot be squared with the intent of the document's authors.

Janot's appeal to the fear of "government by judges" was the standard reductio ad absurdum in French debates over the proper role of the judiciary in public life. He was not the first to raise the familiar specter in connection with the preamble. Pierre-Henri Teitgen had suggested a similar linkage even before Van Graefschepe had moved his ill-starred amendment. Such rhetorical ploys were part of the government's strategy to keep the jurisdiction of the Constitutional Council within manageable bounds. Sensitivity to this matter was evident in Janot's initial discussion of the council before the Advisory Committee. In unveiling the Constitutional Council, Janot insisted it was not a "supreme court" that would lead to "government by judges."[43] His explicit rejection of the term "supreme court" may have been an effort on his part to distance the proposed council from the Supreme Court of the United States which, because of its tumultuous battles with President Roosevelt during the New Deal era, continued to conjure up for French jurists their worst fears of judicial authority run amok.[44] Thus Janot takes pains to assure the Advisory Committee of the modest scope of the proposed council's activities. It will not meddle in the affairs of the ordinary courts because its authority is "limited to the organization and management of public institutions."[45]

This minimalist interpretation of the Constitutional Council's powers is quite consistent with the Gaullist view of the council's purpose as primarily to keep Parliament within its constitutionally defined sphere. As noted above, the council's crucial decision of 16 July 1971 finds no support in the Gaullist orthodoxy of 1958. Without denying this in any way, Bruno Génévois wisely observes that the framers did not do all they could have done to *prevent* the Constitutional Council from going down the path it eventually chose to follow.[46] The Constitution of the Fourth Republic declared its preamble off-limits to the very modest reviewing powers it conferred upon its own hapless Constitutional Committee.[47] The framers of the 1958 Constitution could have done the same but chose not to do so and thereby left open the possibility for the vigorous institutional growth of the Constitutional Council.

Génévois made this point in the paper he presented at Aix-en-Provence in 1988. In the discussion following Génévois's presentation, Raymond Janot did not seem at all perturbed, much less betrayed, that the Constitutional Council had developed in a way that belied his expectations. Looking back over three decades, he shrewdly assessed his own work and that of his colleagues of 1958: "If we did not open the doors of the future, at least we kept ourselves from closing them."[48]

The ideas that prompted the 1974 constitutional amendment permitting sixty members of either house of Parliament to convene the Constitutional Council were discussed in great detail in 1958. Like the government, the Advisory Committee on the Constitution relied on "working groups" to prepare its positions in advance of plenary sessions. At a meeting of one of these groups on 5 August, Raymond Triboulet won approval for a proposal that would have permitted one-third of the members of either parliamentary chamber to convene the Constitutional Council. Thus a parliamentary minority would share a power the government had reserved to the president of the Republic, the prime minister, and the presidents of the two legislative bodies. The Advisory Committee as a whole accepted this bold proposal which signalled a major change in the text submitted to it by the government. The Advisory Committee's purely advisory character became abundantly clear, however, when the government deleted this change from the revised text it submitted to the Council of State, the next step in the drafting process.

Although the Advisory Committee's recommendation did not find its way into the final version of the constitution, the debate over the controversial issue illuminates a major problem many found with the restricted basis for convening the Constitutional Council. This problem culminated in the 1974 amendment, which substituted a mere sixty members for the Advisory Committee's requirement of one-third of the membership of either chamber to convene the council. The National Assembly elected in March 1993 has 577 members. Had the Advisory Committee's recommendation been part of the unamended Constitution, it would take 192 deputies to convene the Constitutional Council today instead of the mere sixty required by the 1974 amendment. This difference is not only numerical but political as well. Given the staggering proportion of the conservatives' legislative victory in 1993—486 rightists versus sixty-seven Socialists and twenty-four Communists on the Left[49]—the conservative government would not have to worry about a constitutional challenge from the Assembly's Left if the Advisory Committee's one-third standard had prevailed thirty-five years earlier. As a matter of fact, however, because of the 1974 amendment the tiny minority of Socialists in the National Assembly is able to muster the required sixty votes even without any help from the unreliable Communists.

François Valentin presented Triboulet's proposal to a plenary session of the Advisory Committee on the afternoon of 5 August. He explained its rationale as resting on the simple proposition that "a door ought to be opened to the minority."[50] Particularly relevant to the unhappy lot of the Socialists in the 1993 Parliament was Valentin's explanation of why the amendment required at least one-third of either chamber to convene the council. Although minority rights were important, Valentin and his allies wanted to be certain that "the minority is sufficiently important in order to avoid the risk of seeing a very small fraction of the Assembly impose its will by introducing a measure that is dilatory."[51] Had the Gaullists of 1958 not brushed aside Triboulet's proposal, the Socialists elected in 1993 would be that "very small fraction" Valentin would have excluded from initiating constitutional appeals. This would have avoided a particularly bitter political battle over the right to asylum *(droit d'asile)* in the late summer and fall of 1993, wherein the Constitutional Council struck down key provisions of a law approved by the conservative majority in Parliament pursuant to certain European Community accords on immigration. The decision provoked predictable outcries from the conservatives of a "government by judges" thwarting the will of the representatives of the people. Instead of revising the law to meet the constitutional standards imposed by the council, the Balladur government, following the lead of its irrepressible interior minister, Charles Pasqua, flexed its political muscle by amending the Constitution in a thinly veiled and rather effective effort to put the Constitutional Council in its place. This unfortunate incident was an acute embarrassment to Frenchmen who value constitutional government and *l'Etat de droit.* Had the Advisory Committee's recommendations been followed in 1958, France would have been spared this ordeal.[52]

Michel Debré was present at the session in which the Advisory Committee's recommendation was discussed and took the lead in opposing the innovation. His main point was the fear of politicizing the Constitutional Council. If one-third of a legislative chamber can raise a constitutional challenge, the opposition press will mount campaigns to encourage such challenges from their champions in Parliament. Partisans will seek out constitutional issues in the most mundane matters such as "setting the price of an agricultural product." He concluded his intervention by voicing his belief that it is best to permit only the four designated officers to convene the Constitutional Council because they ought to possess "the sense of the State" *(le sens de l'Etat).*[53] He did not explain why the presidents of the legislative chambers should be more likely to have "the sense of the State" than the legislators who chose them as their presidents.

Triboulet countered by minimizing the danger of politicization on the idealistic grounds that the whole case for the Constitutional Council presupposes that it will not be a political institution.[54] Debré responded by arguing that politicization is likely to come from increasing the number of those empowered to convene the council. This road leads to "government by judges."

In our earlier discussion of the preamble, we noted Pierre-Henri Teitgen's comment linking the constitutionalization of the preamble to the fearsome "government by judges." He suggested this link in the context of permitting a parliamentary minority to convene the Constitutional Council. Anticipating the danger of the council becoming a third legislative chamber, he predicted that those who lose in Parliament will inevitably see to it that every hotly debated issue goes before the Constitutional Council. Although the preamble was not under discussion in the debate over who should convene the Constitutional Council, Teitgen seems to take it for granted that the preamble will serve as one of the sources for constitutional decisions by which the council will limit the scope of Parliament's authority. This is why he maintains that by increasing the number of those who can invoke the jurisdiction of the council, Tiboulet's proposal will encourage "government by judges."[55]

Paul Coste-Floret attacked Triboulet's proposal on the grounds that it would upset the nice balance achieved by limiting the authority to convene the Constitutional Council to the four officers already mentioned in the government's draft version of the constitution. The balance in question was owing to the position of the four officers as holding a middle ground between the feckless provisions for constitutional review in the 1946 Constitution and a real constitutional court where individual citizens could challenge the constitutionality of laws passed by Parliament. Needless to add, Coste-Floret intoned the ritual chant that such an expansion would lead to the wearisome "government by judges."

Not to be outdone, Triboulet invoked the "government by judges" bogeyman to travel half the way with Coste-Floret by agreeing that what was needed was a middle ground between letting ordinary citizens invoke the council on the one hand and the ineffective review provision of the Constitution of the Fourth Republic on the other. Predictably, he found this middle ground not with the four constitutional officers—as Coste-Floret would have it—but with his own proposal to add to these officers one-third of the members of either legislative chamber.[56]

Perhaps the most telling comment on the proposal to expand the number of those who could convene the council came from René Dejean on 7 August, two days after the Advisory Committee had approved Triboulet's controversial proposal. The Committee was debating the question we have already examined on whether the preamble should be considered part of the Constitution. Dejean rose to say that he had supported the Triboulet amendment on 5 August because he thought it unlikely that many constitutional issues could be raised to challenge legislation and therefore he saw no danger in increasing the number of those who might convene the Constitutional Council. He would have to reconsider his position, however, if the preamble with its references to the great documents of 1789 and 1946 were to be considered part of the Constitution. If this should happen, no law would be passed by Parliament without an unhappy group of outvoted legislators finding some sort of constitutional issue to bring to the council. Therefore, he concluded that if the preamble is considered part of the Constitution, "all the laws are going to be submitted to the Constitutional Council."[57]

In effect, Dejean anticipated the critique of contemporary political scientists to the effect that the Constitutional Council has become a third legislative chamber. Mercifully, however, he had the good sense to spare his weary listeners the obvious conclusion of his argument: "government by judges."

At the beginning of this chapter, we described a movement afoot in French legal circles to permit individual citizens to challenge the constitutionality of laws they believe violate certain fundamental rights. The impetus for this reform came in part from the European Court of Human Rights, which expects member nations to have some form of independent judicial review of the constitutionality of laws passed by national parliaments. The review powers of the Constitutional Council fall short of the standards established in the authentic constitutional *courts* one finds in such countries as Austria, Belgium, Germany, Italy, and Spain.

There are two reasons for this. First, the jurisdiction of the Constitutional Council does not reach laws passed prior to 1958 because its decisions are exclusively *prospective,* that is, they are rendered only before *new* legislation takes effect. Secondly, neither the ordinary citizen nor the council itself can challenge the constitutionality of a statute. The council's jurisdiction, as we know, is utterly dependent upon the president of the Republic, the prime minister, the presidents of the two legislative chambers, or sixty members of either chamber. As a practical matter, the 1974 amendment has assured that few important pieces of legislation escape review by the Constitutional Council, but in principle, a flagrantly unconstitutional law would still be enforced by French courts if all the officials empowered to convene the council chose not to do so.

In 1990 Prime Minister Rocard's government sponsored a far-reaching constitutional amendment that would have permitted a person to raise a constitutional objection to a law being applied against him in actual litigation. This procedure is known as "constitutional control by means of a plea" *(contrôle de la constitutionalité par voie d'exception).*[58] Under the proposed amendment, a judge in a court of first instance would refer a litigant's plea of unconstitutionality to the highest court in his or her jurisdiction—the Council of State for the administrative judge and the Court of Cassation for judges in civil and criminal courts. One of these institutions would then decide whether the claim of unconstitutionality was serious enough to merit the attention of the Constitutional Council which alone could resolve the matter. The National Assembly approved the proposal but all for naught when the Senate withheld its consent, which is a required step in the amending process.[59]

The proposed reform languished in this legal limbo until the fall of 1992 when President Mitterrand announced the appointment of a blue-ribbon committee to examine possible constitutional changes across a broad range of issues that included expanding the jurisdiction of the Constitutional Council along the lines of the aborted 1990 reform. Significantly, the president borrowed a term from 1958, calling the group he had convened the Advisory Committee for Revising the Constitution *(le comité consultatif pour la révision de la constitution)*. The name choice clearly signaled the seriousness the president attached to the Advisory Committee's work, a point reinforced by the selection of Dean Georges Vedel, one of the most distinguished jurists in France, to chair the committee.[60] In February 1993 Vedel's committee submitted its report which, along with a good number of far-reaching considerations, included a proposal quite similar to the reform blocked by the Senate in 1990.[61] On 10 March 1993 the Council of Ministers included this proposal in a package of constitutional reforms it submitted to the Senate. The proposed reform would also delete the provision making former presidents lifetime members and forbid members of the Constitutional Council from serving as presidents of either regional or general (i.e., departmental) councils or as mayors of large or medium-size cities.[62] By keeping former presidents off the council and by reducing the political activities of the constitutional councillors, the reform would clearly underscore the council's heightened judicial character as a body that passes upon the constitutionality of laws challenged in real litigation. Since Prime Minister Balladur's conservative government, which came to power in March of 1993, shows little interest in sweeping constitutional reforms, the prospects for change in the near future are dim.

During the summer of 1958, the framers of the Constitution debated on several occasions the issue of individual citizens' challenging the constitutionality of a law. Not surprisingly, this idea triggered the customary fears of "government by judges";[63] but other, more substantive issues surfaced as well. André Malterre, for example, referred specifically to the American model of judicial review when he asked the government's representatives if they had considered permitting ordinary French citizens to question the constitutionality of laws before a judicial tribunal.[64]

Raymond Janot gave a detailed response to this query. Instead of invoking vague generalities about the French legal tradition, Janot brought the weight of that tradition to bear on the distinction between permitting a judicial body to *prevent* an unconstitutional law from being promulgated on the one hand and annulling such a law *after* it had been promulgated on the other. The latter offends French legal tradition, according to Janot, and that is why he supports the Constitutional Council's prophylactic power to keep unconstitutional laws off the books but opposes permitting citizens in litigation to challenge such laws once they are in effect.[65]

Janot gave an additional reason for opposing citizen challenges that is of particular interest to students of public administration. Many laws will require administrative regulations before they can be implemented and therefore the government would at times be unable to act until the constitutionality of a statute had been judicially confirmed. This could cause "some serious delays in governmental activity and that in turn could have an adverse effect on the institutions of the State as a whole."[66] This is a telling comment that provides some insight into French public administration. In France, a statute is the foundation of an elaborate administrative superstructure—and prior to 1958 its only foundation. To permit a court to nullify a statute would not only embarrass Parliament but it would weaken as well the government's power to govern by regulation. Hence, the stability of law—even an unconstitutional law—had assumed a tremendous importance in France because prior to 1958 law was the *conditio sine qua non* for the State to express its will through regulation.

Janot's intervention suggests two comparative reflections. First, he seems to think that the threat of judicial review would paralyze the government, as though it could not take administrative action until the constitutionality of a law had been confirmed. In the United States, of course, this is not the case, because the rule-making authorities *presume* the constitutionality of the statute and issue administrative directives accordingly. Months, years, and even decades could pass before a suitable "case or controversy" arises to provide the forum for a successful constitutional challenge.[67] Janot seems to see judicial review initiated by citizens as coming into play after a law has been passed but *before* it is implemented by administrative regulations. The American experience suggests an alternative, but perhaps it is one that the Cartesian spirit of French law would find intolerable. There is something untidy about the American practice of courts waiting for decades to strike down an unconstitutional act of Congress; untidy, but perhaps effective nonetheless in confining Congress to its constitutionally appointed powers—especially if the legal imagination discovers a latent constitutional principle in the commonsense maxim of "better late than never."[68]

Secondly, in the United States, as in France (especially before 1958), administrative regulations are normally grounded in statutes and therefore Janot's observation about citizen-initiated constitutional challenges as threats to administrative effectiveness could apply to American judicial review of acts of Congress as well as to the abortive call for such initiatives in France in 1958. It is very unlikely, however, that an American jurist would criticize the institution of judicial review on the grounds of its potentially disruptive effects upon regulations issued pursuant to an unconstitutional law. When Americans criticize the *excesses* of judicial review, they usually do so on grounds that the principles of democracy demand that the considered judgment of elected officials should ordinarily prevail over that of unelected judges holding office during good behavior.[69] It is true that a judicial decision voiding a federal statute could bring down an imposing administrative apparatus, but few Americans indeed would follow Janot's lead in thinking about the problem in this way. It is an important cultural difference. Janot's point of view faithfully reflects how seriously the French take their administrative State.

When the debate on citizen challenges to the constitutionality of statutes moved from the Council of State's Constitutional Commission to its General Assembly, a new consideration emerged. Speaking before the General Assembly on 27 August, Aubert Lefas maintained that such challenges were but the logical conclusion of the decision to establish the Constitutional Council in the first place. Until citizen challenges are allowed "by way of appeal" *(par voie d'exception),* the reform remains incomplete.

René Cassin, the distinguished vice president of the Council of State, disagreed with Lefas but did so in a way that left the door open for further reform. He rehearsed the familiar French traditions in such matters, counseled prudence in introducing broad innovations, and even recalled the abuses of the *parlements* under the *ancien régime.* Behind his obvious discomfort at Lefas's suggestion, one senses, however, a certain sympathy and a certain willingness to concede that the citizen challenge is indeed the logical consequence of the reform set in motion by the creation of the Constitutional Council. He considers the council's limited review powers as an "experiment" *(un essai)* which ought to be tried first before attempting more ambitious reforms.[70] Thus, like Janot commenting sagely on the constitutional status of the preamble thirty years after the event, Cassin may not have opened the door to the future but neither did he close it.

In reviewing the founding documents on the Constitutional Council, one cannot but be impressed by the foresight of the framers in anticipating the great debates that have marked the council's institutional development—constitutionalizing the preamble, the amendment of 1974, and the current efforts to give the individual citizen the right to challenge the constitutionality of a statute. In each case the dread specter of "government by judges" prevailed in 1958, only to be seriously reexamined at a later time. These developments lead one to wonder whether the framers' traditional fear of judicial power was not exaggerated. If not, that is, if the men of 1958 had it right after all, then it would seem to follow from their dire predictions that the changes that actually took place in 1971 and 1974 have surely already delivered France to the dread "government by judges." One recalls Byron's Julia who "whispering 'I will ne'er consent'—consented."

Marbury v. Madison

Earlier in this chapter we noted the similarity between the Constitutional Council's decision on the preamble and the decision of the Supreme Court of the United States in *Marbury v. Madison* (1803). In both cases the jurisdictions in question conferred extensive powers upon themselves that could not be found in the texts of the constitutions they purported to interpret. The Supreme Court of the United States and the French Constitutional Council seemed to expand their own respective powers by what might best be described as a form of "bootstrap jurisprudence."

Marbury v. Madison is an oft-told tale and a good one. For our purposes, a very general description of the case will suffice.[71] At issue was the seemingly insignificant question of President John Adams's appointment of William Marbury as justice of the peace for the District of Columbia in February 1801. From this tiny acorn grew a mighty constitutional oak.

The accession of Thomas Jefferson to the presidency in March 1801 brought the end of the twelve-year "Federalist era" under Presidents Washington and Adams. Knowing they would soon lose control of both the legislative and executive branches, the Federalists looked to the judiciary to preserve their influence over the national government. Before leaving office, President Adams appointed his secretary of state, John Marshall, as chief justice of the United States. Shortly thereafter, the lame-duck Congress dramatically increased the number of federal courts, which Adams and an obliging Senate staffed with reliable Federalists, aptly dubbed "midnight appointments." The jurisdiction of the federal courts was considerably expanded and the number of Supreme Court justices was reduced from six to five, to become effective with the next vacancy. This would delay the new president's opportunity to nominate a justice to the Supreme Court.

These changes, except for the appointment of Chief Justice Marshall, were brought about by the Judiciary Act of 1801 which the next Congress, dominated by Jefferson's Republican party, repealed in 1802. At the same time, Jeffersonian Republicans were voicing ominous threats about impeaching certain Federalist judges whose opinions they considered excessively partisan.

Marbury's appointment to the relatively obscure post of justice of the peace for the District of Columbia must be seen against the backdrop of this politically charged atmosphere. Marbury's commission had been signed and sealed but not delivered before President Adams left office. The duty to deliver commissions fell to the secretary of state, who, as we have just seen, was none other than John Marshall, whom President Adams had appointed chief justice of the United States. Marshall's failure to deliver the commission was probably due to the often hectic rush of events at the end of an administration. When Jefferson became president, he instructed his new secretary of state, James Madison, not to deliver the commission. Marbury brought a suit to compel Secretary Madison to deliver it and thus was born the historic litigation of *Marbury v. Madison.*

Marbury sued under Section 13 of the Judiciary Act of 1789 by which the first Congress had authorized the Supreme Court to issue the legal order he sought—technically, a writ of mandamus. Chief Justice Marshall held that Marbury had a right to the commission but that the Supreme Court could not issue the writ of mandamus he sought because the act of Congress conferring this power on the Court was unconstitutional. Its fatal flaw was that it conferred "original jurisdiction" upon the Supreme Court, contrary to the second section of article 3 that limits the original jurisdiction of the court to "cases affecting ambassadors, other public ministers, consuls and those in which a state shall be a party." In all other cases the Constitution requires that the Supreme Court exercise "appellate jurisdiction." Since Marbury's case had nothing to do with the types of cases reserved for the Court's original jurisdiction, the section of the congressional act under which he brought his original jurisdiction suit was unconstitutional.

In denying Marbury the remedy he sought, Marshall handed the Jeffersonians the petty political triumph of keeping a Federalist partisan out of a relatively insignificant office. This muted the Jeffersonians' complaints about a politicized judiciary because, after all, their side had won the lawsuit. At the jurisprudential level, however, Marshall's Federalist Supreme Court served notice on the Jeffersonian Republican Congress of its power to annul legislation it deemed to violate the Constitution. Hence, it has been aptly called a "judicial *coup d'état.*"[72]

Although there are interesting similarities between *Marbury* and the preamble decision in France of 16 July 1971, the *scope* of the two decisions reveals a marked contrast. As noted above, the Constitutional Council provided the broadest possible rationale to ground its claim to void the law limiting freedom of association. Eschewing both a specific constitutional provision in article 4 protecting political parties and the Declaration of the Rights of Man and of the Citizen, the council expanded its own authority by relying on the notoriously vague "fundamental principles recognized by the laws of the Republic."

Marshall followed a different strategy, basing his decision on narrow, specific, and technical language in the text of the Constitution. The logic of his argument suggested a sweeping conclusion, for he maintained that the Court's task is to interpret law and the Constitution in its own terms is "the supreme Law of the Land." This argument would seem to go beyond textually explicit matters, but the examples he used to illustrate his point are all taken from the very words of the Constitution. Thus he says that if Congress should defy the explicit constitutional prohibition against bills of attainder and ex post facto laws, the federal courts must refuse to enforce them. The same would hold, he says, for constitutionally prohibited taxes on exports or for laws punishing treason with less evidence than the constitutionally required "Testimony of two Witnesses to the same overt Act." Thus while the *logic* of Marshall's argument—the Constitution is law and courts interpret laws—suggests an American version of "government by judges," his examples are far more modest.[73] This may help to explain why, despite *Marbury's* tremendous significance, the Supreme Court waited fifty-four years before declaring another act of Congress unconstitutional.[74]

Although both the Supreme Court's decision in *Marbury v. Madison* and the Constitutional Council's decision on the preamble broke new constitutional ground in their respective countries, neither came as a bolt from the blue. In both cases there was an unofficial jurisprudential tradition which at least hinted at the dramatic decisions that would eventually announce new binding norms.

In France, the tradition went back to the last two decades of the nineteenth century, a period Alec Stone has characterized as a "golden age" of public law.[75] From that time until the founding of the Fifth Republic, there was a strong teleological dimension to French jurisprudence, which, influenced by natural law considerations, developed a principled criticism of the prevailing orthodoxy that celebrated the sovereignty of Parliament and its laws. Léon Duguit and Maurice Harriou were among the leaders of this movement.[76] They and their disciples had long insisted upon the legally binding character of the Declaration of the Rights of Man and of the Citizen of 1789, and of certain unwritten principles as well.[77]

The Constitution of 1946 was approved in October of that year but only after an earlier constitution had been rejected in a referendum on 5 May. The rejected constitution had included *within the body of its text* the Declaration of 1789, which would therefore have had constitutional status had the referendum results been favorable. As we have already seen, the October Constitution, which did go into effect, consigned the Declaration to the preamble which was declared off-limits to the ineffective Constitutional Committee created by the same constitution. This Committee was a disappointment to those who had hoped for more vigorous institutional support for some form of judicial review. It was not to be a "judge who sanctions and condemns" as some jurists had hoped. Rather it would be merely "a consultative commission which absolves and justifies."[78]

The intellectual background of *Marbury v. Madison* has been traced by enthusiasts for judicial review back to a dictum by Sir Edward Coke in *Dr. Bonham's Case* (1610): "When an Act of Parliament is against common right and reason or repugnant, or impossible to be performed, the common law will control it, and adjudge such act to be void."[79] Historians dispute whether Coke's famous remark had anything to do with the sort of judicial review Marshall invoked in *Marbury*, but the dictum entered American law *via* James Otis in the famous *Writs of Assistance Case* in Boston 1761. There the colonials challenged the legitimacy of an Act of Parliament permitting officers of the crown to use "general warrants," that is, search warrants that did not specify what was being sought. Several references favorable to judicial review appeared during the ratification debates on the Constitution, notably in *Federalist* 78. Records of the state ratifying conventions yield supportive comments from James Wilson, Oliver Ellsworth, and Marshall himself. Wilson, as we know, would be appointed to the Supreme Court by President Washington. Ellsworth was Marshall's predecessor as Chief Justice of the United States.[80] In 1796 the Supreme Court upheld an act of Congress challenged on grounds of constitutionality. Although the Court did not address directly the question of its power to annul acts of Congress, the fact that it heard the case strongly implied such a power.[81]

These events prior to *Marbury* are not legal precedents but they serve as indications that the silence of the constitutional text on the subject of judicial review of acts of Congress does not necessarily imply denial. Perhaps the great constitutional scholar Edward S. Corwin put it best during congressional testimony in 1937, when he asserted that those who say the historical records prove that the framers of the Constitution intended to give the courts the power to review acts of Congress are "talking nonsense"; but so are those "who say they did not intend it." Historian Leonard Levy, taking note of Corwin's comment, wryly adds: "A close textual and contextual examination of the evidence will not result in an improvement on these propositions."[82]

A TALE OF TWO COUNCILS

At the beginning of this chapter, we saw that in France there is no "one supreme court" but rather three judicial or at least quasi-judicial bodies, each of which is supreme in its own sphere: the Constitutional Council, the Council of State, and the Court of Cassation. We have also commented on the central role of the councillors of State in drafting the Constitution of the

Fifth Republic. Since the Constitutional Council is a creature of the Fifth Republic, this means that the councillors of State took the unusual step of creating an institutional competitor and endowing it with considerable power. Such an action challenges the received wisdom on the self-interested nature of organizational behavior and therefore merits a close examination on our part.

Administrative and Constitutional Jurisdictions

The framers of the 1958 Constitution resembled their American counterparts of 1787 in that both groups intended to establish a regime that would be governed by a constitution: the "rule of law" for the Americans and a "legal State" *(Etat de droit)* for the French. Despite the similar objectives, the respective tasks at hand bore striking differences. The Americans came about as close as is possible in human affairs to building anew. "Starting from scratch," or, more elegantly, "writing on a tabula rasa"—the metaphors are as abundant as the point is clear; constitutionally speaking, the Americans had a fresh start. Not so the framers of mid-twentieth-century France. They faced the very different problem of erecting their constitutional order as a superstructure upon the foundation of a fully developed administrative State. The constitutional aspiration for "a legal State" could not ignore the progress that had already been made toward that end by an impressive body of administrative law. Concretely, this meant defining the jurisdictional scope of the Constitutional Council on the one hand and of the Council of State on the other.

Raymond Janot alerted the Advisory Committee on the Constitution to this matter on 31 July. In explaining the innovative Constitutional Council, he assured his listeners that it would not interfere with the work of the judicial system already in place. He felt compelled to add, however, that "there is nevertheless a problem which I do not wish to hide."[83] Suppose, he said, that a deputy should introduce a bill which the government thought exceeded the legislative competence of Parliament. Under a provision in the text before the Advisory Committee similar to what would eventually become article 41, the government could challenge the proposal before the Constitutional Council. If the council should uphold the government's position, the latter could then adopt the same measure by means of a decree. That is, it could achieve by decree what it did not want Parliament to bring about by law.

Suppose, further, that a citizen should attack the decree in the administrative courts as an *excès de pouvoir,* that is, an act that exceeds the constitutional powers of the government. Such a plaintiff would contend that the subject matter of the government's decree should have been handled by law.

This case would eventually come before the Council of State, which, as the supreme administrative jurisdiction, rules on the legality and the constitutionality of government actions. (Recall that in 1958 no French jurisdiction could declare a *law*, that is, an Act of Parliament, unconstitutional; but the Council of State could make such a declaration about a government regulation.) How would the Council of State resolve such a question? Could it not, in principle, find for the complaining citizen and declare the matter at hand to be subject to *law* and not to *regulation?* If it did so, it would, of course, flatly contradict the previous ruling of the Constitutional Council.

The draft text submitted to the Advisory Committee provided that there could be no appeal from a decision of the Constitutional Council, but Janot's hypothetical case involved not an appeal but an entirely new legal action within the separate and independent jurisdiction of administrative law. Nothing in the draft text would have obliged the Council of State to follow the decision of the Constitutional Council.

To solve his own problem, Janot suggests as an analogy the situation confronting the Council of State when it must interpret a treaty whose provisions are being applied administratively against a particular citizen or enterprise. In such circumstances, the Council of State would be likely to ask the advice of the minister of Foreign Affairs. Though not obliged to follow this advice, the Council of State, in all likelihood, would let it serve as a guide in reaching its decision. Janot opines that in his hypothetical case the Council of State would treat the previous opinion of the Constitutional Council in the same way.

This ad hoc improvisation is helpful but it fails to solve Janot's problem, because it clearly indicates that *in principle* the Council of State would not be obliged to follow the Constitutional Council and that, consequently, the same subject matter could be found to be of a regulatory character by the Constitutional Council and of a legislative character by the Council of State.

Not surprisingly, the Advisory Committee, dissatisfied with potential juridical gridlock, soon revisited the complex question of the relationship between the two councils. On 5 August, the Advisory Committee discussed the possibility of assigning to the Constitutional Council the task of deciding the constitutionality of both laws and regulations. Jean Gilbert-Jules took the lead in pressing the case for "establishing an equilibrium between the two powers, legislative and executive," by subjecting both laws and regulations to review by the Constitutional Council.[84] Michel Debré rejected this suggestion as unnecessary, since the Council of State already had the authority to nullify regulations on grounds of constitutionality.

René Dejean replied that it mattered little to him which council had the constitutional authority to strike down regulations. What is important is that the constitutional basis for this authority be stated explicitly in the Constitution itself. It is not enough to rely on the Council of State's traditional powers in these matters because these powers have always been exercised very sparingly in the past.

To grasp the import of Dejean's insistence upon an explicit constitutional power to annul regulations, we must recall that the traditional jurisprudence of the Council of State focused primarily on the *legality,* not the constitutionality, of regulations. That is, the Council of State's principal task had been to determine whether a particular regulation conformed to a particular law. The constitutionality of the law itself was, of course, strictly off-limits to the Council of State. Ordinarily, the constitutional rulings of the Council of State were restricted to the relatively rare situations in which a regulation, taken pursuant to a vaguely-worded law, ran afoul of a constitutional principle arising from the council's jurisprudence such as "equality before the law, freedom of conscience . . . [and] the nonretroactivity of administrative acts."[85] Since the new constitution envisioned a scheme of autonomous regulations—that is, regulations unsupported by statute—the Council of State would be called upon routinely to judge their constitutionality. Thus, yesterday's rare event would become tomorrow's commonplace.

Because, Dejean argued, the Council of State had properly been so cautious about reaching constitutional issues in the past, "it must find in the new constitution a boldness which hitherto it has lacked."[86] Without such boldness, the vast scope of activity likely to fall under the regulatory domain will escape *effective* judicial review. "The only way" to embolden the Council of State to assume its new constitutional responsibilities is "to insert in the constitution a clear statement to the effect that the Council of State will judge the constitutionality of regulations."[87]

Dejean and Gilbert-Jules did not prevail but they succeeded in highlighting a serious jurisprudential problem inherent in the effort to reconcile the traditional role of the Council of State as France's supreme administrative court with the proposed innovation of a Constitutional Council. Their probing inquiries set the stage for still another examination, three days later, of the relationship between the two councils. This time Jean Gilbert-Jules began by reviewing fundamentally the same troublesome situation Raymond Janot had outlined on 31 July and which we have just examined—how to avoid the embarrassing possibility of placing the same subject matter before the Council of State as a regulation and before the Constitutional Council as a law with the consequent danger of eliciting contradictory decisions. As we saw above, the text submitted to the Advisory Committee forbade any appeals from the decisions of the Constitutional Council, but Gilbert-Jules correctly stated that this did not go far enough. What is needed, he said, is "that the decisions of the Constitutional Council should not only be unappealable, but that they should also be binding upon every jurisdiction."[88] Such a change would go a long way toward solving the problem of conflicting interpretations but it could do so, of course, only at the price of going an equally long way toward transforming the Constitutional Council into a supreme court. This was a step the government was unwilling to take.[89]

It remained for the Council of State itself to incorporate the substance of Gilbert-Jules's suggestion and to add to the text submitted to it by the government the provision that would eventually comprise the final version of the second paragraph of article 62. The draft text stated: "The decisions of the Constitutional Council may not be appealed to any jurisdiction whatsoever." To this the Council of State added the following self-denying provision: "They [the decisions of the Constitutional Council] must be recognized by all administrative and juridical authorities." A judicious combination of political imagination and poetic license might permit us to borrow an Americanism and call this addition the "supremacy clause" of the Constitution of the Fifth Republic. The "supremacy clause" of the Constitution of the United States appears in article 6 and provides that "this Constitution and the Laws of the United States which shall be made in pursuance thereof . . . shall be the supreme Law of the Land." Article 62 of the Constitution of the Fifth Republic imposes upon all jurisdictions the obligation to follow the decisions of the Constitutional Council and thereby confers a certain supremacy upon it. For the Council of State to add this clause to the Constitution was a self-denying act of statesmanship because, in order to achieve a harmonious legal order, it imposed upon itself the duty to follow the constitutional decisions of the institutional rival that was about to be created.

This decision did not come easily for the Council of State. Before taking leave of the Advisory Committee, Raymond Janot had acknowledged the serious nature of the problem of potentially conflicting jurisdictions and had assured the committee that this topic would receive careful attention from the Council of State whose advice was the next step in the drafting process.

Janot was as good as his word. The Constitutional Committee *(Commission Constitutionnelle)* of the Council of State took up the question of the relationship between the two councils before recommending revisions to the General Assembly of the Council of State. The committee's inquiry focused on what Roger Latournerie called "the juridical meaning" of the decisions of the Constitutional Council. He wanted to know if they had "an impact equal to the authority of res judicata."[90] The French expression he used was *la chose jugée*—literally the judged matter, that is, something that has been settled by a court of law. In the common law tradition, the Latin term res judicata expresses the same idea as the French *la chose jugée*. Unfortunately, there is no equivalent in English. Anglo-American lawyers use res judicata to describe what *Black's Law Dictionary* defines as "a thing judicially acted upon or decided; a thing or matter settled by judgment."

I dwell on the meaning of res judicata only because the Constitutional Committee did the same. At first, they were ready to add to the government's text barring appeals from decisions of the Constitutional Council the further provision that such decisions should "have the authority of res judicata."[91] A debate then ensued on whether the use of this technical legal term would necessarily imply that the Constitutional Council was a "court" *(une juridiction.)* Several committee members thought it would, with Raymond Janot among them. Earlier, Janot had expressed his indifference as to how long the members of the Constitutional Council should hold office. To him it made little difference if they served for five years or for ten. Doctrinal stability on the council was of no importance to him. "Perhaps it would not be a bad thing," he said, "if there were ongoing doctrinal renewal."[92] Clearly, for Janot, the Constitutional Council was something other than a court, a position quite consistent with what he had said on previous occasions.[93] Deferring to Janot, Latournerie suggested replacing res judicata with a statement to the effect that all decisions of the Constitutional Council "must be recognized by all administrative and juridical authorities." Janot agreed but Jean Foyer found the formulation too narrow because it would not apply to Parliament. The statement was then further amended to add *"pouvoirs publics,"* an expression broad enough to include Parliament.[94] Thus the Constitutional Committee forwarded the much-debated sentence to its parent body, the General Assembly of the Council of State, with the exact wording that would eventually appear in the final version of the Constitution. The "supremacy clause" of the Constitution of the Fifth Republic is a creature of the Council of State.

In introducing the proposed constitution to his fellow councillors of State, André Deschamps, one of three "reporters" *(rapporteurs)* charged with explaining the document, candidly acknowledged the possibility of doctrinal conflict between the two councils.[95] Perhaps with the "supremacy clause" in mind, he assured his colleagues that care had been taken to minimize such conflicts but that the possibility still remained.

The possibility became actual once the Constitution went into effect. In a penetrating study of the extent to which decisions of the Constitutional Council have influenced the Council of State, Louis Favoreu draws an important distinction between two ten-year periods: 1960–1969 and 1977–1986. During the first period only ten occasions arose in which the Council of State took into consideration a previous decision of the Constitutional Council; during the second period there were forty-four such occasions. The fourfold jump can be explained in part by the constitutional amendment of 1974 that permitted sixty members of either parliamentary chamber to challenge the constitutionality of an Act of Parliament. As the sheer volume of appeals decided by the Constitutional Council increased, there was a substantial increase in the number of these decisions affecting the Council of State. Further, during the first period the constitutional questions presented to the Constitutional Council dealt exclusively with the distinction between law and regulation, whereas the second period, coming well after the effects of the 1971 preamble decision had been felt, addressed an extremely broad range of substantive, value-laden, constitutional rights.[96]

In 1969, at the end of the first period, an official at the Council of State declared that his organization treated decisions of the Constitutional Council as though they came from a judicial body. Therefore, the Council of State applied the narrow, legal doctrine of res judicata to the other council's decisions. Consequently, the Council of State felt itself obliged to follow only the precise matters that had actually been decided by the Constitutional Council and *not* its jurisprudence or legal reasoning. In other words, the Council of State gave the narrowest possible interpretation to its duty under article 62, paragraph 2, to follow the decisions of the Constitutional Council. The distinction between decision and jurisprudence is still in vogue as the proper description of the dependence of the Council of State upon the Constitutional Council.

Favoreu accepts this distinction but argues persuasively that its stark simplicity masks a richer relationship between the two councils which became increasingly discernable during the second ten-year period. He maintains that even though the Council of State is not *obliged* to follow the jurisprudence of the Constitutional Council, as a matter of fact it does so and thereby contributes more effectively toward building a consistent body of constitutional law than its strict obligation might suggest.

He cites a generous number of "recommendations from representatives of the government" *(conclusions des commissaires du gouvernement)* to support his case. As we saw in the preface, the "representatives of the government" are misnamed councillors of State who analyze an administrative law case and present their recommendations to a panel of their colleagues who render the decision. They are misnamed because in no sense do they represent the government. They are as likely to recommend a decision against the government as for it. Their statements are extremely important in French administrative law because the formal decisions of the Council of State are *very* brief and succinct—indeed, maddeningly so for American jurists, who revel in the rich factual background of the common law tradition. To understand the true basis of a decision by the Council of State, it is often necessary to supplement the bare bones of the official decision with the heartier fare found only in the full and detailed recommendations of the representatives of the government. It is in these documents that Favoreu finds evidence to support his claim that the Council of State often follows the broad jurisprudence of the Constitutional Council as well as its narrow decisions.

Sometimes the representatives of the government will directly cite decisions of the Constitutional Council as bearing on a case before the Council of State. At other times, they will go out of their way to show that a recommended decision is not inconsistent with a previous ruling of the Constitutional Council. On the relatively rare occasions when the Council of State rejects the jurisprudence of the Constitutional Council, the representatives of the government carefully explain their reasons, usually based on the belief that the constitutional councillors did not grasp all the aspects of the problem before them.[97]

On one occasion, a Constitutional Council decision prompted the Council of State to dramatically reverse its jurisprudence on the classification of pollution fees imposed upon industrial enterprises. If a fee is considered "fiscal," litigation concerning it goes before a specialized administrative judge known as a fiscal judge. If it is "nonfiscal," it falls under the jurisdiction of an ordinary administrative judge. The Council of State had traditionally held such fees to be nonfiscal, but in 1982 the Constitutional Council decided otherwise. The next time a similar case came before the Council of State it changed its previous position to bring it into line with the reasoning of the Constitutional Council.[98]

Favoreu applauds these tendencies on the part of the Council of State and its "representatives of the government" as significant steps toward establishing the jurist's ideal of a "legal state." He sees an irrevocable trend on the part of administrative law judges toward moving beyond the narrow confines of res judicata and applying the jurisprudence of the Constitutional Council on a regular basis. To do otherwise would cause them serious embarrassment. Consider the example of an administrative judge obliged to apply res judicata to prohibit the retroactive imposition of a fine. His reliance on res judicata means that he has before him a legal text already interpreted by the Constitutional Council as requiring the prohibition. Hence, his obligation to follow the Constitutional Council in applying *that specific text*. Suppose, however, that at a later date, the same judge has another case before him concerning retroactive fines that are based on a different legal text, one that has never been interpreted by the Constitutional Council. Would he not be embarrassed to uphold such a fine simply on the grounds that the text in question came before him without benefit of an interpretation by the Constitutional Council? Arguing in this way, Favoreu discerns a certain inevitability that will gradually bring the two jurisprudential orders together to the advantage of the Constitutional Council.

The path of influence between the two councils is not a one-way street. If it is inevitable that the Constitutional Council will gradually impose its jurisprudence upon the Council of State, the latter will surely experience a sense of déjà vu in its newfound submission. This is because the *content* of the Constitutional Council's jurisprudence is heavily influenced by "general principles of law" developed by the Council of State. We mentioned above that long before the creation of the Fifth Republic, the Council of State had developed a set of principles to adjudicate the legality and at times even the constitutionality of administrative regulations.[99] They included freedom of conscience, equality before the law, and most notably, "freedom of association," which was to become the basis of the Constitutional Council's celebrated 1971 ruling on the preamble. Thus, the innovative constitutional law announced by the Constitutional Council in what many of its admirers consider its finest hour was simply an elevation of a principle of administrative law to constitutional stature. The Constitutional Council has been in tutelage to the Council of State. This is surely a remarkable example of an administrative state shaping a constitutional state and thereby, in a most dramatic way, reversing the cause and effect relationship of constitution to administration that Americans would take for granted.

This influence of the Council of State upon the Constitutional Council did not end in 1971. Important decisions by the Constitutional Council on the right to strike in 1979 and on nationalization of privately owned companies in 1982 bore unmistakable signs of Council of State jurisprudence.[100] One of the reasons for this influence may be due to the Constitutional Council's marked tendency to recruit its legal staff heavily—and at times exclusively—from the Council of State.[101] Since not all constitutional councillors are legal experts, we may confidently assume that some of them rely heavily on the advice of their specialized legal staff.

The heightened activity of the Constitutional Council since the 1974 amendment marked an important change in the nature of the Council of State's role as legal adviser to the government. Article 39 requires the government to solicit the Council of State's advice on legislation it intends to submit to Parliament. In the early years of the Fifth Republic, this meant that the Council of State would examine proposed legislation to determine its effects on laws or decrees already in force. Since 1974, and especially with the advent of the politically charged 1980s, the Council of State's primary focus has shifted from legal consistency to constitutionality. The Council of State's 1982 annual report states that in examining government bills, "its first concern is to verify their conformity to the Constitution."[102] The Council of State advises in secret, but the government may reveal this advice at its discretion and has done so in order to enlist it as a political weapon in the inevitable parliamentary struggles over the constitutionality of proposed legislation. Thus, the Council of State is "in the position of having its prestige put on the line, but with little control over how or in what context."[103]

This problem is aggravated by the fact that the Council of State cannot make public comments on the proposed legislation, nor can it control the amendments added to the pristine bill it had once approved. Nevertheless, if the Constitutional Council strikes down a proposed law in whole or in part, there is a public perception that the Council of State's authority as legal adviser to the government has been repudiated. This tends, at times, to create ill feeling between the two councils, even though as a matter of fact the precise provisions rejected by the Constitutional Council may never have received the blessing of the Council of State.[104]

Tension between the two councils reached a high-water mark in 1984 when the Constitutional Council voided the main provisions of an extremely controversial Socialist law aimed at reforming the legislation regulating the press. Several provisions approved by the Council of State were struck down by the Constitutional Council. In a most unusual action, Georges Maleville, a prominent member of the Council of State, sent a vitriolic letter to *Le Monde* attacking the decision of the Constitutional Council. Specifically, he called attention to the superior legal training of the councillors of State vis-à-vis their counterparts at the Constitutional Council. Pulling no punches, he accused the Constitutional Council of betraying its judicial role and behaving "more like a third legislative assembly."[105] Outbursts of this sort are precisely what the framers of the 1958 Constitution had hoped to avoid.

In 1981, the newly elected Socialist government launched a bruising constitutional battle over its aggressive nationalization program. In the hope of preserving the program from constitutional grief, the Council of State had succeeded in persuading the government to include a more generous compensation formula than was originally intended for the owners of the industries that were to be nationalized. In its decision of 16 January 1982, the Constitutional Council found even the enhanced compensation formula insufficiently generous to meet the constitutional standards derived from the 1789 Declaration of the Rights of Man and of the Citizen which proclaimed:

> Since the right to private property is sacred and inviolable, no one can be deprived of it except in certain cases legally determined to be essential for public security; in such cases a fair indemnity must first of all be granted.

Robert Badinter, a disappointed Socialist who would later become president of the Constitutional Council, voiced his party's frustration and sense of betrayal at having followed for naught the constitutional advice of the

Council of State. Referring to the physical location of the two councils on opposite sides of the elegant mall at the *Palais Royal,* he complained bitterly, "Constitutional truth on one side of the *Palais Royal,* constitutional error on the other."[106] Badinter's sardonic quip contrasts sharply with Favoreu's happier assessment just five years later.

Although the Socialists would eventually succeed in winning the approval of the Constitutional Council for a nationalization scheme, they did so only by yielding to the exacting compensation standards and to other demands imposed upon them by the Constitutional Council. More significant perhaps than the interesting conflict between the two councils is that both entered the fray with the same goal of imposing constitutional discipline upon the central economic program of a democratically elected government. Enter the legal state; exit majoritarian democracy.

The Administrative Law Judge

The "one Supreme Court" in article 3 of the American Constitution has always been the unchallenged master of the federal judiciary. Its control over state courts has often been disputed, but never its supremacy among the courts of the United States.[107] The dramatic development of administrative agencies from the final decade of the last century until the middle of the present one raised a problem not for the dominance of the Supreme Court but for the proper role of the entire federal judiciary vis-à-vis the emerging administrative institutions. Dicey's diatribe against *droit administratif* created a hostile atmosphere for public administration among Anglo-American jurists. In the United States the problem was aggravated by the fact that some of the most important administrative activities fell to the newly created "independent regulatory commissions" that were strangers to the familiar tripartite regime of legislative, executive, and judicial power. The new agencies—the Interstate Commerce Commission (1887), the Federal Trade Commission (1914), the Federal Communications Commission (1934), the Securities and Exchange Commission (1934), and so forth, seemed to execute law, but they could not be called "executive" because the *independent* regulatory commissions were so called to flag their independence from the president, the chief executive officer of the Republic. Their powers were usually (and very unsatisfactorily) described as quasi-legislative and quasi-judicial. Edward S. Corwin had the nub of it when he reduced hopelessly muddled efforts to explain the constitutional topography of the Federal Trade Commission to the proposition that it is "forsooth, in the uncomfortable halfway situation of Mahomet's coffin, suspended Twixt Heaven and Earth."[108]

Throughout the first half of the twentieth century, the courts gave considerable attention to the jurisdictional question of where administrative issues end and judicial issues begin. All agreed that the line should be drawn somewhere along the fault dividing questions of law from those of fact. This distinction was helpful in those happy circumstances wherein facts could be readily differentiated from law, but the inevitable lawyerly creation of "constitutional facts" and "jurisdictional facts" served only to restate the problem.[109]

At the same time, judges were fretting over how to discharge their responsibility to review agency actions that were the product of "institutional decision making." Critics of this process have described it, not altogether unfairly, as a system designed to conceal the identity of the real decision maker in an administrative proceeding in which the property or some other important interest of an individual or a corporation is at risk. Institutional decision making often meant that decisions would be "drafted for the agency by an anonymous staff team of experts who were unseen by the parties and to whom the parties had no opportunity to address their arguments."[110]

Shortly before World War II, President Franklin Roosevelt gave considerable attention to reforming the nation's burgeoning administrative processes. In 1941 these efforts yielded an important document commonly known as the "Attorney General's Report," which outlined a program of sweeping administrative reform.[111] The Second World War postponed definitive action in this matter but shortly after the war Congress included many of the ideas generated by the attorney general's report in the Administrative Procedure Act of 1946. Among the major features of this act was the attention it lavished on the "hearing examiner" whose title would later be elevated to "administrative law judge." Congress stated in some detail this officer's duties to prepare a written record of the initial stages of agency decision making and strengthened his capacity for independent judgment by providing certain procedural safeguards against possible reprisals from the agency leadership.

One of the most interesting examples of the American version of the interaction between administrative jurisdictions and the ordinary federal courts occurred in the Supreme Court case of *Universal Camera Co. v. National Labor Relations Board* (1951).[112] At issue was the relationship between the hearing examiner as an administrative judge and his agency, the statutorily responsible decision-making authority.

The National Labor Relations Board (NLRB) had found Universal Camera guilty of an unfair labor practice because it fired an employee for testifying against the company at a Labor Board hearing. The company maintained the firing had nothing to do with the man's testimony but was owing to an insulting remark he had made to his supervisor. The hearing examiner who had observed the testimony of all parties to the dispute accepted the company's account of what had happened but his decision was reversed by the Labor Board, which found for the fired employee. An important aspect of the hearing examiner's decision was his finding that certain parties to the dispute had lied. In reversing its hearing examiner's decision, the NLRB rejected this finding, reconstructed events to its own satisfaction, and substituted findings of its own as to who had lied and who had told the truth.

Universal Camera appealed this adverse decision of the NLRB to the United States Circuit Court of Appeals for the second circuit. Company counsel pressed the argument that the NLRB had no business reversing its own hearing examiner's findings on the veracity of various witnesses because the examiner, having actually observed the witnesses, had the advantage of demeanor evidence and the board did not.

The problem for the court was to determine what weight, if any, it should give to the hearing examiner's report. Technically, this was a problem of "scope of review," that is, how deeply a reviewing court should look into the inner workings of an agency. After all, Congress had charged the NLRB, not the hearing examiner, with making the final decision. Congress had also instructed the courts to uphold agency decisions that are supported "by substantial evidence on the record considered as a whole." "Substantial evidence" is a relatively easy standard for an agency to meet, much easier, for example, than if it had to show that the preponderance of evidence supported its decision. In deciding whether the evidence is substantial, however, the court must look at the record "as a whole." This is how the court reached the question indicated at the beginning of this paragraph: whether the hearing examiner's report was part of the record and, if so, what weight it should receive.

In discussing the relationship between the Constitutional Council and the Council of State, we saw that a well-established administrative jurisprudence provided many of the salient norms adopted by the newly-created constitutional jurisdiction. In the United States, the process was reversed. In trying to establish a rule for administrative law, the Court of Appeals looked for guidance to the practices and principles of the ordinary federal courts created pursuant to article 3 of the Constitution.

Judge Learned Hand, writing for the Second Circuit Court of Appeals, turned to judicial analogies for guidance on how to assess the relationship between the hearing examiner and the NLRB. He wondered aloud if the examiner is to the Labor Board as a trial judge is to a court of appeals or as a "master in equity" would be to a trial judge. He found these analogies unsatisfactory because they would give too much independence to the hearing examiner. A trial judge, for example, may not reverse the findings of a master in equity unless they are "clearly erroneous"—an extremely difficult standard for a judge to meet. To hold the NLRB to such an exacting standard would undercut the hierarchical structure of the organization, which is charged not only with adjudicating disputes but with developing labor policy as well. Therefore, Judge Hand reluctantly concluded, the reviewing court could not consider the hearing examiner's report as part of the record submitted to its review by the NLRB. To be sure, the agency should not totally disregard its examiner's report, but the court refused to announce a rule on just how the NLRB should evaluate it. In defending this judicial self-restraint, which some might see as an abdication, the court revealed a remarkable lack of judicial imagination. "We cannot find any middle ground," Judge Hand said, between refusing to treat the examiner's report as part of the record justifying the Labor Board's reversal "and treating such a reversal as error, whenever it would be such, if done by a judge to a master in equity."[113] That is, Judge Hand could find no middle ground between simply ignoring the examiner's report on the one hand and treating it with all the deference due to a report by a master in equity on the other. He chose to ignore it. Judge Hand candidly acknowledged his own displeasure with the outcome of his argument but defended it nonetheless on the grounds that there was no appropriate legal analogue to govern the case. Therefore the NLRB's ruling against Universal Camera was upheld.

The company, of course, appealed to the Supreme Court of the United States, which, fortunately for the development of American administrative law, reversed Judge Hand's decision.[114] Justice Frankfurter delivered the opinion of the Court. As a former professor of administrative law, Frankfurter realized the disastrous implications for the integrity of the administrative process lurking in Judge Hand's opinion. For all practical purposes, the hearing examiners' reports would be rendered useless and the hearing itself would be an empty charade, if Judge Hand's ruling were to prevail.

Frankfurter stoutly maintained that the courts must treat the examiner's report as part of the record but he faltered in addressing the difficult question Judge Hand had set aside: how much weight should the reviewing court give to the report of an examiner whose findings are reversed by his parent agency?

Justice Frankfurter offered several norms that were less than models of clarity. First, he said that nothing in the relevant statutes "suggests that the reviewing courts should not give to the examiner's report such probative force as it intrinsically commands." On the heels of this nebulous standard, there followed the pious affirmation that "high standards of public administration counsel that we attribute to the Labor Board's examiners both due regard for the responsibility which Congress imposes on them and the competence to discharge it." Later, he asserted his belief that the statutes "gave significance" to the examiner's report and that the legislators intended that they "would be of consequence." These vague assertions were balanced by the no less vague disclaimer that "we do not require that the examiner's findings be given more weight than in reason and in the light of judicial experience they deserve."

Clearly, Justice Frankfurter was struggling. He was groping toward that elusive middle ground, whose existence Judge Hand had denied, between simply ignoring the examiner's report on the one hand and insisting that the Labor Board follow it unless it is "clearly erroneous" on the other. Frankfurter realized that the first alternative would make a mockery of the hearing procedure and that the second would undermine legitimate hierarchical control of the Labor Board over its examiners. Hence, he refused to be "pinioned between the horns of his [Judge Hand's] dilemma." Frankfurter was trying desperately to defend a middle ground but his tentative language signaled unmistakably his painful awareness that it was a muddled middle he had found.

French administrative law hoisted a standard to which the newly created Constitutional Council repaired, but in the United States, administrative law, cut loose from the moorings of ordinary constitutional courts, was buffeted by the winds and tides of uncharted seas. American administrative law seeks norms. French administrative law provides them.[115]

The aftermath of *Universal Camera* continued to reveal the unsettled character of the hearing examiner as a major actor in American administrative law. Nowhere was this clearer than in the strange controversy that swirled around the renaming of the hearing examiners as "administrative law judges" in 1972. This decision was taken by the Civil Service Commission after a protracted and surprisingly heated debate involving Congress, the Administrative Conference of the United States, the American Bar Association, and the commission itself. Indeed, the commission acted only after the Federal Power Commission and the Federal Trade Commission virtually forced it to do so by threatening to act on their own in elevating their examiners' title to that of judge.

Over the years, many new names had been suggested for the hearing examiners, for example, administrative trial judge, hearing commissioner, administrative judge, administrative chancellor, administrative law examiner, trial judge, and so forth. This instability in nomenclature was a telling symbol of the deeper uncertainty about the hearing examiner's precise institutional identity and function. One of the proposed changes—"hearing commissioner"—was clearly inappropriate because it would lead to inevitable confusion with the "commissioners" already in place as the heads of the several regulatory commissions.

More interesting, however, was the firm resistance of the Judicial Conference of the United States to any change involving the word *judge*. Constitutional judges, that is, those appointed under article 3 of the Constitution, considered themselves alone as *real* judges. They did not want administrative parvenus poaching on their territory. The contrast with France could not be greater. At the time of the founding of the Fifth Republic, the participants in the lively debates of the Advisory Committee on the Constitution outdid one another in shouting hosannas to the Council of State and voicing their aspirations that the proposed Constitutional Council would follow in the footsteps of its illustrious predecessor.[116]

Shortly after the Civil Service Commission had made the decision to elevate the erstwhile hearing examiner to administrative law judge, Joseph Zwerdling, the chief administrative law judge of the Federal Power Commission, decided to mark the happy event by writing an article offering some guidance to his newly appointed colleagues. Even though he and his readers were now themselves "judges," he followed the customary pattern of looking to constitutional judges for appropriate norms to guide the behavior of the administrative judge. For example, administrative law judges need feel no embarrassment when told that "administrative proceedings are much more liberal and flexible with respect to its rules of evidence and procedure than court proceedings."[117] In a revealing resort to a tu quoque argument, Zwerdling counters that the rules of evidence and procedure applied by federal judges in civil cases without a jury are in many ways even "more liberal and flexible than the approach of some parties and administrative law judges in administrative hearings."[118] Therefore, it must be all right.

Dramatically indicating the insecurity of the newly anointed administrative law judges, Zwerdling felt compelled to prepare a revealing checklist of appropriate behaviors they should enforce at the hearings before them:

1. The participants should not be allowed to sit in their shirtsleeves.
2. Smoking should not be permitted.
3. Reading of newspapers should not be allowed.
4. Counsel should rise when addressing the administrative law judge.
5. Counsel should address their comments to the administrative law judge, and not to each other.[119]

Such advice speaks volumes. The Council of State needs no code of etiquette.

6

Publius and the Gaullists

History is, indeed, like a picture gallery in which there are few originals and many copies.

— ALEXIS DE TOCQUEVILLE

Throughout this book we have had numerous occasions to examine the ideas of Publius and the Gaullists on an ad hoc basis, but in this chapter we shall do so more systematically by considering three specific comparisons: (1) the structure of the argument in defense of the two constitutions; (2) the treatment of separation of powers; and (3) a direct comparison of the political thought of Publius and Michel Debré.[1]

STRUCTURE OF THE ARGUMENT

Uses of History

In structuring the arguments in support of their respective constitutions, both Publius and the Gaullists make frequent use of history, but they do so in very different ways. The Gaullists rely almost exclusively on French history to buttress their arguments, whereas Publius has surprisingly little to say about American colonial history. His references to his own country are, for the most part, confined to the Revolution and its aftermath. He is particularly interested in the constitutions of the several states, but apart from detailed examination of these texts, he is much more likely to ignore the United States and to draw his historical analogies from England, France, Switzerland, the Netherlands, and, above all, from ancient Greece and Rome.

General de Gaulle, steeped as he was in the history of his country, frequently used historical allusions to explain and embellish constitutional texts. Thus, in clarifying the sense of the provision of article 5 that the "President of the Republic . . . shall ensure by his arbitration . . . the continuance of the State," the general recalled President Poincaré's decision during a particularly difficult period of World War I to call upon the controversial Georges Clemenceau to head the government. De Gaulle maintained that Clemenceau was neither a personal favorite of Poincaré nor, more importantly, the choice of a majority of the members of Parliament, but the president knew him to be the man to lead France to victory, which he did.[2] Poincaré had exercised what de Gaulle meant by "arbitration."

André Malraux, a famous author of Gaullist persuasion, relied on history to answer critics of the Constitution who charged that the powers of Parliament were so diminished that the proposed regime failed to meet the republican standards of the Revolutionary era. He responded by rallying to the Gaullist cause two great patron saints of the Revolution, Danton and St. Just, who, said Malraux, proclaimed that a republic requires the *control* of the government by the people but not its paralysis.[3]

Echoing the importance of the Revolution, Pierre Marcilhacy reminded the Advisory Committee of the need to maintain in the text of the preamble an explicit reference to the Declaration of the Rights of Man and of the Citizen of 1789 because "these words have an enormous impact on the public. . . . The French are so attached to the Declaration of 1789."[4]

History was invoked not only for the rhetorical purposes of persuading the French people to adopt the constitution but also in the day-to-day tasks of discussing and refining the text itself. Thus, in a working memorandum on an early draft of the constitution, François Luchaire evaluated the proposed power of the president to dissolve Parliament in the light of the disastrous use of this power in 1877 by Maréchal Mac Mahon, the first president of the Third Republic.[5]

The most interesting trait in the Gaullists' use of history is their marked tendency to justify proposed institutional arrangements as apt means to safeguard against flaws of character in the French people revealed by their history. We saw in chapter three the Gaullists' uneasiness about electing the president on the basis of direct universal suffrage because of the unhappy outcome of this practice under Napoléon III. The way in which those concerns were formulated suggests that the problem lay not just with Napoléon himself but with those who elected him as well. Thus, Gaullist supporter Maurice Clavel, in a radio address urging a "yes" vote on the constitution points to the *absence* of direct universal election of the president as a sound measure to avoid "the popular infatuations" associated with Napoléon.[6]

Long before 1958, General de Gaulle had been calling for stable government and a strong executive as the solution to the political crises that had weakened France. In his famous address at Bayeux on 16 June 1946, he grounded his case for ensuring "the confidence in our laws, the cohesion of our governments, the efficiency of our administrations and the prestige and the authority of the State" in the need to counterbalance "our ancient gallic tendency to be divisive and quarrelsome." He blamed this national trait for the sorry fact that "in the course of a period not more than twice the life of a man, France has been invaded seven times and has seen some thirteen regimes."[7]

The general went on to say that it is "imperative for the future of our country and of our democracy" that we take into consideration that aspect of our "national temperament" which has brought it about that "partisan bickering has assumed among us the character of a national trait which is forever calling everything into question and which leads us to lose sight of greater interests of our country."[8]

Before proposing the specifics of the strong governing institutions he had in mind, the general once again revisited the national character theme, this time reminding his Bayeux listeners that new democratic institutions for France must be designed in such a way as to "offset the effects of our perpetual political agitation."[9]

De Gaulle's frank assessment of his countrymen in 1946 was frequently echoed by the participants in the drafting of the 1958 Constitution. Thus, Pierre-Henri Teitgen urged the Advisory Committee to support constitutional provisions making it more difficult to overthrow a government in power as necessary to offset the excessive individualism of the French which had led to the disturbing pattern of multiple, undisciplined political parties unable to support a government for more than a few months. This governmental instability has been "a national sickness, a sort of gangrene in France and in the nation."[10]

During the same debate, Paul Reynaud, supporting Teitgen's position, called for constitutional provisions "adapted to the weakness and the instability of our temperaments and our customs."[11]

During the campaign to ratify the constitution, Léon Delbecque urged his countrymen to support the proposed new vigorous governing institutions as the best way to avoid repetition of the calamities that had befallen France during the first half of the twentieth century. "Our weakness," he maintained, "has always had the same cause, the decadence of our institutions which leads inevitably to the degradation of public spiritedness on the part of both the citizen and the politician. This sows the seed of foreign intervention and war."[12]

The specter of war and foreign intervention led to a poignant colloquy before the Advisory Committee on the evening of 13 August. The draft text submitted to that body included a title on how the constitution was to be amended. Borrowing a provision from the Constitution of 1946, the proposed text stated that no amendment could be introduced or approved in the event that any part of metropolitan France (i.e., France in Europe as opposed to France overseas) should be under the control of a foreign army of occupation. This provision was, of course, a bitter reminder of the Constitutional Law of 10 July 1940 in which the Parliament of the Third Republic voted its own demise and handed over supreme power to Maréchal Pétain. Edmond Barrachin objected to the "very humiliating tone" of the provision. Reminded by Paul Reynaud of the unhappy precedent of 1940, Barrachin wondered if a less offensive expression could be found to preclude the danger of constitutional amendments taken under foreign duress. He proposed softening the language to prohibit constitutional amendments "when the integrity of the territory is in jeopardy." The Advisory Committee accepted this change, which was eventually incorporated into article 89 of the final version of the constitution.[13] This brief debate illuminated for an instant the stubborn postwar problem that has bedeviled France: what to think and to say and to do about the humiliating experience of defeat and collaboration during World War II. Even today, the solution to this nagging problem remains elusive.[14]

Publius is more generous toward his fellow Americans than the French founders of 1958 were toward their countrymen. As noted above, most of his references to the United States are contemporary rather than historical and tend to emphasize specific legal and constitutional texts rather than broad national characteristics. When Publius wants a historical allusion to support his argument, he is more likely to turn to classical antiquity than to his own country. Thus, he draws lessons for American federalism from the Achaean League and the Lycian and Amphyctionic Confederacies or he buttresses his case for a unified executive by showing the mischief created by the two consuls who headed the executive of the Roman Republic.[15]

Like the French founders of 1958, Publius is fond of anchoring institutional reforms in the need to counteract human weaknesses, but the weaknesses Publius targets are more likely to be found in human nature as such than in any particular people, like his fellow Americans. Relying on a curious blend of philosophical insight, shrewd common sense, and dogmatic assertion, Publius, good eighteenth-century man that he was, takes his cues from human nature as he understands it.

Examples abound in *The Federalist* of Publius appealing to universal human characteristics to support specific constitutional arrangements. At the most general level of the need for some kind of union among the thirteen states, he asserts that without effective union the states would soon be at war with one another. Those who doubt this, says Publius, "forget that men are ambitious, vindictive, and rapacious." To expect harmony from "a number of independent unconnected sovereignties, situated in the same neighborhood would be to disregard the uniform course of human events, and to set at defiance the accumulated experience of ages."[16] He repeats the same grim assessment of his fellow man to explain the extensive military powers the Constitution confers upon the national government. These ample powers are justified because someday they will be needed. How does Publius know this? From what history tells us about human nature:

> To judge from the history of mankind, we shall be compelled to conclude, that the fiery and destructive passions of war, reign in the human breast, with much more powerful sway than the mild and beneficent sentiments of peace; and, that to model our political systems upon speculations of lasting tranquility, is to calculate on the weaker springs of the human character.[17]

At a far less dramatic level, Publius appeals to human nature to explain why the Constitution gives to the Senate rather than to the Supreme Court the power to judge whether to convict an official impeached by the House or Representatives. Reminding his reader that conviction upon impeachment involves only removal from office, Publius states that after the removal, the officer may still face criminal charges for his wrongdoing. A conviction for his crimes could come before the Supreme Court on appeal. It would not be right to have the justices of that august tribunal weigh the guilt or innocence of a man in a criminal trial after they had already judged him sufficiently guilty to be removed from office. "Would there not be the greatest reason," Publius asks, "to apprehend, that error in the first sentence would be the parent of error in the second sentence? That the strong bias of one decision would be apt to overrule the influence of any new lights, which might be brought to vary the complexion of another decision?"[18]

Publius has no trouble answering his own questions:

> Those, who know any thing of human nature, will not hesitate to answer these questions in the affirmative; and will be at no loss to perceive, that by making the same persons Judges in both cases, those who might happen to be the objects of prosecution would in a great measure be deprived of the double security, intended them by a double trial. The loss of life and estate would often be virtually included in a sentence, which, in its terms, imported nothing more than dismission from a present, and disqualification for a future office.[19]

To support his commitment to unity in the executive—one person alone to head the executive branch—Publius points to the dangers of a plural executive which, not surprisingly, we discover are grounded in human nature itself. "Men," asserts Publius, "often oppose a thing merely because they have had no agency in planning it." If, however, they have been consulted and their advice has been rejected, "opposition then becomes in their estimation an indispensable duty of self-love."[20] Herein lies the problem of the plural executive. Those members of the executive whose opinions have lost out will try to undermine the policy that has been adopted. "They seem to think themselves bound in honor, and by all the motives of personal infallibility to defeat the success of what has been resolved upon, contrary to their sentiments."[21] The plural executive would invite manifestations "of this despicable frailty, or rather detestable vice in the human character."[22]

To those Anti-Federalists who thought that the four-year term for president was too long, Publius has a ready answer: "It is a general principle of human nature, that a man will be interested in whatever he possesses, in proportion to the firmness or precariousness of the tenure by which he holds it." From this "general principle of human nature," Publius deduces the behavioral conclusion that a president securely in office for four years is more likely to meet the standard of *energy* in the executive and will work harder at succeeding in his tasks than one who enjoys a shorter term. The same line of reasoning supports the constitutional provision enabling the president to be reelected to an indefinite number of terms.[23] The prospect of reelection, Publius maintains, will energize the president.

The same human nature Publius invoked to support unity in the executive is called upon once again, but this time to justify dividing the treaty power between the Senate and the president. "The history of human conduct does not warrant that exalted opinion of human virtue which would make it wise in a nation to commit interests of so delicate and momentous a kind as those which concern its intercourse with the rest of the world to the sole disposal of a magistrate, created and circumstanced, as would be a president of the United States."[24] Publius grounds this assertion in an interesting argument turning on the distinction between a hereditary monarchy and a republic. A king, "though often the oppressor of his people, has personally too much at stake in the government to be in a material danger of being corrupted by foreign powers." Thus, the treaty power can safely be confided to him alone. The president of a republic, however, is "a man raised from the station of private citizen to the rank of chief magistrate." Consequently, he is likely to be "possessed of but a moderate or slender fortune" and must anticipate an eventual "return to the station from which he was taken." Such a man "might sometimes be under temptation to sacrifice his duty to his interest, which it would require superlative virtue to withstand."[25] Hence, the wisdom of dividing the treaty power in a republic between the chief executive and some other institution, like the Senate of the United States.

In emphasizing human nature, Publius reveals a pronounced tendency to stress its darker side. I think it is fair to say that Publius was a hardheaded realist with no illusions as to the moral capacities of his fellow man. Having said that, however, I must add a word of caution that my selection of texts from *The Federalist* may have overemphasized this aspect of Publius's thought. Happily, he does not entirely neglect the brighter angels of our nature, especially when he gets around to discussing the degree of civic virtue demanded by an authentic republic.[26] If, on balance, Publius offers a rather sober, if not grim, view of his fellow man, it may be that he was following David Hume's advice that lawgivers who establish a regime should assume the worst rather than the best about human nature. Fundamental laws should be designed for the worst of times. The best of times will take care of themselves.[27]

To conclude this section, I should note that there are many explanations for the different ways in which Publius and the French founders of 1958 incorporated history into their arguments. At the simplest level, one might observe that the French relied more upon the history of their country than the late-eighteenth-century Americans relied on theirs, for the excellent reason that there was far more French history than American from which to choose. Or perhaps Publius found the history of each of the thirteen states too diverse to yield meaningful generalizations about Americans as such.

At a more fundamental level, the best explanation may be a function of history itself. In emphasizing human nature, Publius followed the idiom of his day. The same holds for his reliance on classical antiquity. The classics remained the centerpiece of a gentleman's education as long as people took seriously the idea of a constant human nature remaining the same over the centuries. If there is such an abiding nature, then the study of the lives of the men and women of the ancient world will reveal as much about it as the study of the lives of one's contemporaries and of one's own countrymen. Indeed, it will reveal even more because the marked differences between the ancients and ourselves will help us to distinguish the abiding from the ephemeral.

Twentieth-century man, taught by Nietzsche and the existentialists that man is malleable, has trouble taking seriously the idea of an abiding human nature. He is much more at ease in the comfortable relativism of a particular people. Hence, the unremarkable tendency of the French founders of 1958 to stress the history of their own country—even if the depth of their knowledge of French history was both remarkable and impressive.

Our examination of history in the arguments of Publius and the French founders stressed what might best be described as "procedural" or even "methodological" matters, that is, *how* they used history rather than the substantive historical events they used. Now we turn to two substantive points of comparison in the founding arguments in the two countries: political blackmail and national independence.

Political Blackmail

General de Gaulle's critics often complained of the way he formulated great issues. Although he left the final decision-making authority with the French people, he did so in such a way that they had to give the general what he wanted or face the most dire consequences. "Me or chaos" became the shorthand slogan the general's critics used to describe this disturbingly effective tactic they denounced as a form of political blackmail. As president of the Fifth Republic, the general perfected this technique by having recourse on four occasions to referenda which were accompanied by threats, either expressed or implied, to resign if the people denied him what he wanted.[28] This strategy served the general well because his unquestioned integrity left no doubt that he really would resign if the proposal should fail. Indeed, in 1969, on the sole occasion when the people rejected a referendum question supported by de Gaulle, he resigned at once and retired to private life.

As far as the founding of the Fifth Republic is concerned, the first cries of "blackmail" against de Gaulle arose when President Coty asked him to form a government on 29 May 1958, at the height of the Algerian crisis, as talk of chaos—or worse—dominated French politics. On that very day, President Coty sent a message to Parliament with an unprecedented threat that he himself would resign if Parliament should refuse to "invest" de Gaulle as "President of the Council," the title bestowed upon the heads of government under the Fourth Republic.

During the ensuing investiture debate before the National Assembly on 1 June, de Gaulle's critics complained bitterly of the pressure put upon them. Pulling no punches, Pierre Cot called it blackmail, and vowed not to submit.[29] Jacques Duclos, a prominent Communist leader, was called to order by the president of the assembly for openly criticizing President Coty's ultimatum as a form of "unacceptable pressure."[30] Assembly rules forbade any criticism of the person or the role of the president of the Republic. Duclos replied that he would withdraw the president's name but would let the facts speak for themselves. François Mitterrand complained bitterly that "it is intolerable that we find ourselves faced with this choice": either accept de Gaulle as head of the government or submit to the blows of those who threaten the nation.[31] Pierre Mendès-France refused to cast "a vote constrained by insurrection and the threat of a military takeover."[32]

These charges, voiced before the process of constitutional reform had begun, resurfaced as soon as the new constitution was finished and presented to the French people for their approval. During the ratification campaign from 4–28 September, Pierre Poujade on the Right and Pierre Cot and Claude Bourdet on the Left railed against the "blackmail" *(chantage)* that led the French people to believe they had to choose between de Gaulle's constitution and "civil war."[33]

The opponents of the American Constitution of 1787 complained that the Federalists exaggerated the problems under the Articles of Confederation in a deliberate effort to panic their countrymen into accepting the new constitution without carefully considering its true nature. Publius was among the offenders they had in mind. His strategy was to present the constitution in terms of all or nothing at all. If the constitution is rejected, he maintained, there can be no return to the status quo ante. The alternative to ratification is nothing less than "dismemberment of the Union."[34] The objections to the constitution are but "airy phantoms that flit before the distempered imagination of some its adversaries." The rejection of the constitution "would in all probability put a final period to the Union." Then the "airy phantoms" would "quickly give place to the more substantial forms of dangers real, certain, and formidable."[35]

The Anti-Federalists cried "foul" at these alarmist predictions. Federal Farmer caught the spirit of their reply when he charged:

> It is natural for men, who wish to hasten the adoption of a measure, to tell us, now is the crisis—now is the critical moment which must be seized, or all will be lost: and to shut the door against free enquiry, whenever conscious the thing presented has defects in it which time and investigation will probably discover. This has been the custom of tyrants and their dependents in all ages.[36]

Publius, master of rhetoric that he was, was not above presenting his case in terms of "the constitution or chaos." Having asserted that rejection of the constitution would mean the end of the Union, he then dwelt upon the dire consequences of thirteen totally separate states, or at best three or four competing confederacies formed by these states. In either case, disaster awaited his countrymen. A disunited America would soon be the prey of ambitious European powers that would manipulate one state or group of states against the other.[37] If this were not enough to destroy American liberty, it would at the very least put the American states "exactly in the situations [in] which some nations doubtless wish to see us, viz., *formidable only to each other*."[38] This would inevitably lead to "domestic factions and convulsion" and "frequent and violent contests with each other." Nor would the fact that Americans enjoyed republican institutions save them because "there have been, if I may so express it, almost as many popular as royal wars."[39]

Unending civil wars would eventually lead Americans to care more about safety than liberty as they came to rely increasingly upon large standing armies for protection. This, in turn, would lead them to exalt "the executive at the expense of the legislative authority" and finally the soldiers who began as their protectors would finish as their masters.[40]

One of the reasons there can be no return to the Articles of Confederation if the constitution should be rejected is the deplorable state of affairs they have brought about.

> We may indeed with propriety be said to have reached almost the last stage of national humiliation. There is scarcely anything that can wound the pride, or degrade the character of an independent nation, which we do not experience.[41]

Publius goes on to chronicle the miseries of life under the Articles of Confederation: commitments are not honored, debts go unpaid, foreign armies occupy lands rightfully our own, our military forces are pathetic, commerce languishes, credit is unavailable, our embassies abroad are a laughing stock, and so forth and so on. Publius concludes his doleful review by asking "what indication is there of national disorder, poverty, and insignificance that could befall a community so peculiarly blessed with natural advantages as we are, which does not form part of the dark catalogue of our misfortunes?"[42]

> This is the melancholy situation, to which we have been brought by those very maxims and councils, which would now deter us from adopting the proposed constitution; and which not content with having conducted us to the brink of a precipice, seem resolved to plunge us into the abyss, that awaits us below.[43]

Leaving the alarmed reader teetering on the abyss, Publius rests his case for the constitution or chaos.

National Independence

To conclude our discussion of the structure of the arguments at the two foundings, we shall examine very briefly the relationship between national independence and strong institutions of government.

This relationship was so clear to General de Gaulle and his followers that it appears not in the arguments for the constitution but in its very text. National independence is mentioned twice in the Constitution of 1958 and both times, significantly, in connection with the powerful office of the president of the Republic. Article 5 proclaims the president "the guarantor of national independence" and article 16 confers virtually unlimited power upon him when "the independence of the nation . . . [is] threatened in a grave and immediate manner."

The profound link between national independence and powerful institutions of government can be traced ultimately, of course, to the defeat of France in 1940 which General de Gaulle, with considerable justification, always insisted was due not so much to the collapse of the French army as to the collapse of the parliamentary regime of the Third Republic.

In the famous address at Bayeux in 1946, which is often considered a prologue to the 1958 Constitution, de Gaulle made explicit connections between national independence and the new political dispensation he envisioned for his country. Situated in Normandy, Bayeux prompted de Gaulle to recall the glorious events that had taken place there just two years earlier. Before explaining the details of the institutional reforms he had in mind, the general devoted the first half of his speech to glowing accounts of "liberty," "victory," and the heroism of the brave resistants, "on the soil of our ancestors."[44] As for the mass of Frenchmen who spent the war years under the German yoke, their servitude, the general continued, was more apparent than real. If the force of circumstances made them submit, their submission was purely external, for they never forgot that the enemy was really their enemy and his authority only a sham. Happily, few indeed were the Frenchmen who submitted in their minds and hearts.[45]

De Gaulle uses this powerful rhetoric to set the stage for what might otherwise have been a rather tedious talk on institutional reform. In the key transition paragraph in which the general moves from celebration of national glory to institutional analysis, he reminds his listeners of the urgency of the reform because "the position, the independence and the very existence of our country and our French Union are at stake."[46]

Publius offers no statement comparable to the grace and power of de Gaulle's Bayeux address. Nevertheless, he is at one with the general in the need for a strong government in order to maintain national independence.

The most interesting example of this connection in *The Federalist* appears in Publius's defense of the need for a United States navy. Many Anti-Federalists challenged the purpose of the constitutional provision conferring upon Congress the power "to provide and maintain a Navy." Their argument rested on a vision of America's future that looked westward to development of the continent and to a rejection of Europe and its decadent ways. Many of them had no quarrel with Congress' power "to raise and support Armies," which would be needed to fight the Indian wars inevitable in a strategy of westward expansion, but a navy struck them as a useless and possibly dangerous extravagance.[47]

Publius attacked this position by arguing that most Americans wanted to establish a great commercial republic and this meant we must be a seafaring people. A navy was necessary to protect American commerce. Up to this point, Publius's position was quite conventional. Navies have always protected commercial interests. His argument takes a novel twist, however, when he examines the ends of commerce and discovers them to be related to raising revenue for the state which will tax lucrative imports from abroad.

With commerce as a major source of revenue, the tax collector need not rely on unpopular excises and unenforceable personal property taxes. Because of the unreliable character of excises and personal property taxes, the new government would have to rely almost exclusively upon taxes on land to raise its revenues, and this would disproportionately burden the agricultural interests of the nation—unless a vigorous international commerce came to the rescue.

Throughout his long and complicated discussion of these matters, Publius, ever faithful to his mercantilist convictions, focuses his argument on the government's need for revenue. "A nation cannot long exist without revenue," he confidently asserts.[48] And the purpose of this revenue? Nothing less than national independence: "Destitute of this essential support, it [a nation] must resign its independence and sink into the degraded condition of a province. This is an extremity to which no government will of choice accede."[49]

Thus, the Constitution's ambitious plan for a navy is intended to protect commerce, which, in turn, is intended to raise revenue for the government, and this revenue will secure national independence. By means of this complicated scheme, Publius subordinates economics to politics and forges the link between a powerful naval establishment and national independence.[50]

SEPARATION OF POWERS

The reader may wonder why the topic of separation of powers appears yet again when it has already been discussed—sometimes at considerable length—in each of the preceding chapters. The ubiquity of separation of powers in this book faithfully reflects its pervasive character throughout the two founding periods we examine. Separation of powers is the primary organizational principle of both constitutions, although, as so frequently noted already, the principle was understood very differently in 1787 America and 1958 France. Here we shall compare Publius and the Gaullists on their respective understandings of separation of powers.

The President as Arbitrator

Perhaps the most striking difference between Publius and de Gaulle is the latter's felt need to anchor the regime itself in a single unifying institution: the presidency. The constitutional text Publius defends has nothing quite comparable to article 5 of the Constitution of the Fifth Republic:

> The president of the Republic shall see that the Constitution is respected. He shall ensure, by his arbitration, the regular functioning of the governmental authorities, as well as the continuance of the State.

He shall be the guarantor of national independence, of the integrity of
the territory, and of respect for Community agreements and treaties.

The president's role as "arbitrator" was a cardinal tenet of Gaullist political thought—an idea proposed by the general himself long before 1958
and defended by him long afterward. At the Bayeux address of 1946, de
Gaulle had already claimed for the presidential office he envisioned the task
of "serving as arbitrator above and beyond political contingencies . . . [and]
the duty to be the guarantor of national independence."[51] Writing his memoirs after leaving the presidency in 1969, de Gaulle continued to look to the
president as "the keystone of our regime . . . and the guide of France." As
the great unifying force of the nation, his was the task to counter "the de-
mons of our divisions."[52]

The Constitution of the Fifth Republic reveals the logic of article 5 at
three other points in the text. The first is the famous emergency power provision of article 16 which we have already discussed in some detail in chapter
two. As "guarantor of national independence," the president has virtually
unfettered power to act decisively on his own initiative at times of great national peril.

Secondly, articles 64 and 65 anoint the president as "guarantor of the
independence of the judicial authority" and name him presiding officer of
the "High Council of the Judiciary," the organization responsible for recommending judicial appointments and for enforcing judicial discipline.
When the High Council exercises its disciplinary role, the first president of
the Court of Cassation replaces the president of the Republic as presiding
officer. The High Council of the Judiciary is to assist the president in guaranteeing judicial independence. The Constitution of 1958 originally provided that the minister of justice would serve on the High Council ex officio
and that the nine other members would be appointed by the president. Thus,
although the president of the Republic did not preside over the High Council
in its disciplinary capacity, the council itself was totally dominated by presidential appointees. That the president of the Republic should have such influence over a body created to discipline judges is a striking example of the
far-reaching implication of the president's role as arbitrator—an impression
that is convincingly reinforced by his duty to guarantee the judges' independence.

Publius would reject such an arrangement out of hand, insisting with
Montesquieu that "there is no liberty, if the power of judging be not separated from the legislative and executive powers."[53] Far from considering the
president of the United States as the guarantor of judicial independence,
Publius eyes him suspiciously as a potential threat. To assure judicial inde-

pendence, Publius will rely on the Constitution itself, notably the provision that judges shall serve during good behavior (III, 1).

To understand the foundation of the Gaullist position that the president should be able both to influence judicial discipline and to guarantee judicial independence, we must recall our lengthy discussion in chapter three on the prime minister as the chief executive officer and the president as a different kind of officer, that is, a *nonexecutive* arbitrator. Although the history of the Fifth Republic would belie this distinction, it was taken seriously in 1958 and must be kept in mind if one wishes to grasp the Gaullist vision of separation of powers. Since the president was not an executive officer, he stood outside the classic tripartite division of legislative, executive, and judicial powers.[54]

To underscore the broad-based support for the president's role as arbitrator, it is useful to note that the text making the president of the Republic the president of the High Council of the Judiciary as well came not from de Gaulle's government but from the Advisory Committee comprised mainly of parliamentarians. The government text submitted to this body was silent on the presiding officer of the High Council. Noting this silence, Jacques Fourcade urged the Advisory Committee on 5 August to name the president of the Republic as presiding officer of the High Council because he alone could assure its impartiality and he alone "could reconcile the interests of the nation and the independence of the magistrates."[55] Repeating this point during the same debate, René Chazelle added the further consideration that to designate the president of the Republic as president of the High Council of the Judiciary would "give to the judicial corps its dignity and the role which the magistrate ought to hold in our society."[56]

In 1992, President Mitterrand, responding to widespread appeals to enhance the independence of the French judiciary, proposed a constitutional amendment to reduce sharply the president's control over appointments to the High Council. A blue-ribbon committee on constitutional reform reduced Mitterrand's suggestions to appropriate constitutional language that influenced an amendment to article 65 eventually adopted in July of 1993. To reduce presidential influence over the High Council, the amended version of article 65 permits the president to appoint but one member, whereas the appointments of the other nine members are distributed among several officers including the judges themselves. The minister of justice continues to serve ex officio and the president of the Republic retains his position as presiding officer except when the High Council acts as a disciplinary body.[57]

Article 68 offers the third and final text to reflect the logic of the principle of the president as arbitrator expressed in article 5. According to article 68, the "President of the Republic shall not be held accountable for actions performed in the exercise of his office except in the case of high treason."

Thus, treason aside, the president of the Republic is an irresponsible officer which would seem to be consistent with the nature of his role as arbitrator, that is, as one who stands outside politics, above the battle, and from these lofty heights orders all things sweetly. Like a referee at a sporting event, he cannot be accountable to the players in the game but must look to the well-being of the game itself. Or, in the language of article 5, he ensures "by his arbitration, the regular functioning of the governmental authorities, as well as the continuance of the State."

The contrast with the president of the United States is stark. That officer, along with "all civil Officers of the United States shall be removed from Office on Impeachment for, and conviction of, Treason, Bribery, or other high Crimes and Misdemeanors." Thus, the president of the United States can be removed from office for any number of reasons, including whatever skullduggery the two houses of Congress might discover lurking in the open-ended language of "high Crimes and Misdemeanors."[58] To be sure, the constitutional requirement of a two-thirds vote in the Senate affords the president considerable protection. Nevertheless, the imprecise expression, "high Crimes and Misdemeanors" theoretically could have created a form of routine presidential responsibility to Congress, which, of course, would have undermined the American version of separation of powers.

François Luchaire opposed the idea of enshrining in the French Constitution the notion of presidential responsibility, even in the admittedly far-fetched case of high treason. He feared that the reference to treason could be the "germ of a political responsibility for the head of State."[59] Acknowledging that the constitutional requirement for an *absolute* majority of the votes in both chambers of Parliament was a reassuring safeguard, Luchaire nevertheless worried over the political viability of a president who had endured the humiliation of a relative majority in even one chamber voting to accuse him of treason. Luchaire thought it best to delete any reference to treason in the Constitution. Had his advice been followed, the president would have been an absolutely irresponsible officer.

Publius approached the question of removing the president from office very differently. He linked the impeachment clause to the broader question of the exigencies of a republican regime. Arguing that the framers of the American Constitution envisioned an executive as energetic "as republican principles would admit," he states in no uncertain terms that the president is "at all times liable to impeachment, trial, dismission from office, incapacity to serve in any other; and to the forfeiture of life and estate by subsequent prosecution in the common courts."[60] Thus, Publius trumpets the severity of his constitution's impeachment provision; republican principles demand nothing less.

Admittedly, discussions of presidential impeachment for any reason, let alone treason, have a certain fantastic quality about them. Nevertheless, the contrasting attitudes of Publius and Luchaire are instructive for our purposes.

First of all, Luchaire's concern about the term "treason" being used for political purposes could not apply to American politics because the Constitution of the United States defines this crime with admirable clarity:

> Treason against the United States, shall consist only in levying War against them, or in adhering to their Enemies, giving them Aid and Comfort. No Person shall be convicted of Treason unless on the Testimony of two Witnesses to the same overt Act, or on Confession in open Court. [III,1]

Treason is the only crime defined in the Constitution of the United States and goes as far as language allows to head off the possibility that this charge could be used for political purposes. As noted above, however, the vague expression "high Crimes and Misdemeanors" could have led to the politicization of the American impeachment process and did so, according to President Andrew Johnson and his supporters. President Richard Nixon voiced a similar complaint, but less convincingly than Johnson.

Secondly, Luchaire's concern about the adverse effect of even an *unsuccessful* charge of high treason against a president is of considerable relevance to the United States. Neither Andrew Johnson nor Richard Nixon was accused of treason, but the presidencies of both men were hopelessly compromised by the humiliation of the impeachment process itself. Johnson was acquitted by one vote but he was in no position to exercise effective leadership after his narrow escape. The prospect of impeachment immobilized Richard Nixon throughout his last year in office and eventually forced him to resign before the House of Representatives could take a vote on this issue.

More importantly, the office of the president suffered as well. The men who followed Johnson—Grant, Hayes, Garfield, Arthur, Cleveland, Benjamin Harrison, and McKinley—were not notably powerful presidents and were often eclipsed by Congress. Indeed, the post–Civil War period has come to be known as the era of "Congressional government."[61] In the twenty years that have passed since Nixon's resignation, only the early years of Ronald Reagan's first term could be called a period of executive ascendancy. For the rest, it has been a story of gridlock, lost elections, and "failed presidencies." The history of the Fifth Republic has belied Luchaire's fears for France, but interestingly, his admonition on the danger of even an unsuccessful impeachment illuminates American history.

Finally, there remains the curious fact that, treason aside, the Constitution of the Fifth *Republic* provides the very *unrepublican* example of a politically irresponsible officer. François Luchaire, a man of impeccable republican credentials, would have torn away even the figleaf of republican orthodoxy in the treason clause. How can one explain this startling contrast with Publius's proud republican boast of the high visibility of presidential impeachment in the American Constitution?

Perhaps the best explanation is to look upon the French president, with his powers of arbitration, as a vestigial remnant of the French monarchy. The question of presidential responsibility received very little attention throughout the summer of 1958. Indeed, the text prepared by de Gaulle's government as early as 26 July has *exactly* the same wording as the final version submitted to the people on 4 September. Nothing was changed because the issue was not taken seriously enough to merit close attention. It seems as though the founders of 1958, who were willing to argue about almost anything, were quite willing to take their irresponsible head of State as a simple fact of political life.

This easygoing attitude contrasts markedly with the enormous energy expended on how to ensure that the prime minister and his government would be responsible to Parliament. This was one of the most important issues debated in 1958. The same is true of the American framers of 1787. They took excruciating pains in drafting any language pertaining to impeachment. The founders in the two countries busied themselves with these matters because, as serious republicans, they wanted to find that right balance that would safeguard against the likely abuses of executive power without weakening its legitimate role in a republican regime. Hence, the Americans targeted their president and the French their prime minister and his government. The French founders made the president of the Republic an irresponsible officer because they believed the Gaullist assurances that the prime minister would be the real executive in the new regime. They thought that the president of the Republic, especially after the departure of the charismatic de Gaulle, would be an arbitrator vested with residual trappings of the monarchy, who would unify the nation and give dignity to the State. However desirable such an officer might be, he is ill at ease in a republican regime anchored in the principle of separation of powers.

As noted above, the *text* of the Constitution of the United States provides nothing comparable to the arbitration powers of the president of the Fifth Republic. Nevertheless, Publius's commentary suggests that the Senate might provide a unifying aspect to the new regime in a way that bears a certain resemblance to the Gaullist idea of presidential arbitration.

The Senate was a favorite whipping boy of the Anti-Federalists, who delighted in denouncing it as an "aristocratic junto" that would conspire with a monarchical president against the liberties of the people. Their favorite targets were the Senate's executive powers over treaties and appointments and its judicial power to convict impeached officers. Since it was also the second chamber of the legislature, it thereby exercised all three powers of government and, according to the Anti-Federalists, thereby violated the principle of separation of powers. This problem was aggravated by the fact that the senators would serve lengthy (by eighteenth-century standards) six-year terms, could be reelected indefinitely, and were chosen not by the people but by the state legislatures.

Realizing that the role of the Senate required considerable justification, Publius offered some rather far-reaching claims for it. Making a virtue of necessity, he defended the duration of the senators' terms on the grounds that it would give them the firmness they would need to resist "the impulse of sudden and violent passions" by which "factious leaders" might try to induce them to approve "intemperate and pernicious resolutions." Further, the Senate must "possess great firmness and consequently ought to hold its authority by a tenure of considerable duration."

The defense of the six-year senatorial terms appears in *Federalist* 62 and sets the stage for the remarkable statement in number 63 that the Senate will provide nothing less than "a due sense of national character." The expression occurs in the context of foreign affairs, but similar language in other parts of *The Federalist* and in speeches by both Madison and Hamilton at Philadelphia suggests a broader application of these intriguing words. In *Federalist* 75, Publius credits the Senate with "a nice and uniform sensibility to national character," and in number 65 he calls the senators "the representatives of the nation." At the Philadelphia Convention, Hamilton had looked to the Senate, whose members in his plan would have served during good behavior for life, as embodying "a permanent will," a "weighty interest" in the government that would give them a reason to endure "the sacrifice of private affairs which an acceptance of public trust would require." Also at the convention, Madison had looked to the Senate as an institution that would "protect the people against their rulers." By *ruler,* the context makes clear, he meant the elected representatives in the House. On the same day, 26 June, he went on to hail the senators as "impartial umpires and Guardians of justice and general good." As Publius, Madison echoed this theme in *Federalist* 63, where he looked to the Senate for that "cool and deliberate sense of community" that will safeguard against the danger that the country "may possibly be betrayed by the representatives of the people."

Needless to say, the United States Senate, fine institution that it is, has failed to measure up to Publius's extraordinary expectations. The references to "national character," "permanent will," and "representatives of the nation" suggest a certain similarity to the Gaullist notion of arbitration. Unlike arbitration, however, there is no hint of a monarchical residue in Publius's Senate. Rather, his plan for the Senate seems to be the result of a quest for an institution that will serve as an anchor or a balance wheel to stabilize a regime all too prone to capture by the centrifugal forces of both federalism and separation of powers. Perhaps Publius would share the sentiment of William Maclay of Pennsylvania who described the first Senate, of which he was a member, as "the great check, the regulator, the corrector, or, if I may so speak, the balance of this government."[62] I believe General de Gaulle would have understood and approved of this comment.

Trust versus Interest

By a curious coincidence, Publius and two prominent Gaullists, Guy Mollet and Raymond Janot, use the same metaphor to disparage what they see as a common misunderstanding of the principle of separation of powers. The metaphor, "parchment barriers" for Publius and *murs de papier* (walls of paper) and *barrières de papier* (paper barriers) for Mollet and Janot, respectively, is used to characterize a mindset that relies excessively on merely formal constitutional provisions to achieve substantive political results.

Let us look more closely at the context in which the metaphor appears. Guy Mollet used it in his remarks on 1 June before the National Assembly's Committee on Universal Suffrage. There he voiced his displeasure at snide comments on the need for constitutional protections against any plans General de Gaulle might have to establish a dictatorship. Dismissing such fears as preposterous, Mollet added that "if you take that idea as your starting point, then I say that you will never put enough precautions in your texts. You can erect walls of paper, but you will never stop anything that way."[63] His advice was to take the general at his word when he said he posed no threats to republican institutions. Indeed, Mollet, a prominent Socialist who had served as prime minister during the Fourth Republic, offered his trust in de Gaulle as "the sole justification for my presence in this [de Gaulle's] government." For Mollet, the best answer to loose talk about a coming dictatorship was simply to recall that "here it is a problem of confidence, a problem far more political than constitutional."[64] De Gaulle had won Mollet's confidence.

Janot's reference to "paper barriers" occurred in a debate before the Advisory Committee on the procedure to be used to censure and thereby to overthrow a government. There was widespread consensus that this had been done all too easily under the Fourth Republic. The text submitted to the Advisory Committee, which resembled closely the version eventually adopted as article 49, listed several procedural protections for a government in power: the motion of censure must be signed by at least 10 percent of the deputies, the vote to censure may be taken only after a two-day "cooling off" period, an absolute majority is required to bring down the government, and so forth.

Janot supported these provisions but candidly acknowledged that in his "personal opinion" no government can long remain in power if it has lost the confidence of the parliamentary assemblies. Without this substantive support, procedural safeguards mean very little. "You can erect all possible barriers, but they will be paper barriers without the confidence of parliament."[65]

Publius's use of the "parchment barrier" metaphor is solidly integrated into a cardinal point in *The Federalist Papers*. In essays 47 to 51, he explains the importance of separation of powers and how the new constitution will safeguard it in practice. Referring to each of the three great branches of government, he acknowledges that "to provide some practical security for each against the invasion of the other" is nothing less than "the great problem to be solved." In considering likely solutions, he asks: "Will it be sufficient to mark with precision the boundaries of these departments in the Constitution of the government, and to trust to these parchment barriers against the encroaching spirit of power?"[66]

Publius answers his own question in the negative, observing that a naive reliance by the states on the sterile formalism of parchment barriers has doomed "most of the American constitutions." Separation of powers has failed in America with the unhappy result that the "legislative department is every where extending the sphere of its activity, and drawing all power into its impetuous vortex."[67] One must look elsewhere for a "more adequate defence" than parchment barriers alone can provide for the principle of separation of powers.

Publius then tries and finds wanting several other ways of preserving separation of powers, including Thomas Jefferson's reliance on popular conventions to correct breaches of the principle. These unsuccessful efforts set the stage for the question he asks to introduce the famous *Federalist 51*: "To what expedient then shall we finally resort for maintaining in practice the necessary partition of power among the several departments as laid down in the constitution?" His answer is that separation of powers will be preserved only "by so contriving the interior structure of the government, as that its several constituent parts may, by their mutual relations, be the means of keeping each other in their proper places." To do this, "it is evident that each department should have a will of its own." Further, to protect the executive and the judiciary from the "legislative vortex," the salaries of the president and the judges must be free from manipulation at the whim of the legislature—a matter explicitly addressed in articles 2 and 3 of Publius's constitution. Having carefully laid this foundation, Publius is ready at last to present his startling thesis that reliance on the self-interest of the officeholders in the various branches is the best means to preserve separation of powers. Let Publius speak for himself in this important matter:

But the great security against a gradual concentration of the several powers in the same department, consists in giving to those who administer each department, the necessary constitutional means, and personal motives, to resist encroachments of the others. The provision for defence must in this, as in all other cases, be made commensurate to the danger of attack. Ambition must be made to counteract ambition. The interest of the man must be connected with the constitutional rights of the place. It may be a reflection on human nature, that such devices should be necessary to controul the abuses of government. But what is government itself but the greatest of all reflections on human nature? If men were angels, no government would be necessary. If angels were to govern men, neither external nor internal controuls on government would be necessary. In framing a government which is to be administered by men over men, the great difficulty lies in this: You must first enable the government to controul the governed; and in the next place, oblige it to control itself. A dependence on the people is no doubt the primary controul on the government; but experience has taught mankind the necessity of auxiliary precautions.

This policy of supplying by opposite and rival interests, the defect of better motives, might be traced through the whole system of human affairs, private as well as public. We see it particularly displayed in all the subordinate distributions of power; where the constant aim is to divide and arrange the several offices in such a manner as that each may be a check on the other; that the private interest of every individual, may be a centinel over the public rights. These inventions of prudence cannot be less requisite in the distribution of the supreme powers of the state.

This passage reveals the chasm separating Publius from the Gaullists on the question of separation of powers. For Mollet, the fundamental solution to the problem of a possible Gaullist dictatorship was to trust the general. Happily for France, events fully justified Mollet's confidence and that of his countrymen. Publius would not have taken such a gamble. He put his faith not in men but in a constitution so well designed that separation of powers, and therefore liberty itself,[68] would be preserved by counteracting one man's ambition with the ambition of another. Candidly, he acknowledges as his own the "policy of supplying by opposite and rival interests the defect of better motives." This policy reveals a very different view of the world from that of the Gaullists, who looked to a highly motivated president as the great national arbitrator.

Like Mollet, Janot differs from Publius but not in the same way. Janot, it will be recalled, dismissed as "paper barriers" the various constitutional mechanisms to protect a government in place from reckless motions of censure. For him, no government could long survive without the authentic support of Parliament and, without this support, procedural safeguards were to no avail. Publius travels half the road with Janot, acknowledging that a "dependence on the people is no doubt the primary controul on the government." They part company, however, when Publius insists upon "the necessity of auxiliary precautions." These precautions are an effective separation of powers to be achieved only by intricate constitutional designs wherein the "interest of the man must be connected with the constitutional rights of the place."

The Gaullists did not have to invoke the parchment barrier metaphor in order to reveal a much greater readiness to trust than one finds in the suspicious Publius. Michel Debré, for example, urged the Advisory Committee to trust in a "certain civic discipline" from the leaders of the various political parties in a debate over how the president should be elected. As we saw in chapter three, the president of the Fifth Republic was originally chosen, not by direct universal suffrage, but by an electoral college. One of the questions before the committee was how to ensure that a sufficient number of the electors would agree to support one presidential candidate in order to avoid the embarrassment of selecting a president with a plurality of only 20 to 25 percent of the electoral votes. Various proposals were suggested. Debré favored relying on the "civic discipline," noted above, of the various party leaders in order to avoid this danger. In a second round of voting, this discipline would prompt the electors to form alliances behind acceptable candidates they thought could win. Debré saw no need to coerce such behavior by permitting only the two top candidates in the first round to compete in the second. "If the political parties," he asserted, "cannot agree among themselves on the second round, . . . there is no chance that French political life will amount to anything." He went on to assert that if a matter as important as electing a president could not overcome partisan bickering, there is simply no point in writing a constitution. "Democracy will not survive."[69]

Pierre Henri-Teitgen was not impressed with Debré's uncritical reliance upon civic virtue and even went so far as to admonish him that "we have not come here to make a constitution in the clouds."[70] Publius would agree.

Governmental Stability

Before concluding our discussion of separation of powers, a brief comment on the question of governmental stability is in order. As the reader is by now well aware, the Gaullists saw governmental instability as an abiding flaw in French republicanism that they were determined to rectify. Raymond Janot underscored this point in the remarks we have just examined in which he put little faith in procedural safeguards to protect a government from votes of censure. Such safeguards were poor substitutes for authentic parliamentary support for the government.

Janot had little interest in trying to enshrine in a constitution that fine balance that makes it neither too hard nor too easy to overthrow a government. As a practical man, he believed that "rather than trying to solve insoluble problems, we should see to it that such problems do not arise." The way to do this is to give the government adequate powers to govern. "In the modern world, in the world of the twentieth century, governing is not simply a matter of applying legal texts to individual cases but rather, it is a question of making rules of law for a certain number of problems." Here Janot refers to the constitutional distinction between the domains of law and regulation which we examined in some detail in chapter four. His solution to the problem of governmental instability is to endow the government with the powers it will need. In practice, this means constitutionalizing a sphere of independent regulatory power. In Janot's words, "What is absolutely essential in this matter is not paper barriers but a demarcation of domains."[71] Thus, in the crucial matter of governmental stability, Janot relies upon separation of *functions* rather than upon Publius's separation of constitutional powers reinforced by an elaborate scheme of checks designed to maintain the correct constitutional balance. For Janot, the path to stability lies along the road of clearly delineated functions which preserve a certain autonomy for the regulatory powers of the government, even though the government is responsible to Parliament. This is Janot's plan of escape from what Publius called the "legislative vortex." Publius chose a different route. Instead of distributing functions between Parliament and a government responsible to it, Publius would give "to those who administer each department the necessary constitutional means and personal motives to resist encroachments of the others."

MICHEL DEBRÉ

Michel Debré, General de Gaulle's minister of justice, was the undisputed intellectual leader of the Gaullists who drafted the Constitution. He took the lead both in reducing the general's political insights to proper constitutional form and in guiding the working group *(groupe de travail)* of his fellow councillors of State who supplied the actual language of the texts submitted for the approval of such formal participants in the drafting process as the interministerial committee, the Advisory Committee, and the Council of State.

Like James Madison, Debré acknowledges his debt to the "fine Greek and Latin authors from Aristotle to Polybius and Cicero as well."[72] Like Madison masked as Publius, Debré's hardheaded realism prompts him to write without embarrassment about "the natural egoism of states" and "the great political competition which is the law of humanity."[73] Like Publius, he dreads governmental instability, which in France had become so acute "that it would be reprehensible not to react against it."[74] Publius had asserted that "the vigor of government is essential to the security of liberty" and Debré echoed this sentiment by singling out inadequate power as the great defect of French republicanism and by affirming the need for an authentic State—that is, one that can govern—in order to preserve liberty.[75] Finally, where Publius had celebrated ambition in statesmen, Debré applauds their love of power, deploring the fact that in the case of Fourth Republic ministers "power is no longer exercised for its own sake," but instead is sought merely for "the title it gives and the opportunities for one's own career."[76]

Clearly, Publius and Debré share a high-minded view of vigorous statesmanship. Nowhere is this clearer than in their mutual support for a strong president.[77] Interestingly, they both point to defects in the legislature to support their respective cases for a strong president, but no less interestingly, they do so for very different reasons. Debré wants a strong president because Parliament is so weak, but Publius wants the same lest Congress become too strong.

Debré's president is to be the "keystone of our parliamentary regime" precisely because "our historic quarrels" and "internal divisions have so much power over the political scene" that they deprive the government of the powers one would ordinarily expect in a parliamentary system.[78] That is, Parliament is too bitterly divided among perpetually warring factions to support a strong government. Hence the need for a powerful president independent of Parliament and buttressed with exceptional constitutional powers to enable him to fulfill his role as "the highest judge of the national interest."[79]

For Publius, the problem is just the opposite—Congress, with its popularly elected House of Representatives, will threaten the independence of the executive and the judiciary. The danger of legislative usurpation is thematic in *The Federalist*. The president must be fortified with a conditioned veto power and other constitutional prerogatives to empower him to resist the "legislative department" which "is everywhere extending the sphere of its activity, and drawing all power into its impetuous vortex."[80]

These differences between Debré and Publius are instructive. Following the statist tradition of France, Michel Debré, like de Gaulle himself, abhors the idea of incapacity for action. Publius, faithful to the Lockean origins of American politics, fears oppression by unchecked power. Both men seek a common refuge in a strong president.

The method of selecting the president in the two countries raises further significant comparisons between Publius and Michel Debré. As we saw in chapter three, the French Constitution of 1958 provided for an "electoral college" to choose the president, an arrangement that yielded in 1962 to an amendment calling for direct election by universal suffrage. The American electoral college of 1787 survives to this day in principle, but only in principle. Political practice has democratized the presidential electoral process and rendered the college a historical curiosity whose usefulness is subjected to quadrennial journalistic scrutiny. Thus, in both countries the original apparatus has undergone profound changes. Michel Debré's memoires show clearly that he did not mourn the passing of the pristine college. Since Publius wrote no memoires, we do not know what he might have thought about the electoral college's evolution toward practical extinction; but the text of *The Federalist* clearly indicates that he saw far more merit in his electoral college than Debré saw in the French model of 1958.

Let us look at Debré first. Writing in 1988, he has little to say about the defunct electoral college he had helped to create thirty years before. He presents it as though it were merely the result of a process of elimination which had excluded other plausible alternatives. He dismisses direct election by the people as simply not "desirable" in 1958, placing the word *souhaitable* in quotation marks without further explanation. Recalling our lengthy discussion of this matter in chapter three, we can readily understand why Debré declined to reopen this delicate question in 1988. If direct popular election was undesirable, election by Parliament was out of the question. The president's role as arbitrator required that he have more prestige and authority than selection by Parliament could possibly confer. Since he was charged with assuring the regularity of public institutions and entrusted with the right to dissolve Parliament and to summon the people to referenda, he could not be merely the favorite of Parliament. Therefore it was necessary that he be chosen by a special college independent of Parliament.[81]

Debré's jejune treatment of this matter in his memoires is probably due to the overwhelming success of the 1962 amendment that made popular election of the president a fixed star in the constellation of French politics. By 1988, the original electoral college was long forgotten and little lamented.

Unlike Debré, Publius was an enthusiastic defender of his electoral college. He notes with evident pleasure that even the Anti-Federalists find little fault with it. Publius's reasons for supporting the electoral college illuminate his vision of future presidential elections and serve to remind us of how far our present electoral process has departed from what he had in mind. For Publius, the great merit of the electoral college was its low-key, deliberative character—a quality at war with the circus atmosphere of contemporary presidential elections. Publius believed that the electoral college would rescue the selection of the president from the "heats and ferments" that might otherwise mar this important task, assigning it instead to a small number of men "most capable of analyzing the qualities adopted to the station [of the presidential office]." In sharp contrast to current electoral practice, the procedure envisioned by Publius would be entrusted to men "acting under circumstances favourable to deliberation and to a judicious combination of all the reasons and inducements, which were proper to govern their choice."[82]

To understand Publius's enthusiasm for the electoral college, one must recall the difficult struggle the founding fathers had in agreeing upon a suitable electoral mechanism for the president. As we saw in chapter three, the case for direct popular election made little headway. Election by Congress was the preferred method. Indeed, it may come as a surprise to contemporary Americans to learn that on four separate occasions the delegates voted to support congressional election of the president. Never satisfied with this decision, they continued to revisit it because they feared that a president chosen by Congress would not be sufficiently independent of that potentially oppressive body. Even James Madison—somewhat reluctantly it seems—acquiesced in congressional election of the president, but only with the very significant qualification that he could not be reelected. Madison believed that congressional election alone was not incompatible with an independent executive; but if that executive had to please Congress in order to be returned to office, his independence would be fatally compromised.[83]

Some delegates, dissatisfied with this compromise, urged that if the president must be selected by Congress, he should serve during good behavior. That would guarantee executive independence with a vengeance! Historian Forrest McDonald observes that the fact that four state delegations actually voted in favor of this radical proposal for a lifetime executive had a "chilling effect" on the delegates and led them to reexamine the entire question of presidential selection anew.[84]

Understandably, the men who had been through this stressful debate saw nothing but welcome relief in the electoral college. It avoided the problem of congressional selection of the president, which would have sacrificed the principle of re-eligibility on the altar of executive independence. It also avoided the unacceptable alternative of a lifetime executive whose independence would have been won only at the exorbitant price of rendering him unaccountable.

The fact that the central question in the debate over election and reelection of the president focused on his independence provides some insight into the framers' view of that office. During the Philadelphia debates and throughout the ratification process, Madison and his Federalist allies (including Publius) seemed to have had a more legalistic view of the presidency than we have today. As we saw in chapter three, they often referred to the president as a *magistrate*. I believe the reason for Madison's profound concern to preserve the independence of the president—even at the expense of re-eligibility—was primarily to safeguard an even-handed execution of the laws enacted by Congress. For Madison and his contemporaries, it was an article of republican faith, grounded in the principle of republican equality, that those who make the laws should be subject to them along with their fellow citizens. An impartial execution of law by an impartial magistrate would be an indispensable means towards this end.

All this contrasts markedly with Michel Debré's reasons for denying Parliament a role in electing the president. Debré's concerns were far more political than legal. Surely Debré, like all republicans everywhere, applauds the impartial execution of law; but this had nothing to do with his president who, it will be recalled, was no executive but rather an arbitrator with overarching responsibilities for the well-being of the State. Thus Debré's vision of the president of the Fifth Republic is something far more grand than Publius's impartial magistrate and, one might add, much closer to the way in which—for weal or woe—Americans think about *their* president today.

Our comparison of Michel Debré and Publius would be incomplete if we failed to reexamine that hearty perennial, the separation of powers. Here again we find the now familiar pattern of striking similarities alongside meaningful differences. Both Publius and Debré link separation of powers to political questions of the highest order. A wanton disregard of the principle will lead to "tyranny" for Publius and to "dictatorship" for Debré.[85] Despite the seriousness of the principle, however, both men acknowledge its vulnerability to exaggerated claims and excessively rigid interpretations of its meaning in practice. Hence, Debré sympathizes with the many authors who dismiss it as an "obsolete dogma" and Publius finds it at times a "trite topic."[86]

Both Publius and Debré take pains to apply the principle of separation of powers sensibly in order to avoid the rigidities they have observed elsewhere. Publius offers an extraordinarily relaxed interpretation when he says that the principle is violated only when "the *whole* power of one department is exercised by the same hands which possess the *whole* power of another department." (Publius's emphasis.) By "department," Publius means not the executive departments (state, commerce, agriculture, and so forth), but what we call "branches" today—legislative, executive, and judicial. Thus, Publius would find a violation of the principle of separation of powers only in the truly extraordinary—indeed fantastic—circumstances wherein Congress, for example, should take over *all* executive powers. Such a relaxed standard virtually defines out of existence the likelihood of violation of the principle in practice and leaves Publius ample room to justify the "blending of power" that figures so prominently in his constitution; for example, the Senate judges impeached officers, the president vetoes legislation, Congress makes rules for the army and navy, and so forth. Indeed, so broad is Publius's criterion that it might even reconcile the emergency powers of the French president under article 16 with the principle of separation of powers.

Michel Debré does not address the question of what it takes to violate the principle of separation of powers. His focus is on the innovative provision in the Constitution of the Fifth Republic guaranteeing that the president be chosen independently of Parliament. Hence, the new Constitution goes beyond a mere separation of functions and provides different *sources* of power for separate institutions. In this respect, the principle of separation of powers expressed in the Constitution of the Fifth Republic resembles the American Constitution. The similarity is quite limited, however, if one recalls that the president of the Republic is not an executive officer, according to the Gaullist orthodoxy of 1958. Thus, the independent *sources* of presidential and parliamentary power serve to separate the legislature from the arbitrator but not from the executive. The prime minister and his government possess the executive power, a hybrid of sorts. The president is the source of executive power because he appoints the prime minister, but only Parliament can remove him from office. The accountability of the executive to Parliament is, of course, a classic principle of the parliamentary regime and far removed from American-style separation of powers.

It is perhaps significant that in explaining to the Council of State how the proposed constitution implements the principle of separation of powers, Debré never says *which* powers will be kept separate. Indeed, having used the expression "separation of powers" at the outset of his analysis, he concludes by speaking of the "separation of authorities."[87]

As we know, this arrangement was far more complicated in theory than in practice. Periods of cohabitation aside, the president of the Republic has de facto been the chief executive officer of the Fifth Republic throughout its thirty-five-year history. Strengthened by the direct universal suffrage amendment of 1962, the French president is at least as independent of Parliament as the American president is of Congress.

To conclude our discussion of Michel Debré on separation of powers, we should note the curious fact that in the very midst of discussing this topic he observes that separation of powers can never be absolute because "in fact and in law power is 'one'" *(le pouvoir est "un")*.[88] Publius would, of course, agree that the separation of powers is not absolute, but he would surely resist the corollary that power is "one." This was not an offhand or unguarded comment by Debré. He repeats it emphatically in the peroration of his address to the Council of State where he uses the expression "one power" three times in the same paragraph.[89]

Although this forceful language on the unity of power is surprising in view of Debré's remarks on separation of powers, it serves to underscore the fundamental differences between French and American understandings of this cardinal principle. Unified power has played an enormous role in French political history—whether it be an absolute monarch, a sovereign Parliament, or a centralized administrative State. Diversified power has done no less for the United States—e.g., judicial review, federalism, and town meetings. Publius and Debré took separation of powers seriously but they did so as an American and a Frenchman, respectively. In France power is one; in America it is many.

Throughout this section I have compared and contrasted Publius and Michel Debré over a broad range of issues. I shall close this chapter with what I consider to be the most striking difference between them. It appears in Debré's account of how he explained to the general's fiercest partisans why their leader, upon assuming the position as head of government in May 1958, proved so conciliatory toward the leading politicians of the Fourth Republic, whom ardent Gaullists might be forgiven for thinking the general simply despised:

> I reassured them and especially I explained to them that the essential point of our struggle was to restore General de Gaulle to France. Indeed, this had already taken place. Henceforth, we should make every effort that the French people rediscover themselves in him and reassemble around him who is at once France and the State.[90]

Such a statement would be unthinkable in *The Federalist Papers*. Despite the towering presence of George Washington at the time of the American founding, Publius would never yield to Debré's mysticism that identifies the person of General de Gaulle with the nation and the State. Such a statement is all the more remarkable in that it comes from so usually a clear-headed thinker as Michel Debré. It stands as a lasting monument to the overwhelming importance of General de Gaulle at the founding of the Fifth Republic. Debré expresses a sentiment that is absolutely incomprehensible to Americans—and may it ever be so.

7

Administrative Law and Normative Dialogue

Thus the intervention of the courts in administrative matters, though it often told against the good conduct of public business, served sometimes as a safeguard of the freedom of the nation; it was a great mischief, but limited a still greater mischief.

— ALEXIS DE TOCQUEVILLE

In examining the foundings of the French and American republics, our attention has focused perforce on the past. Before concluding our work in the next (and final) chapter, however, it is fitting to say a word about the future. The present chapter says that word. It is a word about launching a normative dialogue among students, professors, and practitioners of public administration in France and the United States. I say *normative* dialogue because of the remarkable interest one currently finds in both countries in questions of professional standards and ethics.[1]

In the United States the normative dialogue often centers on constitutional principles, for several reasons: (1) the American Constitution expresses some of the most profound moral values of the nation; (2) federal public servants take an oath to uphold the Constitution and thereby explicitly affirm its moral relevance; and (3) the salience of concurring and dissenting opinions in major Supreme Court interpretations of the Constitution presents a structured argument among the justices on important questions of societal norms. Only the first of these American characteristics applies to France as well. French public servants take no oaths and French judges issue neither concurring nor dissenting opinions; but in France, as in the United States, constitutional decisions often touch upon moral values deeply rooted in the nation's political culture—most notably questions of individual rights. Consequently, the Supreme Court has been aptly called America's "Republican schoolmaster" and the Council of State no less aptly described as "not only the judge of the administration but also its conscience."[2]

As we saw in chapter five, constitutional jurisprudence in France has relied heavily on French administrative law. In the United States, as in France, there is considerable overlap between administrative and constitutional law; but the causal relationships flow in opposite directions in the two countries. American constitutional law has shaped American administrative law, notably through the principle of separation of powers and the due process clauses of the Fifth and Fourteenth Amendments, whereas in France constitutional law has borrowed some of its most important principles from the well-established and highly regarded administrative jurisprudence of the Council of State. For the purpose of this chapter, however, the mere *fact* of the extensive overlap between the spheres of administrative and constitutional law in both countries is more important than the direction of the causal nexus. The de facto overlap integrates fundamental regime values into administrative practice in the two countries and thereby provides a solid foundation for a Franco-American dialogue on fundamental norms in public administration.

There is nothing original about turning to law to provide the foundation for normative discourse. In so doing, we follow a venerable western tradition that has long recognized the formidable capacity of law to serve as a moral teacher. Both the ethical teaching of classical antiquity and the religious doctrine of the New Testament support the pedagogical function of law. Just before his death, Socrates entered into a dramatic dialogue with the laws of the city to provide moral justification for his actions, and St. Paul compared the Old Law to a teacher preparing the chosen people for the new revelation he preached.[3]

To be sure, the ensuing constitutional-administrative dialogue pales into insignificance at the mere mention of its illustrious socratic and pauline predecessors, but it has the advantage of borrowing from a great tradition that provides the moral focus for the task at hand. The discussion that follows is innocent of any technical advice for French or American lawyers planning to practice their profession abroad. Such matters are far beyond both my competence and my interests. Rather, my purpose is to examine certain principles of constitutional and administrative law in the hope that they will yield ideas that might provide the basis for a normative dialogue between French and American administrators.

First, we shall examine institutional norms and then individual rights.

INSTITUTIONAL NORMS

Actes de gouvernement and Political Questions

Jurists in both France and the United States have long recognized that not all government decisions are amenable to review by an independent judiciary. In the United States, this realization led to the development of what has come to be known as the "political questions" doctrine.[4] In France, the same realization has created a special legal category called "acts of government" *(actes de gouvernement).*[5] Military and diplomatic decisions are the most likely candidates for exemption from judicial review but administrative action in other domains have qualified as well. Prudence counsels caution in expanding the scope of such exemptions because too many decisions escaping judicial review could undermine the rule of law itself.

In 1875, the Council of State rendered an extremely important decision that shaped the subsequent development of the acts of government doctrine. The case, entitled *Prince Napoléon,* involved a cousin of Napoléon III, whom the emperor had appointed a general in 1853. In 1873 a military roster was published for the first time since the collapse of the Second Empire during the Franco-Prussian War of 1870. Prince Napoléon's name was conspicuous by its absence. The prince asked the minister of war, an officer of the fledgling Third Republic, whether the omission was involuntary or deliberate. The minister replied that it was most emphatically deliberate. The prince owed his rank not to the ordinary course of military promotions regulated by law but to "the particular circumstances of a political order which no longer exists today"—that is, to the personal favor of the former emperor.

The prince appealed this decision to the Council of State. The minister of war invoked the acts of government doctrine to challenge the council's jurisdiction over the appeal. Relying on previous Council of State rulings, the minister stressed the political character of the matter at hand, grounded as it most certainly was in the profoundly political change from an imperial to a republican regime.

As we saw in chapter five, the Council of State relies heavily upon its "representative of the government" *(commissaire du gouvernement)* in reaching its decisions. The task of this ill-named officer, it will be recalled, is to recommend legal decisions to the Council of State in his "report" *(conclusion).* He is ill-named because he does not represent the government at all and is as likely to recommend against the government as for it. Some of these *commissaires* or representatives have achieved great renown in French legal history as men who have profoundly influenced the jurisprudence of the Council of State. Among them is Monsieur David, the representative of the government in Prince Napoléon's case. In his report, David recommended that the Council of State reject the effort of the minister of war to escape review of his decision on the grounds of its political character. Stressing the exceptional character of acts of government, David acknowledged that they were political, but insisted that not all politically motivated acts should be exempt from judicial review. In his words: "Although the acts characterized in the language of the law as acts of government are discretionary by their very nature, the sphere to which the characterization pertains cannot be extended arbitrarily at the pleasure of those who govern."[6] The thrust of David's argument was that the government should not be permitted to escape judicial review simply by calling a particular decision "political"—no matter how correctly it might be so called. The Council of State should decide which political decisions were of such a nature as to qualify for exemption from judicial review. In deciding Prince Napoléon's case, the Council of State relied implicitly on David's theory, thereby prompting a contemporary commentary to assert: "This decision marks an extremely important step in the extension of the control of administrative acts by the Council of State."[7]

So important has it become that the Council of State has specifically cited the political character of a government decision as the primary reason for *annulling* it. This took place in the famous *Barel* case of 1954 in which the Council of State forbade the government from denying a Communist the right to compete in the examination for admission to the prestigious National School of Administration. The decision to punish the candidate for his political beliefs was obviously political and for this very reason the Council of State would not allow it.[8] Thus the council came full circle from its pre-1875 jurisprudence which would have exempted all politically motivated decisions from review. By 1954, the council was willing to overturn an administrative decision precisely because it was political.

As a result of *Prince Napoléon* and its progeny, the scope of the acts of government doctrine has been so narrowed that today it applies only to two types of cases: (1) those involving the relationship between the government and Parliament, and (2) those involving the relationship between the government and foreign nations or international organizations.[9]

As for the prince himself, his appeal came to an unhappy end despite the council's rejection of the argument proffered by the minister of war. Although the council dismissed the minister's sweeping interpretation of the acts of government doctrine, it nevertheless upheld his decision to remove the prince from the list of generals. The Council of State reasoned that the imperial decree to which the prince owed his military rank was based on the understanding that the emperor had full authority over members of the imperial family and that therefore the prince had been under the emperor's control as long as the empire existed. The collapse of the empire put an end to this personal relationship of subordination. The prince cannot claim in its stead the status of a regular army officer whose position is grounded in law as opposed to the pleasure of a former emperor.

In disposing of the case in this manner, the Council of State handed the government a pyrrhic victory. The position of its minister of war was upheld but only at the price of surrendering its autonomy from judicial review over all politically motivated decisions. Thereafter, the Council of State would determine which political decisions would qualify as acts of government. The council's action recalls Chief Justice Marshall's strategy in *Marbury v. Madison* whereby he gave President Jefferson the petty triumph of keeping a low-level Federalist functionary out of office, while affirming the power of a Federalist Supreme Court to declare unconstitutional acts passed by a Congress dominated by Jeffersonian Republicans.[10]

Marbury v. Madison is a good starting point to examine the American "political questions" doctrine, which strongly resembles the French *actes de gouvernment*. In *Marbury,* Chief Justice Marshall sowed the seeds of the political questions doctrine by observing that "questions in their nature political" could never be raised "in this court."[11] It remained, however, for Marshall's successor, Roger B. Taney, to articulate the doctrine more fully, which he did in the unusual case of *Luther v. Borden* (1849).[12] Luther brought a trespass suit against Borden, a Rhode Island militiaman, who had searched Luther's home during a period of considerable unrest in that state in the early 1840s. So serious was the unrest that disaffected Rhode Islanders, led by Thomas Dorr, assembled in an extralegal convention and drafted a constitution to replace a royal charter of 1663 that continued to serve as a constitution for the state of Rhode Island. They proceeded to elect officers under the new constitution, which the government in place under the charter rejected as illegitimate. The struggle by the new government to wrest control of the state from the charter government came to be known as Dorr's Rebellion. The charter government responded by declaring martial law. Under these tense circumstances, militiaman Borden searched the home of Luther, a Dorrite supporter, without observing the customary legal niceties.

The principal cause of Dorr's unhappiness and that of his followers was the extremely restricted suffrage under the charter government. After suppressing Dorr's Rebellion, the charter government won ratification for a new constitution that somewhat ameliorated the injustices of the charter but fell far short of the reforms envisioned by the populist Dorrites. Dissatisfied, the erstwhile rebels saw in Luther's trespass suit a vehicle to enlist the federal judiciary on their side. Luther's suit had failed in a Rhode Island court because the jury accepted militiaman Borden's defense that he was simply carrying out lawful orders during the period of civil unrest. Luther sought review of this decision in a federal court, citing the fourth section of the fourth article of the Constitution of the United States, which provides: "The United States shall guarantee to every state in this Union a Republican Form of Government." Using Luther's trespass suit as a point of entry into the federal judicial system, the Dorrites argued that the suffrage in Rhode Island was so restricted that the state's government was not republican and that therefore the United States had to do something about it—such as recognizing Dorr's government as the legitimate government of the state.

In framing the issue in this way, the Dorrites pushed the technicalities of trespass law into the wings and brought weighty questions of federalism to center stage.

The "Guarantee Clause" states that the *United States* shall guarantee a republican form of government in every state without specifying which of the three great branches of government has this duty. Chief Justice Taney held that this general power could not be exercised by the courts because "[m]uch of the argument on the part of the plaintiff turned upon rights and political questions" which were not appropriate for judicial resolution. Political questions of this sort are best left to Congress and the president.

Chief Justice Taney refused to offer a judicial interpretation of the meaning of a "Republican form of Government." Deferring to Congress, he maintained that when that body permits the representatives and senators of a state to take their seats, "the authority of the [state] government under which they are appointed, as well as its republican character, is recognized by the proper constitutional authority." Thus, for Taney, there are no judicially cognizable standards for judging the republican character of a state's government. As far as the courts are concerned, republicanism is a purely formal concept void of substantive content. If Congress seats the senators and representatives of a given state, it ipso facto affirms the state's republican character.

In emptying the rich concept of republicanism of all substantive content, Taney turned his back on the impressive debate at the time of the founding on the nature of a republican regime—a debate we examined in some detail in chapter four. Taney's caution will surely disappoint those who look to the Supreme Court for guidance and perhaps even for inspiration in settling great controversies. Despite its sterile formalism, Taney's "political questions" doctrine has the advantage of giving the court a graceful exit from intractable questions it might not be able to resolve without considerable embarrassment to itself and considerable harm to the nation as a whole.

The development of the French doctrine of "acts of government" after *Prince Napoléon* has been aptly described as creating simply a "list" rather than a "general definition."[13] That is, the doctrine has not been applied in a rigorously consistent manner but rather on an ad hoc basis. The same is true of the American political questions doctrine. Like its French counterpart, the American doctrine by no means declares *all* politically motivated decisions off-limits to the federal judiciary. Such an interpretation would leave the federal courts with precious little to do. For the most part, the doctrine has been applied in the areas of military and foreign policy. Prior to 1962, it had also served to extricate the court from the "political thicket" of trying to resolve charges that congressional and state legislative districts were "malapportioned," that is, that some legislators represented far more people than others and that the suffrage of constituents in heavily populated districts was thereby diluted.

In 1962, however, the Supreme Court reversed course and marched boldly into the thicket with the dauntless Justice Brennan leading the charge. Because of the precedent of *Luther v. Borden,* Brennan could not use the "Guarantee Clause" to address the apportionment questions. Instead, he relied on the equal protection clause of the Fourteenth Amendment, which did not exist at the time of *Luther v. Borden.* It will be recalled that the first section of the Fourteenth Amendment forbids any state from denying "to any person within its jurisdiction the equal protection of the laws." In relying on this clause that protects individual persons, Brennan transformed the question of equal representation in the legislature. At the time of the founding, such a question would have been part of the broader question of the structure of republican government. Brennan's reliance on the equal protection clause meant that equal representation was now a question of individual rights and therefore could be deftly distinguished from the structure-of-government question which Taney had avoided as "political" in 1849.

Anticipating criticism for entering a domain traditionally off-limits to the courts, Justice Brennan articulated the most comprehensive statement on the political questions doctrine ever announced by a Supreme Court justice:

> Prominent on the surface of any case held to involve a political question is found a textually demonstrable constitutional commitment of the issue to a coordinate political department; or a lack of judicially discoverable and manageable standards for resolving it; or the impossibility of deciding without an initial policy determination of a kind clearly for nonjudicial discretion; or the impossibility of a court's undertaking independent resolution without expressing lack of the respect due coordinate branches of government; or an unusual need for unquestioning adherence to a political decision already made; or the potentiality of embarrassment from multifarious pronouncements by various departments on one question.[14]

Despite Brennan's efforts to clarify the meaning of political questions, the Court has continued to apply the doctrine, now graced with Brennan's gloss, in a somewhat haphazard way.[15] As might be expected, military and foreign affairs continue to provide the most fertile field for the political questions doctrine.[16] More importantly, however, in applying the political questions doctrine, the Supreme Court, like the Council of State in identifying acts of government, determines the scope of its own restraint.

Let us close our discussion of acts of government and political questions with three brief points of comparison. First, there is the curious French practice of treating acts of government, which are, of course, administrative acts (usually a decree of some sort), as though they were laws. The administrative judge does this because the Council of State has no jurisdiction over laws.[17] The Supreme Court of the United States, however, proclaims a wide range of governmental activities "political questions" with no need to obfuscate their nature to fit a prejacent legal theory. I have found no explanation in French legal literature as to why French jurists use this legal fiction, but I suspect it is to preserve intact the principle that *all* administrative acts are subject to review by the administrative courts.[18] To reconcile this principle with the doctrine of *actes de gouvernement,* it would be expedient to treat these administrative acts as though they were laws and therefore *necessarily* beyond the reach of the administrative judge.

Second, if one pulls back the veil of legal fiction and regards acts of government as the administrative acts they really are, one cannot ignore the anomaly that all *laws* can be subjected to review by the Constitutional Council before going into effect, but some administrative acts (*actes de gouvernement),* although legally inferior to laws, enjoy immunity from judicial review.[19]

Third, there is an interesting contrast in the way French and American jurists address the problem created by doctrines that exempt some official acts from judicial review. Any jurist would find such an exemption unsettling because it compromises—however modestly—the principle of the rule of law. French jurists tend to see the problem precisely in these terms and therefore are pleased to report that the doctrine of acts of government has been marginalized so as to apply to only a rather narrow range of governmental activities. American jurists share the same concern, but are far more likely to stress the *advantages* of the political questions doctrine for the federal judiciary itself. Rather than focus on the danger that judges might neglect their proper responsibilities and thereby endanger the rule of law, American jurists are more likely to celebrate the political questions doctrine as a prudent expedient empowering courts to extricate themselves from "no-win" situations.

This line of argument is consistent with the genius of *Federalist* 51 wherein American statesmen (including judges) are urged to integrate personal interest and constitutional powers. The constitutional power of avoiding an unwelcome issue by calling it political, which the judges have conferred upon themselves, certainly reinforces their personal interest in avoiding decisions all too likely to prove personally, professionally, and politically embarrassing. At a deeper level, the doctrine, if applied wisely and without cowardice, can safeguard the legitimacy of the courts by taking them out of situations in which they do not belong.

Service Public and State Action

Jurisdictional questions are always of interest to public administrators because in the answers to such questions they discover whose rules they must follow and to whom they must answer. In France, the most interesting jurisdictional disputes arise from the absence of "one supreme court." The Council of State has the final word in deciding questions of administrative law, whereas the Court of Cassation is the supreme judicial authority in civil and criminal matters. The concrete, practical application of this neat principle has been no simple matter.

In the United States, there is "one supreme court" whose supremacy over the lower courts of the national government is as real in practice as it is clear in constitutional theory. Because of American federalism, however, there are fifty additional supreme courts—one in each of the states, although not all of them use the word *supreme* to designate their highest courts. Federalism has, of course, provided a fertile field for jurisdictional conflicts for over two centuries, with no end in sight. The sources of the conflicts are many and varied, but among the most interesting is the curious and problematic doctrine of "state action," whereby the Supreme Court has tried to mark the boundaries of federal intervention in protecting individual rights under the Fourteenth Amendment.[20] Let us look first at the French jurisdictional problem and then at its American counterpart.

The jurisdictional question of the administrative courts, like so many other questions in French politics, can be traced to the time of the Revolution. The revolutionaries gave vent to their hostility toward the courts of the *ancien régime* by passing a series of laws from 16–24 August of 1790 severely restricting the authority of the ordinary courts. So extreme were these measures that they even forbade the judges from interpreting the laws! If a judge found a law unclear, he was not to interpret it himself, but was to seek guidance from the legislature as to its meaning. His task was simply to apply the law, not to interpret it. In such a climate, it was no surprise that the legislature "forbade the judicial tribunals from hindering or from delaying the application and the execution of law."[21] In effect, this precluded any judicial review of administrative action. To leave no doubt of their intentions, the legislators of 1790 provided under pain of prosecution for abuse of authority that "the judges may not disturb in any way whatsoever the activities of the administrative corps nor summon the administrators to appear before them in connection with their official duties."[22]

This text has never been repealed and therefore, technically, is still good law today. Nevertheless, for well over a century French administrative agencies have been called upon to defend themselves before judges as often, if not more often, than comparable institutions in any other country. How can this be? The answer lies in the development of the institutions of administrative law whereby French administrators must answer to *administrative* judges and not to the ordinary judges targeted in the laws of 1790.

This new administrative jurisdiction developed only gradually, largely under the guidance of the Council of State. Several theories were put forward to justify and to define the scope of the newly emerging administrative jurisdiction. For example, the theory of "the State as debtor" *(l'Etat debiteur)* maintained that the ordinary courts could not require the State to pay a sum of money regardless of the nature of the debt. This did not mean that the State could disregard its just debts, but that a jurisdiction other than the ordinary courts was necessary to impose this obligation. The theory rested on the shaky foundation of a decree to the effect that the customary ways of enforcing legal obligations between individual citizens in the ordinary courts could not be applied against the State.

Another theory drew a distinction between the State's "acts of authority" *(actes d'autorité)* and its "acts of management" *(actes de gestion),* with the ordinary courts salvaging some jurisdiction over the latter but not the former. A third theory distinguished public from private management *(gestion publique* and *gestion privée)* to call attention to the fact that the State sometimes conducts its business in the same way private associations conduct theirs. The State is then involved in private management and such acts can be reviewed by an ordinary court.

If these various legal theories were confused and incoherent, it was because the French jurists of the post–Revolutionary era were struggling with a perplexing problem that at once characterizes and bedevils the modern administrative state. On the one hand, there is need for considerable autonomy from judicial control if a powerful, centralized, interventionist State is to carry out its far-flung activities. On the other hand, there is need for the rule of law, embodied in an independent judiciary, to check the all too human tendency to abuse power—however necessary and advantageous it might be.

Americans would wait a century before they faced similar issues with similarly incoherent results. By mid-twentieth century, American courts had come to rely on a distinction between "proprietary" and "governmental" functions to determine when public agencies and their officers could be sued for their torts. Like the earlier French distinctions between acts of authority and acts of management or between public and private management, the American distinction tried to express the difference between official characteristics of the state (governmental) and actions taken by the state in its capacity as a property owner (proprietary). The state, like any property holder, could be sued by those harmed on its land or in its buildings—for example, by a citizen injured by falling down the icy steps of a municipal building. It could not be sued when it was acting in its distinctively governmental role— for example, by a policeman injured in carrying out his duties.

Unfortunately, the proprietary-governmental distinction proved unworkable in practice. Streets, sidewalks, and bridges might favor the proprietary side of the distinction and police departments the governmental side, but what about municipal parks, swimming pools, recreation centers, and airports? Clearly, they would seem to have both governmental and proprietary aspects, thereby leading commentators to speak of "mixed" functions, which undermined the usefulness of the proprietary-governmental distinction. By mid-century, the Supreme Court had begun to complain about the "quagmire" in this legal area, and Kenneth C. Davis, a prominent commentator on administrative law, after finding a state with both "governmental and proprietary manholes," mused that "surely some state must have mixed manholes."[23]

Soon courts abandoned the proprietary-governmental distinction in favor of a distinction between ministerial acts, which are actionable, and discretionary acts, which are not.[24] This distinction, though an improvement on its predecessor, was far from satisfactory because one still searches in vain for a bright line to divide the two functions. The same can be said for yet another distinction between official *planning* activities, for which the government cannot be sued, and *operational* activities, for which it can.[25] None of these distinctions is entirely satisfactory because the problem they address is intractable. Justice Jackson put it best in his characteristically pithy way when he wrote that it "is not a tort for government to govern."[26] This lapidary formula goes to the heart of the problem. The admirable effort to render a government accountable for its actions must not render that same government incapable of action. It has proved extremely difficult, however, to reduce this commonsense proposition to a rule of law.

To return to France, we have seen that by mid-nineteenth century, French jurists had interpreted the absolute prohibition in the Revolutionary-era statute against judicial interference with governmental activity in such a way as to permit some such interference without successfully identifying a principle to explain just how much is enough. All this changed in 1873 because of an extremely important decision rendered by the Tribunal of Conflicts, a body established the previous year to resolve jurisdictional disputes between the Court of Cassation and the Council of State.[27] The case involved a child, Agnès Blanco, who was injured by a wagon driven by a worker at a state-owned tobacco factory. The road where the accident occurred lay between different parts of the factory. The child's father brought suit for damages against the State in an ordinary court. The tribunal of Conflicts was called upon to determine the appropriate jurisdiction for the case. The representative of the government, M. David, whom we met earlier in this chapter, advised the Tribunal that the suit was administrative in character and therefore did not belong in the ordinary courts. The tribunal followed his advice.

There was nothing remarkable about the outcome of the case. The "State-as-debtor" theory mentioned above would have supported the same result. What was remarkable was that David did *not* rely upon this familiar if somewhat questionable theory, but broke new ground in basing his position on the fact that injury resulted from a "public service" *(service public)*. Following David's lead, the Tribunal of Conflicts held that such cases cannot be governed by the civil code as though one individual citizen were suing another. Because the special needs of the public service and of the State itself are involved when public employees cause harm, only an administrative jurisdiction can settle the claims of the injured party.[28]

This conclusion might strike an American reader as unwarranted because American courts have a broad range of means at their disposal to fashion appropriate remedies that would take into consideration the legitimate needs of the state. French courts, however, have a narrower range of powers available to them. If the issue is framed, as David would have it, that the only choice was between an ordinary court applying the civil code that governs relations between individuals, and a special administrative jurisdiction that can take cognizance of the needs of the State, the latter must prevail. And so it did.

Many French commentators have described *Blanco* as effecting "a jurisprudential revolution,"[29] while others have called it nothing less than the "cornerstone" of French administrative law. The fact that it appears first in the collection of administrative law decisions most widely used in French law schools today testifies eloquently to its lasting importance.[30]

Curiously, it took French jurists nearly three decades to recognize the overwhelming importance of *Blanco* and even then the recognition came more from academic commentaries and treatises than from real-world decisions. This may be due simply to the major role played by academicians in the development of French law or perhaps it is because academicians were more likely than busy practitioners to see in *Blanco*'s "public service" standard a principled norm to differentiate an administrative jurisdiction from that of the ordinary courts. In any event, "public service" with its classic definition as "any activity of a public authority aimed at satisfying a public need"[31] became and remains the fundamental principle for defining the proper sphere of administrative courts in France.[32]

Although widely hailed as a marked improvement over the State-as-debtor notion and other disappointing formulae for determining jurisdiction, the "public service" standard was not without ambiguities of its own. For example, it was not clear whether the term applied only to the State, that is, to the central government, or if it included an activity undertaken by a department as a local jurisdiction inferior to the State. This important question came before the Council of State in 1903 in what Vedel and Delvolvé describe as a "colorful" case involving a decision by the department of Saône-et-Loire to undertake a snake eradication campaign. The department promised to pay one-fourth of a franc for every snake a person might kill. Although some officials suspected the snake hunters of inflating their claims, there was no doubt that the snake hunt was a grand success. So successful was it that the department could not afford to pay the promised bounty. M. Terrier, a disappointed hunter, complained to the Council of State of the department's failure to pay him for the snakes he had killed. The Council of State, ruling that the case fell under its jurisdiction, took the important step of including departmental activities within the concept of "public service" and thereby "brought about the unification of juridical questions concerning local governments with those concerning the State."[33] From this case it also became clear that to undertake a public service, a governmental authority need not create a corps of officers to perform the task. The department of Saône-et-Loire was engaged in a "public service" even though it relied upon ordinary citizens to execute the snake eradication policy. Both aspects of the decision expanded the notion of public service, thereby expanding pari passu the jurisdiction of the Council of State.

The Council of State also considerably expanded its jurisdiction by deciding in 1936 that the notion of "public service" could include activities carried on by organizations that were technically private associations. The case involved a complaint from employees of one of France's many social security *caisses,* that is, provident societies, which "are the basic local organizations administering the social-insurance system."[34] These organizations were created toward the end of the last century and are of enormous importance in France today because of their crucial role in administering the national health care system. Because of their original connection with labor unions and charitable organizations, they have always been considered private associations and regulated by private law.

In 1936, Parliament passed a law restricting the number of jobs that could be held by a person employed by a "public service." A governmental decree taken pursuant to this statute applied the restriction to the employees of the provident societies. The employees argued that the private status of their organizations put them beyond the reach of a law aimed only at those employed in a public service.[35] The Council of State rejected this argument, finding that notwithstanding the provident societies' legal status as private, their extensive social welfare responsibilities were so inextricably woven into the fabric of State activities that they fell within the concept of a public service and, not incidentally, under the jurisdiction of the administrative courts. This decision pointed the way to enabling the Council of State to bring a wide range of ostensibly private activities under its jurisdiction—for example, associations of professional athletes and the governing board of the medical profession.[36]

Despite these dramatic conquests for the administrative courts, one should not read the history of French administrative law as an uninterrupted string of jurisdictional victories over the ordinary courts. There have been notable setbacks along the way.[37] For example, an institution will be considered as performing a "public service" only if it has "recourse to methods and prerogatives which would be excluded in relations between private parties." Examples of such methods include operating "the service concerned as a monopoly" or financing "it by compulsory contributions from those it benefits."[38] The purpose of this standard is to preserve the jurisdiction of the ordinary courts over conventional commercial transactions even if a public authority carries them out.

An interesting illustration of this principle can be found in a 1921 decision by the Tribunal of Conflicts in a case commonly called the *Bac d'Eloka* for a ferry boat of that name operated by the government of the Ivory Coast, at that time a French colony.[39] On the night of 5 September 1920, the boat foundered and the owner of an automobile it had been carrying brought an action for damages against the colony in a civil court. The lieutenant-governor of the colony, which was clearly a public authority, maintained that colonial ownership of the boat precluded a civil court from hearing the case. The Tribunal of Conflicts disagreed, holding that "the Ivory Coast colony runs a transportation service in the same way as an ordinary industrial enterprise" and that, consequently, "it pertains only to the judicial authority [i.e., the ordinary courts] to assume jurisdiction over the question of damages resulting from the accident in question."[40]

The tribunal's reasoning recalls the earlier (pre-*Blanco*) distinction between acts of authority and acts of management or what American law would once have called the distinction between proprietary and governmental functions. As we observed above, these distinctions are hard to apply in practice. For example, after *Bac d'Eloka,* the Tribunal of Conflicts assigned to the ordinary courts the case of a boy "injured while playing games at a holiday camp run by the government for the benefit of workpeople in certain state-owned factories and their families." And yet the same tribunal in the same year awarded the administrative courts jurisdiction over a case involving "a syndicate of private firms employed by the administration to undertake schemes of redevelopment in slum areas."[41] Even more bewildering

is the fact that litigation concerning state-owned forests is assigned to the ordinary courts whereas challenges to fire-fighting services in those forests are
heard by the administrative courts.[42]

Difficult as the practical application of the *Bac d'Eloka* principle might
be, the case indicates the remarkable flexibility of the "public service" concept, especially when it is juxtaposed to the ruling in the case brought by the
disgruntled employees of the provident society. Although the provident societies involved in the litigation were private organizations, they were found to
perform a public service. Although the Ivory Coast colonial government
was clearly a public authority, its venture into the transportation industry
was found not to be a public service. Such decisions surely lead juridical for-
malists to despair, but they have the merit of trying to determine the appropriate jurisdiction by the practical consequences of an activity rather than
simply by the legal status of those who perform it.

As noted at the beginning of this section, the most interesting jurisdictional
questions in the United States follow the great fault line of federalism which
divides those questions amenable to definitive solutions in state courts from
those open to federal intervention.[43] The effort to sort out these classic questions has been massive and abiding; indeed, it has shaped the contour of
American constitutional history. Here we shall examine one small aspect of
the jurisdictional consequences of federalism—the judiciary's use of "state
action" to promote racial justice in the decade between the 1954 decision
Brown v. Board of Education and the Civil Rights Act of 1964. The *Brown*
decision took the dramatic step of declaring unconstitutional the practice in
many southern and border states of either requiring or permitting separate
schools for black and white children. The Supreme Court's boldness in
Brown was tempered by its subsequent holding that school desegregation
need not take place at once but only with "all deliberate speed."[44] As the
process of desegregating the public schools unfolded slowly (and by no
means surely), civil rights proponents expanded their agenda to include the
desegregation of public beaches, golf courses, libraries, swimming pools,
and so forth. Since *Brown* had dealt only with children in public schools, it
was technically irrelevant to the claims of, say, a thirty-five-year-old black
man who wanted to play golf on a municipal course reserved for whites
alone. Indeed, the reasoning of *Brown* had relied heavily on the adverse affect of racial segregation on the educational development of vulnerable children. It therefore seemed an unlikely support for adults complaining of exclusion because of their race from state-sponsored activities unrelated to
education.

The overwhelming moral force of the attacks on racial segregation,
however, soon brushed aside the legal technicalities of *Brown* and the federal

courts gradually moved toward a constitutional principle that would prohibit virtually every form of racial segregation sponsored by state or local
governments.[45]

The constitutional text supporting these dramatic changes in American
life was the famous "equal protection" clause, which provides that "no State
shall . . . deny to any person within its jurisdiction the equal protection of
the laws." Prior to 1954, the federal courts had found that this clause permitted "separate but equal" treatment of the races, but all this changed after
Brown rejected this standard for public schools and subsequent decisions extended the moral force of *Brown*—if not its precise legal reasoning—to other
activities sponsored by the states themselves or by local governments, which
are the creatures of the states. Hence, there emerged a new constitutional
standard that promised to prohibit virtually all forms of state-based segregation.

Unfortunately for jurists, the unruly nature of American politics does
not always follow their tidy conceptual categories. The moral force of the
protest against all forms of racial segregation could not be contained within
the banks of the constitutional concept of state action. To the black man
smarting from the sting of injustice, what difference did it make if a sheriff's
deputy told him his children cannot use the municipal pool of his choice or
if a hotel clerk told him his race makes him an unwelcome guest? The jurist
sees a profound constitutional difference between these two situations because the deputy sheriff represents the state and the hotel clerk does not.
Civil rights activists, having wearied of such legalisms, soon launched a
campaign to end segregation in such public accommodations as hotels, motels, restaurants, theaters, and amusement parks that were *privately* owned
and therefore, according to the state action doctrine, beyond the reach of the
Fourteenth Amendment's prohibition against states' denying anyone the
equal protection of the law.[46]

This was the background of the "state action" problem, a problem that
was as much political as legal. Throughout the 1950s and the early 1960s,
most state governments in the South—including the state courts—were hostile to the civil rights movement, whereas the federal government tended to
be sympathetic. If a particular form of racial discrimination could be linked
to "state action," the Fourteenth Amendment would come into play and the
federal courts would then review what the state had done—usually to the advantage of those protesting the discrimination. If, however, no state action
were involved, as in the case of a restaurateur refusing to seat black diners, it
would seem that the federal courts could do nothing.

Within this political and legal framework, there arose in 1961 the interesting case of *Burton v. Wilmington Parking Authority*,[47] which, like the *Bac
d'Eloka* case, examined the legal consequences of a close relationship be-

tween public and private activities. Burton, a black man, was refused service in a privately owned restaurant located in a building belonging to the Municipal Parking Authority of Wilmington, Delaware. The question before the Supreme Court was whether the fact that the privately owned restaurant leased its space from the city was sufficient to make the restaurateur's discrimination a form of state action. In a 6 to 3 decision, Justice Clark found that it was. He based his decision on the congeries of financial arrangements that bound the restaurant to the Parking Authority. These included such considerations as that public agencies "owned the land and the building, had floated bonds, were collecting revenues to pay for the building's construction and maintenance, and received rent payments from the restaurant."[48]

Justice Clark realized, of course, that his opinion invited the criticism that to include the policies of a privately owned restaurant within the concept of state action threatened to erode the significance of that concept. Candidly, he acknowledged that "to fashion and apply a precise formula for recognition of state responsibility under the Equal Protection clause is an impossible task." He justified his decision with the following pragmatic, if somewhat unsatisfying, remark: "Only by sifting facts and weighing circumstances can the non-obvious involvement of the State in private conduct be attributed its true significance."[49]

Clearly, Justice Clark was struggling and was honest enough to admit it. Like the French administrative judges struggling to define the scope of their jurisdiction by articulating a clear standard of "public service," Justice Clark looked for a way to empower the federal courts to protect the rights of an oppressed minority against wayward state governments consistent with the demands of federalism. Just as French administrative judges groped in the conceptual fog generated by provident societies performing public functions and colonial governments running ferry boats, American jurists puzzled over whether state action should include private clubs licensed by the state to sell liquor, privately owned utilities enjoying a monopoly from the state, and "company towns" performing traditional municipal services, even though they were owned by private citizens.[50]

Justice Clark's emphasis on "sifting facts and weighing circumstances" limited the usefulness of his opinion as a precedent for settling subsequent racial discrimination cases involving allegations of state action by private entrepreneurs. New cases would surely present new facts to be sifted and new circumstances to be weighed.

This became apparent in the spate of dramatic confrontations triggered by the "sit-ins" of the early 1960s. National attention was riveted on black college students entering restaurants where they were not welcome and refusing to leave until they had been arrested for trespassing. Federal judges faced an extremely difficult problem when the students called upon them to over-turn their trespass convictions in state courts. What federal question was be-fore them? To be sure, state action was involved in the persons of the police-men who arrested the trespassers and the judges who convicted them. This line of reasoning, however, would prove too much. Police and judicial activ-ity might be found in any trespass case regardless of the motives of the prop-erty owner and the intruder, but such a finding would erode the federal-na-tional distinction. On the other hand, if no state action were involved, how could the federal judge avoid the embarrassment—to say nothing of the sub-stantive injustice—of denying relief to the convicted students and thereby giving the implicit approval of the federal government to the racist senti-ments at the heart of the controversy? To slip between the horns of this di-lemma, federal judges invented some remarkably creative devices to ferret out traces of state action in the highly particularized facts of whatever "sit-in" appeal happened to be before them. Thus, they might find a local mu-nicipal ordinance requiring segregation in the city in which the sit-in oc-curred and conclude—however unrealistically—that the restaurateurs were really acting as agents of the city government. If no ordinance were avail-able, they might find some statement by the mayor encouraging segregation to support their finding of state action on the part of the restaurateur as though he were carrying out the policy of the city as announced by the mayor.[51]

One did not have to be a die-hard segregationist to recognize that the federal courts were straining the state action doctrine to the breaking point. Racial issues aside, this doctrine expressed a principle of American constitu-tional law that was, and still is, a crucial element in maintaining the vitality of American federalism. As it became increasingly clear that the moral case against racial segregation was on a collision course with the firmly estab-lished constitutional doctrine of state action, enlightened opinion turned from the courts to Congress for a definitive solution. The judges' clever ma-nipulation of the state action doctrine to support the morally attractive civil rights cause brought them to the outer limits of their legitimate authority. It was time for the elected representatives of the people to enact a statute for-bidding discrimination in privately owned hotels, motels, restaurants, the-aters, concert halls, and so forth. This they did in the famous Civil Rights Act of 1964. No longer was it necessary for the judges to invent ways to as-sert very questionable federal authority over very unjust state practices. They had done their part in preparing public opinion to support the long-overdue congressional decision to rely on its extensive powers over commerce in order to prohibit discrimination in privately owned public accommoda-tions.[52]

Principe de proportionalité and Balancing Tests

Our final institutional comparison focuses on the problem of courts' substituting their judgments for those of administrative agencies. This comparison leads us to the principle of proportionality *(principe de proportionalité)* in France and to judicial "balancing tests" in the United States.

The principle of proportionality is part of the larger question of judicial control of administrative discretion, a question which Guy Braibant, the author of a leading textbook, places "at the center of administrative law and its political implications."[53] The heart of the problem is to find the path that leads to that happy land wherein administrative agencies have enough discretion to govern effectively but not so much as to slip the bonds of the rule of law imposed by reviewing courts.

Since the early 1960s, the Council of State has relied chiefly upon the principle of "manifest error in the assessment of facts" *(erreur manifeste d'appréciation des faits)* to assure adequate but not excessive judicial control of administrative discretion. Jean-Paul Costa describes this principle as permitting the judge to reverse an erroneous conclusion an administrative officer draws from a given set of facts only if the error is both "obvious and serious."[54] A British commentary characterizes the principle as permitting reversal of an administrative decision only if the judge finds "that no reasonable administrator could have reached that view from those facts." That is, "the administrator has the right to err, to decide wrongly, but not to make a *manifestly* wrong decision."[55] Thus, the manifest error principle somewhat resembles the American legal doctrine found in those cases wherein the courts apply the relaxed standard of "mere reasonableness" to sustain a statute or regulation, while striking down only those that are "arbitrary and capricious."

The principle of proportionality extends the manifest error doctrine in a way that considerably increases the scope of judicial inquiry into administrative decision making. Its origins are traced to "New City East" *(Nouvelle Ville Est),* a Council of State decision in 1971 involving extensive condemnation of private property for an ambitious town planning project near Lille. The plan called for building a university complex east of the city that would relieve pressure on the downtown area. To avoid isolating the students, the university facilities were to be integrated into a new urban setting. As originally conceived in 1966, the project was to accommodate some fifty thousand people in an area covering nearly fifteen hundred acres at an estimated cost running into hundreds of millions of dollars. Further, the plan called for the demolition of 250 private dwellings, some of which had just been built. When home owners who would be displaced protested, the projected demolition was reduced to eighty-eight homes. Still unsatisfied, the homeowners' association proposed extensive revisions to the plan that would save nearly all the homes by changing the location of the main road that was to run through the new city. The planners rejected this suggestion because the new location of the road would isolate the students from the community at large and thereby defeat one of the goals of the plan. After prolonged discussion and negotiations, the housing ministry declared the project a "public benefit" *(d'utilité publique),* thereby conferring official approval upon it. The home owners turned to the administrative courts to reverse the ministry's decision.[56]

The importance of the case was highlighted by the fact that the decision came from the General Assembly of the Council of State instead of its customary legal section. Traditionally, condemnation cases had been settled on grounds of whether an agency's finding of a public benefit could be supported by the evidence. To answer this question, the administrative judge examined only the *purposes* of a given project—that is, is a proposed highway really an undertaking from which the public will benefit? He was not expected to delve into the details of the construction plan nor to examine the specific parcels of land that were to be condemned. Critics of this approach found it too narrow. It dated from a time when an agency might condemn a few rural lots in order to build a country school, but it leaves too much discretion to agencies today when they engage in "huge urban development projects or in the construction of super-highways that affect hundreds of private holdings and sometimes involve the destruction of numerous dwellings."[57]

Guy Braibant, the Council of State's "representative of the government" for this case, argued before his colleagues that in deciding whether a vast development project is really a public benefit, the judge should look beyond its purpose and weigh its specific costs and benefits. The costs should include not only financial considerations but social and environmental consequences as well. Only when he has examined data of this nature can the judge decide whether or not the project represents a public benefit.

This argument broke new ground. It came to be known as the "balance sheet" approach *(le bilan).* It seemed to undermine the traditional distinction between the legality of a proposed undertaking—the sphere of the judge's influence—and its "merits" *(l'opportunité).*

In rendering its decision, the Council of State upheld the housing ministry's finding that the project was a public benefit, but the importance of the case lies in the way the council reached this conclusion. In approving the project, the Council of State, following Braibant's lead, formally announced that "a project can be declared a public benefit only if the burdens on private property, the financial cost and, if applicable, the inconvenience to the social order which it involves are not excessive in view of the advantages it promises."[58]

As we have seen so often in this book, a court establishes a new legal principle while rendering a decision in favor of those who are most likely to be adversely affected by the innovation. By incorporating a cost-benefit calculation into the concept of public benefit, the Council of State clearly limited the discretion of administrative agencies, even though in this particular instance the housing ministry prevailed.

Administrators did not have to wait long to feel the force of the logic underpinning the *New City East* decision. The following year the Council of State, again in full assembly, decided a case in which Assumption Hospital appealed a decree from the prime minister finding that the construction of an access route linking a departmental highway to a superhighway was a public benefit. The hospital, located just north of Nice, cared for mental patients and was the only such facility in the department of the Maritime Alps. No one questioned the value of the proposed access route as an apt means for alleviating local traffic problems, but Morisot, the Council's "representative of the government" in the case, argued that this benefit was not enough to offset the likely harm to the hospital. Thus, the Council of State entered into such practical details of the plan as the likelihood that certain buildings in the hospital complex would have to be destroyed, the future of "green spaces" around the hospital, the effect of increased noise on patient care, and the hospital's chances of expanding its facilities in the future. Having examined these and similar questions, the council concluded that the burdens on the hospital outweighed the plan's advantages and that therefore the designation of the project as a public benefit was illegal.

In presenting the case to his fellow councillors of state, the "representative of the government" pulled no punches. Reminding them of the rule they had announced the previous year in *New City East,* he stated that the jurisprudence of that case called for nothing less than "the substitution of your own conception of the public interest for that which the administration thought should prevail." Candidly, he acknowledged that to treat such a matter as a legal question takes the authority of the Council of State right up to "the outer boundary" of questions of expediency or appropriateness—that is, the very questions that had traditionally been beyond the reach of the administrative courts.[59]

The Council of State has shown restraint in exercising its enhanced role in the administrative process. For example, in a case involving the construction of a superhighway in the hilly northeastern section of France, the government's decision to build over the hills rather than through a valley was upheld on the grounds that the relation of benefits to costs was sufficiently favorable to classify the project as a public benefit. The council refused, however, to examine the claim that a road through the valley would be *better.* To prevail against a challenge to its decision to build in the hills, the government need only establish that the decision it actually made was a public benefit, even if a different route would yield a more favorable cost-benefit ratio. Gentôt, the council's "representative of the government" in this case, acknowledged that some might be disappointed at the choice of the hills over the valley, but concluded nonetheless that "these misgivings concern only the merits *(l'opportunité)* of the decision, not its legality."[60]

The principle of proportionality has spread to many areas other than the condemnation of property for public works, for example, disciplinary actions against civil servants and efforts to ban automobiles from streets set aside exclusively for pedestrians.[61] The most illuminating example, however, appeared in a recent case involving the deportation from France of an Algerian national by the name of Hamid Belgacem.

Born in France in 1958, Belgacem had spent his entire life there, including several years in prison for breaking and entering and for armed robbery. The interior minister decided to expel him from France under a law in effect only from 1986 to 1989 that permitted such an action against persons in Belgacem's situation. He appealed this decision to the administrative tribunal in Paris on the ground that it violated the European Convention on the Rights of Man which had been legally binding upon French governments since 1974.[62]

Specifically, he relied on a provision of the convention requiring member states to respect every person's right to a life with his or her family. The convention permitted member states to interfere with the exercise of this right only by actions approved by law and only for reasons relating "to national security, public safety, the economic well-being of the country, the defense of public order and the prevention of criminal wrong-doing, the protection of health and morals, or the protection of rights and liberties." The Paris tribunal rejected Belgacem's appeal because his deportation was in accordance with French law. It specifically rejected as irrelevant his plea that his right to a life with his family was infringed, because the European Convention permitted such infringement in order to defend "public order." Having taken Belgacem's case on appeal from the tribunal of Paris, the Council of State took a closer look at his family situation. He was the second of thirteen children and contributed to the support of his widowed mother and his younger brothers and sisters who were still of school age. Prior to his release from prison, Belgacem had participated successfully in a furlough program that permitted him to take part-time employment in a dry cleaning establishment whose proprietor certified his readiness to offer him a full-time position with increased responsibilities. A social worker reported that his crimes in the early 1980s were due in part to temporary psychological problems and that now he was ready to reenter society. Having lived all his life in France, he had no close family ties with anyone in Algeria.

Taking all these factors into consideration, the Council of State found that "in view of the gravity of the hardship imposed upon his family life, the decision to deport Belgacem has exceeded that which is necessary for the defense of public order." Thus the Council of State relied upon a proportionality analysis to determine what was necessary to defend public order. The costs imposed upon Belgacem outweighed whatever benefits his deportation might have for the defense of the public order. Therefore, the deportation decision did not meet the requirements of the public order exception the government had relied upon to set aside Belgacem's right to a life with his family under the European Convention.

This is an interesting line of argument because it clearly implies a radically *subjective* notion of the needs of public order. Apparently, these needs wax or wane depending on the burdens imposed upon certain persons. The logic of the council's position suggests that somehow the needs of public order would have been greater if Belgacem's sufferings had been less. That is, the government's reliance on the public order exception might have succeeded if one or more of Belgacem's siblings had lived in Algeria, if his father had still been alive, if his family had been wealthy, and so forth. Thus, the needs of public order are not objective realities in the "already-out-there-now," but they are determined in part by the amount of suffering the State imposes upon a particular person. One wonders if the same analysis would be applied to a case involving national security instead of public order.

The clearest parallel in American law to the French principle of proportionality is the frequent reliance of the federal courts on "balancing tests" to settle competing claims between an individual's right to exercise some sort of personal liberty and the state's authority to limit that exercise. Despite the absolute language of the first amendment, "Congress shall make *no* law" (emphasis added), the courts have consistently recognized the legitimacy of some limitations on the exercise of even the most fundamental rights. A "balancing test" is one important means by which the courts decide the constitutionality of a particular limitation upon a particular right. For example, the courts might use such a test to conclude "that the free speech interests of pamphleteers outweigh the interest in clean streets protected by an antilittering ordinance forbidding the distribution of handbills."[63]

A recent Supreme Court decision on disciplining public servants provides a striking example of the balancing test and one that should be of particular interest to specialists in public administration.

On 30 March 1981, the world was shocked to learn that President Reagan had been wounded in an assassination attempt in Washington, D.C.

When Ardith McPherson, a nineteen-year-old probationary clerical employee in the constable's office of Harris County, Texas, heard the news, she said to one of her coworkers, "If they go for him again, I hope they get him." A third employee overheard this ill-advised remark and reported it to Constable Rankin, who fired McPherson after questioning her briefly. Shortly thereafter, she brought suit for reinstatement in the United States District Court for the Southern District of Texas, relying upon a federal statute which prohibits state officials acting "under color of state law" from depriving any person of his or her rights under the Constitution or laws of the United States. McPherson maintained Rankin had deprived her of her constitutional right to freedom of speech. She argued that although her probationary status made her exceedingly vulnerable to termination, she could not be terminated simply because of her speech. The District Court rejected McPherson's argument, but the United States Court of Appeals for the Fifth Circuit reversed this ruling. Constable Rankin appealed this reversal to the Supreme Court of the United States. In a 5–4 decision, the Supreme Court upheld McPherson's claim.

Justice Marshall delivered the opinion of the Court in which he first established McPherson's comment, despite its offensive character, "as constituting speech on a matter of public concern." He then set up a balancing test between McPherson's free speech interest and Rankin's managerial interest in firing her for what she had said. Just as the Council of State examined the details of Belgacem's family life, Justice Marshall delved into the details of McPherson's employment. "She was not a commissioned peace officer, did not wear a uniform, and was not authorized to make arrests or to carry a gun." Her "duties were purely clerical" and she worked "in a room to which the public did not have ready access." Her offensive remark was heard by only two other persons and there is "no evidence that it interfered with the functioning of the office."[64]

At the end of this fact-driven analysis, Justice Marshall concluded:

> Given the function of the agency, McPherson's position in the office, and the nature of her statement, we are not persuaded that Rankin's interest in discharging her outweighed her rights under the First Amendment.[65]

Justice Scalia wrote a dissenting opinion, which three other justices joined. He got off to a good start by repeating a quip from Rankin's brief to the effect that "no law enforcement agency is required by the First Amendment to permit one of its employees to 'ride with cops and cheer for the robbers.'" He then disputed Justice Marshall's finding that McPherson's speech was of "public concern," but this point is irrelevant for our analysis of balancing tests. What is relevant, however, is the second major argument in his opinion which began as follows: "Even if I agreed that McPherson's statement was speech on a matter of 'public concern,' I would still find it unprotected. It is important to be clear on what the issue is in this part of the case."[66]

In drawing attention to what he considers "the issue in this part of the case," Scalia signals his displeasure with the Court's balancing test. He does not object to balancing tests as such but rather to what Justice Marshall wants to balance in this particular case. For Scalia, the issue "is not, as the Court suggests, whether 'Rankin's interest in *discharging* [McPherson] outweighs her rights under the First Amendment.'" (Scalia's emphasis.) Rankin's interest in this case, according to Scalia, must not be confined to *discharging* a wayward employee, but must be expanded to include his *"interest in preventing the expression of such statements in his agency"* as those McPherson uttered. (Scalia's emphasis.) Scalia criticizes the opinion of the Court for what he sees as its misplaced emphasis on McPherson's termination. He acknowledges that the punishment Rankin imposed may, as a practical matter, have been excessive, but for Scalia, such an assessment is no part of the judicial function. As he puts it: "We are not sitting as a panel to develop sound principles of proportionality for adverse action in the state civil service."[67] That is, the suitability of the punishment visited upon McPherson is properly an administrative, not a judicial, question.

Scalia's reconstruction of the balance illuminates the true nature of balancing tests and reveals their problematic character as well. Scalia would balance McPherson's first amendment interests not against Rankin's interest in firing her, but against his interest in preventing expression of the sentiments McPherson announced. Having reset the balance in this way, he would then find for Rankin. To do otherwise, that is, to find for McPherson once the balance had been reset to Scalia's liking, would mean she had a *right* to say what she said and therefore *no* disciplinary action could be taken against her. Indeed, she could repeat her outrageous comment day after day without fear of *any* disciplinary action at all. Scalia maintains that the court's misplaced focus on the outcome of the incident—McPherson's dismissal—has obscured the true nature of the case. A court should confine itself to deciding whether or not the constable can punish McPherson for what she said. If he can, then the appropriateness of the punishment, for example, a letter of reprimand, a delayed promotion, or even dismissal should be determined by a civil service personnel board.

Scalia's dissent brings out the key problem in balancing tests. It is not to decide which side has the "weightier" claim; once the balance is set, this is often obvious. The real problem is to decide which weights should be placed in the scale. The answer to this question defines the difference between Marshall and Scalia in deciding this case. If Rankin's interest in *firing* McPherson goes in the scale, he loses because the punishment is too severe. If

Rankin's broader interest in being able to take some (unspecified) sort of disciplinary action against an employee like McPherson is put on the scale, he wins because such intemperate speech in the workplace should not be allowed to pass without rebuke. If, as a matter of fact, the unspecified punishment turns out to be dismissal, Rankin still wins because, in Scalia's analysis, the precise nature of the punishment is not a judicial question.

INDIVIDUAL RIGHTS

Thus far in this chapter we have centered our attention on institutional norms, that is, on the powers various state institutions may or should exercise. In doing this, we have touched upon questions of individual rights or at least of individual interests as, for example, in the cases of Hamid Belgacem, Agnès Blanco, and Prince Napoléon. We have touched upon these rights only obliquely as a means of understanding institutional powers such as those of an administrative judge vis-à-vis a minister, a prefect, or a mayor. In the remainder of this chapter we shall focus directly upon individual rights and only obliquely upon the powers of officials who try to curtail them.

L'ordre public and Compelling State Interests

The Council of State upheld Hamid Belgacem's complaint on the grounds that his deportation would impose more hardships upon him than were necessary to satisfy the needs of public order. "Public order" (l'ordre public) is a rich and complex notion in French law with roots running back at least as far as the Declaration of the Rights of Man and of the Citizen of 1789. There we read in article 10: "No one must suffer for his opinions, even for religious opinions, provided that his advocacy of them does not endanger public order." Only the demands, therefore, of public order can justify the otherwise prohibited power to punish a person for advocating his opinions. As we saw above, the Declaration of the Rights of Man and of the Citizen eschews the absolute language of the First Amendment to the Constitution of the United States ("Congress shall make no law") in favor of a prudential accommodation of the rights of the individual on the one hand and the needs of society on the other. Article 10 implies a certain balance between the free advocacy of opinion and the preservation of public order. This balance or prudential accommodation is reinforced by article 11, which provides in part that "every citizen may speak, write, and print his views freely, provided only that he accepts the bounds of this freedom established by law." Therefore, the text of the Declaration suggests that the power of the

State to suppress the spoken or written word would be at its strongest when an officer can point to a *law* to support his effort to do so because of threats he perceives to the public order.

The mayor of Nevers found himself in this strong position in the early 1930s when he decided to forbid René Benjamin from delivering a lecture at the request of the local tourist bureau. Benjamin was known to be a severe critic of the public schools and the prospect of his addressing a meeting in Nevers aroused strong opposition from the teachers' union and other local unions as well. Joined by several leftist groups, the unions threatened a mass demonstration if the lecture should take place. Citing an 1884 law giving mayors the duty to take the measures necessary to maintain public order, the mayor of Nevers forbade the lecture. Benjamin appealed the mayor's decision to an administrative court on the grounds that the order forbidding him to lecture violated laws from 1881 and 1907 guaranteeing the right to hold public meetings.

Even though the mayor's claim to see a threat to public order was buttressed by a statute, he did not prevail. The Council of State held that the mayor's statutory power to maintain public order had to be reconciled with the no less statutory right of Benjamin and his sponsors to hold a meeting. Balancing these competing interests, the council found "that the possibility of trouble alleged by the mayor of Nevers" did not pose so serious a problem as to keep him from relying on routine police measures to maintain order "without forbidding the meeting."[68]

It is important to note that the Council of State did not question the mayor's perception that there was a possible threat to public order, but rather it faulted: (1) his assessment of the *gravity* of the likely disorder, and (2) his failure to address the problem by using means less drastic than simply prohibiting the meeting where the lecture would be delivered.[69] A leading commentary on *Benjamin* summarizes the council's decision as holding that it is possible to prevent a meeting legally but to do so, "it will be necessary that the threat to public order be exceptionally serious and that the mayor does not have at his disposal the police force necessary to let the meeting proceed while assuring the maintenance of public order."[70] Once again, the two key points are the exceptional nature of the danger and the absence of any means to cope with the danger short of prohibiting the meeting to take place. I stress these two points because they provide the basis for an important comparison with American constitutional law which we shall examine below.

Before doing so, however, let us consider the famous *Action Française* decision of 8 April 1935, which involved an order by the prefect of police in Paris to confiscate all copies of a right-wing newspaper from which the case takes its name.[71]

On 6 February 1934, there was a bloody riot in Paris when a variety of rightists, including some fascists, marched on the Palais Bourbon, the seat of the Chamber of Deputies, as the lower house of Parliament was known under the Third Republic. There ensued a violent upheaval that left fifteen persons dead and over one thousand injured. The next morning, the prefect of police ordered all copies of the newspaper *Action Française* to be confiscated throughout all of Paris and its suburbs. When the publisher sued the prefect for having given this order, the case came before the Tribunal of Conflicts to determine whether the plaintiff should seek redress before an administrative or an ordinary court. As a matter of fact, the tribunal assigned the case to the ordinary courts for technical reasons that need not concern us here.[72] For our purposes, the important point is the reason the tribunal gave to support its finding that the prefect had acted improperly despite the violent confrontation on the day preceding his confiscation order. According to the tribunal, the confiscation of a newspaper can be justified only if it is "indispensable for assuring the preservation or the reestablishment of public order."[73] This was not the case in the present instance. In reaching its decision, the tribunal emphasized the sweeping character of the prefect's order, which reached every kiosk in the Paris metropolitan area where the paper was sold. As the representative of the government advised the Tribunal of Conflicts, the confiscation order might have been legal had it been confined "to all the places where its sale would be likely to contribute to disorder: major arteries, locations crucial for defending the streets, etc."[74]

Thus the tribunal's decision seemed to rely on a two-pronged analysis similar to that employed in *Benjamin*. First, the threat to public order must be exceptionally serious, as it surely was in this case. Second, the repressive action must be *indispensable*—not merely suitable or appropriate but indispensable—for maintaining public order. This was the test the prefect failed. He had at his disposal an alternative and considerably less drastic means of protecting the public order. He could have limited the confiscation order to certain key areas of the city.

American courts have relied on a similar structure of argument to handle difficult cases involving the fundamental First Amendment rights of speech, press, assembly, and religion.[75] For over thirty years, the courts have required state and national governments to pass a two-pronged test before their inroads on these cherished liberties will be upheld. Although the precise formula varies from case to case, the courts ordinarily analyze challenges to official actions in First Amendment matters by requiring the government to show that: (1) there was a *compelling* state interest at stake, and (2) there were no alternative means to secure that compelling interest other than suppressing the First Amendment rights in question.[76]

The 1963 case *Sherbert v. Verner*[77] provides a good example of this approach. Appellant Sherbert was a member of the Seventh-Day Adventist Church. She had been discharged by her employer in South Carolina because she would not work on Saturday, the day of rest and worship for Seventh-Day Adventists. She filed a claim for unemployment compensation benefits under the South Carolina Unemployment Compensation Act, which provides that a claimant is ineligible for benefits if he or she has failed, without good cause, to accept available, suitable work when offered. The State Commission denied Sherbert's application on the grounds that she would not accept suitable work when offered and that she therefore failed to meet the statutory requirement of "availability" for work as a condition of receiving unemployment benefits. The Supreme Court of South Carolina upheld the State Commission but the Supreme Court of the United States reversed this decision, finding that South Carolina's failure to accommodate Sherbert's religious scruples was a denial of the free exercise of her religion.

Justice Brennan, who delivered the opinion of the Court, reached this decision by asking "whether some compelling state interest enforced in the eligibility provisions of the South Carolina statute justifies the substantial infringement of appellant's First Amendment right." For Brennan, "no showing merely of a rational relationship to some colorable state interest would suffice" for South Carolina to prevail. The state's interest must be compelling. The record indicated that the state's interest did not go beyond avoiding the administrative inconvenience of reclassifying employers on the basis of whether they required their employees to work on Saturday. This was a legitimate state interest but not a compelling one. This conclusion is similar to the Council of State's finding that the unrest Benjamin's lecture might have occasioned was not sufficiently serious as to warrant its suppression.

In presenting its case before the Supreme Court, South Carolina had argued that if an exemption were granted to Sabbatarians, "the filing of fraudulent claims by unscrupulous claimants feigning religious objections to Saturday work might . . . dilute the unemployment compensation fund." Justice Brennan refused to evaluate this claim on the technical grounds that it had not been raised before the Supreme Court of South Carolina and "we [the justices of the Supreme Court of the United States] are unwilling to assess the importance of an asserted state interest without the views of the state court." Significantly, however, Brennan added:

> Even if the possibility of spurious claims did threaten to dilute the fund and
> disrupt the scheduling of work, it would plainly be incumbent upon the ap-

pellees to demonstrate that no alternative forms of regulation would combat such abuses without infringing First Amendment rights.

Justice Brennan's hypothetical situation is significant because it shows how the Court would have proceeded if South Carolina had successfully shown that the exemption Sherbert sought would have seriously threatened the unemployment compensation fund. Even if the state's interest in avoiding this fiscal problem were found to be "compelling," it would still have to show that there were no alternative means to protect the state's compelling interest other than by discriminating against Sabbatarians. Needless to say, this would be hard to show and, therefore, in all likelihood, Sherbert would still have prevailed even if South Carolina had succeeded in showing a compelling state interest in this case. This line of reasoning recalls that of the Tribunal of Conflicts in *Action Française*. There were serious threats to public order in the metropolitan Paris area on the morning of 7 February 1934, but the confiscation of *all* copies of *Action Française* was not "indispensable" to deal with these threats. As Justice Brennan might have put it, there were "alternative forms of regulation" short of total confiscation.

In comparing the French and American approaches to these individual rights cases, it is instructive to begin with fundamental texts—the Declaration of the Rights of Man and of the Citizen for the French and the First Amendment for the Americans. Although at the time these cases were decided French law forbade the judges from relying expressly on the Declaration, one may confidently assert that the spirit of that great charter informed the principles of French administrative law that emerged in *Benjamin* and in *Action Française*. We have already commented upon the balance struck in the tenth article of the Declaration between the right to advocate one's opinion, on the one hand, and the needs of public order on the other. We have also commented on the specific provision in article 11 that freedom of speech and of the press may be curtailed by law. Finally, we have contrasted this language that invites compromise with the absolute prohibition of the First Amendment. If one were to look at these texts alone, one might surmise that questions of individual rights would be handled entirely differently in the two countries.

To be sure, there are very important differences, but we have just seen that there are remarkable similarities as well. Jurists in both France and the United States recognize that claims involving the rights of speech, press, assembly, and religion deserve special consideration. Where a French jurist will support State suppression of speech only if the threat to public order is "exceptionally serious," his American counterpart will do so only if he finds a compelling state interest. And if the two jurists believe their respective states have passed this first test, they are both ready with a second test that is even more demanding. The French judge will ask if the State action in question was "indispensable" to protect the "exceptionally serious" interest and the American will want to be sure that there were "no alternative forms of regulation" to safeguard the "compelling state interest."

Thus, although jurists in the two countries start with very different organic texts, they reach comparable structures of legal argument. The French start with the spirit of the Declaration of Rights, which seems to be disconcertingly generous toward the State, and build up to a doctrine that places significant limitations on the State without incapacitating it for decisive action when it is really called for. The Americans build down from the absolute language of the First Amendment to reach an eminently sensible, but clearly nontextual, compromise that protects First Amendment rights without crippling the state.

Faute de service and Tort Liability

Despite the elaborate protection of individual rights in France and the United States, judges in both countries have struggled to develop proper remedies for the unpleasant but inevitable situations in which state officials disregard these protections and violate the rights of citizens or wrongfully harm them in some other way.

Prior to the Revolution, such questions were nipped in the bud by the French version of the English common law principle that the king can do no wrong: *"le Roi ne peut mal faire."* The Revolution disposed of the king and made citizens of his former subjects, but did little to ameliorate the sorry plight of those subjected to official injustice. Because of the revolutionaries' extreme hostility to the judiciary and their dread of *gouvernement des juges,* they looked with profound suspicion upon any effort by the ordinary courts to control administrative action. Consequently, as we saw in our discussion of jurisdictional questions, the Council of State throughout most of the nineteenth century had to rely on contrived theories of "the State as debtor" and strained distinctions between "acts of authority" and "acts of management" to impose a modicum of judicial discipline upon wayward administrators. All this began to change, however, with the famous *Blanco* decision of 1873, discussed earlier in this chapter, wherein "the general principle of the liability of the state was established beyond question."[78]

In the same year in which it rendered its *Blanco* decision, the Tribunal of Conflicts in another case "laid down what has become the classic distinction between a *faute de service* and a *faute personnelle.*"[79] *Faute de service* (an official fault) occurs when a representative of the State wrongfully harms someone while carrying on his official activities, whereas *faute personnelle* (a "personal fault") envisions an ordinary human failing by an official or, as the classic phrase put it, a wrong "which is not linked to the public service but reveals the man with his weakness, his passions, his imprudence."[80] Civil servants can be sued in the ordinary courts for their personal faults because such faults are unrelated to State functions, but they are immune from the jurisdiction of these courts for their official faults because of "the principle of separation of powers which prohibits the ordinary courts receiving actions against the administration or its officials."[81] To redress official faults, the aggrieved citizen must seek relief in administrative courts where he sues an administrative agency instead of an erring civil servant.

The distinction between personal and official faults brings conceptual clarity to the problem of wrongdoing by those holding public office, but its practical value is dependent upon how the distinction is applied in practice. A broad interpretation of personal fault runs the considerable risk that a wronged citizen would be "left perhaps with a worthless right of action against a penniless official."[82] That is, the citizen's right to sue the official in the ordinary courts will prove illusory if the official is judgment-proof.

The Council of State addressed this question in its *Anguet* decision of 3 February 1911.[83] The plaintiff entered a Paris post office at eight-thirty on the evening of 11 January 1908 to cash a money order. Upon completing his transaction, he noticed that the door through which the public was to enter and leave the building was closed, even though postal regulations required that it be open at that hour. A postal clerk told him to use another door that brought him into an area reserved for post office personnel. Two employees eyed Anguet suspiciously and, thinking he was too slow in making his exit, pushed him out into the street so brutally that he broke his leg. When Anguet sued the ministry of postal and telegraphic services, the minister defended on the grounds that the injury was due to the *faute personnelle* of the employees and that the ministry, therefore, could not be held accountable for damages. Anticipating a legal doctrine that would eventually become known as the "combination of liabilities" *(combination des responsibilités),* the Council of State upheld Anguet's claim. To be sure, the brutality of the postal workers was a personal fault, but the failure of the post office management to keep its doors open until the official closing time was an official fault which set in motion the unhappy chain of events leading to Anguet's violent expulsion from the premises. That is, "the *faute personnelle* of the postal agents . . . had been made possible only by the *faute de service.*"[84] Therefore, Anguet had correctly brought his suit against the ministry from which he was far more likely to receive the indemnity he deserved than if he had prevailed in a suit against impoverished postal employees in an ordinary court. Although two distinct faults were involved—one by the ministry and the other by its agents—they could be combined to enable Anguet to collect from the ministry the damages he sought.

Seven years later in 1918, the Council of State extended the principles of *Anguet* in its *Lemonnier* decision.[85] On 9 October 1910, the commune of Roquecourbe celebrated its annual fair, which featured a shooting contest at targets afloat in the Agout River. During the year preceding the fair, a tree-lined promenade had been opened on the bank across the river. Several strollers had complained to the mayor of bullets whistling over their heads. The mayor made some changes in the line of fire but not enough to keep a woman from being struck on the cheek by a bullet as she and her husband walked along the promenade. Through a series of complicated legal maneuvers, the Lemonniers brought suits simultaneously against the mayor in an ordinary court and against the commune in the administrative courts.[86] The ordinary courts had already upheld the Lemonniers' claim when the case reached the Council of State. Despite this ruling, the council held it still had jurisdiction because the mayor's failure to protect the strollers was *both* a personal *and* an official fault. Léon Blum, the representative of the government in the case, captured nicely the reasoning the council would make its own when he said:

> If the personal fault has been committed in the public service, or on the occasion of the service, if the means and instruments of the fault have been placed at the disposal of the party at fault by the service, if in short the service has provided the conditions for the commission of the fault, the administrative judge will and must then say: the fault may be severable from the service—that is for the ordinary courts to decide, but the service is not severable from the fault.[87]

Blum's argument went a long way toward assuring that a wronged citizen would usually have the opportunity to sue an administrative body. Granted there may be a personal fault which is "severable from the service," but recourse to the administrative courts is still possible as long as "the service is not separable from the fault." This line of reasoning goes beyond *Anguet,* where the Council of State had found two distinct faults but enabled Anguet to recover from the postal and telegraph ministry because the official fault came first and led to the personal fault of the employees. In *Lemonnier,* there was but one fault and it had both a personal and an official aspect. Hence, *Anguet*'s combination of faults *(cumul des fautes)* becomes a combination of liabilities *(cumul des responsibilités)* in *Lemonnier* with no need to show which came first in order to give the wronged citizen access to the deeper pockets of an administrative body.

Lemonnier was the touchstone for a series of cases in which the combination of liabilities doctrine carefully folded questions of personal fault into larger questions of official fault to the financial advantage of wronged citizens. Typical was the case of a soldier driving a gasoline tanker who made an unauthorized detour to his hometown, where he crashed the vehicle into a private residence. Clearly, the soldier was at fault for departing from his assigned route, but the home owner was nevertheless "able to recover [from the State] since the tanker had been entrusted to the driver to perform a public service."[88]

The jurisprudence developed by the Council of State in cases involving the personal faults of public employees "demonstrates a clear desire of the administrative judge to extend as far as possible, out of consideration of justice, the guarantee of compensation which the finding of liability on the part of the public authority alone can provide the victim."[89] So zealous has the Council of State been in trying to guarantee compensation to wronged citizens by expanding the notion of official fault that "one finds oneself in some cases having to make do with a pure fiction."[90] Thus, the family of a man who was killed by the accidental discharge from the service revolver of an off-duty policeman was able to recover for his death. The deceased shared an apartment with a policeman who was required to keep his gun at home. This requirement "created a danger for third parties such as to make the accident not unconnected with the service."[91] Clearly, this is an extremely generous interpretation of official wrongdoing. But, alas, all good things must come to an end. The Council of State refused to find an official fault in the action of a uniformed off-duty customs officer who used his weapon to commit a murder.[92]

An important qualification of the combination of liabilities doctrine announced in *Lemonnier* is that it does not permit a victim to collect twice for the same wrong. If the victim prevails in both the ordinary and the administrative courts, the debtor who actually pays the victim retains a right to seek partial or full compensation from the other debtor. In technical terms, the rights of the victim against the debtor who has *not* paid are "subrogated" to the debtor who has paid. That is, the debtor who has paid "succeeds to" the victim's rights. Consequently, in *Lemonnier,* once the commune of Roquecourbe had compensated the injured woman, it could seek some reimbursement from the mayor.

This arrangement was acknowledged to be a "clumsy device" because it required the victim to sue in both the ordinary and the administrative courts. Few victims were likely to be so gracious to the State as to pursue this two-track litigation since, as a practical matter, the pay-off in the administrative court would almost always be far more lucrative. If no suit were initiated against delinquent officials, the State would bear the full financial burden and the officials themselves would have no liability whatsoever for their misdeeds. Thus, the Council of State's strategy of expanding the notion of official fault in order to ensure adequate compensation to victims would have the unintended consequence of encouraging irresponsible behavior on the part of officials whose victims would not bother to sue them.

Eventually, the Council of State solved this problem by giving the administrative agency "a direct action for contribution or indemnity against the official."[93] Thus, there would be no need for the agency to succeed to any rights the victim might have won against the erring official in the ordinary courts. The administrative agency, after having compensated the victim, would simply bring an action before an administrative judge who would determine how much each of the offending parties should pay.

For example, a government truck was involved in an accident which was determined to have been caused by defective brakes in the vehicle (an official fault) and by the inebriated condition of the driver (a personal fault). Both the government and the driver paid one-half of the victim's compensation. In a more complicated case, a soldier used an army vehicle without authorization for a private journey in the course of which he struck a pedestrian. The victim sued in the administrative courts and the Council of State found that the army's failure to maintain adequate supervision over the garage from which the soldier had taken the vehicle was an official fault and required the State to compensate the victim. The State then initiated proceedings against the soldier to recover the entire amount it had paid the victim. The soldier appealed this action in the administrative courts, but to no avail. The Council of State upheld the army. Even though there was a combination of personal and official faults, the soldier could not invoke the latter to shield himself since the official fault "had been caused by the deception which he had practiced upon the guard in charge of the garage where the vehicle was kept."[94]

After having explained these vehicular cases, Brown and Bell correctly conclude that

> the Conseil d'Etat has completed its construction of a logically satisfying system of administrative liability. Where there is personal fault combined with service fault, the victim can sue either the official or the administration in the appropriate court. The ultimate division of responsibility rests, however, with the administrative courts. In this way the official who is at fault can be made to contribute appropriately towards the damage done, where, as is usual, only the administration has been sued by the victim.[95]

The most important contrast between the French and the American approaches to the problem of official wrongdoing reveals the different understandings of separation of powers in the two countries. As we have just seen, the elaborate structure of French administrative justice rests on "the principle of separation of powers which prohibits the ordinary courts receiving actions against the administration or its officials." That is, the administrative courts came into being to fill the gap created by the doctrinal prohibition against the ordinary courts reviewing official acts of public servants. The exclusion of ordinary courts from administrative affairs led inevitably to the creation of a new order of judges called councillors of State who, pursuant to the French understanding of separation of powers, exercised their judicial functions independently of the regular courts and, eventually, independently of the government as well. Their independence from the government came in no small part from the prestige they had won over the years.

In the United States, all roads lead to the ordinary courts because the American understanding of separation of powers most emphatically does not preclude judges from passing judgment upon official acts. Indeed, because of the close connection between separation of powers and the rule of law, American judges include their jurisdiction over such acts among their most important duties. As the Supreme Court of the United States announced over a century ago: "Courts of justice are established, not only to decide upon controverted rights of the citizens as against each other, but also upon rights in controversy between them and the government."[96]

Thus, following different interpretations of the "separation of powers" formula, the French and the Americans have followed diametrically opposed paths to a remarkably similar result: independent institutions—the administrative courts in France and the ordinary courts in the United States—that effectively discipline wayward officials in both countries.

Despite the salient role of American courts in the governing process, there is a curious countervailing principle that provides still another interesting contrast with French administrative justice. I refer to the common law principle of "sovereign immunity." Tracing its origins back to the thirteenth century, sovereign immunity meant that "the king was immune from suit by his subjects,"[97] which, in turn, undergirds the expression so offensive to republican ears that "the king can do no wrong." This expression, of course, "does not mean that everything done by the government is just and lawful, but that whatever is exceptionable in the conduct of public affairs is not to be imputed to the king."[98] The rationale for the royal exemption was not moral but jurisdictional: "Since law emanated from the sovereign, he could not be held accountable in courts of his own creation."[99]

Just how and why this royalist doctrine survived in American jurisprudence is something of a mystery. Indeed, the Supreme Court of the United States once confessed that although sovereign immunity has "been repeatedly asserted here, the principle has never been discussed or the reasons for it given, but it has always been treated as an established doctrine."[100]

We noted above that the French once had a similar legal principle that their king could do no wrong and that this principle, purged of its royal overtones, survived the Revolution and contributed substantially to preventing the ordinary courts from reviewing acts of French officialdom. We have also seen that by the time of the *Blanco* decision in 1873, the administrative courts had brought it about that "the general principle of the liability of the state was established beyond question." This is a principle that even to this day has not been established in the United States because of sovereign immunity.

To be sure, sovereign immunity gives off today but a pale reflection of its medieval splendor. Long before the American Revolution, it had been "riddled with exceptions." Since that time, many judicial decisions at both the state and federal levels have interpreted sovereign immunity so narrowly that "the ambit of the exemption has been drastically reduced."[101] Statutory enactments by both Congress and state legislatures have contributed to the same result by waiving immunity in many areas. At the federal level, the most significant actions of this nature have been the creation of the Court of Claims in 1855, the Federal Tort Claims Act of 1946, and important amendments to sections 702 and 703 of the Administrative Procedure Act in 1976.[102]

Today one can assert without fear of contradiction that "sovereign immunity has become a narrow and ill-defined jurisdictional bar, whose contemporary legitimacy and utility are doubtful."[103] For our comparative purposes, however, the significant point is not that sovereign immunity is no longer important but that it exists at all in latter-day republican America. The very notion of sovereignty—"[t]he supreme, absolute and uncontrollable power by which any independent state is governed"—is ill at ease in the American framework of separation of powers which is at war with the idea of a single "supreme, absolute and uncontrollable power."[104] It would seem to find a more hospitable home in the sovereign parliaments of the Third and Fourth Republics. And yet the concept, though but a shadow of its former self, survives to this day in the United States, whereas its French version disappeared in *Blanco* over a century ago. This is a curious phenomenon in view of the statist tradition in France and its absence in the United States.

Sovereign immunity, however, is more than a curiosity. It has explanatory power as well, for it accounts in no small part for the plethora of suits in American courts against public officials. Precisely because the doctrine of sovereign immunity impeded suits against the state and national governments, the tradition of suing *officials* took root and flourished.[105] These suits have often been thinly veiled subterfuges for circumventing the harshness of the sovereign immunity doctrine.[106] Governmental jurisdictions, even when theoretically immune from lawsuits, have often joined the charade by paying the fines incurred by their officers for their torts. Thus, just as the French practice of excluding ordinary judges from reviewing official actions spawned a new system of administrative courts, so the American doctrine of sovereign immunity has institutionalized the legal fiction of the individual officer as personally responsible for his wrongful actions in carrying out his official duties.

A civil rights statute passed in 1871 has been a rich source of suits in federal courts brought by aggrieved citizens against state officials. Originally intended to protect recently emancipated freedmen from Ku Klux Klan violence, the statute today covers virtually every area of governmental activity. In 1980, for example, it was the basis of over nine thousand suits filed in federal courts.[107] These legal actions are often called "section 1983 suits" after the section of the U.S. Code where the statute is found today.[108] As codified, the statute provides:

> Every person who, under color of any statute, ordinance, regulation, custom or usage, of any State or Territory or the District of Columbia, subjects, or causes to be subjected, any citizen of the United States or other person within the jurisdiction thereof to the deprivation of any rights, privileges, or immunities secured by the Constitution and laws, shall be liable to the party injured in an action at law, suit in equity, or other proper proceeding for redress.

For our comparative purposes, it is important to note that the statute clearly targets government officials—*persons* who deprive other persons of some federal right. Just recently, the Supreme Court explicitly rejected the argument that state governments are included within the word *person* at the beginning of section 1983, thereby reinforcing the traditional American practice of suing officials of state governments rather than the states themselves.[109]

Interestingly, however, the Supreme Court has held that local governments, unlike states, are "persons" under section 1983.[110] This holding is consistent with a long-standing practice dating back to colonial times by which state governments have conferred "political power upon public and municipal corporations for the management of local concerns." The Court has found that "by 1871 municipalities—like private corporations—were treated as natural persons for virtually all purposes of constitutional statutory analysis." Consequently, local governments have been "routinely sued in federal and state courts."[111] Because they are creatures of state governments, local governmental jurisdictions, by definition, are not "sovereign," and consequently have never enjoyed sovereign immunity.

In finding local governments to be persons under section 1983, the Supreme Court gave wronged citizens bringing actions for money damages direct access to the deep pockets of the public fisc. In so doing, however, the Court made an interesting qualification that recalls the French distinction between *faute de service* and *faute personnelle*. A local jurisdiction can be held liable when "the action that is alleged to be unconstitutional implements or executes a policy statement, ordinance, regulation or decision officially adopted and promulgated by that body's officers." This language approximates the French notion of official fault. Conversely, the local government will not be liable for the wrongs of its employees "unless action pursuant to official municipal policy of some nature caused a constitutional tort." The Court summarized its holding as follows: "We conclude that a municipality cannot be held liable *solely* because it employs a tortfeasor—or, in other words, a municipality cannot be held liable under §1983 on a *respondeat superior* theory."[112]

Respondeat superior means "let the master answer" for the wrongs of his servant. Under this theory, the mere fact of an employer-employee relationship would suffice to render a local government liable for its employee's torts. In rejecting this notion, the Court allows some scope for personal accountability on the part of the erring public servant and thereby recalls the French notion of personal fault.

Because American local governments have never been affected by the sovereign immunity doctrine, their situation is closer to that of French administrative agencies since *Blanco* than is the case with state and federal governments. It is not surprising, therefore, that American courts should develop a legal theory of responsibility for local governments that resembles the theory developed in France.

Voie de fait and Absolute Immunity

The doctrine of *voie de fait* (flagrant irregularity) extends the discussion of official and personal faults to administrative acts that are so flagrantly illegal as to be "denatured" of their administrative character in the forceful language of a leading administrative law textbook.[113] *Voie de fait* (literally "way of fact") has no common law equivalent. "Flagrant irregularity" is the translation suggested by Brown and Bell and the one we shall follow in this section. The principle applies only to situations in which a citizen has been deprived of "some fundamental right . . . , such as liberty of the person, sanctity of property, or inviolability of the home."[114]

The expression's strongly pejorative connotation is underscored by its appearances in criminal law as the French counterpart of assault and battery, although its administrative law version does not necessarily imply violence. The word *fait* (fact or deed) emphasizes the nature of the flagrant irregularity as simply an event that has taken place—a deed or a fact—but something that is "manifestly incapable of being connected with the application of a law or a regulation."[115] That is, the flagrant irregularity has no basis in law. It is an event that took place, but it is not an administrative act.

The practical significance of the flagrant irregularity doctrine is that lawsuits for damages brought by victims of such illegal actions fall under the exclusive jurisdiction of the ordinary courts.[116] That is, the perpetrators of the flagrant irregularity—whether individual administrators or an agency itself—are deprived of the customary protection of an administrative court. This is perfectly consistent with the firmly established principle that only administrative courts should have jurisdiction over administrative actions because, by definition, a *voie de fait* means that no administrative action has taken place. As a practical matter, however, *voie de fait* provides one of the few examples in French law where an ordinary court sits in judgment on activities associated with the State.

To grasp the significance of the flagrant irregularity doctrine, it is important to recall that it does not include all forms of official illegality. Thus, while every flagrant irregularity is illegal, not every illegal act constitutes a flagrant irregularity.[117] The Council of State's *Carlier* decision in 1950 clarifies this point nicely.

Carlier was a vocal critic of the Fine Arts administration, charging it with negligence in its appointed task of preserving the great national monuments of France. One day he was busily photographing the exterior of the cathedral at Chartres, "no doubt in order to add to his brief against the Fine Arts Administration," when suddenly he was arrested and taken to the police station. There his negatives were confiscated and he was then released. Undaunted, he returned to the cathedral at once and joined the line of tourists waiting to visit the tower. The guard, a public official acting under orders from his superiors, refused to admit Carlier to the tower.

Carlier sued in the administrative courts for damages because of the wrongs he had suffered. The Council of State agreed to hear that part of his suit dealing with the denial of access to the cathedral tower but not his complaint about his arrest and the confiscation of his negatives. These were *voies de fait* because, in the absence of some dire emergency, there was no basis in law or regulation for the police to arrest Carlier and to confiscate his property. Administrative courts adjudicate administrative cases, but the police action taken against Carlier had no administrative significance. And yet Carlier had clearly been wronged. Consequently, he should seek redress before the ordinary courts.

The cathedral guard's refusal to let Carlier visit the tower was also illegal, but it was nonetheless an administrative act because access to the cathedral was governed by legitimate regulations. That is, the routine management of the cathedral as a national monument included regulations specifying the hours of public access to the building. The regulations were applied illegally to Carlier; but since there were regulations to apply, the illegal action did not lose its administrative character and therefore his complaint could be heard by an administrative court. Hence the aphorism that every flagrant irregularity is illegal but not every illegal act is a flagrant irregularity.

The doctrine of flagrant irregularity has been criticized by many French jurists for a variety of reasons but principally because it dims the bright line dividing the jurisdictions of the administrative and the ordinary courts. Vedel and Delvolvé, however, raise a spirited defense of *voie de fait,* seeing in it "one of the most precious guarantees for civil liberties and for the right to both real and chattel property."[118] They give several reasons for this encomium. The first concerns certain technical questions on the power of the ordinary courts to issue injunctions against administrative officers under the *voie de fait* doctrine. Injunctions enable judges to right wrongs in a matter of days or even hours, whereas the same matter as an after-the-fact action for damages might drag on for years in the administrative courts. Secondly, the injunctions of the ordinary courts reach not only administrative agencies but the administrators themselves. Under the flagrant irregularity doctrine, administrators for good reason lose the customary protection from ordinary courts that they enjoy as a result of the separation of powers doctrine. Bereft of their customary protection, they feel the discipline of personal accountability before an ordinary judge. As Vedel and Delvolvé put it: "The bureaucrat becomes an ordinary man like every one else and experience shows in a striking way that in this situation, even the most stubborn administrator becomes a simple citizen once again and readily obeys the judge and the law."[119]

Thus, Vedel and Delvolvé see in *voie de fait* something that is good for the soul of the bureaucrat because, like an ordinary citizen, he must answer to an ordinary judge for his misdeeds.

To this salutary reflection we might add the observation that *voie de fait* reveals an important normative element of the French understanding of separation of powers. Significantly, Vedel and Delvolvé say the *protection* administrators ordinarily enjoy under separation of powers is appropriately withdrawn in cases of *voie de fait* because there is simply no administrative action to protect.[120] The notion of separation of powers as a means to protect the integrity of administration marks a sharp difference between the French and American understandings of this venerable doctrine. Although Publius defends the president's veto as a means of protecting him from the "legislative vortex," it is clear that this protection is instrumental to the broader purpose of American separation of powers which includes not only institutional integrity but personal liberty as well.[121]

There is no flagrant irregularity doctrine in American law nor could there be because of the subordination of administrative courts to the ordinary courts in the United States. The importance of flagrant irregularity in France is that—by way of exception—it subjects the State and its officers to the jurisdiction of the ordinary courts. In the United States, however, despite the sovereign immunity doctrine, ordinary courts routinely sit in judgment on the government itself and on its officials.

Nevertheless, the aspect of the flagrant irregularity doctrine that characterizes certain actions taken by public officials as merely facts or deeds without legal meaning might illuminate some of the dark corners in the problematic area of official immunity in the United States. Our earlier discussion of tort liability touched on questions of official immunity, but our present concern with *voie de fait* invites a closer look at it.

Not surprisingly, the American law on official immunity, like virtually everything else in American government, tracks the separation of powers doctrine with different standards for each of the three great branches of government. Congressional standards focus on the meaning of the constitutional provision that "for any Speech or Debate in either House, they [the members of Congress] shall not be questioned in any other place." Since a courtroom would be "another place," this provision clearly means that no member of Congress can be made to answer before a court for anything he or she may have said on the floor of the Senate or the House of Representatives. Thus, the senators and the representatives enjoy an absolute immunity within the narrow confines of the legislative chambers. But what about questionable actions by congressmen in other circumstances? Specifically, what about a senator who defames a citizen during a congressional debate and then circulates his defamatory remarks in a press release? Or the remarks of a legislator's aide as opposed to the legislator himself? Or state legislators who are not protected by the "speech and debate clause" of the federal constitution? These are the sorts of questions with which the federal courts have struggled in trying to define the boundaries of legislative immunity from accountability to the courts.[122]

Executive officers enjoy what is commonly called a "qualified immunity," which the Supreme Court has described as meaning that

> government officials performing discretionary functions generally are shielded from liability for civil damages insofar as their conduct does not violate clearly established statutory or constitutional rights of which a reasonable person would have known.[123]

This standard is also known as "good faith immunity," a somewhat misleading expression because it stresses the subjective disposition of the officer—his state of mind, as it were—at the expense of the objective standard the Supreme Court clearly implies in the passage quoted above: "clearly established statutory or constitutional rights of which a reasonable person would have known."

Judges and other significant participants in the adjudicatory process, notably prosecutors, are more fortunate than both their executive and legislative colleagues. More fortunate than the former because their immunity is absolute, and more fortunate than the latter because the absolute immunity of judges rests on a broader foundation than the "speech and debate" clause. A sweeping Supreme Court opinion rendered over a century ago in *Bradley v. Fisher* held that

> judges of courts of superior or general jurisdiction are not liable to civil actions for their judicial acts, even when such acts are in excess of their jurisdiction, and are alleged to have been done maliciously or corruptly.[124]

The absolute immunity of judicial officers was put to a severe test in the startling case of *Stump v. Sparkman*.[125] Linda Sparkman, a young married woman, brought suit against Judge Harold Stump of the Circuit Court of DeKalb County, Indiana, for an order he had signed in 1971 authorizing a physician at the DeKalb Memorial Hospital to perform a tubal ligation upon her without her knowledge. At the time Linda was a fifteen-year-old minor. Her mother, alleging that Linda was "mildly retarded" and prone to stay out all night with older men, petitioned the judge to authorize the sterilization as something that would be in the "best interest" of her child. Judge Stump granted the mother's request on the same day it was made. Within a week, Linda entered the hospital after being told that she was to undergo an appendectomy. Unaware of the true nature of her surgery, Linda married two years later. Her inability to conceive led to tests revealing that she had been sterilized in 1971. This discovery prompted a section 1983 suit against Judge Stump, which charged that, acting under color of state law, he had deprived her of a broad range of constitutional rights. Prominent among the nine rights listed in the complaint was the right not to be deprived of liberty—here the liberty to procreate—without due process of law. Sparkman maintained Judge Stump's actions were arbitrary and therefore failed to meet minimal due process standards.

The federal District Court, citing the principle of judicial immunity, held that no action could lie against Judge Stump. The United States Court of Appeals for the Seventh Circuit reversed, "holding that the 'crucial issue' was 'whether Judge Stump acted within his jurisdiction' and concluding that he had not."[126] The Supreme Court in turn reversed the Court of Appeals decision that had favored Linda Sparkman.

The question of jurisdiction was indeed, as the Court of Appeals suggested, the "crucial issue." In announcing the broad immunity of judges in *Bradley v. Fisher,* the Supreme Court had added one important qualification: the judge "will be subject to liability only when he has acted in the 'clear absence of all jurisdiction.' " Since judges are not liable even for their malicious acts, the jurisdictional issue seemed to be the only way to attack the mighty fortress of judicial immunity. Justice White, who delivered the opinion of the Court, examined the Indiana law conferring jurisdiction upon circuit court judges and found that there was "indeed a broad jurisdictional grant"—broad enough to reverse the Court of Appeals' finding that Judge Stump had no jurisdiction over Sparkman's mother's plea for the duplicitous sterilization order.[127] The tone of Justice White's opinion hinted at his disgust with Judge Stump's shameful behavior, but, however reluctantly, he found that the law—as settled over a century earlier in *Fisher v. Bradley*—supported the judge's authority to make the decision.

Justice Stewart, joined by Justices Marshall and Powell, filed a dissenting opinion, which brings us back to *voie de fait,* for it seems that the dissenters sought something akin to this principle as they struggled to justify in law the basis of their displeasure with the outcome of *Stump v. Sparkman.* Citing the language of *Bradley v. Fisher* to the effect that judges are absolutely immune from monetary liability "for their judicial acts," Stewart maintained that Judge Stump's behavior in this case was so outrageous that it ceased to be a "judicial act" and therefore could not be protected by judicial immunity. Just as *voie de fait* "denatures" an administrative act of its administrative character, so, according to Justice Stewart, Judge Stump's irresponsible acquiescence to the request for the sterilization order "was beyond the pale of anything that could sensibly be called a judicial act."[128]

Stewart offered impressive arguments to support his position. Without belaboring technical procedural matters, he simply noted the following points in passing: (1) The petition for the sterilization order "was not given a docket number" nor was it "placed on file with the clerk's office"; (2) The petition was granted "in an ex parte proceeding without notice to the minor, without a hearing, and without the appointment of a guardian *ad litem;* and (3) Stump did not appear "in his judge's robes" and the proceeding did not take place "in the courtroom itself."

Having touched on these technical points, Stewart then focused on the legal precedents supporting absolute immunity for judges. They rested on three sound public policy considerations. First, a judge should be immune from lawsuits as reprisals from disappointed litigants, because at times it is inevitable that he will anger many people, since it is his "duty to decide all cases within his jurisdiction that are brought before him including cases that arouse the most intense feelings in the litigants." Second, a judge's errors can always be corrected on appeal and, third, the fear of being relentlessly pursued by disappointed litigants would "contribute not to principled and fearless decision-making but to intimidation."[129]

Having reviewed the policy reasons for judicial immunity, Stewart maintained that none of them applied to Judge Stump: "There were no litigants. There was and could be no appeal. And there was not even the pretext of principled decision-making." He then concluded that "the total absence of *any* of these normal attributes of a judicial proceeding" had convinced him that Judge Stump's action "was not a judicial act."

Unfortunately for Linda Sparkman and, in my opinion, for the sake of justice itself, Stewart's argument did not prevail against Justice White's reliance on the admittedly strong precedents in favor of absolute judicial immunity. These precedents were too well-entrenched in the law to permit Justice Stewart's innovative reasoning on the absence of a judicial act to carry the day. Perhaps if American law harbored a principle somewhat akin to *voie de fait,* Stewart might have prevailed.

As stated at the outset of this chapter, its purpose has been to initiate "a normative dialogue among students, professors and practitioners of public administration in France and the United States." I have tried to ground this normative dialogue in the traditions of constitutional and administrative law in the two countries. I hope I have succeeded in showing how legal argument invites normative reflection. I also hope I have shown how remarkably similar many of the legal norms are in the two countries despite the profound differences in language, legal culture, and general history. Perhaps an awareness of these similarities and differences will help to define the role of law in developing an administrative culture across national boundaries.

8

Conclusion

Men are not corrupted by the exercise of power or debased by the habit of obedience, but by the exercise of a power which they believe to be illegitimate, and by obedience to a rule which they consider to be usurped and oppressive.
— ALEXIS DE TOCQUEVILLE

The preface to this book explained its origins. To refresh the reader's memory, I stated that having struggled in an earlier book with the problem of legitimating the contemporary American administrative state in terms of the "intent of the framers" of the Constitution, I began to wonder what might happen in a country whose normative foundations were the opposite of those of the United States—that is, a country in which administrative institutions embodied the abiding norms while constitutions were unstable. France was the obvious choice to satisfy my curiosity and the pages between the preface and this conclusion answer my question.

In this concluding chapter, I shall develop four points that I hope will recall, highlight, and extend some of the major findings in our investigation: (1) the crucial role of the Council of State in developing the Constitution of the Fifth Republic; (2) the importance for public administration of the demise of the sovereign Parliament; (3) an in-depth examination of how an important and perennial administrative problem—the control of the political activity of civil servants—is addressed in France where administrative and constitutional principles are so closely linked; and (4) a closing reflection on the American practice of requiring civil servants to take an oath to uphold the Constitution of the United States.

THE COUNCIL OF STATE

To the careful reader it will come as no surprise to learn of my profound admiration for the Council of State. Indeed, I fear my admiration may at times have crossed the boundary into cheerleading; but, if so, I draw some comfort from the company I keep. For decades, distinguished British and American scholars have struggled to find the appropriate superlatives to express their enthusiasm for the Council of State. Consider the following descriptions: The Council of State

- has a unique record in European administrative law, and a unique reputation amongst administrative courts. For impartiality, intellectual brilliance, common sense, administrative wisdom and experience, and ability to reconcile the interests of efficient administration with the rights of a citizen, it has no equal.
- is a remarkably successful institution. . . . It is composed of the cream of the French civil service.
- is the saving grace [of the French administrative system].
- became the unshakeable cornerstone of the French administrative system.
- is one of the most remarkable institutions of France.
- has enriched the concept of civil liberties by "deducing" them from existing laws. Thus, its decisions have contributed to promoting sexual equality before the law, limiting the administrative internment of foreigners; and affirming civil servants' right to strike, freedom of the press, the principle of public trials, and the equality of access of candidates to state examinations regardless of their political orientations.
- [The Council of State's] advice is never binding [upon the government], but its prestige is so high that, now more than before, its recommendations are seldom ignored.[1]

For the immediate purpose of this study, the most obvious contribution of the councillors of State to the Constitution of the Fifth Republic is their absolutely crucial role in drafting the text. As we saw in chapter one, Michel Debré, himself a councillor of State, relied heavily upon a "working group" of younger councillors in the challenging task of subjecting General de Gaulle's lofty aspirations for his country to the discipline of a legal text that would be at once feasible in practice and politically acceptable.

Less obvious, but important nonetheless, was the decisive role played by the Council of State itself, not just Debré's working group, in fashioning the language that gave final form to the Constitutional Council. I refer in particular to what in chapter five we called the "supremacy clause"—that is, the following provision from article 62:

> The decisions of the Constitutional Council may not be appealed to any jurisdiction whatsoever. They must be recognized by the government authorities and by all administrative and judicial authorities.

This provision must give pause to critics of administrative behavior who are all too ready to pontificate on the self-aggrandizing nature of administrative institutions. The Council of State offers a clear counterexample of an administrative agency displaying a statesmanlike willingness to confer substantial power and authority upon a potential institutional rival.

American students of public administration who admire the Council of State must do so at a distance because such an institution would be unthinkable in the United States. The Council of State is too deeply rooted in French history, especially in the relatively weak tradition of judicial independence for the ordinary courts in France, to provide anything faintly resembling a model for the United States. That is, the origin and development of the Council of State is inextricably linked to a serious flaw in the French constitutional tradition which, fortunately, does not exist in the United States. What Americans can and should learn from the Council of State is that an administrative institution can play a leading role—indeed, in France, *the* leading role—in protecting individual rights. This point was developed at some length in chapter seven as well as in chapter five, where we saw that many of the legal principles used by the Constitutional Council to defend individual rights were drawn from the jurisprudence of the Council of State. Staffed as it is with seasoned administrators, the Council of State stands as a concrete refutation of the facile assumption that vigorous administration is somehow at war with individual rights. This is a lesson Americans should find congenial, for in the first of *The Federalist Papers* Publius asserts that "the vigor of government is essential to the security of liberty."[2]

THE DEMISE OF THE SOVEREIGN PARLIAMENT

The demise of the sovereign Parliament under the Fifth Republic has been a major theme in this book. At the risk of wearying the reader, I believe it worthwhile to review the background of this important development in French constitutional history. Let us begin our review by recalling that separation of powers is understood very differently in the two countries, a point that has been touched upon, in one way or another, in every chapter of this book.

Prior to 1958, French republicans insisted upon parliamentary sovereignty and, in so doing, excluded any possibility of serious consideration of separation of powers as Americans understand that principle. For Americans, separation of powers precludes the possibility of any *institution* possessing sovereign power. In the American tradition, sovereign power and separation of powers are mutually exclusive ideas. The American people are sovereign; but, unlike the French Parliament, they are not an institution. They divide their sovereign power between their state and national governments and then subdivide these powers into legislative, executive, and judicial institutions at both levels. Such an arrangement is utterly at odds with sovereign power which, by definition, is one and supreme. Throughout the history of the United States, despite occasional grumblings about an "imperial presidency," "congressional government," and an "imperial judiciary," there has never been one supreme institution of government.

As long as the French Parliament remained sovereign, French administration was necessarily subordinate to it, at least in principle. I add the qualification "at least in principle," because as a matter of fact French governments under the Third and Fourth Republics occasionally wielded considerably broad powers Parliament had delegated to them by decree-laws *(décrets-lois)* or by other means of sometimes dubious legality.[3] Thus, strong governments were not necessarily incompatible with a sovereign Parliament, but their strength was always held hostage to parliamentary whim. Hence, even strong governments were unstable and all too many governments were, of course, neither strong nor stable.

All this changed in 1958 with the enumeration in article 34 of specific areas reserved for parliamentary action by law followed by the provision in article 37 consigning all other matters to the regulatory power of the government. Parliament was no longer sovereign, since certain areas of French life were beyond its control. As we saw in chapter four, the Constitutional Council, notably in its decision of 20 July 1982, has interpreted these provisions more favorably to Parliament than the framers of 1958 might have expected; but by the 1980s, the parliamentary excesses of the Third and Fourth Republics were but a distant memory. By that time, the revolution in constitutional theory envisioned in the text of the 1958 document had been sufficiently integrated into French political practice that the Constitutional Council could slacken the reins holding Parliament in check without endangering the fundamental constitutional innovation of the Fifth Republic. French politicians, especially members of the parliamentary majority, can still be heard carrying on about a "sovereign Parliament," but their complaints are patently partisan and, as a matter of legal doctrine, are taken no more seriously than those of their American counterparts who celebrate the long-moribund "sovereign states" of the Union.

The demise of the sovereign French Parliament is important for Americans for three reasons. First, it enhances the opportunity for Franco-American dialogue on constitutional principles. Neither country has a sovereign *institution*. In both countries the people exercised their sovereignty by approving constitutions that distribute less-than-sovereign power to specific governing institutions. Therefore, the fundamental principles of government in the two republics resemble one another more closely than they did prior to 1958.

Second, this consideration offers Americans a salutary reminder of the preeminent role of the Constitution in our own political life. At times we forget that it is the Constitution of the United States that confers legitimate power upon those whom we elect. More seriously, our elected officials themselves sometimes forget this as well, and assume a certain arrogance of power as they boast of the authority the people have conferred upon them. As we observed in chapter four, whatever authority our elected officials possess comes to them, not directly from the people, but from the Constitution whose officers they are. In our elections, we the people simply name the officers who will exercise the authority we gave to a constitutional order, which, in turn, distributes certain powers among certain offices.

Prior to 1958, French parliamentarians played fast and loose with their republican constitutions and they did so with impeccable logic. If Parliament is sovereign, no legal text, not even a constitution, can prevail against it. The demise of the sovereign Parliament highlights its character as but one of several institutions exercising limited powers as provided in the constitutional text that won the approval of the sovereign people in 1958. This is the clear implication of Raymond Janot's comment, which we have already examined:

> If the French people adopt this constitution, it is they who are sovereign and the commands of the sovereign bind the Assembly. To say that the Assembly is sovereign is simply an abuse of language. There is but one sovereign and that is the people. The people may distribute their powers as they see fit.[4]

Janot's wise words remind Americans of their own tradition and inspirit them against the unwholesome demagoguery one occasionally detects in elected officials.

Third, the idea of legitimate authority flowing from the Constitution is helpful for harried American administrators whose participation in the governing process is often challenged by posturing elected officials and disgruntled citizens. Just as the Constitution explicitly created Congress and the Supreme Court, so too it explicitly empowers Congress to create other offices "by law," states how these offices are to be staffed, and for good measure, gives Congress all the means "necessary and proper" to carry out these powers. This is the constitutional basis of the administrative state created gradually by Congress over the past two centuries. The fact that administrative officers are not elected has no effect whatsoever upon their constitutional legitimacy.[5]

POLITICAL ACTIVITIES OF CIVIL SERVANTS

Since the focus of this book has been on the relationship between administration and constitutionalism, we have had little chance to observe in detail the workings of the French administrative system. To be sure, there is an abundant literature on French administration readily available in English.[6] Before concluding our work, however, I believe it would be useful to examine in some detail at least one substantive area of French public administration in which fundamental regime values and administrative behavior come together. I have chosen the problem of regulating the political activities of civil servants, a hearty perennial in the garden of any nation's public service and one in which Americans may have something to learn from the French. I say this because public administration theory in this country has failed to catch up with the fact that "political responsiveness" is rapidly replacing the traditional norm of "neutral competence" as the salient *operational* standard for high-ranking American civil servants.[7] This neglect is puzzling when one recalls that Congress enshrined in law something closely akin to a standard of political responsiveness for the Senior Executive Service in the Civil Service Reform Act of 1978.[8]

The French and American approaches to regulating the political activities of civil servants are diametrically opposed. For the most part, Americans prohibit such activities, whereas the French positively encourage them. For over half a century, American career personnel have endured the severe restrictions of the Hatch Act, which, despite certain relaxations recently signed into law by President Clinton, remain strict today. On two occasions, the Supreme Court of the United States has rejected First Amendment arguments challenging the constitutionality of these restrictions.[9]

France encourages the political activity of its civil servants by permitting them to run for and to hold public office without losing their civil service status. Many civil servants hold office in local governments through partisan elections. They can even be members of the French Parliament, provided they take a temporary leave of absence from their civil service positions. After having served in Parliament, they may return to the civil service at the same rank they held when they left. This practice is very common in France. From 1958 until 1986, 33 percent of the members of the National Assembly came from the civil service. The percentage was lower in the earlier years of the Fifth Republic, but grew to 38.8 percent in 1978 and to 49.9 percent in 1981 before falling off to 41.9 percent in 1986.[10] Once elected to the National Assembly, many civil servants make an impressive career in politics without losing the right to return to their erstwhile status. Remarkably, twelve of the fourteen prime ministers of the Fifth Republic have been former civil servants. So prominent are civil servants in French politics that, as we saw in chapter one, some have called the present republic *la République des fonctionnaires.*

Despite the easy access to politics for French civil servants, French law and tradition impose effective restraints on what civil servants may say, write, or do in relation to matters of public interest. This is done through the *obligation de réserve,* a complicated and somewhat amorphous standard that puts both legal and moral pressure on civil servants to be circumspect in their political statements and, indeed, in any other statements relating to the State or to the government of the day. A careful examination of the obligation of reserve will help to show the differences between the French and American approaches to regulating political excesses by career civil servants.

The obligation of reserve is grounded in the principle of the neutrality of the public service, which in turn is grounded in the fundamental right of the citizen to enjoy an impartial administration of the laws of the French Republic. The services provided by the State should serve general interests, not the particular interests of a political party, not even the party that happens to be in power.[11] Thus civil servants are expected to be neutral in their deportment as they go about their business of delivering public services. They are not to give the slightest impression that a particular public service favors persons adhering to a particular political, philosophical, or religious belief.[12] The civil service statute of 1983 guarantees that personnel files will have no entries on the political, philosophical, or religious beliefs of any civil servant. The principle of neutrality, in turn, obliges the civil servant to avoid giving any outward sign of such beliefs in order to discourage suspicions on the part of the citizen that these beliefs might have an effect on the administration of the laws and regulations of the State. So important is the principle of neutrality that one knowledgeable commentary claims that the citizen's right to impartial public service may well be the "first freedom" in a democratic State.[13]

The principle of neutrality silences the civil servant and therefore, taken alone, presents a one-sided view of the role of the civil servant, who, like every other citizen, has a right to express and to act upon his or her deepest convictions. The obligation of reserve modifies the principle of neutrality in such a way as to accommodate the needs of the civil servant as citizen without reneging on his duty to provide services impartially; that is, by avoiding even the appearance of favoritism to persons of a particular political, religious, or philosophical persuasion.

In its most elementary sense, the obligation of reserve is an obligation to be cautious and moderate in the expression of one's views in order to maintain public confidence in the impartiality of French public administration.[14] Thus a customs official given to using racial epithets to vent his hostility toward immigrants would violate the obligation of reserve.[15] So would a judge who indulges in bitter diatribes against capitalist exploitation of the working class. An employer with litigation before such a judge would rightfully harbor misgivings on his chances of receiving even-handed justice.[16] Both the judge and the customs official are free to believe whatever they please and, more important, they may express their opinions; but they must do so discreetly and in such a way as not to undermine public confidence in the impartiality of French law and administration.

Central to the notion of reserve is the question of *circumstances*. More important than *what* the officials say are the time, place, and manner in which they say it. For example, the Council of State upheld the Ministry of Education in disciplining a school inspector for voicing an intemperate criticism of French foreign policy in a private interview while he was residing abroad. In advising the Council to uphold the sanction against the inspector, the representative of the government (that ill-named officer whom we first met in the preface) conceded that Plenel's remarks might not have warranted disciplinary action if they had been made by a civil-service academic in France. School Inspector Plenel's problem was that the time, place, and manner were all wrong. The time was 1963—in the immediate aftermath of the Algerian war. The place was Algeria itself. The manner was to let his critical remarks be tape-recorded. An Algerian newspaper published his statement, much to the embarrassment of the French government. Plenel maintained he had not given anyone permission to give the tapes to the newspaper, but the Council of State was unimpressed. Plenel never should have allowed his remarks to be recorded in Algeria at that particular time.[17]

Nowhere is the circumstantial character of reserve clearer than in the case of civil servants who are labor union officials. At one time in France, it was thought that public service labor unions were logically incompatible with the obligation of reserve. The strike is a union's most effective weapon in its struggle with an employer—including the State as employer. But the strike is a form of combat, whereas reserve is a principle of subordination. The role of combatant is incompatible with that of subordinate, and therefore the two cannot be reconciled. Whatever the logical merits of this argument, the Council of State, driven by the constitutional mandate for labor unions, carved out an exception to the obligation of reserve for union officials.[18] The exception was carefully tailored to apply to officials as opposed to rank-and-file members. Further, to maintain their privileged position, the officials had to be acting in defense of the interests of the union membership, as opposed to acting in pursuit of some broader political agenda. If these conditions are met, the civil servant who holds office in a public service union may write and speak to his or her superiors in the forceful manner that is customary among union officials, even though such language from an ordinary civil servant would violate the obligation of reserve.

The circumstantial emphasis in the Plenel case and in the cases involving civil service union officials pervades the jurisprudence of the Council of State's treatment of the obligation of reserve. When French civil servants are accused of violating this obligation, the salient issues are the alleged offender's position in the State hierarchy,[19] the specific nature of his or her function—e.g., judges, who are civil servants in France, are held to particularly strict standards,[20] one's status as a candidate for elective office or as one who holds such office,[21] and the distinction between questionable actions taken before one enters a civil service career and afterward.[22]

In sum, the flexible nature of the obligation of reserve is captured by the frequent appearances in the literature of such words as "prudence," "good taste," "common sense," and even the word "gentleman" without translation from the English.[23] As one author put it: "The civil servant may proclaim his loyalty to the proletarian revolution and may glorify the red flag; but in his zeal, he may not drag the tricolor through the mud."[24]

The French attention to circumstances in regulating the political activities of civil servants introduces a degree of flexibility that contrasts sharply with the rigid American approach to the same question. Despite recent relaxations of some of the more burdensome restrictions, federal civil servants are still considerably disadvantaged in comparison to their French colleagues where *partisan* activities are concerned. Interestingly, however, American civil servants are remarkably free—shockingly free by French standards—to express their political views in a nonpartisan context. French civil servants may not drag the tricolor through the mud; but outside the workplace, an American civil servant, like any American citizen, may burn the stars and stripes with impunity.[25] Indeed, as we saw in chapter seven, the Supreme Court of the United States has held that an employee of the state of Texas could not be fired for on-the-job remarks applauding the news that President Reagan had been shot and for then adding that "if they go for him again, I hope they get him."[26]

The efforts of the American personnel system to regulate political behavior is easily driven to the opposing extremes of severity on the one hand and laxity on the other. The French system, with its emphasis on circumstances, has been more successful in finding a middle ground. One possible explanation for this difference is that in France such matters are adjudicated by the Council of State, a group of seasoned administrators, whereas in the United States these matters reach their conclusion before the Supreme Court, which is staffed by judges the French would call *juges judiciaires* (judiciary judges). Not surprisingly, the analysis of the Supreme Court is "legalistic," that is, it tends to polarize the issue before it in the classic but abstract terms of individual rights versus the legitimate powers of the state. Such considerations are not irrelevant in the jurisprudence of the Council of State, but these abstractions are tempered by pragmatic attention to the circumstances and the foreseeable results of the questionable words or deeds.

In some ways, however, the strength of the jurisprudence of the Council of State is also its weakness. The attention to circumstance and detail exacts a price, and that price is a striking lack of clear principles to give solid doctrinal support to the decisions enforcing the obligation of reserve.[27] For example, as noted above, the obligation of reserve is grounded in the principle of neutrality; but how, we might ask, did School Inspector Plenel's ill-starred remarks in Algeria offend against the principle of neutrality? He surely embarrassed the government of the day and probably the French State itself. He may have outraged the vast majority of his fellow country-men. But what does all this—unpleasant as it might be—have to do with neutrality? There was no evidence that in exercising his duties as school inspector, Plenel showed any favoritism to anyone on the grounds of political, religious, or philosophical opinions.

The same question might be asked of the civil servant who is free to honor the red flag but may not drag the tricolor through the mud. To desecrate the flag of one's nation is a shameful deed that stirs the righteous indignation of true patriots. But what does it have to do with neutrality? Why should such behavior—outrageous as it might be—be considered a violation of the obligation of reserve and therefore of neutrality? Indeed, one might argue that the man who desecrates his country's flag shows his contempt for *all* his fellow citizens and does so with stunning impartiality. One can argue that he certainly should be punished, but not for violating an obligation grounded in the principle of neutrality.

As one might suspect, there is a second principle that supports the obligation of reserve—*le bon fonctionnement du service* (the orderly management of the agency).[28] It is this principle, not the principle of neutrality, that has been the grounds for the substantial number of cases in which civil servants have been charged with violating the obligation of reserve because of disobedience or disrespectful behavior toward their superiors. Violations of reserve have been found in such situations as the following:

- A striking municipal worker is recalled to work against his will and insults his superiors with offensive language.[29]
- An employee of the postal service participates in a demonstration after an explicit warning from her minister not to do so.[30]
- A policeman, temporarily suspended from his duties, permits a cartoon critical of President de Gaulle to appear in a newspaper he edits.[31]

The relationship between the two principles that ground the obligation of reserve, neutrality on the one hand and orderly management on the other, is not entirely clear. One of the few authors to address the issue suggests that neutrality is a means to achieve the end of orderly management, but it is only one means toward this end. A second means is a certain deference on the part of the civil servant toward his superior—not servility nor syco-phancy to be sure—but deference just the same.[32]

Within this frame of reference, the obligation of reserve can be violated by behavior that has little or no relation to neutrality. This broadening of the obligation of reserve is unfortunate because it deprives reserve of its admirable focus on safeguarding the citizens' confidence in the impartiality of the public administration. This confidence reinforces the bedrock republican principle of equality before the law, announced in the Declaration of the Rights of Man and of the Citizen of 1789. Thus the obligation of reserve, grounded in the principle of neutrality, gives an upward tilt to French public administration, linking it to what is best in the French political tradition.

The obligation of reserve based on orderly management, as opposed to neutrality, runs the risk of collapsing into a mere instrument of hierarchical control. Jean Rivero detects in the jurisprudence of the obligation of reserve based on orderly management a thinly veiled remnant of *lèse majesté*. That is, a broadly interpreted principle of orderly management provides rhetorical cover for punishing as violations of reserve words and deeds that do nothing more than offend the self-esteem of officials in high positions. In a manner quite inappropriate for a contemporary liberal democracy, obligation of reserve grounded in the needs of orderly management revives the notion of "the sacral character of the prince."[33]

For example, the offense taken by President de Gaulle because of the cartoon that appeared in a newspaper edited by a policeman had nothing to do with the orderly management of the policeman's activities. It would have been different if the policeman had seriously and publicly insulted his immediate supervisor whom he encountered on a day-to-day basis; but the connection between the policeman and the president of the Republic is too tenuous to have any impact on routine management. The policeman's offense was really one of *lèse majesté* masquerading as a violation of the obligation of reserve.[34]

This aspect of the obligation of reserve would seem to be at odds with calls for dramatic changes in French administration that were afoot even before Prime Minister Rocard's widely publicized call for administrative reform in May 1988.[35] For example, at a 1985 roundtable on "The Public Service and Deontology," Guy Braibant, a prominent scholar in French administrative law whom we met in chapter seven, commented on the notable shift in French administrative thought away from "duties of the civil servant and the authority of the State" toward public service.[36] At the same conference, Bernard Gournet, a leading author on French administrative science, remarked upon the way the classic notion of the Weberian administrator has been modified by new norms that stress the role of the administrator as an "effective manager" and one who is "eager to enter into dialogue with the citizens."[37] A decree of 11 February 1977 supported the "accessibility of public administration documents to the public" despite the "pathological obsession with secrecy which characterizes the French administrative tradition."[38] In 1991, an international group of scholars assembled in Paris to discuss efforts at "coproduction" in French transportation services.[39]

These innovations surely challenge that aspect of reserve that is linked to *lèse majesté*. Such an understanding of reserve runs counter to the notion of *transparence* (openness), which dominates the current move toward administrative reform in France.[40] This is not surprising. The origin of the obligation of reserve is judicial. It is borrowed from the jurisprudence of the Court of Cassation in the area of judicial discipline, where it is associated with such notions as "honor," "dignity," "dedication," and "the State."[41] President Pompidou once assured an assembly of high-ranking civil servants that it is "the obligation of reserve that creates the grandeur and the dignity of their mission."[42] This high-toned language is appropriate as long as administration is looked upon as "the detailed and systematic execution of public law."[43] In this setting, administrators are judgelike figures—remote, aloof, and above the battle. They must exude dignity and reserve because they represent the majesty of the State. They are not "transparent," dynamic, or outgoing. As the image of the administrator changes—as it certainly is in contemporary France[44]—the obligation of reserve may change as well.

The friends of administrative reform have good reason to hope that the obligation of reserve will adapt to the changing administrative environment—*adapt* but not disappear. The obligation of reserve is too valuable a part of the French administrative tradition to be sacrificed on the altar of managerial innovation. The obligation of reserve deserves some of the credit for the fact that France successfully avoided the excesses of McCarthyism in the early 1950s.[45] Reserve showed the way to a middle ground between the competing claims for individual liberty on the one hand and the State imperative for loyal civil servants on the other. A middle ground, I might add, that proved so elusive in the United States at that time.

THE OATH OF OFFICE

The Constitution of 1958 has been a resounding success. Prior to that year, one might have described French republicanism as a political culture of brittle brilliance. By marrying institutional stability to republican principle, the 1958 text purged French republicanism of much of its brittleness but none of its brilliance. The 1962 constitutional amendment that brought about the direct election of the president, despite its irregularity, has had the happy effect of making the Fifth Republic a more democratic regime than it was at the outset. The 1974 constitutional amendment permitting sixty senators or deputies to challenge an Act of Parliament before the Constitutional Council, combined with the dramatic development of that council itself, has gone a long way toward realizing the French jurists' dream of an *Etat de droit* (a legal State, i.e., a State subject to the rule of law). Finally, the relatively tranquil relationship between a conservative prime minister and a Socialist president during the second cohabitation augurs well for the capacity of the Constitution of the Fifth Republic to rise above its most problematic provisions.

Despite its accomplishments, the Constitution of the Fifth Republic does not enjoy in France the same prestige and reverence the American Constitution enjoys in the United States. A good illustration of this can be found in the very different reactions in the two countries to the question of whether public servants should be required to take an oath to uphold the Constitution. In the United States, such a requirement is taken for granted. The oath to uphold the Constitution is the moral foundation of the American public service. Not so in France. Indeed, one knowledgeable commentator maintains that "the very thought of such an oath makes Frenchmen shiver."[46] This rather striking cultural difference demands further analysis before our work is finished.

The French have not always opposed compulsory oaths for public officials. Both before and after the Revolution of 1789, mandatory oaths to support the established order were commonplace. Even kings were required to take oaths before ascending their thrones. The precise wording of royal oaths would vary from time to time to respond to the great issues of the day. For example, one king would swear to preserve the territorial integrity of the realm, another to banish heretics, and a third to live in peace with the Church.[47] The Constitution of 1791, which established the ill-starred constitutional monarchy, prescribed a royal oath that clearly reflected the principles of the Revolution and the diminished status of the king. He was required to swear "to be faithful to the Nation, and to the Law, to use all the power delegated to him to uphold the Constitution established by the National Constituent Assembly in the years 1789, 1790, and 1791 and to see to it that the Laws are executed."[48] The same constitution required all civil servants to take the following oath: "I swear to be faithful to the Nation, to the law and to the King, and to uphold with all my power the Constitution of the realm established by the National Constituent Assembly in the years 1789, 1790, and 1791.[49]

As France lurched and reeled from one regime to another in the chaotic aftermath of the Revolution, civil servants continued to swear their loyalty to whatever form of government happened to be in power—constitutional monarchy, republic, directorate, consulate, empire, or restored monarchy. The oaths assumed a "fill-in-the-blank" character depending on the regime of the day. Thus civil servants who had pledged their fidelity to the constitutional monarchy of 1791 found within themselves sufficient moral flexibility to swear their "hatred for royalty" four years later, their "fidelity to the Emperor" a few years after that, and finally their "obedience and fidelity to the King" once the monarchy had been restored. There were at least 726 relatively high-ranking officers who survived the constant political upheaval between 1789 and 1815 and solemnly pledged their fidelity to each regime in its turn. They came to be known as *les girouettes* (the weathercocks). The most famous of them was Talleyrand, truly a world-class survivor. When he came out of retirement to swear his loyalty to a new king after still another revolution in 1830, he is reported to have said somewhat wearily, "Sire, this is my seventeenth oath."[50]

Despite this unhappy history, oaths continued to be required from civil servants until 1870 with only a brief hiatus during the Second Republic (1848-1851).[51] In 1870, during the stressful conditions of the Franco-Prussian War, oaths for civil servants were again abolished shortly after the collapse of the Second Empire and the establishment of a provisional government that would eventually lead to the Third Republic (1871-1940). Throughout the long history of the Third Republic, there were no compulsory oaths because they were considered to be incompatible with republican institutions.[52] Oaths for high-ranking civil servants were reinstated with the establishment of Maréchal Pétain's collaborationist regime at Vichy in 1940.

Today in France the idea of compulsory oaths carries fascist overtones because of their reinstatement under the disgraced Pétain regime. The oath required at that time was particularly offensive because it required high-ranking civil servants to pledge their fidelity to the person of the chief of state, the maréchal himself, who was also the author of the act requiring the oath.[53]

Although the Vichy era oath was offensive, it was not illogical. The only periods in French history in which civil service oaths had been prohibited were the Second and Third Republics, 1848-1851 and 1871-1940, respectively. Republicans looked upon such oaths as unsavory relics of discredited authoritarian regimes. Maréchal Pétain had no intention of establishing a Republic. With the fall of France in 1940, *la République Française* gave way to Pétain's *Etat Français,* which was unabashedly authoritarian in fact and in principle. The reinstatement of civil service oaths was a policy entirely compatible with the spirit and form of the Vichy regime.

The link in the French political tradition between civil service oaths and authoritarian government should be of considerable interest to thoughtful Americans. There is no such link in our own tradition. Like most contemporary Frenchmen, we are uncompromising republicans but, unlike them, we have no reservations whatsoever about requiring affirmative oaths from our civil servants.[54] Perhaps an examination of the French republican tradition of rejecting compulsory oaths will illuminate our own republican practice of demanding them. To do this, we must go beyond the vagaries of French history and return, once again, to the French understanding of the nature of republicanism.

As we have mentioned so often in this book, parliamentary supremacy dominated the republican tradition in France until 1958. This was especially true during the era of the Third Republic (1871–1940), the longest republican regime in French history. Strictly speaking, the legal foundation of the Third Republic was not a constitution, but a series of "constitutional laws" passed in 1875.[55] Unlike the American constitutional practice, these constitutional laws were not anchored in a "higher" written constitution. Thus the American practice of requiring civil servants to swear to uphold the Constitution of the United States as a "higher law" than a mere act of Congress or a presidential executive order would have been utterly irrelevant under the Third Republic.

The reader will also recall that before 1958 the dominant theory of French republicans maintained that the elected representatives of the people truly *re-presented*—that is, presented a second time, in microcosm—the sovereign people themselves. Therefore it would be illogical to demand from civil servants—or even from parliamentarians themselves—an oath to uphold something higher than a legislative enactment because this "something higher" would be higher than the people themselves who are *re-presented* in their legislative assembly. But in republican theory in France and in the United States (and probably everywhere else) there can be no authority higher than the people themselves. In addition, such an oath might furnish civil servants a principled basis for refusing to obey laws duly passed by the representatives of the people, and this too would violate the republican principle of parliamentary supremacy as the surrogate of the supremacy of the people.

A second argument against civil service oaths in a republican regime focused on the individual rights of the civil servant himself as citizen. To require a citizen to swear to uphold a particular form of government implies an impermissible intrusion upon his personal beliefs.[56] The Declaration of the Rights of Man and of the Citizen guarantee that no one will be troubled because of his opinions as long as these opinions are not manifested in such a way as to disturb the public order. It would seem that as long as a civil servant performs his assigned tasks satisfactorily, his beliefs would not disturb the public order and therefore he should not be obliged to swear his loyalty to a particular form of government in which he may not necessarily believe. As we saw in our discussion of the obligation of reserve, French civil servants are free to express their political views outside of the workplace, provided they do so in a prudent and restrained manner. The logic of an oath to uphold a particular constitution precludes fundamental criticism of that constitution—on the job or off the job, restrained or unrestrained.[57] This is because an oath, if taken seriously at all, is a profoundly personal statement that touches the very soul of the juror and therefore cannot be confined to working hours. In the French republican tradition, however, it is a cardinal principle that there should be no state restriction whatsoever on what one *believes*. *Expressions* of belief may be regulated by law as the needs of the public order will require, but the freedom to believe as one wishes is absolute.[58] State-imposed oaths would seem to come perilously close to demanding as a condition of public employment the surrender of that most fundamental right.

What lessons might Americans learn from the checkered history of civil service oaths in France? To answer this question, let us review briefly the reasons why such oaths are out of favor in France today.

1. Oaths are redolent of Vichy.
2. The cynicism of the *girouettes* (weathercocks) in the chaotic quarter century after the Revolution irreparably compromised the character of the civil service oath as a serious statement of moral commitment.
3. Throughout the longest period of republicanism in France, there was no formal constitution to serve as a "higher law" than the laws passed by Parliament.
4. Prior to 1958, the political theory of French republicanism rested on the foundation of legislative supremacy.
5. Compulsory oaths violate the individual rights of civil servants.

The first three reasons are purely historical. They arise out of circumstances peculiar to France and, hence, are of no particular relevance to the United States. The fourth and fifth reasons, however, are quite relevant because, like the French, we Americans are republicans (reason 4) committed to a serious belief in individual rights (reason 5). Let us look first at republicanism and then at individual rights.

Republicanism

In the second section of this chapter, we reviewed the demise of the sovereign Parliament. Since Parliament is no longer sovereign, its acts must follow the "higher law" of the Constitution as interpreted by the Constitutional Council. Interestingly, the nine appointed members of the Constitutional Council must take an oath to discharge their constitutional responsibilities faithfully.[59] This is the only exception under the Fifth Republic to the traditional French republican antipathy toward oaths for civil officers. It is a fitting exception because the constitutional councillors were originally tasked with the serious duty of preventing a collapse into a regime of parliamentary supremacy that would have undermined the regime of constitutional supremacy so clearly intended by the founders of the Fifth Republic. The oath imposed upon the constitutional councillors makes sense because—and only because—the Constitution is superior to Parliament. Once the connection between parliamentary supremacy and republicanism is severed, there is no logical reason why a compulsory oath could not be required of all French civil servants without violating republican principles. No *logical* reason, indeed, but, as we have seen above, there are abundant *historical* reasons why this will not and should not happen in France.[60] Descartes notwithstanding, in France, as in the United States, "a page of history is worth a volume of logic."

What Americans can learn from all this is that one reason why the oath to uphold the Constitution of the United States fits into our political culture so easily is because of our profound belief in constitutional supremacy. At the time of the founding of our own republic, some Anti-Federalists vigorously championed the principle of legislative supremacy and, quite consistently, opposed ratification of the proposed constitution they correctly perceived as rejecting this principle. In the United States this issue was settled definitively with the ratification of our Constitution over two hundred years ago. Neither Congress, nor the president, nor the judiciary is supreme because all three are creatures of the Constitution, which alone is supreme and which alone is a worthy object of a compulsory oath.[61]

Individual Rights

As noted above, French republicans have a second reason for rejecting compulsory civil service oaths: they violate the individual rights of civil servants. Significantly, the oath required of members of the Constitutional Council is carefully worded to avoid this objection. The statute prescribing the oath provides that before assuming office those nominated to the council must

> swear to fulfill their duties well and faithfully, to carry them out with complete impartiality with respect to the constitution, to preserve the secrecy of deliberations and of votes, and not to take any public position nor to give any advice on any questions within the Council's jurisdiction.[62]

Although the oath requires the constitutional councillor to swear to base his or her decision on the Constitution, it does not require that he swear to uphold, defend, or even believe in it. It is a *professional* oath, that is, an oath to observe certain professional standards, rather than a *political* oath demanding adherence to the prevailing State orthodoxy.[63] The duty to exercise his constitutional responsibilities faithfully appears alongside such other routine judicial duties as maintaining secrecy and not speaking out on questions before the council.[64] A constitutional councillor could take this oath in perfectly good conscience even if he despises the Constitution and looks forward to its eventual overthrow.

All this contrasts sharply with the oath required of American civil servants. The exact wording may vary from agency to agency and from time to time, but the text that follows is typical:

> I, _____, do solemnly swear (or affirm) that I will support and defend the Constitution of the United States against all enemies, foreign and domestic; that I will bear true faith and allegiance to the same; that I take this obligation freely, without any mental reservation or purpose of evasion; and that I will well and faithfully discharge the duties of the office on which I am about to enter, so help me God.

There can be no doubt that this oath touches the soul of the American civil servant. He or she must swear to "support" and "defend" the Constitution "against all enemies" and bear "true faith and allegiance" to it. That is, the civil servant must *believe* in the Constitution. The oath is not confined to on-the-job behavior. Civil servants cannot leave their "true faith and allegiance" in the office at five o'clock and pick them up the next morning at nine. Finally, in taking this oath, the civil servant surrenders his natural right to revolution as long as he remains a civil servant; no small matter this for the spiritual heirs of John Locke.

Given the strong American tradition of civil liberties, this is an astounding requirement as a condition of employment. If such an oath were required of all citizens, the courts would almost certainly find it unconstitutional.[65] As a rule the courts are suspicious of governmental requirements to surrender constitutional rights as a condition of employment,[66] but judicial tolerance of affirmative oaths to uphold the Constitution is a notable exception.[67]

Why is it that despite our strong civil libertarian tradition we are so comfortable in demanding that civil servants publicly proclaim their belief in our Constitution—precisely the sort of demand that French republicans would find offensive?

I believe the reason is because it is our Constitution—and perhaps our Constitution alone—that holds us together as a people. This is not true in France. The Constitution of the Fifth Republic is a splendid document that has brought France over thirty years of civic peace and unprecedented prosperity. Admirable as it is, however, it would be absurd to say that the Constitution of the Fifth Republic holds France together. The French have many unifying symbols other than their Constitution to hold them together; "nation," "people," and "State" come readily to mind as powerful symbols that were shaping France centuries before the Fifth Republic. This is not true of the United States. We can speak of an American "nation," "people," or "state" only because our Constitution has made us a people and a nation and has given us a state.[68] The Constitution is absolutely essential for our life together as a people organized in civic friendship for action in history. This is why it is so natural for us to require our civil servants to pledge their allegiance to our Constitution. So important is our Constitution to us that we depart from our customary abhorrence of compulsory political orthodoxy in order to be sure that anyone who exercises any sort of governmental authority shares our most cherished beliefs. To borrow a line from the courts, we impose this duty on civil servants because we believe it is a "compelling state interest."

To close our study, let us reflect upon a passage from the second of *The Federalist Papers,* wherein Publius affirms that

> Providence has been pleased to give this one connected country, to one united people, a people descended from the same ancestors, speaking the same language, professing the same religion, attached to the same principles of government, very similar in their manners and customs, and who, by their joint counsels, arms and efforts, fighting side by side throughout a long a bloody war, have nobly established their general Liberty and Independence.

These words surely strike contemporary Americans as strange and puzzling. It would seem that today we have few indeed of the attributes Publius believes held us together as a people in 1787. We are *not* descended from the same ancestors. We do *not* speak the same language. We do *not* profess the same religion. We are *not* very similar in manners and customs. Indeed, we celebrate our diversity in these matters. Ever since Alaska and Hawaii attained statehood in the 1950s, we are no longer a "connected country." Unlike Publius and his contemporaries, we have no memory of uniting our "arms and efforts" in "just counsels" in order to support the noble endeavor of "fighting side by side throughout a long and bloody war," which issued in successfully winning our "Liberty and Independence." Quite the contrary. Aside from a brief moment of glory in the Persian Gulf, our memory of war bears the burden of Vietnam, a sorry undertaking which was probably unjust and certainly unsuccessful.

In rehearsing Publius's litany of unifying forces, one would be tempted to despair if it were not for one phrase buried in the middle of his statement that still applies today: "attached to the same principles of government." These principles are expressed in the Constitution that Publius exhorted his countrymen to approve. History has swept away all the other props Publius rallied to support our unity as a people—ancestors, language, religion, and so forth. All that remains is our attachment to the "same principles of government" as expressed in our Constitution. Since it is all we have, let us hope it is all we need.

Appendices

The translations of the French texts in Appendices A, B, and C have been supplied by the Press and Information Service of the French Embassy. Permission to reproduce these translations is hereby gratefully acknowledged. To avoid confusion with terminology used throughout my book, I have taken the liberty of rendering the word *premier* in the French Embassy's translation as *prime minister.* Otherwise, the embassy translation is reproduced verbatim. Since several recent amendments to the Constitution of the Fifth Republic have not yet been translated by the Press and Information Service, I have translated these texts myself. They all appear in Appendix C. They are articles: 53–1, 65, 68–1, 68–2, 88–1, 88–3, and 93.

Appendix A:
DECLARATION OF THE RIGHTS OF MAN AND OF THE CITIZEN

Adopted by the National Assembly during the French Revolution on 26 August 1789 and reaffirmed by the Constitution of 1958.

PREAMBLE

The Representatives of the French People, formed into a National Assembly, considering ignorance, forgetfulness, or contempt of the rights of man to be the only causes of public misfortunes and the corruption of Governments, have resolved to set forth, in a solemn Declaration, the natural, inalienable, and sacred rights of man, to the end that this Declaration, constantly present to all members of the body politic, may remind them unceasingly of their rights and their duties; to the end that the acts of the legislative power and those of the executive power, since they may be continually compared with the aim of every political institution, may thereby be the more respected; to the end that the demands of the citizens, founded henceforth on simple and uncontestable principles, may always be directed toward the maintenance of the Constitution and the happiness of all.

In consequence whereof, the National Assembly recognizes and declares, in the presence and under the auspices of the Supreme Being, the following Rights of Man and of the Citizen.

ARTICLE 1

All men are born and remain free, and have equal rights. Social distinctions are unjustifiable except insofar as they may serve the common good.

ARTICLE 2

The purpose of political association is to preserve the natural and inalienable rights of man, *i.e.,* liberty, private property, the inviolability of the person, and the right to resist oppression.

ARTICLE 3

Sovereignty resides essentially in the nation as a whole; no group or individual can exercise any authority not expressly delegated to it or him.

ARTICLE 4

Liberty is the right to do anything which does not harm others. Thus, each man's natural rights are limited only by the necessity to assure equal liberty to others. Only the law can determine what restrictions must be made.

ARTICLE 5

The law can proscribe only those actions which harm society. Any action not forbidden by law cannot be disallowed, nor can anyone be forced to do what the law does not specifically command.

ARTICLE 6

Law is the overt expression of the general will. All citizens have the right to participate in legislation, either in person or through their representatives. The law must be framed to operate completely impartially. Since all are equal before the law, all are equally eligible, in accordance with their abilities, for all public offices and positions.

ARTICLE 7

No man can be indicted, arrested, or held in custody except for offenses legally defined, and according to specified procedures. Those who solicit, transmit, execute, or cause to be executed arbitrary commands must be punished; but if a citizen is summoned or arrested in due legal form it is his duty to obey instantly.

ARTICLE 8

The law must impose only penalties that are obviously necessary. No one can be punished except under the correct application of an established law which must, moreover, have existed before he committed the offense.

ARTICLE 9

Everyone must be presumed innocent until he is pronounced guilty. If his arrest and detention are thought necessary, then no more force may be used than is necessary to secure his person.

ARTICLE 10

No one must suffer for his opinions, even for religious opinions, provided that his advocacy of them does not endanger public order.

ARTICLE 11

Free communication of thought and opinion is one of the most valuable rights of man; thus, every citizen may speak, write, and print his views freely, provided only that he accepts the bounds of this freedom established by law.

ARTICLE 12

Some form of military or police force is necessary to guarantee the maintenance of the rights of man and of the citizen; thus, such a force exists for the benefit of all and not for the particular ends of those who command it.

ARTICLE 13

To maintain the police force and to meet administrative expenses, a financial levy is essential; this must be borne equally by all citizens, in accordance with their individual means.

ARTICLE 14

All citizens have the right to decide, either personally or through their representative, the necessity of a financial levy and their free assent to it must be obtained. They can appropriate it, and decide its extent, duration, and assessment.

ARTICLE 15

Society has the right to require of every public official an account of his administration.

ARTICLE 16

A society in which rights are not guaranteed, and in which there is no separation of powers, has no constitution.

ARTICLE 17

Since the right to private property is sacred and inviolable, no one can be deprived of it except in certain cases legally determined to be essential for pubic security; in such cases a fair indemnity must first of all be granted.

Appendix B:
PREAMBLE TO THE CONSTITUTION OF THE FOURTH REPUBLIC
OF 27 OCTOBER 1946

As Amended by the Constitutional Law of 7 December 1954

PREAMBLE

On the morrow of the victory of the free peoples over the regimes that attempted to enslave and degrade the human person, the French people proclaim once more that every human being, without distinction as to race, religion, or creed, possesses inalienable and sacred rights. They solemnly reaffirm the rights and freedoms of man and of the citizen ordained by the Declaration of Rights of 1789 and the fundamental principles recognized by the laws of the Republic.

They further proclaim as most vital to our time the following political, economic, and social principles:

The law shall guarantee to women equal rights with men, in all domains.

Anyone persecuted because of his activities in the cause of freedom shall be entitled to the right of asylum within the territories of the Republic.

Everyone shall have the duty to work and the right to obtain employment. No one may suffer in his work or his employment because of his origin, his opinions, or his beliefs.

Everyone may defend his rights and interests by trade-union action and may join the union of his choice.

The right to strike may be exercised within the framework of the laws that govern it.

Every worker, through his delegates, may participate in collective bargaining to determine working conditions, as well as in the management of the enterprise.

All property and all enterprises that now have, or subsequently shall have, the character of a national public service or of a monopoly in fact, must become the property of the community.

The Nation shall ensure to the individual and to the family the conditions necessary to their development.

The Nation shall guarantee to all, and particularly to the child, the mother, and the aged worker, protection of health, material security, rest, and leisure. Any individual who, because of his or her age, his or her physical or mental condition, or because of the economic situation, shall find himself or herself unable to work shall have the right to obtain from the community the means for a decent existence.

The Nation shall proclaim the solidarity and equality of all the French people with respect to burdens resulting from national disasters.

The Nation shall guarantee equal access of children and adults to education, professional training, and culture. The establishment of free, secular, public education on all levels shall be a duty of the State.

The French Republic, faithful to its traditions, shall abide by the rules of international public law. It shall not undertake wars of conquest and shall never use force against the freedom of any people.

On condition of reciprocal terms, France shall accept the limitations of sovereignty necessary to the organization and defense of peace.

France shall form with the peoples of her overseas territories a Union based upon equality of rights and duties, without distinction as to race or religion.

The French Union shall be composed of nations and peoples who shall place in common or coordinate their resources and their efforts in order to develop their respective civilizations, further their well-being, and ensure their security.

Faithful to her traditional mission, France shall guide the peoples for whom she has assumed responsibility toward freedom to govern themselves and toward the democratic administration of their own affairs; rejecting any system of colonization based upon arbitrary power, she shall guarantee to all equal access to public office and the individual or collective exercise of the rights and liberties hereinabove proclaimed or confirmed.

Appendix C:
EXCERPTS FROM THE CONSTITUTION OF THE FIFTH REPUBLIC
OF 4 OCTOBER 1958

PREAMBLE

The French people hereby solemnly proclaims its attachment to the Rights of Man and the principles of national sovereignty as defined by the Declaration of 1789, reaffirmed and complemented by the Preamble of the Constitution of 1946.

By virtue of these principles and that of the free determination of peoples, the Republic hereby offers to the Overseas Territories that express the desire to adhere to them, new institutions based on the common ideal of liberty, equality, and fraternity and conceived with a view to their democratic evolution.

ARTICLE 1

The Republic and the peoples of the Overseas Territories who, by an act of free determination, adopt the present Constitution thereby institute a Community.

The Community shall be based on the equality and the solidarity of the peoples composing it.

Title I
On Sovereignty

ARTICLE 2

France is a Republic, indivisible, secular, democratic, and social. It shall ensure the equality of all citizens before the law, without distinction of origin, race, or religion. It shall respect all beliefs.

The language of the Republic is French.

The national emblem is the tricolor flag, blue, white, and red.

The national anthem is the "Marseillaise."

The motto of the Republic is "Liberty, Equality, Fraternity."

Its principle is government of the people, by the people, and for the people.

ARTICLE 3

National sovereignty belongs to the people, which shall exercise this sovereignty through its representatives and by means of referendums.

No section of the people, nor any individual, may attribute to themselves or himself the exercise thereof.

Suffrage may be direct or indirect under the conditions stipulated by the Constitution. It shall always be universal, equal, and secret.

All French citizens of both sexes who have reached their majority and who enjoy civil and political rights may vote under the conditions to be determined by law.

ARTICLE 4

Political parties and groups shall be instrumental in the expression of the suffrage. They shall be formed freely and shall carry on their activities freely. They must respect the principles of national sovereignty and democracy.

Title II
The President of the Republic

ARTICLE 5

The President of the Republic shall see that the Constitution is respected. He shall ensure, by his arbitration, the regular functioning of the governmental authorities, as well as the continuance of the State.

He shall be the guarantor of national independence, of the integrity of the territory, and of respect for Community agreements and treaties.

ARTICLE 6 [as amended 6 November 1962]

The President of the Republic shall be elected for seven years by direct universal suffrage.

The procedures implementing the present article shall be determined by an organic law.

ARTICLE 7 [as amended 6 November 1962 and 18 June 1976]

The President of the Republic shall be elected by an absolute majority of the votes cast. If this is not obtained on the first ballot, there shall be a second ballot on the second Sunday following. Only the two candidates who have received the greatest number of votes on the first ballot shall present themselves, taking into account the possible withdrawal of more favored candidates.

The voting shall begin at the formal summons of the Government.

The election of the new President shall take place twenty days at the least and thirty-five days at the most before the expiration of the powers of the President in office.

In the event that the Presidency of the Republic has been vacated, for any cause whatsoever, or impeded in its functioning as officially noted by the Constitutional Council, to which the matter has been referred by the Government, and which shall rule by an absolute majority of its members, the functions of the President of the Republic, with the exception of those provided for by Articles 11 and 12 below, shall be temporarily exercised by the President of the Senate and, if the latter is in his turn impeded in the exercise of these functions, by the Government.

In case of a vacancy, or when the impediment is declared definitive by the Constitutional Council, the voting for the election of a new President shall take place, except in case of an emergency officially noted by the Constitutional Council, twenty days at the least and thirty-five days at the most after the beginning of the vacancy or the declaration of the definitive character of the impediment.

* * * * *

There may be no application of either Articles 49 and 50 or of Article 89 of the Constitution during the vacancy of the Presidency of the Republic or during the period that elapses between the declaration of the definitive character of the impediment of the President of the Republic and the election of his successor.

ARTICLE 8

The President of the Republic shall appoint the Prime Minister. He shall terminate the functions of the Prime Minister when the latter presents the resignation of the Government.

On the proposal of the Prime Minister, he shall appoint the other members of the Government and shall terminate their functions.

ARTICLE 9

The President of the Republic shall preside over the Council of Ministers.

ARTICLE 10

The President of the Republic shall promulgate the laws within fifteen days following the transmission to the Government of the law which has been definitively adopted.

He may, before the expiration of this time limit, ask Parliament for a reconsideration of the law or of certain of its articles. This reconsideration may not be refused.

ARTICLE 11

The President of the Republic, on the proposal of the Government during [Parliamentary] sessions, or on joint motion of the two assemblies, published in the *Journal Officiel,* may submit to a referendum any bill dealing with the organization of the governmental authorities, entailing approval of a Community agreement, or providing for authorization to ratify a treaty that, without being contrary to the Constitution, might affect the functioning of [existing] institutions.

When the referendum decides in favor of the bill, the President of the Republic shall promulgate it within the time limit stipulated in the preceding article.

ARTICLE 12

The President of the Republic may, after consultation with the Prime Minister and the Presidents of the assemblies, declare the dissolution of the National Assembly.

General elections shall take place twenty days at the least and forty days at the most after the dissolution.

The National Assembly shall convene by right on the second Thursday following its election. If this meeting takes place between the periods provided for ordinary sessions, a session shall, by right, be held for a fifteen-day period.

There may be no further dissolution within a year following these elections.

ARTICLE 13

The President of the Republic shall sign the ordinances and decrees decided upon in the Council of Ministers.

He shall make appointments to the civil and military posts of the State.

Councilors of State, the Grand Chancellor of the Legion of Honor, Ambassadors and envoys extraordinary, Master Councilors of the Audit Office, prefects, representatives of the Government in the Overseas Territories, general officers, rectors of academies [regional divisions of the public educational system], and directors of central administrations shall be appointed in meetings of the Council of Ministers.

An organic law shall determine the other posts to be filled in meetings of the Council of Ministers, as well as the conditions under which the power of the President of the Republic to make appointments to office may be delegated by him and exercised in his name.

ARTICLE 14

The President of the Republic shall accredit Ambassadors and envoys extraordinary to foreign powers; foreign Ambassadors and envoys extraordinary shall be accredited to him.

ARTICLE 15

The President of the Republic shall be commander of the armed forces. He shall preside over the higher councils and committees of national defense.

ARTICLE 16

When the institutions of the Republic, the independence of the nation, the integrity of its territory, or the fulfillment of its international commitments are threatened in a grave and immediate manner and when the regular functioning of the constitutional governmental authorities is interrupted, the President of the Republic shall take the measures commanded by these circumstances, after official consultation with the Prime Minister, the Presidents of the assemblies, and the Constitutional Council.

He shall inform the nation of these measures in a message.

These measures must be prompted by the desire to ensure the constitutional governmental authorities, in the shortest possible time, the means of fulfilling their assigned functions. The Constitutional Council shall be consulted with regard to such measures.

Parliament shall meet by right.

The National Assembly may not be dissolved during the exercise of emergency powers [by the President].

ARTICLE 17

The President of the Republic shall have the right of pardon.

ARTICLE 18

The President of the Republic shall communicate with the two assemblies of Parliament by means of messages, which he shall cause to be read, and which shall not be followed by any debate.

Between sessions, Parliament shall be convened especially for this purpose.

ARTICLE 19

The acts of the President of the Republic, other than those provided for under Articles 8 [first paragraph], 11, 12, 16, 18, 54, 56, and 61, shall be countersigned by the Prime Minister and, should circumstances so require, by the appropriate ministers.

Title III
The Government

ARTICLE 20

The Government shall determine and direct the policy of the nation.

It shall have at its disposal the administration and the armed forces.

It shall be responsible to Parliament under the conditions and according to the procedures stipulated in Articles 49 and 50.

ARTICLE 21

The Prime Minister shall direct the operation of the Government. He shall be responsible for national defense. He shall ensure the execution of the laws. Subject to the provisions of Article 13, he shall have regulatory powers and shall make appointments to civil and military posts.

He may delegate certain of his powers to the ministers.

He shall replace, should the occasion arise, the President of the Republic as chairman of the councils and committees provided for under Article 15.

He may, in exceptional instances, replace him as chairman of a meeting of the Council of Ministers by virtue of an explicit delegation and for a specific agenda.

ARTICLE 22

The acts of the Prime Minister shall be countersigned, when circumstances so require, by the ministers responsible for their execution.

ARTICLE 23

The office of member of the Government shall be incompatible with the exercise of any Parliamentary mandate, with the holding of any office at the national level in business, professional, or labor organizations, and with any public employment or professional activity.

An organic law shall determine the conditions under which the holders of such mandates, functions, or employments shall be replaced.

The replacement of members of Parliament shall take place in accordance with the provisions of Article 25.

Title IV
The Parliament

ARTICLE 24

The Parliament shall comprise the National Assembly and the Senate.

The deputies to the National Assembly shall be elected by direct suffrage.

The Senate shall be elected by indirect suffrage. It shall ensure the representation of the territorial units of the Republic. French nationals living outside France shall be represented in the Senate.

ARTICLE 25

An organic law shall determine the term for which each assembly is elected, the number of its members, their emoluments, the conditions of eligibility and ineligibility, and the offices incompatible with membership in the assemblies.

It shall likewise determine the conditions under which, in the case of a vacancy in either assembly, persons shall be elected to replace the deputy or senator whose seat has been vacated until the holding of new complete or partial elections to the assembly concerned.

ARTICLE 26

No member of Parliament may be prosecuted, sought, arrested, detained, or tried as a result of the opinions or votes expressed by him in the exercise of his functions.

No member of Parliament may, during Parliamentary sessions, be prosecuted or arrested for criminal or minor offenses without the authorization of the assembly of which he is a member except in the case of *flagrante delicto.*

When Parliament is not in session, no member of Parliament may be arrested without the authorization of the Secretariat of the assembly of which he is a member, except in the case of *flagrante delicto,* of authorized prosecution, or of final conviction.

The detention or prosecution of a member of Parliament shall be suspended if the assembly of which he is a member so demands.

ARTICLE 27

All binding instructions [upon members of Parliament] shall be null and void.

The right to vote of the members of Parliament shall be personal.

An organic law may, under exceptional circumstances, authorize the delegation of a vote. In this case, no member may be delegated more than one vote.

ARTICLE 28 [as amended 30 December 1963]

Parliament shall convene, by right, in two ordinary sessions a year.

The first session shall begin on October 2; it shall last eighty days.

The second session shall open on April 2; it may not last longer than ninety days.

If October 2 or April 2 is a holiday, the session shall begin on the first working day following.

ARTICLE 29

Parliament shall convene in extraordinary session at the request of the Prime Minister, or of the majority of the members comprising the National Assembly, to consider a specific agenda.

When an extraordinary session is held at the request of the members of the National Assembly, the closure decree shall take effect as soon as Parliament has exhausted the agenda for which it was called, and at the latest twelve days from the date of its meeting.

Only the Prime Minister may ask for a new session before the end of the month following the closure decree.

ARTICLE 30

Apart from cases in which Parliament meets by right, extraordinary sessions shall be opened and closed by decree of the President of the Republic.

ARTICLE 31

The members of the Government shall have access to the two assemblies. They shall be heard when they so request.

They may call for the assistance of commissioners of the government.

ARTICLE 32

The President of the National Assembly shall be elected for the duration of the legislature. The President of the Senate shall be elected after each partial reelection [of the Senate].

ARTICLE 33

The meetings of the two assemblies shall be public. An *in extenso* report of the debates shall be published in the *Journal Officiel.*

Each assembly may sit in secret committee at the request of the Prime Minister or of one tenth of its members.

Title V
On Relations Between Parliament and the Government

ARTICLE 34

All laws shall be passed by Parliament.
Laws shall establish the regulations concerning:

- civil rights and the fundamental guarantees granted to citizens for the exercise of their public liberties; the obligations imposed by national defense upon the persons and property of citizens;
- nationality, status, and legal capacity of persons, marriage contracts, inheritance and gifts;
- determination of crimes and misdemeanors as well as the penalties imposed therefor; criminal procedure; amnesty; the creation of new juridical systems and the status of magistrates;
- the basis, the rate, and the methods of collecting taxes of all types; the issuance of currency.

Laws shall likewise determine the regulations concerning:

- the electoral system of the Parliamentary assemblies and the local assemblies;
- the establishment of categories of public institutions;
- the fundamental guarantees granted to civil and military personnel employed by the State;
- the nationalization of enterprises and the transfer of the property of enterprises from the public to the private sector.

Laws shall determine the fundamental principles of:

- the general organization of national defense;
- the free administration of local communities, the extent of their jurisdiction, and their resources;
- education;
- property rights, civil and commercial obligations;
- legislation pertaining to employment, unions and social security.

The financial laws shall determine the financial resources and obligations of the State under the conditions and with the reservations to be provided for by an organic law.

Laws pertaining to national planning shall determine the objectives of the economic and social action of the State.

The provisions of the present article may be developed in detail and amplified by an organic law.

ARTICLE 35

Parliament shall authorize the declaration of war.

ARTICLE 36

Martial law shall be decreed in a meeting of the Council of Ministers.

Its prorogation beyond twelve days may be authorized only by Parliament.

ARTICLE 37

Matters other than those that fall within the domain of law shall be of a regulatory character.

Legislative texts concerning these matters may be modified by decrees issued after consultation with the Council of State. Those legislative texts which may be passed after the present Constitution has become operative shall be modified by decree, only if the Constitutional Council has stated that they have a regulatory character as defined in the preceding paragraph.

ARTICLE 38

The Government may, in order to carry out its program, ask Parliament to authorize it, for a limited period, to take through ordinances measures that are normally within the domain of law.

The ordinances shall be enacted in meetings of the Council of Ministers after consultation with the Council of State. They shall come into force upon their publication, but shall become null and void if the bill for their ratification is not submitted to Parliament before the date set by the enabling act.

At the expiration of the time limit referred to in the first paragraph of the present article, the ordinances may be modified only by law in those matters which are within the legislative domain.

ARTICLE 39

The Prime Minister and the members of Parliament alike shall have the right to initiate legislation.

Government bills shall be discussed in the Council of Ministers after consultation with the Council of State and shall be filed with the Secretariat of one of the two assemblies. Finance bills shall be submitted first to the National Assembly.

ARTICLE 40

Bills and amendments introduced by members of Parliament shall not be considered when their adoption would have as a consequence either a diminution of public financial resources, or the creation or increase of public expenditures.

ARTICLE 41

If it appears in the course of the legislative procedure that a Parliamentary bill or an amendment is not within the domain of law or is contrary to a delegation [of authority] granted by virtue of Article 38, the Government may declare its inadmissibility.

In case of disagreement between the Government and the President of the Assembly concerned, the Constitutional Council, upon the request of either party, shall rule within a time limit of eight days.

ARTICLE 42

The discussion of Government bills shall pertain, in the first assembly to which they have been referred, to the text presented by the Government.

An assembly, given a text passed by the other assembly, shall deliberate on the text that is transmitted to it.

ARTICLE 43

Government and Parliamentary bills shall, at the request of the Government or of the assembly concerned, be sent for study to committees especially designated for this purpose.

Government and Parliamentary bills for which such a request has not been made shall be sent to one of the permanent committees, the number of which shall be limited to six in each assembly.

ARTICLE 44

Members of Parliament and of the Government shall have the right of amendment.

After the opening of the debate, the Government may oppose the examination of any amendment which has not previously been submitted to committee.

If the Government so requests, the assembly concerned shall decide, by a single vote, on all or part of the text under discussion, retaining only the amendments proposed or accepted by the Government.

ARTICLE 45

Every Government or Parliamentary bill shall be examined successively in the two assemblies of Parliament with a view to the adoption of an identical text.

When, as a result of disagreement between the two assemblies, it has become impossible to adopt a Government or Parliamentary bill after two readings by each assembly, or, if the Government has declared the matter urgent, after a single reading by each of them, the Prime Minister shall have the right to have a joint committee meet, composed of an equal number from both assemblies and instructed to offer for consideration a text on the matters still under discussion.

The text prepared by the joint committee may be submitted by the Government for approval of the two assemblies. No amendment shall be admissible except by agreement with the Government.

If the joint committee fails to approve a common text, or if this text is not adopted under the conditions set forth in the preceding paragraph, the Government may, after a new reading by the National Assembly and by the Senate, ask the National Assembly to rule definitively. In this case, the National Assembly may reconsider either the text prepared by the joint committee or the last text adopted [by the National Assembly], modified, when circumstances so require, by one or several of the amendments adopted by the Senate.

ARTICLE 46

The laws that the Constitution characterizes as organic shall be passed and amended under the following conditions:

A Government or Parliamentary bill shall be submitted to the deliberation and to the vote of the first assembly to which it is submitted only at the expiration of a period of fifteen days following its introduction.

The procedure of Article 45 shall be applicable. Nevertheless, lacking an agreement between the two assemblies, the text may be adopted by the National Assembly on final reading only by an absolute majority of its members.

The organic laws relative to the Senate must be passed in the same manner by the two assemblies.

Organic laws may be promulgated only after a declaration by the Constitutional Council on their constitutionality.

ARTICLE 47

Parliament shall pass finance bills under the conditions to be stipulated by an organic law.

Should the National Assembly fail to reach a decision on first reading within a time limit of forty days after a bill has been filed, the Government shall refer it to the Senate, which must rule within a time limit of fifteen days. The procedure set forth in Article 45 shall then be followed.

Should Parliament fail to reach a decision within a time limit of seventy days, the provisions of the bill may be enforced by ordinance.

Should the finance bill establishing the resources and expenditures of a fiscal year not be filed in time for it to be promulgated before the beginning of that fiscal year, the Government shall immediately request Parliament for the authorization to collect the taxes and shall make available by decree the funds needed to meet the Government commitments already voted.

The time limits stipulated in the present article shall be suspended when Parliament is not in session.

The Audit Office shall assist Parliament and the Government in supervising the implementation of the finance laws.

ARTICLE 48

The discussion of the bills filed or agreed upon by the Government shall have priority on the agenda of the assemblies in the order set by the Government.

One meeting a week shall be reserved, by priority, for questions asked by members of Parliament and for answers by the Government.

ARTICLE 49

The Prime Minister, after deliberation by the Council of Ministers, may pledge the responsibility of the Government to the National Assembly with regard to the program of the Government, or with regard to a declaration of general policy, as the case may be.

The National Assembly may question the responsibility of the Government by the vote of a motion of censure. Such a motion shall be admissible only if it is signed by at least one tenth of the members of the National Assembly. The vote may only take place forty-eight hours after the motion has been filed; the only votes counted shall be those favorable to the motion of censure, which may be adopted only by a majority of the members comprising the Assembly. Should the motion of censure be rejected, its signatories may not introduce another motion in the course of the same session, except in the case provided for in the paragraph below.

The Prime Minister may, after deliberation by the Council of Ministers, pledge the Government's responsibility to the National Assembly on the vote of a text. In this case, the text shall be considered as adopted, unless a motion of censure, filed in the succeeding twenty-four hours, is voted under the conditions laid down in the previous paragraph.

The Prime Minister shall be entitled to ask the Senate for approval of a general policy declaration.

ARTICLE 50

When the National Assembly adopts a motion of censure, or when it disapproves the program or a declaration of general policy of the Government, the Prime Minister must submit the resignation of the Government to the President of the Republic.

ARTICLE 51

The closure of ordinary or extraordinary sessions shall by right be delayed, should the occasion arise, in order to permit the application of the provisions of Article 49.

Title VI
On Treaties and International Agreements

*   *   *   *   *

ARTICLE 53

Peace treaties, commercial treaties, treaties or agreements relative to international organization, those that imply a commitment for the finances of the State, those that modify provisions of a legislative nature, those relative to the status of persons, those that call for the cession, exchange, or addition of territory may be ratified or approved only by a law.

* * * * *

ARTICLE 53-1 [added 25 November 1993]

The Republic may conclude agreements with those European States bound by commitments identical to those of France in matters concerning asylum and the protection of human rights and fundamental liberties in order to determine their respective powers for examining requests for asylum presented to them.

However, even if a request does not fall within their power by reason of these agreements, the authorities of the Republic shall always have the right to give asylum to any foreigner persecuted because of his activities in defense of liberty or requesting the protection of France for some other reason.

ARTICLE 54

If the Constitutional Council, the matter having been referred to it by the President of the Republic, by the Premier, by the President of one or the other assembly, or by sixty senators or sixty deputies, shall declare that an international commitment contains a clause contrary to the Constitution, the authorization to ratify or approve the commitment in question may be given only after amendment of the Constitution.

ARTICLE 55

Treaties or agreements duly ratified or approved shall, upon their publication, have an authority superior to that of laws, subject, for each agreement or treaty, to its application by the other party.

Title VII
The Constitutional Council

ARTICLE 56

The Constitutional Council shall consist of nine members, whose term of office shall last nine years and shall not be renewable. One third of the membership of the Constitutional Council shall be renewed every three years. Three of its members shall be appointed by the President of the Republic, three by the President of the National Assembly, three by the President of the Senate

In addition to the nine members provided for above, former Presidents of the Republic shall be members ex officio for life of the Constitutional Council.

The President shall be appointed by the President of the Republic. He shall have the deciding vote in case of a tie.

ARTICLE 57

The office of member of the Constitutional Council shall be incompatible with that of minister or member of Parliament. Other incompatibilities shall be determined by an organic law.

ARTICLE 58

The Constitutional Council shall ensure the regularity of the election of the President of the Republic.

It shall examine complaints and shall announce the results of the vote.

ARTICLE 59

The Constitutional Council shall rule, in the case of disagreement, on the regularity of the election of deputies and senators.

ARTICLE 60

The Constitutional Council shall ensure the regularity of referendum procedures and shall announce the results thereof.

ARTICLE 61 [as amended 29 October 1974]

Organic laws, before their promulgation, and regulations of the Parliamentary assemblies, before they come into application, must be submitted to the Constitutional Council, which shall rule on their constitutionality.

To the same end, laws may be submitted to the Constitutional Council, before their promulgation, by the President of the Republic, the Prime Minister, the President of the National Assembly, the President of the Senate, or by 60 deputies or 60 senators.

In the cases provided for by the two preceding paragraphs, the Constitutional Council must make its ruling within a time limit of one month. Nevertheless, at the request of the Government, in case of emergency, this period shall be reduced to eight days.

In these same cases, referral to the Constitutional Council shall suspend the time limit for promulgation.

ARTICLE 62

A provision declared unconstitutional may not be promulgated or implemented.

The decisions of the Constitutional Council may not be appealed to any jurisdiction whatsoever. They must be recognized by the governmental authorities and by all administrative and juridical authorities.

ARTICLE 63

An organic law shall determine the rules of organization and functioning of the Constitutional Council, the procedure to be followed before it, and in particular the periods of time allowed for laying disputes before it.

Title VIII ⁻
On Judicial Authority

ARTICLE 64

The President of the Republic shall be the guarantor of the independence of the judicial authority.

He shall be assisted by the High Council of the Judiciary.

An organic law shall determine the status of magistrates.

Magistrates may not be removed from office.

ARTICLE 65 [as amended 27 July 1993]

The High Council of the Judiciary shall be presided over by the President of the Republic. The Minister of Justice shall be its Vice President ex officio. He may preside in place of the President of the Republic.

The High Council of the Judiciary shall include two sections, one with authority over judges and the other with authority over public prosecutors.

The section with authority over judges shall include, in addition to the President of the Republic and the Minister of Justice, five judges, one public prosecutor, one Councilor of State appointed by that council, and three other qualified persons belonging neither to Parliament nor to the judiciary, who shall be appointed respectively by the President of the Republic, the president of the National Assembly, and the president of the Senate.

The section with authority over public prosecutors shall include, in addition to the President of the Republic and the Minister of Justice, five public prosecutors, one judge, and the Councilor of State and the three persons mentioned in the preceding paragraph.

The section of the High Council of the Judiciary with authority over judges shall nominate the judges on the Court of Cassation, the first presidents of the Courts of Appeals, and the presidents of the tribunals of first instance. All other judges shall be appointed with its consent.

The same section shall serve as the disciplinary council for judges, in which case the first president of the Court of Cassation shall be the presiding officer.

The section of the High Council of the judiciary with authority over the public prosecutors advises on the appointment of those officers with the exception of such positions as shall be provided by the Council of Ministers.

The same section shall advise on disciplinary sanctions concerning public prosecutors, in which case the procurator general at the Court of Cassation shall be the presiding officer.

An organic law shall determine the conditions in which the present article shall be applied.

ARTICLE 66

No one may be arbitrarily detained.

The judicial authority, guardian of individual liberty, shall ensure respect for this principle under the conditions stipulated by law.

Title IX
The High Court of Justice

ARTICLE 67

A High Court of Justice shall be instituted.

It shall be composed of members [of Parliament] elected, in equal number, by the National Assembly and the Senate after each general or partial election to these assemblies. It shall elect its president from among its members.

An organic law shall determine the composition of the High Court, its rules, and also the procedure to be followed before it.

ARTICLE 68 [as amended 27 July 1993]

The President of the Republic shall not be held accountable for actions performed in the exercise of his office except in the case of high treason. He may be indicted only by the two assemblies ruling by identical vote in open balloting and by an absolute majority of the members of said assemblies. He shall be tried by the High Court of Justice.

Title X
Criminal Liability of Members of the Government

ARTICLE 68-1 [added 27 July 1993]

Members of the government shall be fully accountable for acts performed in the exercise of their duties which were considered as crimes or misdemeanors when they were committed.

They shall be tried before the Court of Justice of the Republic.

The Court of Justice of the Republic shall be bound by the definition of crimes and punishments provided by law.

ARTICLE 68-2 [added 27 July 1993]

The Court of Justice of the Republic shall consist of fifteen judges: twelve members of parliament—six from the National Assembly and six from the Senate—elected in their respective chambers after every general or partial election, and three judges from the Court of Cassation, one of whom shall preside over the Court of Justice of the Republic.

Any person who maintains he has been harmed by a crime or a misdemeanor committed by a member of the government in the exercise of his duties may bring a complaint before a committee on petitions.

This committee shall decide either to dismiss the complaint or to forward it to the procurator general at the Court of Cassation for the purpose of convening the Court of Justice of the Republic.

The procurator general at the Court of Cassation may thereupon convene the Court of Justice of the Republic forthwith pursuant to the recommendation of the committee on petitions.

An organic law shall determine the conditions in which the present article shall be applied.

* * * * *

Title XI
On Territorial Units

ARTICLE 72

The territorial units of the Republic are the communes, the Departments, the Overseas Territories. Other territorial units may be created by law.

These units shall be free to govern themselves through elected councils and under the conditions stipulated by law.

In the departments and the territories, the Delegate of the Government shall be responsible for the national interests, for administrative supervision, and for seeing that the laws are respected.

* * * * *

Title XIV
The European Communities and the European Union

ARTICLE 88-1 [added 26 June 1992]

The Republic shall participate in the European Communities and in the European Union, comprised of states which have chosen freely to exercise some of their powers pursuant to the treaties which have created these communities and this union.

* * * * *

ARTICLE 88-3

Subject to reciprocity and in accordance with the provisions of the Treaty on the European Union of 7 February 1992, the right to vote and the right to be elected in municipal elections may be granted only to citizens of the Union residing in France. These citizens may not serve as mayor or as deputy mayor, nor may they participate in the selection of senatorial electors nor in the election of senators. An organic law passed by the two assemblies in identical terms shall determine how the present article will be applied.

* * * * *

Title XV
On Amendment

ARTICLE 89

The initiative for amending the Constitution shall belong both to the President of the Republic on the proposal of the Prime Minister and to the members of Parliament.

The Government or Parliamentary bill for amendment must be passed by the two assemblies in identical terms. The amendment shall become definitive after approval by a referendum.

Nevertheless, the proposed amendment shall not be submitted to a referendum when the President of the Republic decides to submit it to Parliament convened in Congress; in this case, the proposed amendment shall be approved only if it is accepted by a three-fifths majority of the votes cast. The Secretariat of the Congress shall be that of the National Assembly.

No amendment procedure may be undertaken or followed when the integrity of the territory is in jeopardy.

The republican form of government shall not be subject to amendment.

* * * * *

Title XVI
Temporary Provisions

ARTICLE 90

The ordinary session of Parliament is suspended. The mandate of the members of the present National Assembly shall expire on the day that the Assembly elected under the present Constitution convenes.

Until this meeting, the Government alone shall have the authority to convene Parliament.

The mandate of the members of the Assembly of the French Union shall expire at the same time as the mandate of the members of the present National Assembly.

ARTICLE 91

The institutions of the Republic, provided for by the present Constitution, shall be established within four months after its promulgation.

This time limit shall be extended to six months for the institutions of the Community.

The powers of the President of the Republic now in office shall expire only when the results of the election provided for in Articles 6 and 7 of the present Constitution are proclaimed.

The member States of the Community shall participate in this first election under the conditions derived from their status at the date of the promulgation of the Constitution.

ARTICLE 92

The legislative measures necessary for the setting up of the institutions and, until they are set up, for the functioning of the governmental authorities, shall be taken in meetings of the Council of Ministers, after consultation with the Council of State, in the form of ordinances having the force of law.

During the time limit set in the first paragraph of Article 91, the Government shall be authorized to determine, by ordinances having the force of law and passed in the same way, the system of elections to the assemblies provided for by the Constitution.

During the same period and under the same conditions, the Government may also adopt measures, in all matters, which it may deem necessary to the life of the nation, the protection of citizens, or the safeguarding of liberties.

ARTICLE 93 [added 27 July 1993]

The provisions of Article 65 and of Title X, as they appear in constitutional law #93-952 of 27 July 1993, shall go into effect at the time of the publication of the organic laws passed for their application.

The provisions of Title X, as they appear in constitutional law #93-952 of 27 July 1993, shall be applicable to acts committed prior to their coming into effect.

Appendix D:
EXCERPTS FROM THE CONSTITUTION OF THE UNITED STATES

We the People of the United States, in Order to form a more perfect Union, establish Justice, insure domestic Tranquility, provide for the common defence, promote the general Welfare, and secure the Blessings of Liberty to ourselves and our Posterity, do ordain and establish this Constitution for the United States of America.

ARTICLE I

Section 1. All legislative Powers herein granted shall be vested in a Congress of the United States, which shall consist of a Senate and House of Representatives.

Section 2. The House of Representatives shall be composed of Members chosen every second Year by the People of the several States, and the Electors in each State shall have the Qualifications requisite for Electors of the most numerous Branch of the State Legislature.

*   *   *   *   *

When vacancies happen in the Representation from any State, the Executive Authority thereof shall issue Writs of Election to fill such Vacancies.

The House of Representatives shall chuse their Speaker and other Officers; and shall have the sole Power of Impeachment.

Section 3. The Senate of the United States shall be composed of two Senators from each State, chosen *by the Legislature thereof,* for six Years; and each Senator shall have one Vote. [The italicized clause was changed by the Seventeenth Amendment, q.v.]

*   *   *   *   *

The Vice President of the United States shall be President of the Senate, but shall have no Vote, unless they be equally divided.

The Senate shall have the sole Power to try all Impeachments. When sitting for that Purpose, they shall be on Oath or Affirmation. When the President of the United States is tried, the Chief Justice shall preside: And no Person shall be convicted without the Concurrence of two thirds of the Members present.

Judgment in Cases of Impeachment shall not extend further than to removal from Office, and disqualification to hold and enjoy any Office of honor, Trust, or Profit under the United States: but the Party convicted shall nevertheless be liable and subject to Indictment, Trial, Judgment, and Punishment, according to Law.

* * * * *

Section 6. The Senators and Representatives shall receive a Compensation for their Services, to be ascertained by Law, and paid out of the Treasury of the United States. They shall in all Cases, except Treason, Felony and Breach of the Peace, be privileged from Arrest during their Attendance at the Session of their respective Houses, and in going to and returning from the same; and for any Speech or Debate in either House, they shall not be questioned in any other Place.

No Senator or Representative shall, during the Time for which he was elected, be appointed to any civil Office under the Authority of the United States, which shall have been created, or the Emoluments whereof shall have been encreased during such time; and no Person holding any Office under the United States, shall be a Member of either House during his Continuance in Office.

Section 7. All Bills for raising Revenue shall originate in the House of Representatives; but the Senate may propose or concur with Amendments as on other Bills.

Every Bill which shall have passed the House of Representatives and the Senate, shall, before it becomes a Law, be presented to the President of the United States; If he approve he shall sign it, but if not he shall return it, with his Objections to the House in which it shall have originated, who shall enter the Objections at large on their Journal, and proceed to reconsider it. If after such Reconsideration two thirds of that House shall agree to pass the Bill, it shall be sent, together with the Objections, to the other House, by which it shall likewise be reconsidered, and if approved by two thirds of that House, it shall become a Law. But in all such Cases the Votes of both Houses shall be determined by yeas and Nays, and the Names of the Persons voting for and against the Bill shall be entered on the Journal of each House respectively. If any Bill shall not be returned by the President within ten Days (Sundays excepted) after it shall have been presented to him, the Same shall be a Law, in like Manner as if he had signed it, unless the Congress by their Adjournment prevent its Return, in which Case it shall not be a Law.

Every Order, Resolution, or Vote, to which the Concurrence of the Senate and House of Representatives may be necessary (except on a question of Adjournment) shall be presented to the President of the United States; and before the Same shall take Effect, shall be approved by him, or being disapproved by him, shall be repassed by two thirds of the Senate and House of Representatives, according to the Rules and Limitations prescribed in the Case of a Bill.

Section 8. The Congress shall have Power To lay and collect Taxes, Duties, Imposts and Excises, to pay the Debts and provide for the common Defence and general Welfare of the United States; but all Duties, Imposts and Excises shall be uniform throughout the United States;

To borrow Money on the credit of the United States;

To regulate Commerce with foreign Nations, and among the several States, and with the Indian Tribes;

To establish an uniform Rule of Naturalization, and uniform Laws on the subject of Bankruptcies throughout the United States;

To coin Money, regulate the Value thereof, and of foreign Coin, and fix the Standard of Weights and Measures;

To provide for the Punishment of counterfeiting the Securities and current Coin of the United States;

To Establish Post Offices and Post Roads;

To promote the Progress of Science and useful Arts, by securing for limited Times to Authors and Inventors the exclusive Right to their respective Writings and Discoveries;

To constitute Tribunals inferior to the supreme Court;

To define and punish Piracies and Felonies committed on the high Seas, and Offenses against the Law of Nations;

To declare War, grant Letters of Marque and Reprisal, and make Rules concerning Captures on Land and Water;

To raise and support Armies, but no Appropriation of Money to that Use shall be for a longer Term than two Years;

To provide and maintain a Navy;

To make Rules for the Government and Regulation of the land and naval Forces;

To provide for calling forth the Militia to execute the Laws of the Union, suppress Insurrections and repel Invasions;

To provide for organizing, arming, and disciplining, the Militia, and for governing such Part of them as may be employed in the Service of the United States, reserving to the States respectively, the Appointment of the Officers, and the Authority of training the Militia according to the discipline prescribed by Congress;

To exercise exclusive Legislation in all Cases whatsoever, over such District (not exceeding ten Miles square) as may, by Cession of particular States, and the Acceptance of Congress, become the Seat of the Government of the United States, and to exercise like Authority over all Places purchased by the Consent of the Legislature of the State in which the Same shall be, for the Erection of Forts, Magazines, Arsenals, dock-Yards, and other needful Buildings;—And

To make all Laws which shall be necessary and proper for carrying into Execution the foregoing Powers, and all other Powers vested by this Constitution in the Government of the United States, or in any Department or Officer thereof.

* * * * *

ARTICLE II

Section 1. The executive Power shall be vested in a President of the United States of America. He shall hold his Office during the Term of four Years, and, together with the Vice President, chosen for the same Term, be elected, as follows:

Each State shall appoint, in such Manner as the Legislature thereof may direct, a Number of Electors, equal to the whole Number of Senators and Representatives to which the State may be entitled in the Congress; but no Senator or Representative, or Person holding an Office of Trust or Profit under the United States, shall be appointed an Elector.

The Electors shall meet in their respective States, and vote by Ballot for two Persons, of whom one at least shall not be an Inhabitant of the same State with themselves. And they shall make a List of all the Persons voted for, and of the Number of Votes for each; which List they shall sign and certify, and transmit sealed to the Seat of the Government of the United States, directed to the President of the Senate. The President of the Senate shall, in the Presence of the Senate and House of Representatives, open all the Certificates, and the Votes shall then be counted. The Person having the greater Number of Votes shall be the President, if such Number be a Majority of the whole Number of Electors appointed; and if there be more than one who have such Majority, and have an equal Number of Votes, then the House of Representatives shall immediately chuse by Ballot one of them for President; and if no Person have a Majority, then from the five highest on the List the said House shall in like Manner chuse the President. But in chusing the President, the Votes shall be taken by States, the Representation from each State having one Vote; A quorum for this Purpose shall consist of a Member or Members from two thirds of the States, and a Majority of all the States shall be necessary to a Choice. In every Case, after the Choice of the President, the Person having the greater Number of Votes of the Electors shall be the Vice President. But if there should remain two or more who have equal Votes, the Senate shall chuse from them by Ballot the Vice President. [The italicized sentences have been changed by the Twelfth Amendment, q.v.])

The Congress may determine the Time of chusing the Electors, and the Day on which they shall give their Votes; which Day shall be the same throughout the United States.

No Person except a natural born Citizen, or a Citizen of the United States, at the time of the Adoption of this Constitution, shall be eligible to the Office of President; neither shall any person be eligible to that Office who shall not have attained to the Age of thirty five Years, and been fourteen Years a Resident within the United States.

*   *   *   *   *

The President shall, at stated Times, receive for his Services, a Compensation, which shall neither be encreased nor diminished during the Period for which he shall have been elected, and he shall not receive within that Period any other Emolument from the United States, or any of them.

Before he enter on the Execution of his Office, he shall take the following Oath or Affirmation: "I do solemnly swear (or affirm) that I will faithfully execute the Office of President of the United States, and will to the best of my Ability, preserve, protect and defend the Constitution of the United States."

Section 2. The President shall be Commander in Chief of the Army and Navy of the United States, and of the militia of the several States, when called into the actual Service of the United States; he may require the Opinion, in writing, of the principal Officer in each of the executive Departments, upon any Subject relating to the Duties of their respective Offices, and he shall have Power to grant Reprieves and Pardons for Offenses against the United States, except in Cases of Impeachment.

He shall have Power, by and with the Advice and Consent of the Senate, to make Treaties, provided two thirds of the Senators present concur; and he shall nominate, and by and with the Advice and Consent of the Senate, shall appoint Ambassadors, other public Ministers and Consuls, Judges of the supreme Court, and all other Officers of the United States, whose Appointments are not herein otherwise provided for, and which shall be established by Law: but the Congress may by Law vest the Appointment of such inferior Officers, as they think proper, in the President alone, in the Courts of Law, or in the Heads of Departments.

The President shall have Power to fill up all Vacancies that may happen during the Recess of the Senate, by granting Commissions which shall expire at the End of their next Session.

Section 3. He shall from time to time give to the Congress Information of the State of the Union, and recommend to their Consideration such Measures as he shall judge necessary and expedient; he may, on extraordinary Occasions, convene both Houses, or either of them, and in Case of Disagreement between them, with Respect to the Time of Adjournment, he may adjourn them to such Time as he shall think proper; he shall receive Ambassadors and other public Ministers; he shall take Care that the Laws be faithfully executed, and shall Commission all the Officers of the United States.

Section 4. The President, Vice President and all civil Officers of the

United States, shall be removed from Office on Impeachment for, and Conviction of, Treason, Bribery, or other high Crimes and Misdemeanors.

ARTICLE III

Section 1. The judicial Power of the United States, shall be vested in one supreme Court, and in such inferior Courts as the Congress may from time to time ordain and establish. The Judges, both of the supreme and inferior Courts, shall hold their Offices during good Behaviour, and shall, at stated Times, receive for their Services, a Compensation, which shall not be diminished during their Continuance in Office.

Section 2. The judicial Power shall extend to all Cases, in Law and Equity, arising under this Constitution, the Laws of the United States, and Treaties made, or which shall be made, under their Authority;—to all Cases affecting Ambassadors, other public Ministers and Consuls;—to all Cases of admiralty and maritime Jurisdiction,—to Controversies to which the United States shall be a Party;—to Controversies between two or more States;—*between a State and Citizens of another State*;— between Citizens of different States;—between Citizens of the same State claiming Lands under the Grants of different States, *and between a State, or the Citizens thereof, and foreign States, Citizens or Subjects.* [The italicized clauses have been changed by the Eleventh Amendment, q.v.]

In all Cases affecting Ambassadors, other public Ministers and Consuls, and those in which a State shall be a Party, the supreme Court shall have original Jurisdiction. In all the other Cases before mentioned, the supreme Court shall have appellate Jurisdiction, both as to Law and Fact, with such Exceptions, and under such Regulations as the Congress shall make.

The trial of all Crimes, except in Cases of Impeachment, shall be by Jury; and such Trial shall be held in the State where the said Crimes shall have been committed, but when not committed within any State, the Trial shall be at such Place or Places as the Congress may by Law have directed.

Section 3. Treason against the United States, shall consist only in levying War against them, or, in adhering to their Enemies, giving them Aid and Comfort. No Person shall be convicted of Treason unless on the Testimony of two Witnesses to the same overt Act, or on Confession in open Court.

The Congress shall have Power to declare the Punishment of Treason, but no Attainder of Treason shall work Corruption of Blood, or Forfeiture except during the Life of the Person attainted.

ARTICLE IV

* * * * *

Section 4. The United States shall guarantee to every State in this Union a Republican Form of Government, and shall protect each of them against

Invasion; and on Application of the Legislature, or of the Executive (when the Legislature cannot be convened) against domestic Violence.

ARTICLE V

The Congress, whenever two thirds of both Houses shall deem it necessary, shall propose Amendments to this Constitution, or, on the Application of the Legislatures of two thirds of the several States, shall call a Convention for proposing Amendments, which, in either Case, shall be valid to all Intents and Purposes, as part of this Constitution, when ratified by the Legislatures of three fourths of the several States, or by Conventions in three fourths thereof, as the one or the other Mode of Ratification may be proposed by the Congress; Provided that no Amendment which may be made prior to the Year One thousand eight hundred and eight shall in any Manner affect the first and fourth Clauses in the Ninth Section of the first Article; and that no State, without its Consent, shall be deprived of its equal Suffrage in the Senate.

ARTICLE VI

This Constitution, and the Laws of the United States which shall be made in Pursuance thereof; and all Treaties made, or which shall be made, under the Authority of the United States, shall be the supreme Law of the Land; and the Judges in every State shall be bound thereby, any Thing in the Constitution or Laws of any State to the Contrary notwithstanding.

The Senators and Representatives before mentioned, and the Members of the several State Legislatures, and all executive and judicial Officers, both of the United States and of the several States, shall be bound by Oath or Affirmation, to support this Constitution; but no religious Test shall ever be required as a Qualification to any Office or public Trust under the United States.

ARTICLE VII

The Ratification of the Conventions of nine States, shall be sufficient for the Establishment of this Constitution between the States so ratifying the Same.

Done in Convention by the Unanimous Consent of the States present the Seventeenth Day of September in the Year of our Lord one thousand seven hundred and Eighty seven and of the Independence of the United States of America the Twelfth In Witness whereof We have hereunto subscribed our Names,

G°. Washington—Presid'.
and deputy from Virginia

* * * * *

Amendments to the Constitution of the United States of America

AMENDMENT I [The first ten amendments (Bill of Rights) were ratified effective 15 December 1791]

Congress shall make no law respecting an establishment of religion, or prohibiting the free exercise thereof; or abridging the freedom of speech, or of the press, or the right of the people peaceably to assemble, and to petition the Government for a redress of grievances.

* * * * *

AMENDMENT IV

The right of the people to be secure in their persons, houses, papers, and effects, against unreasonable searches and seizures, shall not be violated, and no Warrants shall issue, but upon probable cause, supported by Oath or affirmation, and particularly describing the place to be searched, and the persons or things to be seized.

AMENDMENT V

No person shall be held to answer for a capital, or otherwise infamous crime, unless on a presentment or indictment of a Grand Jury, except in cases arising in the land or naval forces, or in the Militia, when in actual service in time of War or public danger; nor shall any person be subject for the same offence to be twice put in jeopardy of life or limb; nor shall be compelled in any criminal case to be a witness against himself, nor be deprived of life, liberty, or property, without due process of law; nor shall private property be taken for public use, without just compensation.

AMENDMENT VI

In all criminal prosecutions, the accused shall enjoy the right to a speedy and public trial, by an impartial jury of the State and district wherein the crime shall have been committed; which district shall have been previously ascertained by law, and to be informed of the nature and cause of the accusation; to be confronted with the witnesses against him; to have compulsory process for obtaining witnesses in his favor, and to have the Assistance of Counsel for his defense.

* * * * *

AMENDMENT XI [ratified 7 February 1795]

The Judicial power of the United States shall not be construed to extend to any suit in law or equity, commenced or prosecuted against one of the

United States by Citizens of another State, or by Citizens or Subjects of any Foreign State.

AMENDMENT XII [ratified 15 June 1804]

The Electors shall meet in their respective states and vote by ballot for President and Vice-President, one of whom, at least, shall not be an inhabitant of the same state with themselves; they shall name in their ballots the person voted for as President, and in distinct ballots the person voted for as Vice-President, and they shall make distinct lists of all persons voted for as President, and of all persons voted for as Vice-President, and of the number of votes for each, which lists they shall sign and certify, and transmit sealed to the seat of the government of the United States, directed to the President of the Senate;—The President of the Senate shall, in the presence of the Senate and House of Representatives, open all the certificates and the votes shall then be counted;—The person having the greatest number of votes for President, shall be the President, if such number be a majority of the whole number of Electors appointed; and if no person have such majority, then from the persons having the highest numbers not exceeding three on the list of those voted for as President, the House of Representatives shall choose immediately, by ballot, the President. But in choosing the President, the votes shall be taken by states, the representation from each state having one vote; a quorum for this purpose shall consist of a member or members from two-thirds of the states, and a majority of all the states shall be necessary to a choice. *And if the House of Representatives shall not choose a President whenever the right of choice shall devolve upon them, before the fourth day of March next following, then the Vice-President shall act as President, as in the case of the death or other constitutional disability of the President.—* The person having the greatest number of votes as Vice-President, shall be the Vice-President, if such number be a majority of the whole number of Electors appointed, and if no person have a majority, then from the two highest numbers on the list, the Senate shall choose the Vice-President; a quorum for the purpose shall consist of two-thirds of the whole number of Senators, and a majority of the whole number shall be necessary to a choice. But no person constitutionally ineligible to the office of President shall be eligible to that of Vice-President of the United States. [The italicized sentence has been superseded by the third section of the Twentieth Amendment, q.v.]

AMENDMENT XIII [ratified 6 December 1865]

Section 1. Neither slavery nor involuntary servitude, except as a punishment for crime whereof the party shall have been duly convicted, shall exist within the United States, or any place subject to their jurisdiction.

Section 2. Congress shall have power to enforce this article by appropriate legislation.

AMENDMENT XIV [ratified 9 July 1868]

Section 1. All persons born or naturalized in the United States, and subject to the jurisdiction thereof, are citizens of the United States and of the State wherein they reside. No State shall make or enforce any law which shall abridge the privileges or immunities of citizens of the United States; nor shall any State deprive any person of life, liberty, or property, without due process of law; nor deny to any person within its jurisdiction the equal protection of the laws.

*   *   *   *   *

Section 5. The Congress shall have power to enforce, by appropriate legislation, the provisions of this article.

AMENDMENT XV [ratified 3 February 1870]

Section 1. The right of citizens of the United States to vote shall not be denied or abridged by the United States or by any State on account of race, color, or previous condition of servitude.

Section 2. The Congress shall have power to enforce this article by appropriate legislation.

AMENDMENT XVI [ratified 3 February 1913)

The Congress shall have power to lay and collect taxes on incomes, from whatever source derived, without apportionment among the several States, and without regard to any census or enumeration.

AMENDMENT XVII [ratified 8 April 1913)

The Senate of the United States shall be composed of two Senators from each State, elected by the people thereof, for six years; and each Senator shall have one vote. The electors in each State shall have the qualifications requisite for electors of the most numerous branch of the State legislatures.

When vacancies happen in the representation of any State in the Senate, the executive authority of such State shall issue writs of election to fill such vacancies: *Provided,* That the legislature of any State may empower the executive thereof to make temporary appointments until the people fill the vacancies by election as the legislature may direct.

This amendment shall not be so construed as to affect the election or term of any Senator chosen before it becomes valid as part of the Constitution.

* * * * *

AMENDMENT XIX [ratified 18 August 1920]

The right of citizens of the United States to vote shall not be denied or abridged by the United States or by any State on account of sex.

Congress shall have power to enforce this article by appropriate legislation.

AMENDMENT XX [ratified 23 January 1933]

Section 1. The terms of the President and Vice President shall end at noon on the 20th day of January, and the terms of Senators and Representatives at noon on the 3d day of January, of the years in which such terms would have ended if this article had not been ratified; and the terms of their successors shall then begin.

Section 2. The Congress shall assemble at least once in every year, and such meeting shall begin at noon on the 3d day of January, unless they shall by law appoint a different day.

Section 3. If, at the time fixed for the beginning of the term of the President, the President elect shall have died, the Vice President elect shall become President. If the President shall not have been chosen before the time fixed for the beginning of his term, or if the President elect shall have failed to qualify, then the Vice President elect shall act as President until a President shall have qualified; and the Congress may by law provide for the case wherein neither a President elect nor a Vice President elect shall have qualified, declaring who shall then act as President, or the manner in which one who is to act shall be selected, and such person shall act accordingly until a President or Vice President shall have qualified.

Section 4. The Congress may by law provide for the case of the death of any of the persons from whom the House of Representatives may choose a President whenever the right of choice shall have devolved upon them, and for the case of the death of any of the persons from whom the Senate may choose a Vice President whenever the right of choice shall have devolved upon them.

Section 5. Sections 1 and 2 shall take effect on the 15th day of October following the ratification of this article.

Section 6. This article shall be inoperative unless it shall have been ratified as an amendment to the Constitution by the legislatures of three-fourths of the several States within seven years from the date of its submission.

* * * * *

AMENDMENT XXII [ratified 27 February 1951]

Section 1. No person shall be elected to the office of the President more than twice, and no person who has held the office of President, or acted as

President, for more than two years of a term to which some other person was elected President shall be elected to the office of President more than once. But this Article shall not apply to any person holding the office of President when this Article was proposed by the Congress, and shall not prevent any person who may be holding the office of President, or acting as President, during the term within which this Article becomes operative from holding the office of President or acting as President during the remainder of such term.

Section 2. This article shall be inoperative unless it shall have been ratified as an amendment to the Constitution by the legislatures of three-fourths of the several States within seven years from the date of its submission to the States by the Congress.

AMENDMENT XXIII [ratified 29 March 1961]

Section 1. The District constituting the seat of Government of the United States shall appoint in such manner as the Congress may direct:

A number of electors of President and Vice President equal to the whole number of Senators and Representatives in Congress to which the District would be entitled if it were a State, but in no event more than the least populous state; they shall be in addition to those appointed by the states, but they shall be considered, for the purposes of the election of President and Vice President, to be electors appointed by a state; and they shall meet in the District and perform such duties as provided by the twelfth article of amendment.

Section 2. The Congress shall have power to enforce this article by appropriate legislation.

* * * * *

AMENDMENT XXV [ratified 10 February 1967]

Section 1. In case of the removal of the President from office or of his death or resignation, the Vice President shall become President.

Section 2. Whenever there is a vacancy in the office of the Vice President, the President shall nominate a Vice President who shall take office upon confirmation by a majority vote of both Houses of Congress.

Section 3. Whenever the President transmits to the President pro tempore of the Senate and the Speaker of the House of Representatives his written declaration that he is unable to discharge the powers and duties of his office, and until he transmits to them a written declaration to the contrary, such powers and duties shall be discharged by the Vice President as Acting President.

Section 4. Whenever the Vice President and a majority of either the principal officers of the executive departments or of such other body as

Congress may by law provide, transmit to the President pro tempore of the Senate and the Speaker of the House of Representatives their written declaration that the President is unable to discharge the powers and duties of his office, the Vice President shall immediately assume the powers and duties of the office as Acting President.

Thereafter, when the President transmits to the President pro tempore of the Senate and the Speaker of the House of Representatives his written declaration that no inability exists, he shall resume the powers and duties of his office unless the Vice President and a majority of either the principal officers of the executive departments or of such other body as Congress may by law provide, transmit within four days to the President pro tempore of the Senate and the Speaker of the House of Representatives their written declaration that the President is unable to discharge the powers and duties of his office. Thereupon Congress shall decide the issue, assembling within forty-eight hours for that purpose if not in session. If the Congress, within twenty-one days after receipt of the latter written declaration, or, if Congress is not in session, within twenty-one days after Congress is required to assemble, determines by two-thirds vote of both Houses that the President is unable to discharge the powers and duties of his office, the Vice President shall continue to discharge the same as Acting President; otherwise, the President shall resume the powers and duties of his office.

AMENDMENT XXVI [ratified 1 July 1971]

Section 1. The right of citizens of the United States, who are eighteen years of age or older, to vote shall not be denied or abridged by the United States or by any State on account of age.

Section 2. The Congress shall have power to enforce this article by appropriate legislation.

AMENDMENT XXVII [ratified 7 May 1992]

No law, varying the compensation for the services of the senators and Representatives, shall take effect until an election of Representatives shall have intervened.

Notes

1. John A. Rohr, *To Run a Constitution: The Legitimacy of the Administrative State* (Lawrence: University Press of Kansas, 1986).

2. I say "at least" because, depending on how one defines the term *constitution,* there may have been as many as fifteen.

3. *Documents pour servir à l'histoire de la constitution du 4 octobre 1958,* 3 vols. (Paris: La Documentation française, 1987, 1988, 1991). These volumes are cited frequently throughout this book. The citation form I have adopted uses a Roman numeral for the volume and an arabic numeral for the page. Many of the pages reporting debates have two columns. When citing these pages, I indicate the column and the position of the cited material at the top, middle, or bottom of the column. Thus, (1a) means the top of the first column, (2c) means the bottom of the second column, and so on.

4. Rudyard Kipling, "The English Flag," *Departmental Ditties: Barrack Room Ballads and Other Verses* (New York: Doubleday, Page, 1925), pp. 274–78.

5. Alan Riding, "France Approved Use of AIDS-Tainted Blood," *New York Times* (International), 20 October 1991, p. 7; Alan Riding, "Ex-French Officials Go on Trial in AIDS Case," *New York Times,* 25 June 1992, p. A22; Philip Hilts, "Doctor Accused Anew on AIDS Studies," *New York Times,* 25 June 1992, p. A18; "France Convicts 3 in Case of H.I.V.-Tainted Blood," *New York Times,* 24 October 1992, p. 1; Declan Butler, "Verdict in French Blood Trial Shames Science," *Nature* 359 (29 October 1992): 764; Declan Butler, "French Appeals Court Sends Allain to Jail," *Nature* 364 (22 July 1993): 269; "Justice Unevenly Spread in Paris," *Nature* 364 (22 July 1993): 267; "French Assembly Votes to Try Ex-Premier," *New York Times,* 20 December 1992, p. 18.

6. Remarks by Constance Horner, Director, Office of Personnel Management, at the rotunda of the University of Virginia, 14 October 1988 (Federal Executive Institute: Charlottesville, Va.); David H. Rosenbloom and James D. Carroll, *Toward Constitutional Competence: A Casebook for Public Administrators* (Englewood Cliffs, N.J.: Prentice-Hall, 1990); Phillip J. Cooper, *Public Law and Public Administration,* 2d ed. (Englewood Cliffs, N.J.: Prentice-Hall, 1988); "Forum: Public Administration and the Constitution," *Public Administration Review* 53 (May–June 1993): 237–67; John A. Rohr, *Ethics for Bureaucrats: An Essay on Law and Values,* 2d ed. (New York: Marcel Dekker, 1989); Paul Van Riper, "The American Administrative State: Wilson and the Founders—An Unorthodox View," *Public Administra-*

tion Review 43 (November–December 1983): 477–90; Ralph C. Chandler, ed., *A Centennial History of the American Administrative State* (New York: Free Press, 1987); Richard J. Stillman, ed., "The American Constitution and the Administrative State: A Symposium," *Public Administration Review* 47 (January–February 1987): 3–120; William D. Richardson and Lloyd G. Nigro, "Administrative Ethics and Founding Thought: Constitutional Correctives, Honor, and Education," *Public Administration Review* 47 (September–October 1987) 367–77; Jeffrey Leigh Sedgwick, "Of Centennials and Bicentennials: Reflections on the Foundations of American Public Administration," *Administration and Society* 19 (November 1987): 285–308; John Nalbandian, "The U.S. Supreme Court's 'Consensus' on Affirmative Action," *Public Administration Review* 49 (January–February 1989): 38–45; Donald J. Maletz, "The Place of Constitutionalism in the Education of Public Administrators," *Administration and Society* 23 (November 1991): 374–94; William D. Richardson and Lloyd G. Nigro, "The Constitution and Administrative Ethics in America," *Administration and Society* 23 (November 1991): 275–87; Brian J. Cook, "The Representative Function of Bureaucracy: Public Administration in Constitutive Perspective," *Administration and Society* 23 (February 1992): 403–29; Richard T. Green, "Constitutional Jurisprudence: Reviving Praxis in Public Administration," *Administration and Society* 24 (May 1992): 3–21; David H. Rosenbloom, "Public Administrative Liability for Constitutional Torts: The Rehnquist Court and Public Administration," *Administration and Society* 24 (August 1992): 115–31. The American debate over constitutionalism and administration has caught the attention of German scholars: Ranier Prätorius, "Administrative Standortsuche: Der neue Konstitutionalismus in den USA," *Staatswissenschaften und Staatspraxis* 2 (1991): 482–502.

7. See, for example, Dorothy Pickles, *The Fifth French Republic: Institution and Politics* (New York: Frederick Praeger, 1962), chapters 7 and 8; F. Ridley and J. Blondel, *Public Administration in France* (New York: Barnes & Noble, 1969); Ezra N. Suleiman, *Politics, Power, and Bureaucracy in France: The Administrative Elite* (Princeton, N.J.: Princeton University Press, 1974): chapters 1, 13, and *passim;* J. V. Poulard, "The French Double Executive and the Experience of Cohabitation," *Political Science Quarterly* 105 (1990): 243–67; Harvey Feigenbaum, "Recent Evolution of the French Executive," *Governance* 3 (1990): 264–78; William Safran, *The French Polity,* 3d ed. (New York: Longman, 1991), chapters 6 and 8; Henry W. Ehrmann and Martin A Schain, *Politics in France,* 5th ed. (New York: Harper-Collins, 1992), chapters 8 and 9; Robert Elgie, "The Prime Minister's Office in France: A Changing Role in a Semi-Presidential System," *Governance* 5 (1992): 104–21.

8. For a discussion of the meaning of "regime values," see Rohr, *Ethics for Bureaucrats,* chapter 2.

9. Alexis de Tocqueville, *Democracy in America,* Phillips Bradley trans. (New York: Random House, 1990), vol. I, p. 14. The chapter headings are presented without citations. The headings for the preface and for chapters 3, 4, 5, and 8 are from volume I of *Democracy in America,* as follows: preface and chapter 3 are from "Author's Preface to the 12th edition," pp. xxi and xx; chapters 4 and 5 are from chapter 8, pp. 155 and 139; chapter 8 is from Introduction, p. 9. The headings for chapters 1, 2, 6, and 7 are from de Tocqueville's *The Old Regime and the French Revolution,* Stuart Gilbert trans. (Garden City, N.Y.: Doubleday, 1955), as follows: chapter 1 is

from part III, chapter 7, p. 202; chapter 2 is from part III, chapter 8, p. 209; chapter 6 is from part II, chapter 6, p. 65; and chapter 7 is from part II, chapter 11, p. 116.

10. I add "but not exclusively" because we shall encounter a "representative of the government," Raymond Janot, before an ad hoc body called the Advisory Committee on the Constitution *(Comité Consultatif Constitutionnel)* who has nothing to do with the Council of State. Neither in my reading nor in my discussions with French jurists was I able to ascertain just why Janot was given this title. It is the only time I can recall running across the title given to one really representing the government's interests outside the Council of State. See the entry under "Commissaire du gouvernement" in Olivier Duhamel and Yves Mény, eds., *Dictionnaire constitutionnelle* (Paris: Presses Universitaire de France, 1992), p. 170.

11. Jean-Paul Costa, *Le Conseil d'Etat dans la société contemporaine* (Paris: Economica, 1993), p. 36; L. Neville Brown and J. F. Garner, *French Administrative Law,* 3d ed. (London: Butterworths, 1993), pp. 45, 64.

INTRODUCTION

1. Elizabeth Schemla, "Ecole: le piège religieux," *Le Nouvel Observateur* (26 October–1 November 1989): 74.

2. Youssef M. Ibrahim, "Arab Girls' Veils at Issue in France," *New York Times,* 12 November 1989, p. 8. For a recent statement from a rabbi distinguishing the *foulard* issue from the Jewish complaint about Saturday morning classes, see Josy Eisenberg, "Laïcité: l'exception culturelle," *Le Monde,* 20 April 1994, p. 2.

3. Schemla, "Ecole," p. 75.

4. Jean-Claude William, "Le Conseil d'Etat et la laïcité," *Revue française de science politique* 41 (February 1991): 28–44, at 37. I do not read Hebrew, but those who do tell me that "shield of David" is a better translation than the more customary "star of David." The star appeared on the shield.

5. Elisabeth Schemla, "Jospin: Accueillez les foulards," *Le Nouvel Observateur* (26 October–1 November 1989): 78.

6. Elizabeth Schemla, "Le casse-tête islamo-laïque de Jospin," *Le Nouvel Observateur* (9–15 November 1989): 67.

7. For example, on the evening news of 10 November 1993, French television (TF1) reported that four Muslim girls in Nantua had been suspended from school for wearing the *foulard.* The incident came to prominence because of a local imam who attracted the unfriendly attention of Charles Pasqua, the minister of the interior, when he remarked that it was more important to obey the laws of Allah than the laws of France. The minister was not amused. The imam, who was not a French citizen, was deported shortly thereafter. See "Un Entretien avec Charles Pasqua," *Le Monde,* 17 November 1993, p. 1. On 10 September 1994, another television station (France 2) reported a new effort by Education Minister François Bayroux to address the *foulard* issue.

8. *Le Monde,* 28–29 January 1990, p. 8; Maurice Peyrot, "Intégrisme et bonne

foi: le principal de Creil devant le tribunal de Senlis," *Le Monde,* 4 April 1990, p. 15; Ibrahim, "Arab Girls' Veils," p. 8.

9. Ivan Rioufol, "Ernest Chenière: 'établir des clotures,'" *Le Figaro,* 21 May 1993, p. 9. For a full account of the *foulard* controversy in English, see David Beriss, "Scarves, Schools, and Segregation: The *Foulard* Affair," *French Politics and Society* 8 (Winter 1990): 1–13.

10. Alfred H. Kelly, Winfred A. Harbison, and Herman Belz, *The American Constitution: Its Origins and Development,* 7th ed. (New York: W. W. Norton, 1991), vol. 2, p. 736.

11. *Tinker v. Des Moines Independent Community School District,* 393 U.S. 503 (1969). The scope of *Tinker* seems to have been narrowed in *Bethel School District No. 403 v. Fraser,* 478 U.S. 675 (1986), and in *Hazelwood School District v. Kuhlmeier,* 108 S. Ct. 562 (1988).

12. *Goldman v. Weinberger,* 475 U.S. 503 (1986). For overviews on the question of the legal status of religious garb, see Holly M. Bastian, "Religious Garb Statutes and Title VII: An Uneasy Coexistence," *Georgetown Law Journal* 80 (1991): 211–32.

13. There could be a serious political problem, however, depending on the public attitude in the United States toward Muslims at the time in question. Consider the likely repercussions, for example, if Muslim girls had taken to wearing *foulards* at the height of the Iran hostage crisis or immediately after the arrest of the World Trade Center bombers. The *foulard* problem became front-page news in France because of the chronic popular unrest over French immigration policy, which many Frenchmen believe is too generous.

14. As of 1992, a member of the clergy may not. See *Lee v. Wiseman,* 112 S. Ct. 2649 (1992).

15. This ideal is not shared by all French republicans. Since at least the end of World War II, most Catholics have been "reconciled" to the Republic, even though they do not share the secularist world view that has a been a central tenet in the historical development of French republicanism. Indeed, at the end of the nineteenth century, Pope Leo XIII urged French Catholics to "rally" to the Republic; but a series of unfortunate events, culminating in the notorious "Dreyfus Affair," muted the pontiff's call. Readers familiar with French schools may be surprised to see them described as "temples of reason." Although French public schools have been spared the horrors of inner-city schools in the United States, they are not without their problems. Despite the rigorous academic standards in French schools, drugs and violence are by no means unknown. In describing the public schools as "temples of reason," I present what I understand to be the ideals of French republicanism.

16. Olivier Mongin and Joel Roman, "La France confuse," *Esprit* 157 (December 1989): 129.

17. Jacques Minot, "Droits de l'homme et neutralité de l'Etat: A propos de l'affaire du foulard," *La Revue Administrative* 43 (1990): 32–39.

18. Ibid., p. 38.

19. Ibid. Minot develops this point in the context of criticizing Education Minister Jospin for failing to ban the *foulards.* He makes the interesting argument that Jospin has confused the principle of secularism with toleration.

20. Not all French observers think along these lines. For a position that closely

resembles the American idea of negative obligation, see Guy Sitbon, "La Laïcité a bon dos," *Le Nouvel Observateur* (9–15 November 1989): 69. The Supreme Court of the United States addressed the distinction between negative and affirmative obligations in *DeShaney v. Winnebago County Department of Social Services,* 109 S. Ct. 998 (1989).

21. Guy Coq, "La Laïcité, une idée neuve," *Esprit* 157 (December 1989): 122–23.

22. Claude Allegre, "La Meilleure façon d'enlever le voile," *Le Nouvel Observateur* (9–15 November 1989): 67.

23. Jean Daniel, "L'Autre pari," *Le Nouvel Observateur* (2–8 November 1989): 60.

24. Elisabeth Badinter, "Je suis fière des profs," *Le Nouvel Observateur* (9–15 November 1989): 71; Laurent Joffrin, "Lettre à Harlem Désir," *Le Nouvel Observateur* (2–8 November 1989): 63; Jean-Jacques Rousseau, *The Social Contract,* G. D. H. Cole, trans. (Chicago: Encyclopedia Britannica, 1977) book I, chapter 7, p. 393.

25. For an interesting variation on this theme, see Justice William Douglas's opinion in *Wisconsin v. Yoder,* 406 U.S. 205 (1972), wherein he dissents in part from the opinion of the Court. The case involved Amish parents who refused to send their daughter to high school, arguing that the elementary school education she had already received was all she needed for the "simple life" she would lead and that the local public high school would expose her to ways of the world the parents found objectionable. The Supreme Court overturned the parents' conviction for violating Wisconsin's truancy laws. Justice Douglas agreed with much of the Court's analysis, but disagreed with its assumption "that the only interests at stake are those of the Amish parents on the one hand, and those of the State on the other." He believed that the child's interest in her own free exercise of religion could only be vindicated if her own views about attending or not attending public high school were taken into consideration in deciding the case. Douglas thus emphasized the individual character of the free exercise guarantee, even going so far as to offer the startling theological opinion that "religion is an individual experience."

26. Allegre, "La Meilleure façon," p. 67. *Intégrisme* is the French equivalent of the English word *fundamentalism.* Strictly speaking, I believe the English word originally referred to the insistence upon a literal interpretation of the Bible and, therefore, pertained only to certain traditions in Protestant Christianity. Today, the word seems to have a broader meaning dealing more with moral teaching than with exegesis. We even hear of "Moslem fundamentalists." I believe the French *intégrisme* has this broader meaning and refers more to conservative religious practices than to a particular way of reading a sacred text.

27. Minot, "Droits de l'homme," p. 33.

28. Alfred Cobban, *A History of Modern France* (Middlesex, England: Penguin Books, 1965), vol. 3, p. 236.

29. For a fuller discussion of the founding procedures, see François Luchaire, "Introduction," in François Luchaire and Gérard Conac, eds., *La Constitution de la république francaise,* 2d ed. (Paris: Economica, 1987), pp. 37–45. For full contemporaneous accounts in English, see Stanley H. Hoffman, "The French Constitution of 1958: The Final Text and Its Prospects," *American Political Science Review* 53

(March 1959): 332–57, and Nicholas Wahl, "The French Constitution of 1958: The Initial Draft and Its Origins," *American Political Science Review* 53 (March 1959): 358–82. For a more recent study, see Robert A. Harmsen, *Of Grandeur and Compromise: The Constitution of the French Fifth Republic,* unpublished dissertation (University of Kent at Canterbury, 1988), pp. 358–407. For the testimony of participants, see Jean Foyer, "The Drafting of the French Constitution of 1958," and François Luchaire, "Commentary," in Robert A. Goldwin and Art Kaufman, eds., *Constitution Makers on Constitution Making* (Washington, D.C.: American Enterprise Institute, 1988), pp. 7–55.

30. The names and affiliations of members of the working group can be found in *Documents pour servir à l'histoire de la constitution du 4 octobre 1958* (Paris: La Documentation Française, 1987, 1988, 1991), vol. 1, p. 241.

31. Their names appear at ibid., vol. 1, p. xxiv. Some members of the working group appear on the list of experts as well.

32. The French Community outlined in the 1958 Constitution should not be confused with French departments overseas: Guadeloupe, Martinique, French Guiana, and Réunion. These departments are part of France and are fully represented in parliament. France also retains several overseas possessions. They are either "overseas territories" (French Polynesia, New Caledonia, and Wallis & Futuna Islands) or "territorial collectives" (St. Pierre & Miquelon and Mayotte). Some of these places play an important role in contemporary French foreign policy, especially in connection with the French space program and with France's role as a nuclear power.

33. In using the word *presidentialist,* I follow Fred Riggs's helpful distinction between regimes that are "presidential" as opposed to those that are "presidentialist." Presidential regimes merely have presidents, e.g., Iraq's President Saddam Hussein. Presidentialist regimes are those in which the president is the head of government but is elected for a fixed term. Thus, the United States is a presidentialist regime. The French Fifth Republic poses a difficult case for Riggs's distinction because the president of the Republic is elected for a fixed term but does not head the government. Cohabitation periods aside, however, he has sufficient control over the prime minister that he might be considered as closely akin to a de facto head of government. Hence, my vacillation in the text between calling the Fifth Republic a presidentialist regime or a semipresidentialist regime. Riggs offers a full discussion of presidentialism in a forthcoming publication: "Presidentialism: An Empirical Theory," in Mattei Dogan and Ali Kazancigil, eds., *Comparing Nations: The Pendulum Between Theory and Practice* (London: Basil Blackwell). See also Riggs, "Bureaucracy and the Constitution," *Public Administration Review* 54 (January–February 1994): 65–72.

34. "President of the Republic" is the title by which the French refer to their president. This is to distinguish him from many other presidents: the president of the Senate, the president of the National Assembly, and the presidents of a host of governmental councils. He is never called "president of France."

35. Letter from Georges Vedel to the author, 27 October 1992 (my translation).

36. William Safran, *The French Polity,* 3d ed. (New York: Longman, 1991), p. 50.

37. A recent episode involving very bitter expressions of hostility by politicians

toward the Constitutional Council arose in connection with that body's decision to strike down key provisions in a far-reaching immigration statute enacted by the conservative parliament that was elected in March 1993. See Thierry Bréhier, "Le Conseil constitutionnel atténue la rigueur de la loi sur l'immigration," *Le Monde,* 15–16 August 1993, p. 1; "'Le Conseil constitutionnel empêche le gouvernement d'appliquer sa politique,' affirme M. Pasqua," *Le Monde,* 17 August 1993, p. 7.

38. The origin of the jurisdiction of both the Supreme Court of the United States and the inferior courts mentioned in article 3 of the Constitution has been the subject of considerable discussion in American constitutional law. The discussion focuses on the distinction between jurisdiction arising from the Constitution itself, on the one hand, and from statutes voted by Congress, on the other. See *Ex parte McCardle,* 74 U.S. (7 Wallace) 506 (1868) and *Sheldon v. Sill* 49 U.S. (8 Howard) 441 (1850). For a concise discussion of this question, see Louis Fisher, *Constitutional Structures: Separated Powers and Federalism,* 2d ed. (New York: McGraw-Hill, 1994), pp. 580–84.

39. Martin M. Shapiro, "Judicial Review in France," *Journal of Law and Politics* 6 (Spring 1990): 531–48; Alec Stone, *The Birth of Judicial Politics in France* (New York: Oxford University Press, 1992), pp. 108–10.

40. Hardy Wickwar, *Power and Service: A Cross-National Analysis of Public Administration* (New York: Greenwood Press, 1991), pp. 6–7 and *passim.*

41. I have in mind primarily the use of *state* as an English noun. When used as an adjective, the word has a better chance of shaking its pejorative connotations, as in such expressions as a "state funeral" or "state papers." The former suggests great dignity and solemnity; the latter official importance. *Stately* has no pejorative connotation: "She carries herself in a stately manner." *Statesmen* are usually a cut above politicians.

42. The careful reader will have already observed a certain inconsistency on my part in capitalizing the English word *state.* Throughout this book, I have capitalized it when I refer to the French State and left it in lowercase when referring to the American state. I believe that the inconsistency in capitalization is justified by the continuing reminder it provides of the profound differences between the two countries on this matter.

43. Charles de Gaulle, *Memoirs of Hope: Renewal and Endeavor,* Terence Kilmartin, trans. (New York: Simon & Schuster, 1971), p. 3. General de Gaulle wrote two sets of memoirs. The first were his war memoirs, published in three volumes, titled *The Call to Honor, Unity, and Salvation.* The second memoirs were intended to cover the period from his return to power in 1958 until his resignation as president of the Fifth Republic in 1969. The general died before these could be completed. He had envisioned another three-volume work, with the titles *Renewal, Endeavor, and Completion.* At the time of his death, he had completed the first volume and two chapters of the second. Hence, the subtitle of the English translation is *Renewal and Endeavor.*

44. Don Cook, *Charles de Gaulle: A Biography* (New York: Putnam, 1983), p. 245.

45. Ibid., p. 248.

46. François Mauriac, *De Gaulle,* Richard Howard, trans., (New York: Doubleday, 1966), p. 180.

47. De Gaulle, *Memoirs of Hope,* p. 23.

48. Mauriac, *De Gaulle,* p. 160.

49. André Malraux, *Felled Oaks: Conversations with de Gaulle* (New York: Holt, Rinehart & Winston, 1971), pp. 82-83.

50. Mauriac, *De Gaulle,* p. 68.

51. Ibid., pp. 108-9.

52. Ibid., pp. 91-92.

53. Ibid., p. 7; see also pages 35 and 88 of this source for similar remarks.

54. *Le Monde,* 3 March 1990, p. 12.

55. "'Je crois encore aux chances de la paix,' déclare M. Mitterrand," *Le Monde,* 2 January 1991, p. 3.

56. *Le Monde,* 17 January 1991, p. 8.

57. *Le Monde,* 28 November 1990, p. 6.

58. "Renault-Volvo: L'Etat repoussoir," *L'Express,* 16 December 1993, p. 14; Peter Gumbel, "France's Bureaucracy Finds It Hard to Stop Meddling in Industry," *Wall Street Journal,* 17 June 1994.

59. "France," in *OECD Country Profiles* (Paris: OECD, 1993), p. 107.

60. *L'Express,* 20 January 1989, pp. 5-9. See also, in the same edition of *L'Express,* Nicolas Grabar, "COB et SEC," p. 21.

61. *News from France,* 15 April 1994, p. 2.

62. "France," in *Public Management Developments: Survey 1993,* (Paris: OECD, 1993), p. 70.

63. Yves Mény, "France," in Donald Rowat, ed., *Public Administration in Developed Democracies: A Comparative Study* (New York: Marcel Dekker, 1988), pp. 273-74.

64. Ezra H. Suleiman, *Private Power and Centralization in France: The Notaries and the State* (Princeton, N.J.: Princeton University Press, 1987).

65. Safran, *The French Polity,* p. 199.

66. F. F. Ridley and J. Blondel, *Public Administration in France,* 2d ed. (London: Barnes & Noble, 1970), p. 36.

67. The leading study on this topic is Ezra N. Suleiman, *Politics, Power and Bureaucracy: The Administrative Elite in France* (Princeton, N.J.: Princeton University Press, 1974).

68. Marie-Christine Kessler, *Les Grands corps de l'Etat,* (Paris: Presses de la Fondation Nationale des Sciences Politiques, 1986), p. 208.

69. Ibid., pp. 16-18. Like *grands corps,* the expression *hauts fonctionnaires* is not as clear as it is common. Just which *fonctionnaires* are really *hauts* is a matter of some dispute. See J.-L. Bodiguel and J.-L. Quermonne, *La Haute fonction publique sous la Ve République* (Paris: Presses Universitaires de France, 1983), pp. 11-81.

70. Jean-Louis Barsoux and Peter Lawrence, "The Making of a French Manager," *Harvard Business Review* (July-August 1991): 64.

71. Kessler, *Les Grands corps,* p. 81, citing *Unité* of 31 October 1975.

72. J.-L. Bodiguel, "Political and Administrative Traditions and the French Se-

nior Civil Service," *International Journal of Public Administration* 13 (1990): 711–13.

73. Guy Braibant, *Le Droit administratif français* (Paris: Dalloz, 1988), p. 172.

74. Cook, *Charles de Gaulle,* p. 203.

75. See chapter 8, note 53 and accompanying text, and chapter 6, note 14.

76. Cook, *Charles de Gaulle,* p. 254.

77. Suleiman, *Politics, Power and Bureaucracy,* p. 35.

78. Francis de Baecque, "Les Fonctionnaires à l'assaut du pouvoir politique?" *Pouvoirs* 40 (1987), p. 61–80. To put into proper perspective the extraordinarily high number of civil servants who serve in Parliament, one should take into account that in France teachers are civil servants. Since teachers are very heavily represented in the Socialist party, a substantial number of them won parliamentary seats when the Socialists came to power in 1981.

79. Henry W. Ehrmann and Martin A. Schain, *Politics in France,* 5th ed. (New York: Harper-Collins, 1992), p. 155.

80. The civil servant he appointed was Bernard Tricot. The story is told by Stephen H. Bornstein, "The Greenpeace Affair and the Peculiarities of French Politics," in Andrei S. Markovits and Mark Silverstein, ed., *The Politics of Scandal* (New York: Holmes & Meier, 1988), pp. 91–121. A more recent example involves the weighty responsibilities given to Hubert Prévot in the extremely important question of immigration. See Robert Solé, "Le Haut Conseil à l'integration a été constitué," *Le Monde,* 22 February 1990, p. 44; and Guillaume Malaurie and Sylviane Stein, "Hubert Prévot: un vrai-faux ministre," *L'Express,* 23 February 1990, p. 55.

81. Thierry Bréhier, "Rocard, Michel: inspecteur general des finances," *Le Monde,* 17–18 November 1991, p. 9.

82. *Le Monde,* 25 January 1990, p. 9.

83. "M. Mitterrand exhorte les fonctionnaires à éviter 'l'esprit de caste,'" *Le Monde,* 5–6 January 1992, p. 6.

84. L. Neville Brown and John Bell, "Recent Reforms of French Administrative Justice, *Civil Justice Quarterly* 8 (January 1989), p. 71.

85. Canal, Robin, and Godot, C.E. Ass. 19 October 1962; Rec. 552; in M. Long et al., eds., *Les Grands arrêts de la jurisprudence administrative,* 9th ed. (Paris: Sirey, 1990), pp. 608–14.

86. For the relationship between the Council of State and the Constitutional Council, see Jean-Paul Costa, *Le Conseil d'Etat dans la société contemporaine* (Paris: Economica, 1993), pp. 117–23.

87. F. F. Ridley, *The French Prefectoral System: An Example of Integrated Administrative Decentralization* (London: Commission on the Constitution, Research Paper 4, HMSO, 1974). See also F. F. Ridley, "The French Prefectoral System Revived," *Administration and Society* (May 1974), p. 48–72.

88. There is extensive literature both in French and in English on decentralization in France. See François-Xavier Aubry, *Essai sur la Décentralisation* (Paris: Groupe des Publications Périodiques Paul Dupont, 1988); François Aubry, *La Décentralisation contre l'Etat: l'Etat semi-centralise* (Paris: Librairie Générale de Droit et de Jurisprudence, 1992); Vivien A. Schmidt, *Democratizing France: The Political*

and Administrative History of Decentralization (Cambridge: Cambridge University Press, 1990).

89. Kessler, *Les Grands corps,* p. 212, citing an article from *Le Monde* of 20 April 1982.

90. For a good discussion of *concertation* see David Wilsford, "Running the Bureaucratic State: The Administration in France," in Ali Farazmand, ed., *Handbook of Comparative and Development Administration* (New York: Marcel Dekker, 1991), pp. 611–24. Wilsford explores this question in greater depth with regard to the medical profession in *Doctors and the State: The Politics of Health Care in France and the United States* (Durham, N.C.: Duke University Press, 1991).

91. Max Farrand, ed., *The Records of the Federal Convention of 1787* (New Haven, Conn.: Yale University Press, 1966), vol. 3, p. 14. For a recent study comparing forms of political argument at the the Philadelphia Convention of 1787 and at the French Constituent Assembly (1789–1791), see Jon Elster, "Argumenter et négocier dans deux assemblées constituantes," *Revue française de science politique* 44 (April 1994): 187–256.

92. Bruce Ackerman, "Discovering the Constitution," *Yale Law Journal* 93 (1984), p. 1058. The best contemporary effort to justify the ratification procedure is Forrest McDonald, *Novus Ordo Seclorum: The Intellectual Origins of the Constitution* (Lawrence: University Press of Kansas, 1985), p. 279. I have given a brief summary of the Federalists' efforts to defend the legality of their work in *To Run a Constitution: The Legitimacy of the Administrative State* (Lawrence: University Press of Kansas, 1986), p. 6.

93. Constitution of the Fourth Republic, article 90. The text of this constitution can be found in Yves Mény, ed., *Textes constitutionnels et documents politiques* (Paris: Montchrestien, 1989), p. 240.

94. *Documents pour servir à l'histoire de la constitution du 4 octobre 1958,* vol. 1, p. 211. See also the "lettre rectificative au projet de loi constitutionnelle, 1er juin 1958" (vol. 1, pp. 165–66), and the extended debates in 1955 on proposed changes to the amending procedures for the Constitution of the Fourth Republic (vol. 1, pp. 11–99, *passim*).

95. Herbert Storing speculates on Brutus's identity in Herbert J. Storing, ed., *The Complete Anti-Federalist* (Chicago: University of Chicago Press, 1983), vol. 2, p. 358.

96. Prior to the 1980s, the leading book on the Anti-Federalists was Jackson Turner Main's *The Anti-Federalists: Critics of the Constitution, 1781–1788* (Chapel Hill: University of North Carolina Press, 1961).

97. M. J. C. Vile, *Constitutionalism and the Separation of Powers* (London: Oxford University Press, 1967), pp. 119–211. See also Terence Marshall, "Separation of Powers, Human Rights and Constitutional Government: A Franco-American Dialogue at the Time of the Revolution," in Peter Schramm and Bradford Wilson, eds., *Separation of Powers and Good Government* (Lanham, Md.: Rowman & Littlefield, 1994), pp. 17–45.

98. *Federalist* 78.

99. Ibid.

100. I have discussed these points at some length in *To Run a Constitution,* pp.

77–84, 181–84, and part I, *passim.* The twenty-two ways of achieving office under the Constitution are listed on p. 260, note 31.

FRENCH CONSTITUTIONALISM AND ADMINISTRATION

1. For a concise overview of French constitutional development written in English, see William Safran, *The French Polity,* 3d ed. (New York: Longman, 1991), pp. 1–20.

2. Jean V. Poulard, "The French Double Executive and the Experience of Cohabitation," *Political Science Quarterly* 105 (November 1990): 243–67, 249; Pascal Robert-Diard, "En attendant la VIe République," *Le Monde,* 8 December 1990, p. 8.

3. Constitutional Council, 16 July 1971; 71–44 DC, Rec. 29. This decision, along with a commentary by the editors appears in Louis Favoreu and Loïc Philip, eds., *Les Grandes décisions du conseil constitutionnel,* 6th ed. (Paris: Sirey, 1991), pp. 237–53.

4. At least for now the President is re-eligible. A movement is afoot to shorten the President's term of office. Some would reduce the present seven-year term to five years and retain re-eligibility. Others would retain the seven-year term but prohibit re-eligibility. For President Mitterrand's thoughts on this matter, see *Le Monde,* 12 November 1991, pp. 2–5.

5. Throughout this book, references to the Constitution of the United States will use a Roman numeral to indicate the article number and an Arabic number to indicate the section number.

6. This is not to say that no controversy or confusion surrounds the nature and effect of such varying administrative instruments as the ordinances and decrees adopted by the Council of Ministers, those adopted elsewhere, and the rule-making power *(pouvoir réglementaire)* that article 21 vests not in the president but in the prime minister. For invaluable guidance through the maze of ministerial rule-making powers, see Céline Wiener, *Recherches sur le pouvoir réglementaire des ministres* (Paris: Librairie Générale de Droit et de Jurisprudence: R. Pichon & R. Durand-Auzias, 1970).

7. Phillip Cooper, "By Order of the President: Administration by Executive Order and Proclamation," *Administration and Society* 18 (1986): 233–62.

8. John A. Rohr, "Public Administration, Executive Power, and Constitutional Confusion," *Public Administration Review* 49 (March–April 1989): 108–15.

9. Didier Maus, "La Constitution jugée par sa pratique," in Olivier Duhamel and Jean-Luc Parodi, eds., *La Constitution de la cinquième république* (Paris: Presses de la Fondation Nationale des Sciences Politiques, 1988), p. 298. See also Jean-Louis Quermonne, "Bilan Juridique: Introduction," in Duhamel and Parodi, *La Constitution,* pp. 283–94 at 284.

10. M. J. C. Vile, *Constitutionalism and the Separation of Powers* (London: Oxford University Press, 1967), pp. 119–211.

11. Jean Chatelain, "Article 16," in François Luchaire and Gérard Conac, eds.,

La Constitution de la république française, 2d ed. (Paris: Economica, 1987), pp. 541–53.

12. Ibid., pp. 545–46.

13. Favoreu and Philip, *Les Grandes décisions,* p. 124.

14. Constitutional Council, 23 April 1961; Rec. 69. Favoreu and Philip, *Les Grandes décisions,* p. 123.

15. On this point, Favoreu and Philip cite J. Lamarque, "L'article 16," *Revue de Droit Public et de la Science Politique* (1961): 613ff. The argument recalls U.S. Supreme Court Chief Justice Frederick Vinson's statement in his plurality opinion in the *Dennis* case that the "clear and present danger" test does not mean that before the state can intervene to prohibit potentially subversive speech "it must wait until the *putsch* is about to be executed, the plans have been laid and the signal is awaited." See *Dennis v. U.S.,* 341 U.S. 494 (1951).

16. Favoreu and Philip, *Les Grandes décisions,* p. 123.

17. Chatelain, "Article 16," p. 548.

18. Alfred H. Kelly, Winfred A. Harbison, and Herman Belz, *The American Constitution: Its Origins and Development,* 6th ed. (New York: W. W. Norton, 1983), chapters 16, 22, and 27.

19. Elijah Ben-Zion Kaminisky, *The Contemporary French Executive: Stable Governments, Unstable Institutions* (Atlanta: American Political Science Association, 1989), p. 2.

20. Michel Debré, "La Nouvelle Constitution," *Revue française de science politique* 9 (1959): 7–29.

21. Bruno Génévois, *La Jurisprudence du conseil constitutionnel* (Paris: Les Editions STH, 1988), pp. 73–125; Leo Hamon, *La Loi et réglement: Articles 34, 37, et 38 de la constitution de 1958* (Paris: La Documentation Française, 1988); Jean-Louis Pezant, "Loi/Réglement: La Constitution d'un nouvel équilibre," in Duhamel and Parodi, *La Constitution,* pp. 342–74.

22. The constitutional powers of Congress are not limited to I,8. Elsewhere in the Constitution, one finds references to congressional powers to create offices; to vest the appointing power in certain officers; to choose its own officers; to judge the qualifications of its members; to regulate state powers over the times, manners, and places of holding elections; and so on. Likewise the French Parliament enjoys constitutional powers beyond those of article 34, e.g., the powers to declare war (article 35) and to ratify treaties (article 53).

23. In May 1991, President Mitterrand appointed Edith Cresson to be prime minister. She was the first woman to serve as the head of government in France.

24. See articles 10 and 11 of the Declaration of the Rights of Man and of the Citizen.

25. Article 37 is not innovative in the sense that an autonomous regulatory power is unprecedented in French law. Such a power was recognized by the Council of State in the early years of this century, but it was limited to police administration and the organization of public services. See François Luchaire, "Article 37," in Luchaire and Conac, *La Constitution,* p. 788. The innovation of article 37 lies in its broad application to everything that is not committed to the domain of law by article 34.

26. An American administrative agency could be granted rule-making power pur-

suant to an executive order of the president, which, in turn, could be grounded either in statute or in the constitutional powers of the president. Administrative agencies have an inherent power to issue interpretive rules; but to exercise this power they must first be presented with a statute, an executive order, or some other authoritative document to be interpreted. See *Skidmore v. Swift & Co.,* 323 U.S. 134 (1944). On interpretive rules, see Phillip Cooper, *Public Law and Public Administration,* 2d ed. (Englewood Cliffs, N.J.: Prentice-Hall, 1988), pp. 121–23. At times the U.S. Supreme Court has given remarkable latitude to administrative agencies to issue far-reaching rules on the basis of very scant statutory support. See, for example, *Haig v. Agee,* 453 U.S. 280 (1980), and *Meritor Savings Bank v. Vinson,* 477 U.S. 63 (1986). In principle, *some* statutory basis always underlies the sweeping administrative regulations; but in practice, some agencies at times enjoy virtually autonomous rule-making power.

27. The governmental rule-making power is autonomous in the sense that it need not have a statutory foundation. This is not to say it is simply unfettered power. It remains subject to the general principles of legal constraint imposed on administrative organizations by the Council of State. See Luchaire, "Article 37," pp. 788–89; Quermonne, "Bilan juridique," p. 287.

28. For an illuminating comparative study of the philosophical foundations of the principle of separation of powers in France and in the United States, see Terence Marshall, "Préface" and "Les droits de l'homme et l'art politique à l'époque révolutionnaire: la France et les Etats-Unis," in Terence Marshall, ed., *Théorie et pratique du gouvernement constitutionnel* (Paris: Editions de l'Espace Européen, 1992), pp. 9–22, 389–406.

29. The Constitutional Council bears some resemblance to the Council of Revision proposed by James Madison and James Wilson at the Constitutional Convention of 1787. See Max Farrand, *The Records of the Federal Convention of 1787* (New Haven, Conn.: Yale University Press, 1966), vol. 1, pp. 138–39, and vol. 2, pp. 73–80.

30. Michael H. Davis, "A Government of Judges: An Historical Review," *American Journal of Comparative Law* 35 (Summer 1987): 559–80.

31. The notion of sovereignty in French history is exceedingly complex, as it is in the history of the United States. The Constitution of the Fifth Republic states that the people are sovereign; in so doing, it uses almost the same language as the Constitution of the Fourth Republic. It is quite likely that this language was adopted to stress the continuity between the Fourth and Fifth Republics. See Jean Chatelain, "Article 3," in Luchaire and Conac, *La Constitution,* pp. 179–89. The mention of sovereignty in article 3 does not seem to have any connection with the implications of the division of powers made in articles 34 and 37.

32. Laws enacted by previous parliaments are not the only directives that can be modified by the government under the second paragraph of article 37. The wording of the paragraph in question is *"les textes de forme legislative,"* which includes texts approved by nonlegislative authorities that happened to exercise legislative power due to peculiar historical circumstances—for instance, certain acts taken by Napoléon I, Napoléon III, and General de Gaulle (as the head of Free France). These texts can also be modified by the government. One commentator is not happy with the ex-

pression used in the second paragraph of article 37. He would have preferred *"textes ayant force de loi."* See Luchaire, "Article 37," p. 791.

33. The 1974 amendment to article 61 permits sixty members of the National Assembly or sixty members of the Senate to convene the Constitutional Council. In practice this has given the parliamentary opposition a chance to challenge the constitutionality of laws passed by Parliament. Not surprisingly, this has led to a remarkable increase in the number of cases brought before the Council. For example, between 1959 and 1974, only nine cases were brought before the Constitutional Council under article 61. Between 1974 and 1985, ninety-five such cases were submitted. See Loïc Philip, "Bilan et effets de la saisine du conseil constitutionnel," in Duhamel and Parodi, *La Constitution,* p. 411.

34. In France today, there is serious talk of amending the Constitution to permit ordinary citizens to challenge the constitutionality of laws passed by Parliament. Depending on the subject matter involved, these challenges would originate either in administrative or in ordinary courts, but eventually they would reach the Constitutional Council. If such an amendment were ever passed, the power of the Constitutional Council would increase dramatically. Since such an amendment would introduce judicial review into French law, it would represent a very important change. See Thierry Bréhier, "Les Embûches politiques d'une réforme de la Constitution," *Le Monde,* 29 March 1990, p. 7; Olivier Duhamel, "Déni de justice constitutionelle," *Le Monde,* 15–16 July 1990, p. 6; Georges Vedel, "Réforme de la Constitution: ni gadget ni révolution," *Le Monde,* 6 April 1990, p. 2. This question will be discussed more fully in chapter 5.

35. Article 38 does not mention the president of the Republic explicitly, but article 13 provides that the president must sign ordinances deliberated by the Council of Ministers. Since article 38 explicitly mentions ordinances enacted by the Council of Ministers, it appears that the president's signature is required. See Pierre Levigne, "Article 13," in Luchaire and Conac, *La Constitution,* p. 521.

36. Didier Maus, "Article 44," in Luchaire and Conac, *La Constitution,* p. 865.

37. Leo Hamon, "Article 42," in Luchaire and Conac, *La Constitution,* pp. 840–41.

38. Ibid., p. 846.

39. Maus, "Article 44," p. 864, citing Marcel Prelot, *Précis de droit constitutionnel* (Paris: Dalloz, 1952), p. 462.

40. Ibid., p. 872.

41. The government of Prime Minister Rocard took considerable criticism for what its critics saw as an excessive use of "49,3." See André Passeron, "Crise des institutions," *Le Monde,* 18 December 1990, p. 9; Pierre Servent, "Les Députés rêvent de moderniser la République," *Le Monde,* 25 December 1990, p. 7.

42. Maus, "La Constitution jugée," pp. 311, 325–27.

43. Leo Hamon, "Article 43," in Luchaire and Conac, *La Constitution,* p. 856.

44. Maus, "La Constitution jugée," p. 370; Pezant, "Loi/Réglement," p. 354.

45. See Pezant, "Loi/Réglement," p. 357, where he quotes from an article by Louis Favoreu, in *Actes du colloque d'Aix-en-Provence* (Paris: PUF, 1978), p. 31. The "moving boundary" mentioned by Favoreu seems to have shifted in favor of Parliament in a decision by the Constitutional Council on 30 July 1982; 82–113 DC,

Rec. 57. In this decision, which is reported in Favoreu and Philip, *Les Grandes décisions,* pp. 540–55, the Constitutional Council held that Parliament could include certain matters of a regulatory nature in a law without necessarily violating the Constitution. The council's reasoning rested in part on the fact that the government could protect its interests by invoking article 41 during the legislative process and the second paragraph of article 37 after the law had been passed. See chapter 4 for a further discussion of this case.

46. President Mitterrand, a former parliamentarian, has not forgotten his roots. In a televised interview in November 1991, he promised to offer soon a constitutional amendment that would reinvigorate Parliament, which he thought was in danger of "suffocating." See *Le Monde,* 12 November 1991, pp. 2–3. In 1988, when he was running for reelection as president of the Republic, he called for a strengthening of parliamentary committees. See *Le Monde,* 13 November 1991, p. 11. Such a statement from an incumbent president seeking reelection is a powerful reminder of just how differently the principle of separation of powers is interpreted in France and in the United States.

47. General de Gaulle's views on the independence of the executive from Parliament can be found in the famous address he delivered at Bayeux on June 16, 1946. See *Documents pour servir à l'histoire de l'elaboration de la constitution du 4 octobre 1958* (Paris: La Documentation Française, 1987), vol. 1, pp. 3–7.

48. François Luchaire, "Introduction," in Luchaire and Conac, *La Constitution,* pp. 36–37.

49. The fact that the trappings of contemporary American government are strangers to the text of the Constitution does not necessarily mean that they are unconstitutional. The Supreme Court has upheld most of these arrangements, starting with its confirmation of the power of Congress to create a government corporation (*McCulloch v. Maryland,* 4 Wheat. 316 [1819]) and continuing through the recent Supreme Court decision confirming the constitutionality of the special prosecutor (*Morrison v. Olson,* 108 S. Ct. 2597 [1988]). The most important constitutional authority in the development of this remarkable expansion of federal power has been the famous "necessary and proper" clause of I,8.

50. François Luchaire and Gérard Conac, *Le Droit constitutionnel de la cohabitation* (Paris: Economica, 1989); Kaminsky, *The Contemporary French Executive;* Harvey Feigenbaum, "Recent Evolution of the French Executive," *Governance* 3 (July 1990): 264–78; Poulard, "The French Double Executive"; Olivier Duhamel and Jean-Luc Parodi, "A L'Epreuve de la cohabitation," in Duhamel and Parodi, *La Constitution,* pp. 541–50; Safran, *The French Polity.*

51. Feigenbaum, "Recent Evolution," p. 272; Poulard, "The French Double Executive"; Safran, *The French Polity.*

52. Duhamel and Parodi, "A L'Epreuve de la cohabitation," p. 545.

53. Lloyd N. Cutler, "To Form a Government," *Foreign Affairs* 59 (Fall 1980); 126–43; Theodore Sorenson, *A Different Kind of Presidency* (New York: Harper & Row, 1984).

54. Jim Hoagland, "President Bush Needs a Prime Minister," *Washington Post,* 23 October 1990, p. 17.

55. Kaminsky, *The Contemporary French Executive,* pp. 2–8; Poulard, "The

French Double Executive," p. 252; Gérard Conac, "Article 20" in François Luchaire and Gérard Conac, *Le Droit constitutionnel de la cohabitation,* pp. 143-46.

56. Conac, "Article 20," p. 144.

57. John A. Rohr, *To Run a Constitution: The Legitimacy of the Administrative State* (Lawrence: University Press of Kansas, 1986), p. 185.

58. The acquiescence is less than cheerful, however, when the public suspects that the justices are basing their decisions on something other than the Constitution. Such suspicions have largely fueled today's Interpretist-Activist debate with regard to the Supreme Court.

59. Rohr, *To Run a Constitution,* pp. 181-86.

THE EXECUTIVE POWER

1. For Publius's position that executive power was problematic, see the opening paragraph of *Federalist* 70. Problematic though it was, he recognized its indispensability as well. He concluded that the friends of republican government would do well to hope that the two can be reconciled because, without an effective executive, republican government will never be good government. On the crucial role to be played by the executive in rendering French republicanism effective, see François Luchaire, "Introduction," in Françoise Luchaire and Gérard Conac, eds., *La Constitution de la république française,* 2d ed. (Paris: Economica, 1987), pp. 35-37.

2. For the various characterizations of the executive of the Fifth Republic, see William Safran, *The French Polity,* 3d ed. (New York: Longman, 1991), pp. 133-34. For a vague hint in French constitutional history of what would eventually become the Fifth Republic executive, see the Constitution of the short-lived Second Republic: "La Constitution Républicaine du 4 novembre 1848," in Jacques Godechot, ed., *Les Constitutions de la France depuis 1789* (Paris: Flammarion, 1979), pp. 253-77.

3. *Federalist* 70.

4. Abundant literature is available in English on the French executive. See Preface, note 7.

5. John A. Rohr, *To Run a Constitution: The Legitimacy of the Administrative State* (Lawrence: University Press of Kansas, 1986), chapter 3.

6. II, 97(1a) and 95-98 *passim.* For an explanation of this reference form, see Preface, note 3.

7. II, 104(2c).

8. II, 496(2c).

9. II, 333(2a).

10. III, 81(1b).

11. II, 95(2c)-96(1a). Barrachin attributed the term *bicephalisme* to an article by Georges Vedel which had appeared in *Le Monde.* In developing this point, Barrachin clearly anticipated the cohabitation problem, without using that word (II, 88[2a]-89[1a]).

12. II, 28. (Avant-projet de Constitution des 26/29 juillet 1958.)

13. II, 278(1b).

14. Ibid.

15. II, 372(2c).

16. I, 6.

17. I, 180(2a).

18. III, 303(1c-2a). The English words *arbitrator* and *arbitration* do not really do justice to the French *arbitre* and *arbitrage*. *Arbitrator* suggests labor negotiations and, in particular, those involving contract disputes between professional baseball players and their teams' management. Despite these problems, the English translation of the Constitution issued by the public information office of the French Embassy turns *arbitrage* into *arbitration*. I cannot think of a better substitute. Part of the problem is that the English word *arbitrage* is archaic except for its technical meaning in financial circles. One has difficulty picturing General de Gaulle negotiating a leveraged buy-out!

19. III, 54(2b).

20. II, 328(2b).

21. III, 277.

22. II, 175(2c).

23. Debré acknowledges his own decisive role but recognizes the important contribution of others as well. See Michel Debré, *Trois républiques pour une France: Mémoires, 1946-1958* (Paris: Albin Michel, 1988), pp. 348-53. Luchaire calls Debré the linchpin of the enterprise. See Luchaire, "Introduction," p. 41.

24. III, 264-65.

25. III, 333-34. The texts to which Cassin objected became articles 13 and 21 of the 1958 Constitution. The history of the Fifth Republic has done little to clarify the ambiguities Cassin noted in 1958. For a good discussion pinpointing the confusion in this matter, see "Pouvoir réglementaire" in Olivier Duhamel and Yves Mény, *Dictionnaire constitutionnel* (Paris: Presses Universitaire de France, 1992), pp. 782-85. See also Pierre Lavigne, "Article 13," and Raymond Barrillon, Georges Dupuis, and Marie-José Guédon, "Article 21," in François Luchaire and Gérard Conac, *La Constitution de la république française* (Paris: Economica, 1987), pp. 519-25 and 589-603.

26. III, 554-55.

27. On the appointing power, see articles 13 and 21 of the Constitution of the Fifth Republic.

28. See the text accompanying note 18.

29. I, 518. It is hard to reconcile Debré's comment on this early text with the interpretation of the president's power he put forward in his address to the Council of State, noted in the text accompanying note 24. To be sure, the constitutional text underwent considerable changes, but the two powers Debré called "executive" in the red book text—signing important documents and presiding over the Council of Ministers—are in the text presented to the Council of State.

30. The "necessary and proper" clause appears in article 1, section 8. Known as "the elastic clause," it provides that Congress shall have power "to make all Laws which shall be necessary and proper for carrying into Execution" all the other powers conferred on the government of the United States by the Constitution. It is one of the most important clauses in the U.S. Constitution; perhaps more than any other

clause, it has contributed to the expansion of U.S. national power during the past two centuries.

31. See, for example, the dissenting opinion of Justice Scalia in *Morrison v. Olson* 487 U.S. 654 (1988).

32. The Supreme Court addressed this important issue in *Kendall v. Stokes,* 12 Peters 522 (1838). For its contemporary relevance, see President Reagan's Executive Orders 12291 [46 *Federal Register* 13193 (1981)] and 12498 [50 *Federal Register* 11036 (1986)]. For a discussion of these executive orders, see Phillip J. Cooper, *Public Law and Public Administration,* 2d ed. (Englewood Cliffs, N.J.: Prentice-Hall, 1988), pp. 298–99. See also the opinion of Attorney General William Wirt submitted to President Monroe in 1823 (1 Op. Att'y. Gen. 624).

33. *Federalist* 68.

34. *Federalist* 73.

35. For a recent criticism of excessive reliance on "independent counsels" (the statutory name for the special prosecutors), see the remarks of Reagan-era Solicitor General Charles Fried, "Messing with the Constitution," *Washington Post* 26 August 1994, p. A25.

36. Thomas Ferenczi, "La Maison Mitterrand," *Le Monde,* 4 April 1992, pp. 1, 7.

37. Safran, *The French Polity,* p. 133. The term *premier* is used in place of *prime minister* by some authors to describe the same officer in the Fifth Republic.

38. II, 96(2b).

39. II, 96(2c)–97(1a).

40. The text presented to the Advisory Committee provided: "*Article 6.* The president of the Republic shall appoint the prime minister. On the proposal of the prime minister, he shall appoint the other members of the Government and terminate their functions." Janot argued that the explicit provision for the president, on the prime minister's recommendation, to terminate ministers other than the prime minister implies that the president has no power to remove the prime minister. As we shall see below, Michel Debré argued just the opposite. From the text's silence on removal of the prime minister, Debré infers that he can be removed by the same authority that appointed him—that is, by the president.

41. II, 97(1a).

42. II, 690.

43. II, 689.

44. II, 300.

45. II, 320(1b).

46. II, 625. The text submitted to the Advisory Committee provided:

"The President of the Republic shall appoint the prime minister.

"On the proposal of the prime minister, he shall appoint the other members of the Government and terminate their functions."

The text drafted on 19 August by de Gaulle's advisers provided:

"The President of the Republic shall appoint the prime minister. He may terminate his functions only upon the presentation by the prime minister of the resignation of the government.

"On the proposal of the prime minister, he shall appoint the other members of the Government and terminate their functions."

47. Pierre Avril, "Article 8," in François Luchaire and Gérard Conac, *La Constitution de la république française* (Paris: Economic, 1978), pp. 374–75.

48. Ibid., p. 374.

49. I, 271.

50. Ibid.

51. I, 312. For confirmation that Council of State jurisprudence presumes that the removal power tracks the appointing power, see III, 321(1a).

52. I, 307.

53. I, 530.

54. II, 83(2c).

55. III, 312.

56. III, 562.

57. III, 675–76.

58. I, 277–78.

59. For an explanation of the relationship between the verbatim transcript and the analytic summary of the constitutional debates of 1958, see François Luchaire, "Présentation du deuxième volume," II, vii–viii.

60. II, 752.

61. II, 300.

62. II, 752.

63. The negative force of the English word *only* is less clear than the French *ne . . . que* construction.

64. Avril, "Article 8," p. 372.

65. See articles 13 and 21. For a commentary on these articles, see Lavigne, "Article 13," pp. 523–25; and Barrillon, Dupuis, and Guédon, "Article 21," pp. 596–97; see also "Nomination," in Duhamel and Mény, *Dictionnaire constitutionnel,* pp. 660–61.

66. On delegated and subdelegated power, see the remarks of René Cassin at III, 320(2a). For one of many discussions on the legal status of civil servants, see II, 159–63.

67. For an expansive interpretation of this seemingly rather narrow language, see Raoul Berger, *Impeachment: The Constitutional Problems* (Cambridge, Mass.: Harvard University Press, 1973).

68. The "decision of 1789" has often been analyzed. For discussions of the rich and complex issues that surfaced in the debate, see Edward S. Corwin, *The President's Removal Power Under the Constitution* (New York: National Municipal League, 1927); James Hart, *The American Presidency in Action, 1789: A Study in Constitutional History* (New York: Macmillan, 1948); John A. Rohr, *The President and the Public Administration* (Washington, D.C.: American Historical Association, 1989).

69. *Federalist* 77.

70. The constitutional basis of "the decision of 1789" was not settled conclusively until 1926, when the U.S. Supreme Court held that the president's removal power

over officers he had appointed was a constitutional power of the president and not merely a statutory grant from Congress. *Myers v. U.S.,* 272 U.S. 52 (1926).

71. For a clear statement of the de facto dominance of the president in Fifth Republic practice, see "Président de la République" and "Exécutif," in Duhamel and Mény, *Dictionnaire constitutionnel,* pp. 804-8 and 427-28.

72. III, 326.

73. II, 80(2a). In the passage cited, Coste-Floret mentions article 14 instead of 16. In the text presented to the Advisory Committee, article 14 was the forerunner of the provision that eventually became article 16 of the Constitution as adopted.

74. II, 80(2b).

75. The document discussed by Coty appears at I, 429ff.

76. III, 553.

77. II, 672. See also page 314, where Valentin softens his position by saying that the president is sovereign "in a certain way."

78. Ibid.

79. *Sovereign* is a word that is seldom applied to an officer in American politics. Occasionally the phrase "sovereign states" occurs, but usually in a historical context. An interesting exception, however, appeared in a deposition by former President Nixon to the Senate Select Committee to Study Governmental Operations with Respect to Intelligence Activities (the "Church Committee"). Nixon referred to the president as the sovereign in the following context: "It is quite obvious that there are certain inherently governmental actions which if undertaken by the sovereign in protection of the interest of the nation's security are lawful but which if undertaken by private persons are not." Ordinarily Americans do not view their president or their Congress as sovereign. If there is any sovereign in American political thought other than the people, it is their Constitution, which distributes *limited* (and therefore less than sovereign) powers to the several branches of the government. For an interesting statement on Richard Nixon's "Gaullist" view of the U.S. presidency, see Aaron Wildavsky, "Government and the People," *Commentary* (August 1973), pp. 25-32.

80. III, 683.

81. Ibid.

82. I, 309; see also I, 285.

83. Remarks of Isorni, I, 106(2c)-107(2a).

84. Remarks of de Menthon, I, 130(2c).

85. Remarks of Tixier-Vignancour, I, 172(1b). These three statements (notes 83-85) capture nicely the French idea that members of the National Assembly represent not only those who elect them but all of France as well. For a clear statement to this effect, see article 34 of the Constitution of 4 November 1848 in Godechot, *Les Constitutions,* p. 268.

86. I, 131.

87. III, 681.

88. I, 255-56, 266.

89. III, 307.

90. II, 538. The proposal in question was suggested by Bruyneel; it called for two rounds in the electoral college, with only the leading candidates reappearing in the

second round. This would ensure that the president would be selected by an absolute majority (rather than by a potentially weak plurality) of the electoral college.

91. Debré, *Trois républiques pour une France,* pp. 405–11.

92. Ibid., p. 410.

93. Ibid., pp. 405–6.

94. Ibid., pp. 405–6. The problem of the proper role of citizens overseas in selecting the president was very much on the minds of the framers of the 1958 Constitution. See, for example, I, 269; I, 275–76; I, 285–86.

95. Ibid., p. 410.

96. Such an argument would not make much headway in the United States, where appeals to the Constitution usually trump appeals to democracy on both moral and legal grounds. In France, the moral commitment to democracy expressed through universal suffrage is much stronger than in the United States; and not surprisingly, the moral commitment to the Constitution is correspondingly weaker.

97. For a probing study of the framers' thoughts on how the president should be selected, see James Ceasar, *Presidential Selection: Theory and Development* (Princeton, N.J.: Princeton University Press, 1979), chapter 1.

THE LEGISLATIVE POWER

1. From my reading of the lengthy 1958 debates, I can recall only one statement suggesting a divorce between republicanism and parliamentary government. André Malterre, a member of the Advisory Committee on the Constitution, noted a strong antiparliamentary mood in the country and wondered whether it might not be best for France to manifest its republican spirit in some other form of government. In the course of his remarks, he referred several times to various American institutions without explicitly stating that France should follow the American example of grounding a republican regime in a presidential form of government (II, 86–87). For an explanation of the citations, see Preface, note 3.

2. I, 119(2b).

3. I, 130(2b).

4. I, 128(2c).

5. For a discussion of the role of the Advisory Committee on the Constitution, see Richard Ghevontian, "Rôle du comité consultatif constitutionnel dans l'écriture de la constitution," in Didier Maus, Louis Favoreu, and Jean-Luc Parodi, eds., *L'Ecriture de la constitution de 1958* (Paris: Economica, 1992), pp. 785–810.

6. I, 204(1b).

7. III, 674.

8. I, 106(2b).

9. The Constitutional Law of 3 June 1958 added a fourth principle of judicial independence and a directive that the new constitution should address "the relations of the Republic with the peoples who are associated with it"—a veiled reference to the Empire.

10. I, 203(2b).

11. I, 191(2b).

12. I, 517-18; III, 659.

13. *Federalist* 10.

14. *Federalist* 37.

15. *Federalist* 39.

16. Herbert J. Storing, ed., *The Complete Anti-Federalist* 7 vols. (Chicago: University of Chicago Press, 1981). [Hereafter cited as *CAF*.] References include the name or pseudonym of the Anti-Federalist author and three numbers indicating, respectively, the volume, the author's position in the volume, and the paragraph in the author's speech or pamphlet. Thus the present citation is Brutus, *CAF* 2.9.12. References to volume 1 (Storing's introductory essay) and to Storing's notes throughout the seven volumes will be given by a Roman numeral indicating the volume and an arabic number indicating the page.

17. Federal Farmer, *CAF* 2.8.15.

18. Centinel, *CAF* 2.7.9. As an indication of just how distant Centinel was from Publius politically, compare his call for a "pretty equal" division of property with the following from *Federalist* 10: "The diversity in the faculties of men, from which the rights of property originate, is not less an insuperable obstacle to a uniformity of interests. The protection of these faculties is the first object of Government."

19. Brutus, *CAF* 2.9.16.

20. George Mason, *CAF* 5.17.1.

21. *Federalist* 10.

22. John A. Rohr, *To Run a Constitution: The Legitimacy of the Administrative State* (Lawrence: University Press of Kansas, 1986), p. 132, citing Patrick Henry, *CAF* I, 54.

23. I, 411.

24. I, 450.

25. I, 451.

26. I, 450.

27. For a clear and concise description of the parliamentarian-turned-minister and the *suppléant* who replaces him, see William Safran, *The French Polity,* 3d ed. (New York: Longman, 1993), pp. 184-86.

28. For example, Michel Rocard resumed his civil service position with the *Inspection des Finances* after resigning his position as prime minister. Thierry Bréhier, "Rocard, Michel, inspecteur général des finances," *Le Monde,* 17-18 November 1991, p. 9.

29. Michel Céoara, "Article 23," in François Luchaire and Gérard Conac, *La Constitution de la république française,* 2d ed. (Paris: Economica, 1987), pp. 628-32. Céoara describes civil servants as being "detached" when they serve as members of the government. For a discussion of the distinction in French civil service regulations between *détachement* and *disponibilité,* see Alain Plantey, *La Fonction publique: Traité général* (Paris: Editions Litec, 1991), pp. 262-83.

30. I, 235.

31. II, 303-4(1a); II, 221(2a).

32. III, 260.

33. II, 216-31, 539-44. See also I, 292.

34. II, 228(2b).

35. II, 218(1c-2b).

36. II, 539(1c-2a).

37. II, 225(1b).

38. II, 219(2b).

39. II, 541(2a). See also the remarks of Dejean at II, 217(2a) and of Baillien-court at II, 543(1c).

40. This theme pervades the Advisory Council's discussion. See II, 226(1b); II, 302(2b); II, 550(2b); and especially Paul Reynaud's letter to General de Gaulle at II, 733.

41. II, 220(2b).

42. II, 227(1b).

43. II, 218(1b).

44. Max Farrand, ed., *The Records of the Federal Convention of 1787* (New Haven, Conn.: Yale University Press, 1966), vol. 1, pp. 235, 386. For a further statement of the states' rights rationale, see remarks in Luther Martin's *Genuine Information* in *CAF* 2.4.46.

45. For an early example of state action barring federal officials from state office, see the address of James Wilson of 19 January 1790. As a recently appointed justice of the Supreme Court of the United States, Wilson strenuously but unsuccessfully opposed the following amendment to the Pennsylvania constitution: "No member of Congress from this state, nor any person holding or exercising any office of trust or profit under the United States, shall, at the same time, hold and exercise any office whatever in this state." Robert G. McCloskey, ed., *The Works of James Wilson* (Cambridge, Mass.: Harvard University Press, 1967), vol. 2, pp. 794-802. As new states entered the union, they often inserted in their constitutions provisions forbidding members of Congress and federal officeholders from holding certain state government positions. See, for example, the Mississippi constitution of 1817, article IV, section 15, pp. 2044-45; the Missouri constitution of 1820, article III, section 11, p. 2152; and the Michigan constitution of 1835, article IV, section 2, pp. 1936-37. Page references are taken from volume 4 of Francis Newton Thorpe, ed., *The Federal and State Constitutions, Colonial Charters, and Other Organic Laws of the States, Territories, and Colonies Now or Heretofore Forming the United States of America* (Washington, D.C.: Government Printing Office, 1909).

46. For a lucid critique of the *cumul des mandats* system, see Yves Mény, *La Corruption de la république* (Fayard: Paris, 1992), pp. 61-95. For recently proposed reforms, see the report of the *Comité Consultatif pour la révision de la Constitution* appointed by President Mitterrand and chaired by Georges Vedel. *Le Monde,* 17 February 1993, p. 8.

47. Louis Fisher, "Separation of Powers: Interpretation Outside the Courts," *Pepperdine Law Review* 18 (1990), p. 57-93.

48. "Standing" is the legal doctrine that requires plaintiffs in federal courts to show that they have suffered some "injury in fact" before the court will hear their case. For a discussion of appointments in apparent violation of the ineligibility and incompatibility clauses, see Fisher, "Separation of Powers," pp. 75-77. For the most part, these violations appear to be merely technical, with one notable exception: the

flagrant violation of the incompatibility clause by congressmen holding commissions as reserve officers in the armed forces. The Supreme Court denied a group of plaintiffs standing to challenge this practice in *Schlesinger v. Reservists to Stop the War,* 418 U.S. 208 (1974).

49. *Congressional Record,* 103rd Congress, 1st sess., 5 January 1993: Senate 9–10. In discussing Senator Bentsen's situation, the senators relied primarily on President Nixon's nomination of Senator Saxbe as attorney general and, to a lesser extent, on President Carter's nomination of Senator Muskie as secretary of state. An interesting aspect of the Bentsen nomination was that Congress authorized legal challenges in court to its disposition of the problem presented by the ineligibility clause.

50. Philip B. Kurland and Ralph Lerner, *The Founders' Constitution,* 5 vols., (University of Chicago Press: Chicago, 1987), II, 356(1b). The quotation is from Grayson; for a similar statement from Henry, see Kurland and Lerner, *Founders' Constitution,* II, 355(1a).

51. Kurland and Lerner, *Founders' Constitution,* II, 354(1a).

52. Ibid., II, 354(1b).

53. Ibid., II, 353(2a).

54. Farrand, *Records of the Federal Convention of 1787,* vol. 1, p. 235.

55. Kurland and Lerner, *Founders' Constitution,* II, 350(2b).

56. Ibid., II, 349(2b).

57. Ibid. For Renaud's comment, see the text accompanying note 35 of this chapter.

58. Ibid., II, 351(1a).

59. Ibid., II, 349(1c).

60. Ibid., II, 350(1c–2a).

61. Ibid., II, 373(1a).

62. Ibid., II, 373(2c).

63. Lynton Caldwell, *The Administrative Theories of Hamilton and Jefferson* (Chicago: University of Chicago Press, 1944 [reissued New York: Russel & Russel, 1964]), p. 99.

64. II, 717.

65. Article 13 of the Constitution of the Fourth Republic prohibited delegation of legislative authority, but this prohibition was systematically ignored.

66. I underscore "text" because, in practice, Fifth Republic parliaments have fared better than one might expect from a literal reading of the Constitution unencumbered by history. See, in particular, the decision of the Conseil Constitutionnel of 30 July 1982 (82–143 DC, *Rec.* 57), which is discussed later in this chapter. See also John Bell's illuminating discussion, "The Division of Lawmaking Powers: The Revolution That Never Happened?" in John Bell, *French Constitutional Law* (New York: Oxford University Press, 1992, pp. 78–111).

67. Jean-Louis Pézant, "Les Dispositions instituant un système de délimitation des compétences législatives et réglementaires," in Maus, Favoreu, and Parodi, *L'Ecriture de la constitution de 1958,* pp. 511–65 at 512.

68. I, 325–26; I, 333; Pézant, "Les Dispositions," pp. 516–17. A draft text clearly anticipating two constitutionally distinct domains of law and regulation appears at I, 255, along with other documents believed to have been written in mid-

June. According to an editorial note at the bottom of I, 251, the precise dates of these documents are uncertain. Pézant offers strong evidence to support his judgment that the earliest references to what eventually became articles 34 and 37 do not appear until 1 July. Pézant's argument for the crucial role of Jérôme Solal-Céligny in developing the case for the separate domains of law and of regulation is particularly persuasive.

69. I, 328; I, 353; I, 373.

70. I, 247.

71. I, 420; I, 434.

72. I, 420. Freedom of speech and freedom of religion are not mentioned specifically in this text, but they are included in the broader term "public liberties."

73. I, 507–8; articles 31 and 33.

74. II, 269(1c–2a).

75. Regulations can be autonomous under the 1958 Constitution in the sense that they need not be based on a statute. "Autonomy" does not mean that no judicial control exists over actions taken under the regulatory authority of the State. For an important statement on constitutional control of administrative action, see the Council of State decision of 26 June 1959, *Syndicat Général des Ingénieurs-Conseils, Rec. 394.*

76. III, 12.

77. III, 107(1b).

78. III, 509.

79. The translation of this paragraph is the one used in the text released by the Press and Information Service of the French Embassy. The original wording is *Les dispositions du présent article pourront être précisées et complétées par une loi organique.* One might question "developed in detail" as the best way to render *précisées.* Perhaps "clarified" would be better. In commenting on this text, Luchaire states: *"une loi organique peut préciser les dispositions de l'article 34, notamment en cas de divergences d'interpretation."* If conflicting interpretations between, say, the *Cour de Cassation* and the *Conseil Constitutionnel* are the problem, "clarification" rather than "development in detail" would seem to be the solution. Presumably, Parliament could clarify a constitutional provision by law without either usurping a judicial function or simply "developing in detail." "Amplify" is a good translation of *compléter,* which has a broader meaning than the English "complete." The Collins-Robert dictionary gives "complement" and "supplement" as secondary meanings of *compléter* and offers *augmenter* as a French synonym. Luchaire interprets it as meaning *étendre le domaine réservé à la loi.* However, see also Luchaire's commentary on article 37 and, in particular, his references to the Constitutional Council's decisions of 8 September 1961, 30 January 1968, and 3 November 1977. François Luchaire, "Article 34" and "Article 37," in Luchaire and Conac, *La Constitution,* pp. 772, 788.

80. The case in question was decided on 7 January 1988 (87–234 DC). It is discussed in François Luchaire, "Article 34" in François Luchaire and Gérard Conac, eds., *Le Droit constitutionnel de la cohabitation* (Paris: Economica, 1989), p. 198. In a fuller discussion of the last paragraph of article 34, Luchaire reports no deci-

sions interpreting it. See his "Article 34" in Luchaire and Conac, *La Constitution,* pp. 769-71.

81. Brutus, *CAF* 2.9.5. To bring Brutus up to date, consider the frequent complaint by contemporary officials in state government that crucial state services must be curtailed because federal taxes are so high that state governments cannot impose additional burdens on their citizens.

82. *U.S. v. Butler,* 297 U.S. 1 (1936).

83. II, 106.

84. Henry W. Ehrmann and Martin A. Schain, *Politics in France* 5th ed. (New York: Harper-Collins, 1992), p. 327.

85. Robert A. Harmsen, *Of Grandeur and Compromise: The Constitution of the French Fifth Republic,* unpublished dissertation (University of Kent at Canterbury, 1988), p. 265.

86. II, 105-6.

87. III, 100.

88. II, 105-6.

89. III, 100.

90. *Immigration and Naturalization Service v. Chadha,* 462 U.S. 952 (1983). For a thorough discussion of this case and the entire legislative veto issue, see Barbara Hinkson Craig, *Chadha: The Story of an Epic Constitutional Struggle* (Berkeley: University of California Press, 1988). On several occasions when the Constitution of the Fifth Republic was being written, the framers discussed practices quite similar to the American legislative veto. In addition to Burnay's remark, see also II, 494; II, 483-84; II, 525-26; and III, 366-67. My discussion of *Chadha* follows closely my treatment of that case in John A. Rohr, *The President and the Public Administration* (Washington, D.C.: American Historical Association, 1989), pp. 59-66.

91. Stanley C. Brubaker, "Slouching Toward Constitutional Duty: The Legislative Veto and the Delegation of Authority," *Constitutional Commentary* 1 (Winter 1984), p. 81.

92. CC, 30 July 1982; 82-143 DC, Rec. 57. This decision, along with a commentary by the editors, appears in Louis Favoreu and Loïc Philip, eds., *Les Grandes décisions du conseil constitutionnel,* 6th ed. (Paris: Sirey, 1991), pp. 540-55.

93. Ibid., pp. 547-49.

94. Ibid., p. 549.

95. Fisher, "Separation of Powers," p. 84.

96. Comité consultatif pour la révision de la Constitution, présidé par le doyen Georges Vedel, *Rapport au Président de la République: Propositions pour une révision de la Constitution* (Paris: La Documentation Française, 1993).

97. Favoreu and Philip, *Les Grandes décisions,* pp. 549-50. See also Louis Favoreu, "Les Réglements autonomes n'existent pas," *Revue Française de Droit Administratif* 3 (1987): 872-84.

98. This is not the place to join the great debate on the jurisprudence of "original intent." See Paul Brest, "Constitutional Interpretation," in Leonard W. Levy, Kenneth L. Karst, and Dennis J. Mahoney, eds., *Encyclopedia of the American Constitution* (New York: Macmillan, 1986), vol. 1, pp. 464-71. My criticism of the *Chadha* court is not based on opposition to original-intent jurisprudence. Indeed, I

am rather sympathetic to it, especially when I consider the appalling alternatives. My complaint is with the inconsistency of the Supreme Court in applying original-intent jurisprudence in separation-of-powers cases. Contrast, for example, the rigid formalism of the Court in *Northern Pipeline Construction Co. v. Marathon Pipe Line Co.,* 458 U.S. 50 (1982), *Bowsher v. Synar,* 478 U.S. 714 (1986), and *Chadha* with its free and easy ways in *Morrison v. Olson,* 487 U.S. 654 (1988), *Mistretta v. U.S.,* 488 U.S. 361 (1989), and *CFTC v. Schor,* 478 U.S. (1986). These cases are discussed in Fisher, "Separation of Powers," pp. 57–62. As long as the Court sees fit to vacillate between strict and loose interpretations of the separation-of-powers clauses in the constitution, I wish it would be more statesmanlike in deciding which path it will follow in a given case. Had *Chadha* been part of a long-standing, well-established jurisprudence, I would find it much easier to accept.

99. Luchaire was not a member of the working group but of a group of experts who advised the working group and the interministerial committee. The names of the members of the group of experts and the working group appear at I, xxiv, and I, 241, respectively. In 1958, Luchaire was professor of law at Nancy and technical counsellor in the cabinet of Louis Jacquinot, a minister of State in the de Gaulle government. I, 235.

100. I, 327.

101. I, 295.

102. I, 533.

103. I, 532.

104. For a cogent analysis of the tension between the notion of general will on the one hand and separation of powers on the other, see Terence Marshall, "Préface" in Terence Marshall, ed., *Théorie et pratique du gouvernement constitutionnel: La France et les Etats-Unis* (La Garenne-Colombes: Editions de l'Espace Européen, 1992), pp. 11–22.

105. Rousseau's disciples can be forgiven for departing from the straight and narrow. The master himself modified his teachings considerably when he faced the practical problem of designing a constitution for Poland.

106. Keith M. Baker, "Constitution," in François Furet and Mona Ozouf, eds., *A Critical Dictionary of the French Revolution,* trans. Arthur Goldhammer (Cambridge, Mass.: Harvard University Press, 1989), p. 488.

107. Ibid., p. 489.

108. Ibid. When Sieyès said that France could not be a democracy, he meant that it could not be a direct democracy as envisioned by Rousseau.

109. Ibid.

110. The text of the suspensive veto appears in Title III, chapter III, Section III of the Constitution of 3 September 1791. The full text can be found in Jacques Godechot, ed., *Les Constitutions de la France depuis 1789* (Paris: GF Flammarion, 1979), p. 53.

111. An illuminating discussion of broader themes comparing and contrasting some fundamental principles in French and American political thought can be found in Terence Marshall, "Les droits de l'homme et l'art politique à l'époque révolutionnaire: La France et les Etats-Unis," in Marshall, ed., *Théorie et pratique,* pp. 389–406.

112. III, 399(2b).

113. III, 400(2a); III, 401(1a).

114. III, 401(1a).

115. I, 211.

116. Favoreu and Philip maintain that one of the effects of the Constitutional Council's decision of 30 July 1982 was to abolish the distinction between matters inherently legislative and matters inherently regulatory. In more technical terms, the council imposed a purely formal understanding of legislative power—the position defended by Juillot de la Morandière—for the material understanding of such power that had previously dominated the council's jurisprudence. See Favoreu and Philip, *Les Grandes décisions,* p. 549.

117. III, 403(2a).

118. See the text accompanying notes 25-36 in chapter 3.

119. III, 405(1b).

120. III, 405(2b). Solal-Céligny's assessment accurately states what the Gaullist reformers had in mind. It contrasts sharply with the relaxed interpretation of article 34 in the Constitutional Council's decision of 30 July 1982.

121. III, 509.

122. III, 401(1b).

123. McCloskey, *Works of James Wilson,* vol. 2, p. 770.

124. Ibid.

125. Ibid. One might question Wilson's assertion that the people are superior to their constitution. After all, the people are obliged to abide by it and, hence, do not possess power that is "supreme, absolute, and uncontrollable." For example, they elect members of Congress every two years because the Constitution tells them to do so, even if 90 percent of the people would prefer annual elections. They may, of course, amend the Constitution, but only in the manner the Constitution itself prescribes. The right to revolution can always be invoked to set aside the Constitution, but this right is not exactly the same thing as sovereignty.

126. Ibid.

127. Ibid. This assertion is open to the question discussed in note 125.

128. On *Federalist* 10, see the text accompanying notes 21 and 22 in this chapter.

129. McCloskey, *Works of James Wilson,* vol. 2, p. 772.

130. Ibid., vol. 2, p. 778.

131. Ibid., vol. 2, p. 786. Speech delivered on 31 December 1789.

132. Ibid.

133. Ibid., vol. 1, pp. 292-93.

134. After the Constitutional Council's decision of 30 July 1982, perhaps one should add article 41 as an other essential means of denying sovereignty to Parliament.

THE JUDICIAL POWER

1. Although each institution is supreme in its own sphere, some decisions from

the mid-1980s suggest that, to paraphrase Orwell, the *Conseil Constitutionnel* is a little "more supreme" than the others. See, for example, the decision of the *Conseil d'Etat* of 20 December 1985 (Soc. anon. "Etabl. Outters" C. Agence financière du bassin Seine-Normandie) and the decisions of the *Cour de Cassation* in *Vuckovic* and *Bogdan* of 25 April 1985. Louis Favoreu has commented on these decisions in *Recueil Dalloz Sirey,* 1986; Chronique XXVIII for the *Cour de Cassation;* 169–77 and Jurisprudence 283–86 for the *Conseil d'Etat.*

2. The three articles were quite short in the original Constitution, but a recent amendment has considerably lengthened article 65. The purpose of the amendment was to enhance the independence of the judiciary from the influence of elected officials. See *Le Monde,* 20 July 1993, p. 7.

3. Yves Mény, *Government and Politics in Western Europe: Britain, France, Italy, and West Germany,* Janet Lloyd, trans. (New York: Oxford University Press, 1990), p. 296.

4. Marie-Christine Kessler, *Le Conseil d'Etat* (Paris: Presses de la Foundation Nationale des Sciences Politiques, 1968), p. 28.

5. II, 81(2b) [see Preface, note 3]; and Yves Mény, *Le Système politique français* (Paris: Montchrestien, 1991), p. 147.

6. Mény, *Le Système,* p. 150.

7. For an explanation of the term *Etat de droit,* see Bernard Chantebout, *Droit constitutionnel et science politique,* 6th ed. (Paris: Armand Colin, 1985), pp. 24–26. In this book, we have already noted several times the traditional weakness of the French judiciary vis-à-vis parliament. French jurists have had good reason to complain about the need for an *Etat de droit,* and their complaints have proved effective. For a recent survey of judicial power in France, see Jaqueline Lucienne Lafon, "La Judicialization de la politique en France," *International Political Science Review* 15 (April 1994): 135–42. Significantly, this article appears in an issue of the *International Political Science Review* devoted exclusively to the theme "The Judicialization of Politics." Edited by Torbjorn Vallinder, the issue examines the growing power of courts in nine countries. The increasing power of the judiciary has evoked some sharp criticism in France. See, for example, Gilles Gaetner, "La Conversation secrète de Tapie," *L'Express,* 14 July 1994, pp. 6–7; "Longuet et le juge," *L'Express,* 9 June 1994, pp. 12–13; Dominique de Montvalon, "La Colère calculée de Pasqua," *L'Express,* 26 August 1993, pp. 8–9. Judges in Italy, Germany, and Belgium have also been criticized recently for interfering inappropriately in politics. See William Drozdiak, "Relentless Italian Judges Smell More and More Bribery," *International Herald Tribune,* 18 August 1994, p. 2; Sabine Delanglade, "Schneider: L'Engrenage," *L'Express,* 16 June 1994, pp. 6–8; Christine Landfried, "The Judicialization of Politics in Germany," *International Political Science Review* 15 (April 1994): 113–24.

8. For a good discussion of how the Supreme Court manages its docket, see David M. O'Brien, *Storm Center: The Supreme Court in American Politics* (New York: W. W. Norton, 1986), especially chapters 3 and 4.

9. See the text in this chapter accompanying notes 56–68.

10. Important political events sometimes force the Supreme Court to accelerate its procedures, with deleterious effects on the quality of the Court's opinions. See, in

particular, *New York Times v. U.S.*, 403 U.S. 713 (1971), and *United States v. Nixon*, 418 U.S. 683 (1974).

11. Alec Stone, *The Birth of Judicial Politics in France* (New York: Oxford University Press, 1992), p. 61.

12. Ibid., citing François Luchaire, *Le Conseil constitutionnel* (Paris: Economica, 1980), p. 31.

13. Ibid., p. 60, citing François Mitterrand, *Le Coup d'Etat permanent* (Paris: Plon, 1964), pp. 144, 146.

14. Didier Maus, "La Constitution jugée par son pratique: Réflexions pour un bilan," in Olivier Duhamel and Jean-Luc Parodi, *La Constitution de la cinquième république* (Paris: Presses de la Foundation Nationale des Sciences Politiques, 1988), p. 319. I have translated Maus's expression *"le protecteur des libertés"* as "the guardian of liberty." I substituted the English singular for the French plural because Anglo-American law does not make the distinction between public and private liberties that one often finds in French legal treatises. For an explanation of this distinction, see Jacques Robert, *Libertés publiques et droits de l'homme* (Paris: Montchrestien, 1988), pp. 12–15. Not all French jurists are pleased with this distinction. See Jean Rivero, *Les Libertés publiques* (Paris: Presses Universitaires de France, 1987), vol. 1, pp. 22–23.

15. See article 61 of the 1958 Constitution.

16. James Beardsley, "Constitutional Review in France," *Supreme Court Review* (1975): pp. 189–259 at pp. 225–26. For a full discussion of the 16 July 1971 decision, see James Beardsley, "The Constitutional Council and Constitutional Liberties in France," *American Journal of Comparative Law* (1972): 431–52.

17. CC, 16 July 1971; 71–44 DC, Rec. 29. This decision is included in a collection of the Constitutional Council's most important decisions. See Louis Favoreu and Loïc Philip, eds., *Les Grandes décisions du conseil constitutionnel,* 6th ed. (Paris: Sirey, 1991), pp. 237–53.

18. In a decision rendered on 19 June 1970 (70–39 D.C.), the Constitutional Council may have hinted at the legal force of the preamble. See "Préambule de la Constitution de 1946," in Olivier Duhamel and Yves Mény, eds., *Dictionnaire constitutionnel* (Paris: Presses Universitaires de France, 1992), pp. 791–92.

19. Beardsley, "Constitutional Review in France," p. 226; Stone, *Birth of Judicial Politics,* p. 77.

20. Loïc Philip, "Bilan et effets de la saisine du conseil constitutionnel," in Duhamel and Parodi, *La Constitution,* pp. 408–21 at p. 411.

21. Ibid., and Mény, *Le Système,* p. 152.

22. Martin M. Shapiro, "Judicial Review in France," *Journal of Law and Politics* 6 (Spring 1990): 531–48; Louis Henkin, "Revolutions and Constitutions," *Louisiana Law Review* 49 (1989): 1023ff.

23. Louis Favoreu, "Le Conseil constitutionnel et l'alternance," in Duhamel and Parodi, *La Constitution,* pp. 422–49 at p. 428.

24. Stone, *Birth of Judicial Politics,* p. 86. Stone's book was published in 1992. The conservatives' outrage with the Constitutional Council at the beginning of the second cohabitation in 1993 was probably as great as it had been in 1986.

25. Ibid., p. 114.

26. *Marbury v. Madison,* 1 Cranch 137 (1803). For a comparison of *Marbury* with the Constitutional Council's decision of 16 July 1971, see G. D. Haimbaugh, "Was It France's *Marbury v. Madison?" Ohio State Law Journal* 35 (1974), p. 910ff.

27. William E. Nelson, "The Fourteenth Amendment," in Leonard W. Levy, Kenneth L. Karst, and Dennis J. Mahoney, eds., *Encyclopedia of the American Constitution* (New York: Macmillan, 1986), vol. 2, p. 787.

28. Max Farrand, ed., *The Records of the Federal Convention of 1787* (New Haven, Conn.: Yale University Press, 1966), vol. 1, p. 21. The proposed council of revision would have shared certain powers with Congress over state legislation as well. For purposes of our comparison with France (a unitary state), I have set aside questions of federalism and concentrated on the proposed distribution of powers at the national level.

29. Ibid., vol. 1, p. 138.

30. Ibid., vol. 2, p. 73.

31. Herbert J. Storing, ed., *The Complete Anti-Federalist,* 7 vols. (Chicago: University of Chicago Press, 1981); hereafter cited as *CAF* 2.9.150–51. [For an explanation of this citation form, see chapter 4, note 16.]

32. Philip B. Kurland and Ralph Lerner, *The Founders' Constitution* (Chicago: University of Chicago Press, 1987), vol. 2, p. 15.

33. Dennis J. Mahoney, "Preamble," in Levy, Karst, and Mahoney, *Encyclopedia of the American Constitution,* vol. 3, p. 1436, citing Story's *Commentaries.*

34. *Jacobson v. Massachusetts,* 97 U.S. 11 (1905).

35. Kurland and Lerner, *The Founders' Constitution,* vol. 2, p. 14.

36. Mahoney, "Preamble," p. 1436, citing Edward S. Corwin.

37. Invitations would surely be sent to John Adams and Thomas Jefferson, even though their duties as ambassadors in London and Paris, respectively, kept them from attending the Constitutional Convention in 1787. Unfortunately, many of the convention's outstanding figures, such as James Wilson, George Mason, Edmund Randolph, Gouverneur Morris, and Alexander Hamilton, had died before 1817.

38. See especially the statement prepared by Jérôme Solal-Céligny at the request of Michel Debré at I, 525. This document states unequivocally that the Constitutional Council was an outgrowth of the Fourth Republic's Constitutional Committee and merely extended the powers of its predecessor.

39. III, 601.

40. Philip, "Bilan et effets," p. 467.

41. II, 254(1c).

42. II, 254(2b).

43. I, 73(2a).

44. Philip, "Bilan et effets," p. 468.

45. I, 73(2a).

46. Bruno Génévois, "Le Préambule et les droits fondamenteaux," in Didier Maus, Louis Favoreu, and Jean-Luc Parodi, eds., *L'Ecriture de la constitution de 1958* (Paris: Economica, 1992), p. 411.

47. See paragraph 3 of article 92 of the Constitution of 1946.

48. Génévois, "Le Préambule," in Maus, Favoreu, and Parodi, p. 502.

49. *Le Monde,* 30 March 1993, p. 8.

50. II, 174(1a).

51. II, 174.

52. The constitutional amendment appears as new article 53-1 of the Constitution. The debate over the right of asylum dominated the news media from August to November of 1993. See in particular the following articles: Thierry Bréhier, "Le Conseil constitutionnel atténue la rigueur de la loi sur l'immigration," *Le Monde,* 15-16 August 1993, p. 1; " 'Le Conseil constitutionnel empêche le gouvernement d'appliquer sa politique,' affirme M. Pasqua," *Le Monde,* 17 August 1993, p. 7; Thierry Bréhier, "M. Balladur est encouragé à réviser la Constitution, *Le Monde,* 25 September 1993, p. 1; Olivier Biffaud, "M. Balladur a transmis au Conseil d'Etat un projet constitutionnel tenant compte des exigences de M. Mitterrand," *Le Monde,* 9 October 1993, p. 22; Olivier Biffaud and Thierry Bréhier, "Le texte sur le droit d'asile est une victoire pour M. Pasqua," *Le Monde,* 10-11 October 1993, p. 10; Olivier Duhamel, "Une Révision sans précédent," *L'Express,* 4 November 1993, p. 7; Thierry Bréhier, "Le Congrès du Parliament est convoqué le 19 novembre," *Le Monde,* 17 November 1993, p. 10; "M. Pasqua souligne que le 'pouvoir suprême' appartient au 'peuple,' " *Le Monde,* 23 November 1993, p. 8. See also Jean-Louis Quermonne, "Chronique d'une révision constitutionnelle boulversée," *French Politics and Society* 12 (Winter 1994), p. 1-15. American constitutional history offers four examples of constitutional amendments that had the effect of overturning decisions of the Supreme Court of the United States. See amendments 11, 14, 16, and 26.

53. II, 175(1c-2a).

54. II, 176(1b).

55. II, 176(1c-2a); II, 179(1c-2a).

56. II, 178(2c).

57. II, 257(1b).

58. "Exception d'inconstitutionalité," in Duhamel and Mény, *Dictionnaire constitutionnel,* p. 425.

59. See article 89. The proposed amendment received considerable press coverage throughout 1990. See Thierry Bréhier, "Les Citoyens pourront saisir le Conseil constitionnel," *Le Monde,* 25-26 March 1990, p. 1; Thierry Bréhier, "Les Embuches politiques d'une réforme de la Constitution," *Le Monde,* 29 March 1990, p. 7; Thierry Bréhier, "Les Précédents: Cinq réussites, quatre échecs," *Le Monde,* 29 March 1990, p. 7; George Vedel, "Réforme de la constitution: Ni gadget, ni revolution," *Le Monde,* 6 April 1990, p. 2; André Passeron, "De l'usage du référendum," *Le Monde,* 25 April 1990, p. 10.

60. The creation of the Advisory Committee led to some lively controversies over its constitutional legitimacy. For a particularly forceful critique, see François Goguel, "D'étranges projets de révision," *Le Figaro* 3 December 1992, p. 8.

61. *Propositions pour une révision de la Constitution 15 février 1993* (Paris: Documentation Française, 1993). [Hereafter cited as the "Vedel Commission."] A lengthy summary of the report, by Thierry Bréhier, appeared in *Le Monde,* 17 February 1993, p. 8.

62. Thierry Bréhier, "Les Projets de réforme de la Constitution s'inspirent très largement des travaux du Comité consultatif," *Le Monde,* 12 March 1993, p. 8.

63. II, 176(2b).

64. II, 86(2b).

65. II, 104(1b).

66. II, 104(1c).

67. Article 3, section 2, of the U.S. Constitution limits the jurisdiction of federal courts to "cases or controversies"—that is, to real litigation. The Vedel Commission's proposal contains a similar provision, limiting the right to challenge the constitutionality of a law to *justiciables* (citizens involved in litigation). See Vedel Commission, pp. 76-77, 126. The leisurely pace of American courts can be accelerated by such legal maneuvers as declaratory judgments, facial challenges, temporary restraining orders, and permanent injunctions.

68. Should the maxim "better late than never" achieve constitutional status, it would do so only in the face of a maxim to the contrary: "Justice delayed is justice denied." Such, however, is the unhappy lot of proverbial wisdom, as Glendon Schubert pointed out long ago. "Many hands make light work," but "too many cooks spoil the broth." "You can't teach an old dog new tricks," but "you are never too old to learn."

69. I emphasize "excesses," because nowadays one hardly ever sees an argument against judicial review of acts of Congress as such. As is evident from the end of the last chapter, I do not agree with the argument assigning constitutional superiority to elected congressmen over unelected judges.

70. III, 377(2b).

71. Discussions of the case can be found in Alfred H. Kelly, Winfred A. Harbison, and Herman Belz, *The American Constitution: Its Origins and Development,* 7th ed. (New York: W. W. Norton, 1991): vol. 1, pp. 170-75; Leonard W. Levy, *"Marbury v. Madison,"* in Levy, Karst, and Mahoney, *Encyclopedia of the American Constitution,* vol. 3, pp. 1199-1202; Herbert A. Johnson, *"Marbury v. Madison,"* in Kermit L. Hall et al., eds., *The Oxford Companion to the Supreme Court of the United States,* (New York: Oxford University Press, 1992), pp. 521-22. For further reading suggestions, see the excellent bibliographical essay that follows the appendices at the end of the first volume of Kelly, Harbison, and Belz, especially the readings suggested on page A55.

72. Levy, *"Marbury v. Madison,"* p. 1202, citing Albert J. Beveridge, *The Life of John Marshall,* 4 vols. (Boston: Houghton-Mifflin, 1916-1919). Levy also cites Edward S. Corwin, *The Doctrine of Judicial Review* (Princeton, N.J.: Princeton University Press, 1914), as calling the first part of Marshall's *Marbury* opinion "a deliberate partisan *coup.*" The reason for Corwin's remark was that Marshall's opinion went into great detail to affirm Marbury's right to the commission and spared neither President Jefferson nor his followers for having treated the unhappy Marbury so shabbily. All this, of course, was quite irrelevant since the outcome of the case was to tell Marbury he had brought his suit in the wrong court. Corwin correctly maintains that Marshall's public scolding of President Jefferson was politically motivated. In basing his finding of unconstitutionality on Section 13 of the Judiciary Act of 1789, however, Marshall carefully avoided politics. Marbury had been appointed under the Judiciary Act of 1801, which was nullified by the Repeal Act of 1802. Many Federalists thought that the Repeal Act was unconstitutional because it abolished certain federal courts and, therefore, in effect, removed federal judges from of-

fice. Had the Supreme Court declared the Repeal Act unconstitutional, the judicial claim of such power would have been inextricably intertwined with partisan politics. Wisely, Marshall chose as his constitutional target a low-profile section of an act passed fourteen years earlier by a Federalist Congress.

73. For an expansive reading of *Marbury*—tantamount to a claim of judicial supremacy—see the unanimous opinion of the Supreme Court in *Cooper v. Aaron,* 358 U.S. 1 (1958): "the federal judiciary is supreme in the exposition of the law of the Constitution, and that principle has ever since *[Marbury]* been . . . a permanent and indispensable feature of our constitutional system." Herbert A. Johnson says *Cooper* "marked the high tide of expanded judicial review." Johnson, *"Marbury v. Madison,"* p. 522. The *Cooper* Court's interpretation of *Marbury* is questionable at best.

74. The case in question was the notorious *Dred Scott v. Sandford,* 19 Howard 393 (1857).

75. Stone, *Birth of Judicial Politics,* p. 32.

76. Somewhat problematic is the role of Raymond Carré de Malberg, dismissed by M. J. C. Vile as an unflinching champion of legislative supremacy whose work "represents a low point in the prestige of the theory of separation of powers in French thought." M. J. C. Vile, *Constitutionalism and the Separation of Powers* (Oxford: at the Clarendon Press, 1967), p. 251. Vile bases this assessment on Carré de Malberg's best-known work, *Contribution à la théorie de l'Etat,* 2 vols. (Paris: Sirey, 1920–1922). Robert A. Harmsen, however, offers a very different interpretation of Carré de Malberg as a critic of parliamentary excesses. He relies heavily on an article written by Carré de Malberg that appeared in 1931. ("Considérations théoriques sur la question de la combinaison du référendum avec le parlementisme," *Révue de Droit Public,* 225–44.) Harmsen cites a 1902 article by Adhémar Esmein that is critical of parliamentary supremacy as having influenced this aspect of Carré de Malberg's thought: "Deux formes de gouvernement," *Révue de Droit Public.* See Robert A. Harmsen, *Of Grandeur and Compromise: The Constitution of the French Fifth Republic,* unpublished dissertation (University of Kent at Canterbury, 1988), pp. 168–92.

77. Stone, *Birth of Judicial Politics,* p. 36.

78. Ibid., p. 41, citing Julien Laferrière, *Manuel de droit constitutionnel,* 2d ed. (Paris: Domat, 1947), p. 952; and J. Lemasurier, *La Constitution de 1946 et le contrôle de la constitutionnalité des lois* (Paris: Librairie Générale de Droit et de Jurisprudence, 1953), p. 116.

79. Cited by John Brigham, "Judicial Review," in Kermit Hall et al., eds, *The Oxford Companion to the Supreme Court of the United States,* p. 464.

80. Ibid., p. 465.

81. *Hylton v. United States,* 3 Dallas 171 (1796).

82. Cited by Gerald Gunther in Levy, Karst, and Mahoney, *Encyclopedia of the American Constitution,* p. 1056.

83. II, 73(2a).

84. II, 180(2b).

85. Beardsley, p. 196.

86. II, 181(1b).

87. Ibid.

88. II, 280(2b). Gilbert-Jules repeats virtually the same point at II, 285(2b).

89. II, 73(2a).

90. III, 163(2b).

91. III, 164(1b).

92. III, 162(2b).

93. See, for example, Janot's remarks before the Advisory Committee on the Constitution at II, 73(2b).

94. *Pouvoirs publics* is a difficult expression to translate. "Governmental authorities" is probably the best translation, but one must bear in mind that *governmental* is used here in the American sense of the word, as when one says "the Department of the Treasury is part of the government." The French *pouvoir* is broader than the English *power,* and it has a stronger legal connotation than is often found in *power.*

95. III, 282. For an explanation of the role of the "reporters" at the Council of State, see J. Neville Brown and John S. Bell, *French Administrative Law,* 4th ed. (Oxford: Oxford University Press, 1993), pp. 91-100. See also Jean Paul Costa, *Le Conseil d'Etat dans la société contemporaire* (Paris: Economica, 1993), pp. 29-39.

96. Louis Favoreu, "L'application des décisions du Conseil constitutionnel par le Conseil d'Etat et le Tribunal des conflits," *Révue Française de Droit Administratif* 3 (March-April, 1987): 263-80.

97. Ibid., p. 273.

98. Ibid., pp. 274-75. For a summary of the case in English, see Cynthia Vroom, "Constitutional Protection of Individual Liberties in France: The Conseil Constitutionnelle Since 1971," *Tulane Law Review* (December 1986), p. 24 (downloaded version).

99. See the text that accompanies note 83. For a clear and balanced overview of the relationship between the two councils, see Costa, *Le Conseil d'Etat,* pp. 117-23.

100. Stone, *Birth of Judicial Politics,* pp. 75 and 160. The Constitutional Council's decision on nationalization (January 16, 1982) is usually presented as a defeat for the Council of State, but in that decision the salience of the doctrine of "manifest error" is a tribute to the importance of administrative jurisprudence.

101. Ibid., p. 129.

102. Ibid., p. 124, citing *Rapport annuel 1982, Conseil d'Etat,* p. 15.

103. Ibid., p. 125.

104. Ibid., p. 125.

105. Ibid., pp. 189-90.

106. Ibid., p. 161, citing *Le Monde,* 21 January 1982.

107. Jurisdictional disputes between state and federal courts have been a product of American federalism. In the early years of the Republic, the problem was acute. See *Martin v. Hunter's Lessee,* 1 Wheaton 304 (1816), and *Cohens v. Virginia,* 6 Wheaton 264 (1821).

108. Edward S. Corwin, *The President: Office and Powers,* 4th ed. (New York: New York University Press, 1957), p. 93. Corwin made this comment in the context of criticizing Justice Sutherland's opinion in *Humphrey's Executor v. U.S.,* 295 U.S. 602 (1935).

109. *Crowell v. Benson,* 285 U.S. 22 (1932); *Ohio Valley Water Co. v. Ben Avon Borough* 253 U.S. 287 (1920).

110. Joseph Zwerdling, "Reflections on the Role of an Administrative Law Judge," *Administrative Law Review* 25 (1973), p. 9–40. Although institutional decision making is more salient in administrative agencies than elsewhere, such agencies have no monopoly on the practice. Consider, for example, in the judicial branch of government, the important role of law clerks and the use of *per curiam* opinions.

111. For a manageable, abridged version of this multivolume work, see Charles K. Woltz, ed., *Administrative Procedure in Government Agencies* (Charlottesville: University Press of Virginia, 1967).

112. 340 U.S. 474 (1951). Since this case involved labor relations, the primary statute governing it was the Taft-Hartley Act of 1947. Its provisions for judicial review of agency action were almost the same as those of the Administrative Procedure Act of 1946.

113. *NLRB v. Universal Camera Corp.* 179 F.2d 749 (2d Cir., 1950).

114. *Universal Camera Corp. v. NLRB* 340 U.S. 474 (1951).

115. At the end of the day, the holding of the Court in *Universal Camera* was the following: "We intend only to recognize that evidence supporting a conclusion may be less substantial when an impartial, experienced examiner who has observed the witnesses and lived with the case has drawn conclusions different from the Board's than when he has reached the same conclusion."

116. II, 155–85, especially 175–85.

117. Zwerdling, "Reflections on the Role," p. 32.

118. Ibid.

119. Ibid., p. 14. The role of the administrative law judge continues to be controversial. For a recent examination, see Paul Verkuil et al., "The Federal Administrative Judiciary: Executive Summary and Recommendations 92-7" (Washington, D.C.: Administrative Conference of the United States, January 1993). For a more detailed statement of the issues discussed in the Executive Summary, see Paul Verkuil et al., "The Federal Administrative Judiciary" (Washington, D.C.: Administrative Conference of the United States, August 1993). On the broader question of the distinction between judges whose authority stems from the first article of the constitution and "article III" judges, see *Northern Pipeline Construction Co. v. Marathon Pipe Line Co.,* 458 U.S. 50 (1982).

PUBLIUS AND THE GAULLISTS

1. For a discussion of certain similarities between Publius and General de Gaulle himself, see Bernard E. Brown, "De Gaulle and Publius," *French Politics and Society* 6 (October 1988): 51–55. The author stresses the fear of legislative tyranny in both authors. His discussion of de Tocqueville as a possible link between Publius and de Gaulle is particularly interesting.

2. III, 277.

3. III, 598. Compare the discussion of *Federalist* 51 below wherein Publius as-

serts: "You must first enable the government to control the governed; and in the next place, oblige it to control itself."

4. II, 553(1b).

5. I, 312–13. For further references to Mac Mahon's dissolution of Parliament, see III, 319, and III, 563.

6. III, 662.

7. I, 4.

8. Ibid.

9. I, 5.

10. II, 497(1c–2a).

11. II, 500(2b).

12. III, 666.

13. II, 532(2c)–533(1a).

14. For recent examples of the controversies that still swirl around the memory of Marshal Pétain, see Eric Conan, "Enquête sur le retour d'une idéologie," *L'Express,* 17 July 1992, pp. 20–27; Alain Rollat, "M. Mitterrand et le maréchal," *Le Monde,* 23 July 1992, p. 7. For recent examples of what should be done about those who collaborated with the Nazis' efforts to deport Jews who were French citizens, see "La mémoire et la douleur," *L'Express,* 24 July 1992, p. 14; Eric Conan, "Vel' d'Hiv: un geste très calculé," *L'Express,* 18 February 1993; Philippe du Tanney, "Touvier: Cassation partielle," *Le Figaro,* 29 November 1992, p. 7. The 1994 trial of Paul Touvier, an intelligence officer for Klaus Barbie, the Gestapo chief in Lyon, was particularly important because it marked the first time a French citizen was prosecuted in a French court for crimes against humanity committed during World War II. See Eric Conan, "La Justice contre l'Histoire," *L'Express,* 14 April 1994, p. 13; and William Drozdiak, "Frenchman on Trial for Collaboration with Nazis," *Washington Post,* 18 March 1994, p. A23. The trial received extensive coverage throughout the month of April in *Le Monde.* In September 1994, allegations about President Mitterrand's activities on behalf of the Vichy regime during World War II reopened some old wounds that many Frenchmen would just as soon forget. See Pierre Péan, *Une Jeunesse française* (Paris: Fayard, 1994).

15. *Federalist* 9, 10, 16, 18, 38, 43, 45, and 70.

16. *Federalist* 6.

17. *Federalist* 34.

18. *Federalist* 65.

19. Ibid.

20. *Federalist* 70.

21. Ibid.

22. Ibid.

23. *Federalist* 71 and 72. The unamended Constitution placed no limit on the number of terms a president could serve, but the twenty-second amendment imposed a two-term limit.

24. *Federalist* 75.

25. Ibid.

26. *Federalist* 55, 57, and 76. See Charles R. Kesler, "*Federalist* 10 and American Republicanism," and Harvey C. Mansfield, Jr., "Republicanizing the Executive"

(especially pp. 181-84), in Charles R. Kesler, ed., *Saving the Revolution: The Federalist Papers and the American Revolution* (New York: Free Press, 1987), pp. 13-39 and 168-184.

27. See David Hume, "Of the Independency of Parliament," in Hume, *Essays Moral, Political, and Literary* (Indianapolis: Liberty Classics, 1987), pp. 42-46. The influence of this essay (first published in 1741) on Alexander Hamilton is discussed in Richard T. Green, *Oracle at Weehawken: Alexander Hamilton and the Development of the Administrative State,* unpublished Ph.D. dissertation, Virginia Polytechnic Institute and State University (Blacksburg, Va., 1987): 109-11.

28. A brief summary of the substantive issues in these referenda is given in Jean-Louis Quermonne and Dominique Chagnollaud, *Le gouvernement de la France sous la Ve République,* 4th ed. (Paris: Dalloz, 1991), pp. 105-7.

29. I, 124(2b).

30. I, 114(2b).

31. I, 123(1b).

32. I, 108(2a).

33. III, 675. The reference to civil war came from Claude Bourdet. For the remarks of Poujade and Cot on "blackmail," see III, 677, and III, 672. Since our discussion has focused on the structure of the argument rather than its substance, I have not attempted to assess the accuracy of the contention that France really was faced with a choice of de Gaulle or chaos. Suffice it to recall that when de Gaulle came to power in 1958, France was in real danger of a military coup d'etat and possibly even civil war.

34. *Federalist* 1.

35. *Federalist* 8.

36. Federal Farmer, *CAF* 2.8.3. [See chapter 4, note 16, for the full reference to this source.]

37. *Federalist* 3 and 4. There was nothing surprising in Publius's prediction that a disunited America would prove an irresistible target for European powers. This concern over the danger of foreign wars, however, was supplemented by a concern that a disunited America would be more likely to give European powers *just* cause to go to war with one or more states. Publius was particularly concerned about impetuous actions by states that bordered possessions of the British and Spanish empires. A strong national government would exert a restraining influence. In the event, however, that the strong national government gave just cause to another nation to go to war, the very strength of a united America would greatly improve the chances of a favorable outcome. This remarkable American indulgence in *raison d'état* appears in *Federalist* 3.

38. *Federalist* 5.

39. *Federalist* 6.

40. *Federalist* 8.

41. *Federalist* 15.

42. Ibid.

43. Ibid. For a more optimistic view of America, see Federal Farmer, *CAF* 283.

44. I, 3.

45. Ibid.

46. I, 5.

47. John A. Rohr, "Constitutional Foundations of the United States Navy: Text and Context," *Naval War College Review* 45(337) (Winter 1992): 68–84.

48. *Federalist* 12.

49. Ibid.

50. This is why I refer to Publius as a "mercantalist." If this is not the precise word to describe Publius's position, perhaps a contemporary term such as "industrial policy" or "managed competition" would be more on target. In any event, the point is that, for Publius, economics is subordinated to politics.

51. I, 5.

52. Charles de Gaulle, *Memoirs of Hope: Renewal and Endeavor,* trans. Terence Kilmartin (New York: Simon & Shuster, 1971), p. 312.

53. *Federalist* 78. Publius attributes the quotation to the "celebrated Montesquieu": *Spirit of the Laws* I, 181.

54. Although the tripartite division indicated in the text deserves to be called "classic," one should keep in mind John Locke's formulation of legislative, executive, and federative powers, with the judiciary considered part of the executive. For the most part, French jurists have the distinction between legislative and executive power in mind when they discuss separation of powers.

55. II, 156(2b).

56. II, 161(2a).

57. *Le Monde,* 20 July 1993, p. 1.

58. Article II, section 4. For a comprehensive examination of the impeachment power, see Raoul Berger, *Impeachment: The Constitutional Problems* (Cambridge, Mass.: Harvard University Press, 1973).

59. I, 534.

60. *Federalist* 77.

61. See, for example, Woodrow Wilson's famous book *Congressional Government* (Boston: Houghton-Mifflin, 1885). Interestingly, the target of Wilson's polemic is less Congress itself than its committees.

62. I have discussed the framers' view of the Senate more fully in chapter 3 of *To Run a Constitution.* The present discussion follows the earlier version closely. The paragraph beginning "The defense of the six-year senatorial term . . ." is taken virtually verbatim from page 37 of that earlier book of mine.

63. I, 157(1a).

64. I, 157(1b).

65. II, 103(2b).

66. *Federalist* 48.

67. Ibid.

68. See *Federalist* 47 for the explicit link between separation of powers and the preservation of liberty.

69. II, 538(1a).

70. II, 538(1b).

71. II, 103(2b).

72. Michel Debré, *Trois républiques pour une France* (Paris: Albin Michel, 1988), p. 348. Of the ancient authors Debré had read, he seems to have been especially fond of Polybius; see p. 423. Among the French authors he mentions are Bodin, Montesquieu, and Carré de Malberg. Conspicuous by his absence is Jean-Jacques Rousseau.

73. Ibid., pp. 365–66.

74. III, 260.

75. *Federalist* 1; Debré, *Trois républiques,* p. 347; III, 269.

76. III, 260.

77. I say "president" rather than "executive" by design, because of the Gaullist doctrine during the founding period that the president of the Republic was not an executive officer. Publius was much more likely to speak of "the executive" than of "the president."

78. III, 264.

79. Ibid.

80. *Federalist* 48. The discussion of the president's veto as a means to resist the legislature appears in *Federalist* 73. On the general theme of legislative usurpation, see *Federalist* 49, 69, and 71.

81. Debré, *Trois républiques,* pp. 355–56.

82. *Federalist* 68.

83. John A. Rohr, *To Run a Constitution: The Legitimacy of the Administrative State* (Lawrence: University Press of Kansas, 1986), p. 20. Michel Debré discusses the question of reelection of the president in his memoirs. Although his thoughts on this topic have no relevance to our comparison with Publius, it is nevertheless interesting that he favored a seven-year term for the president, with no possibility of reelection. He decided not to press this point because General de Gaulle would be only seventy-five years of age at the end of his first seven-year term. Debré did not think it advisable to erect a constitutional barrier against a second term for the general if he should desire it when the time came. Debré, *Trois républiques,* pp. 374–75.

84. Forrest McDonald, *Novus Ordo Seclorum: The Intellectual Origins of the Constitution* (Lawrence: University Press of Kansas, 1985), p. 244.

85. *Federalist* 47 and III, 267.

86. *Federalist* 75 and III, 267.

87. III, 266–67.

88. III, 267.

89. III, 269.

90. Debré, *Trois républiques,* p. 328.

ADMINISTRATIVE LAW AND NORMATIVE DIALOGUE

1. "Morale et Politique," *Pouvoirs* 65 (1993): 5–109; Yves Mény, "L'Imparfait démocratique," *Projet No. 232* (Winter 1992–1993): 48–55; Alain Blanchot, "Devant les tribunaux," *Projet No. 232* (Winter 1992–1993): 79–84; Yves Mény, *La Corruption de la république* (Paris: Fayard, 1992); Frédéric Perier, "La Déontologie des

activités financières," *Revue d'Éthique et Théologie Morale No. 176* (March 1991): 89-101; Marie-France Toinet, "La morale bureaucratique: Perspectives transatlantiques et franco-américaines," *Revue Internationale de Science Politique* 9 (July 1988): 193-204; Paul Valadier, *Agir en politique: Décision morale et pluralism en politique* (Paris: Cerf, 1980); Robert Catherine and Guy Thuillier, *Conscience et pouvoir* (Paris: Editions Montchrestien, 1974); Terry L. Cooper, ed., *Handbook of Administrative Ethics* (New York: Marcel Dekker, 1994); H. George Fredrickson, ed., *Ethics and Public Administration* (Armonk, N.Y.: M. E. Sharpe, 1993); Terry L. Cooper and N. Dale Wright, *Exemplary Public Administrators: Character and Leadership in Government* (San Francisco: Jossey-Bass, 1992); James S. Bowman, ed., *Ethical Frontiers in Public Management* (San Francisco: Jossey-Bass, 1991); John A. Rohr, *Ethics for Bureaucrats: An Essay on Law and Values,* 2d ed. (New York: Marcel Dekker, 1989).

2. Ralph Lerner, *Supreme Court Review, 1967* (Chicago: University of Chicago Press, 1967), pp. 127-80; Bernard Ducamin, "Recent Case Law of the French Conseil d'Etat," *American Journal of Comparative Law* 35 (Spring 1987): 341-57.

3. *Crito,* 50A-54B; and *Galatians,* 3:24-25. See also Plato, *Laws* 718, 719, and Aristotle, *Nicomachean Ethics,* 10.9 (1179B-81A).

4. For clear and concise summaries of the political questions doctrine, see Joel B. Grossman, "Political Questions," in Kermit L. Hall, ed., *The Oxford Companion to the Supreme Court of the United States* (New York: Oxford University Press, 1992), pp. 651-53; and Philippa Strum, "Political Question," in Leonard W. Levy, Kenneth L. Karst, and Dennis J. Mahoney, eds., *Encyclopedia of the American Constitution* (New York: Macmillan, 1986): vol. 3, pp. 1420-22. The judicial doctrines of "ripeness" and "standing" can also be traced to an awareness of the inherent limitations on judicial power.

5. "Acte de gouvernement," in Olivier Duhamel and Yves Mény, eds., *Dictionnaire constitutionnel* (Paris: Presses Universitaire de France, 1992), pp. 6-8; L. Neville Brown and John S. Bell, *French Administrative Law,* 4th ed. (Oxford: Oxford University Press, 1993), pp. 151-57; M. Long et al., *Les Grands arrêts de la jurisprudence administrative,* 9th ed. (Paris: Sirey, 1990), pp. 29-38. [Hereafter I shall cite this book as GAJA, the name used by French law students when referring to it.]

6. GAJA, p. 30.

7. Ibid., p. 31. My comment in the text that the Council of State relied "implicitly" on David's position is based on this same commentary (p. 30). The commentator does not explain this remark, but I believe it reflects the fact that the Council of State upheld the decision of the minister of war without accepting the minister's broad interpretation of "acts of government" as encompassing all acts motivated by political considerations. That is, the council found a different reason to uphold the minister from the reason he himself put forward and it thereby implicitly rejected his position.

8. Ibid. *Barel* is reported in GAJA at pp. 524-31.

9. The acts of government doctrine has been further narrowed by the theory of the *acte détachable,* by which the administrative judge retains jurisdiction over a "detachable" administrative act that occurs within the broader context of an act of government. See Brown and Bell, *French Administrative Law,* p. 156. Despite these

inroads on the doctrine of "acts of government," the doctrine itself retains considerable vitality. See, for example, the extremely important decision of the Council of State in *Rubin de Servens* on 2 March 1962, reported in GAJA at pp. 589–607.

10. See the text that accompanies notes 71–82 in chapter 5.

11. *Marbury v. Madison,* 1 Cranch 137 (1803) at 168.

12. *Luther v. Borden,* 7 Howard 1 (1849).

13. GAJA, p. 32.

14. *Baker v. Carr* 369 U.S. 186 (1962) at 217.

15. See in particular *Powell v. McCormack* 395 U.S. 486 (1969), and *INS v. Chadha,* 462 U.S. 919 (1983). Both of these cases seem to fall within Brennan's description of a political question, and yet the Supreme Court rendered a decision in each of them.

16. For a discussion of recent cases, see Grossman, "Political Questions."

17. "Acte de gouvernement" in Duhamel and Mény, pp. 6–7.

18. See *Lamotte,* CE 17 February 1950, which is discussed in Brown and Bell, *French Administrative Law,* pp. 162–65. These citations establish the importance of judicial review of administrative action in French law. The speculation in the text is my own.

19. Duhamel and Mény, "Acte de gouvernement," p. 8.

20. I characterize the "state action" doctrine as "curious and problematic" because, despite its enormous importance in American constitutional history, informed critics have often challenged its validity as an accurate interpretation of the meaning of the Fourteenth Amendment. The reasoning underlying the Supreme Court's decisions in the *Civil Rights Cases,* 109 U.S. 3 (1883) is particularly suspect. For a compelling critique of the "state action" doctrine within the broader context of explaining the Fourteenth Amendment as an effort to "complete" the Constitution, see Michael P. Zuckert, "Completing the Constitution: The Fourteenth Amendment and Constitutional Rights," *Publius: The Journal of Federalism* 22 (Spring 1992): 69–91.

21. Georges Vedel and Pierre Delvolvé, *Droit administratif,* 12th ed. (Paris: Presses Universitaires de France, 1992), vol. 1, p. 101.

22. Ibid., p. 102.

23. Kenneth C. Davis, *Administrative Law: Cases, Texts, Problems,* 6th ed. (St. Paul: West Publishing, 1976), p. 189.

24. *Muskopf v. Corning Hospital District,* 359 P.2d 457 (Cal. 1961). This case is discussed in Davis, *Administrative Law,* pp. 189–95.

25. *Dalehite v. U.S.,* 346 U.S. 15 (1953). The planning/operational distinction was applied in this case to the Federal Tort Claims Act. For a discussion of *Dalehite,* see Davis, *Administrative Law,* pp. 197–204. See also Bernard Schwartz, *Administrative Law,* 2d ed. (Boston: Little, Brown, 1984), pp. 569–72; and Walter Gellhorn, Clark Byse et al., *Administrative Law: Cases and Comments,* 8th ed. (Mineola, N.Y.: Foundation Press, 1987), pp. 1201–3.

26. *Dalehite v. U.S.,* at 57.

27. T. C., 8 February 1873, *Blanco,* Rec. 1er supplt. 61. GAJA, pp. 15–21.

28. GAJA, p. 15.

29. Vedel and Delvolvé, *Droit administratif,* p. 111. These authors refer to other

authors who so describe *Blanco*. Vedel and Delvolvé are more guarded in their assessment.

30. I refer to GAJA.

31. Brown and Bell, *French Administrative Law*, p. 125. I follow these authors' translation of *un besoin d'intérêt général* as "a public need." See Vedel and Delvolvé, *Droit administratif,* p. 112.

32. Guy Braibant, *Le Droit administratif français* (Paris: Presses Universitaires de France, 1988), p. 125.

33. GAJA, p. 79.

34. Brown and Bell, *French Administrative Law,* p. 127.

35. GAJA, p. 321.

36. Brown and Bell, *French Administrative Law,* pp. 127-28.

37. For a full discussion of the questions that escape the jurisdiction of the administrative courts, see ibid., pp. 131-44. Particular attention should be paid to the extremely important decision of the Constitutional Council of 23 January 1987 (#86-224 DC), discussed by ibid., pp. 131-33.

38. Ibid., p. 128.

39. T. C., 22 January 1921, Société Commerciale de l'Ouest Africain, Rec 91. (Reported in GAJA, pp. 219-28.)

40. GAJA, p. 220; Brown and Bell, *French Administrative Law,* pp. 128-29.

41. Brown and Bell, *French Administrative Law,* p. 129.

42. Ibid., p. 137.

43. Within the federal government, the struggle between ordinary courts and administrative courts is much more one-sided than in France. The ordinary courts— i.e., the federal courts created under article 3 of the U.S. Constitution—almost always have the last word. In American administrative law, the major jurisdictional questions turn on what sorts of actions can be *initiated* before an administrative law judge and on how much deference a reviewing court should show to the findings of an administrative tribunal. See the discussion of *Universal Camera Corp. v. NLRB,* 340 U.S. 474 (1951), in chapter 5.

44. The two *Brown* cases, commonly known as *Brown I* and *Brown II,* are reported at 347 U.S. 483 (1954) and 349 U.S. 294 (1955), respectively.

45. See, for example, *Loving v. Virginia,* 388 U.S. 1 (1967).

46. On the validity of the "state action" doctrine as an interpretation of the Fourteenth Amendment, see note 20 of this chapter.

47. *Burton v. Wilmington Parking Authority,* 365 U.S. 715 (1961).

48. Kenneth L. Karst, *"Burton v. Wilmington Parking Authority"* in Levy, Karst, and Mahoney, *Encyclopedia of the American Constitution,* vol. 1, p. 185.

49. *Burton v. Wilmington Parking Authority,* at 722.

50. *Moose Lodge v. Irvis,* 407 U.S. 163 (1972); *Jackson v. Metropolitan Edison Co.,* 419 U.S. 163 (1972); *Marsh v. Alabama,* 326 U.S. 501 (1946).

51. See, for example, *Peterson v. Greenville,* 373 U.S. 244 (1963); *Robinson v. Florida,* 378 U.S. 153 (1964); *Lombard v. Louisiana,* 373 U.S. 267 (1963); *Griffin v. Maryland,* 378 U.S. 130 (1964).

52. For the Supreme Court's treatment of private discrimination cases after 1964, see *Jones v. Alfred H. Mayer Co.,* 392 U.S. 409 (1968); *Moose Lodge v. Irvis,*

407 U.S. 163 (1972); *Runyon v. McCrary,* 427 U.S. 160 (1976); *Patterson v. McLean,* 491 U.S. 164 (1989); and the Civil Rights Act of 1991. Prior to the great changes brought about by the civil rights movement of the 1960s, the most important "state action" case was *Shelley v. Kraemer,* 334 U.S. 1 (1948).

53. Braibant, *Le Droit administratif français,* p. 231.

54. Jean-Paul Costa, "Le Principe de proportionalité dans la jurisprudence du Conseil d'Etat," *L'Actualité Juridique—Droit Administratif* (20 July/20 August 1988): 434–37.

55. Brown and Bell, *French Administrative Law,* p. 241.

56. GAJA, pp. 659–60.

57. Ibid., p. 661.

58. Ibid., p. 659.

59. *Recueil des décisions du Conseil d'Etat* (Lebon) (Paris: Editions Sirey, 1972): *Société civile Sainte-Marie de l'Assomption,* 20 October 1972.

60. GAJA, p. 666.

61. Brown and Bell, *French Administrative Law,* p. 219.

62. Ronny Abraham, "La Convention européenne des droits de l'homme et les mesures d'éloignement d'étrangers,' *Revue française de droit administratif* 7 (May–June 1991): 497–571.

63. Martin Shapiro, "Balancing Test," in Levy, Karst, and Mahoney, *Encyclopedia of the American Constitution,* vol. 1, p. 94.

64. *Rankin v. McPherson,* 483 U.S. 378, 107 S. Ct. 2891 (1987) at 2895.

65. Ibid., at 2901.

66. Ibid., at 2902 and 2904.

67. Ibid., at 2904. For a discussion of the constitutional principles underlying *Rankin,* see *Connick v. Myers,* 103 S. Ct. 1684 (1983), and *Cleveland Board of Education v. Loudermill,* 470 U.S. 532 (1985). The best known criticism of the balancing test will be found in two famous dissents by Justice Black: *Konigsberg v. State Bar of California,* 366 U.S. 36 (1961) and *Barenblatt v. U.S.,* 360 U.S. 109 (1959).

68. GAJA, p. 286. C. E., 19 May 1933, *Benjamin,* Rec. 541. This case is discussed in Braibant, *Le Droit administratif francais,* p. 227.

69. Benjamin claimed that the mayor's action was motivated by political considerations rather than any genuine concern for public order. The Council of State did not address this issue. GAJA, p. 287.

70. GAJA, p. 287.

71. T. C., 8 April 1935, *Action Française,* rec. 1226. GAJA, pp. 297–302.

72. The Tribunal of Conflicts found that the case involved *une voie de fait.* GAJA, p. 297. The meaning of *voie de fait* is discussed in the last section of this chapter.

73. GAJA, p. 297.

74. Ibid., p. 298.

75. The structure of constitutional argument described in the text also applies to certain questions of racial discrimination, *Regents of the University of California v. Bakke,* 438 U.S. 265 (1978), and to certain "fundamental" rights unrelated to the first amendment, *Shapiro v. Thompson,* 394 U.S. 618 (1969).

76. Variations on the tests mentioned in the text are "paramount" interests for "compelling" ones and "least restrictive means" for "no alternative means."

77. 374 U.S. 398 (1963). The scope of the holding in *Sherbert v. Verner* seemed to be sharply narrowed by the Supreme Court's opinion in *Employment Division v. Smith,* 494 U.S. 872 (1990). Three years later, however, in *Church of the Lukumi Babalu Aye, Inc. v. City of Hialeah,* 113 S. Ct. 2217 (1993), the court seemed to return to its traditionally generous interpretation of the free exercise of religion. See Stephen L. Carter, "The Resurrection of Religious Freedom," *Harvard Law Review* 107 (November 1993): 118–42.

78. Brown and Bell, *French Administrative Law,* pp. 175–76. My discussion of *faute de service* follows Brown and Bell very closely. See ibid., pp. 174–83.

79. Ibid., p. 177. The case in question was *Pelletier,* T.C., 30 July 1873, rec. 1er supplt 117. It is reported in GAJA, pp. 22–29.

80. Brown and Bell, *French Administrative Law,* p. 177. The quotation is from M. Laferrière, the representative of the government before the Tribunal of Conflicts in the *Laumonnier-Carriol* decision of 5 May 1877, Rec. 437. GAJA, p. 27.

81. Brown and Bell, *French Administrative Law,* p. 177.

82. Ibid.

83. Rec. 146; GAJA, pp. 143–46.

84. GAJA, p. 144; pp. 199–204.

85. GAJA, p. 199. 26 July 1918, rec. 761.

86. The legal maneuvers are explained in GAJA, p. 199.

87. Brown and Bell, *French Administrative Law,* p. 178. The French text is given in GAJA, p. 202.

88. Brown and Bell, *French Administrative Law,* p. 178, commenting on *Mimeur,* C.E., 18 November 1949, rec. 492; GAJA, pp. 425–30.

89. Brown and Bell, *French Administrative Law,* p. 179, citing the conclusion of Antoine Bernard in "another case," which the authors do not identify.

90. Ibid.

91. Ibid., p. 179, citing *Sadoudi,* C.E., 26 October 1973.

92. Ibid., citing *Litzler,* C.E., 23 June 1954.

93. Ibid., p. 180.

94. Ibid., citing *Delville* and *Laruelle.* Both cases were decided by the Council of State on 28 July 1951. GAJA, pp. 471–84.

95. Brown and Bell, *French Administrative Law,* pp. 180–81.

96. *U.S. v. Lee,* 106 U.S. 196 (1882) at 220.

97. Philip L. Merkel, "Sovereign Immunity," in Hall, *Oxford Companion to the Supreme Court,* p. 806.

98. *Black's Law Dictionary,* p. 1010.

99. Merkel, "Sovereign Immunity," p. 806.

100. *U.S. v. Lee,* at 207. Cited by Kenneth C. Davis, *Administrative Law and Government,* 2d ed. (St. Paul: West Publishing, 1975), p. 96. Davis heads the list of American jurists who savagely criticize the sovereign immunity doctrine. See Davis, *Administrative Law,* p. 220. Justice Holmes was singing out of chorus when he defended sovereign immunity in his majority opinion in *Kanananakoa v. Polybland,* 205 U.S. 349 (1906) at 353.

101. Clyde Jacobs, "Sovereign Immunity," in Levy, Karst, and Mahoney, *Encyclopedia of the American Constitution,* vol. 4, p. 1714.

102. 5 U.S.C. §§702-3. See Davis, *Administrative Law,* p. 220.

103. Jacobs, "Sovereign Immunity," p. 1714.

104. *Black's Law Dictionary,* p. 1568.

105. A good overview of the development of the substantive legal principles governing the liability of public officials will be found in Phillip J. Cooper, *Public Law and Public Administration* (Englewood Cliffs, N.J.: Prentice-Hall, 1988), pp. 361-95.

106. See, for example, *Ex parte Young,* 209 U.S. 123 (1908).

107. Alfred H. Kelly, Winfred A. Harbison, and Herman Belz, *The American Constitution: Its Origin and Development,* 7th ed. (New York: W. W. Norton, 1991), vol. 2, p. 703.

108. 42 U.S.C. §1983. Other surviving remnants of the 1871 Civil Rights Act are codified at 42 U.S.C. §1985 and 28 U.S.C. §1343. Important provisions retained from other civil rights legislation of the Reconstruction era include 18 U.S.C. §§241, 242, and 1581 and 42 U.S.C. §§1981, 1982, 1986, and 1994.

109. *Will v. Michigan Department of State Police,* 109 S. Ct. 2304 (1989). *Will* provides a discussion of the circumstances under which the immunity of the state itself is extended to its officers in suits for money damages. Officials, however, are far more vulnerable in suits for injunctive relief. See David H. Rosenbloom, "Public Administrative Liability for Constitutional Torts, the Rehnquist Court, and Public Administration," *Administration and Society* 24 (August 1992): 122-23. Whatever comfort state officials might have found in *Will's* discussion of suits for money damages was removed by *Hafer v. Melo,* 116 L. Ed. 2d 301 (1991). Without disturbing *Will's* holding that states are not "persons" under 42 U.S.C. 1983, the *Hafer* Court clearly affirmed the liability of state officers in suits brought against them for wrongs committed even when acting in their official capacity.

110. *Monell v. New York City Department of Social Services,* 436 U.S. 658 (1978).

111. Cooper, *Public Law and Public Administration,* p. 373, citing *Owen v. City of Independence,* 445 U.S. 622 (1980) at 638-39.

112. 98 S. Ct. 2018 at 2036.

113. Vedel and Delvolvé, *Droit administratif,* vol. 1, p. 145.

114. Brown and Bell, *French Administrative Law,* p. 136.

115. Braibant, *Le Droit administratif francais,* p. 181.

116. Both administrative and ordinary courts may declare a *voie de fait* null and void, but ordinary courts alone adjudicate the perpetrators' responsibility. See Raymond Guillien and Jean Vincent, *Lexique de termes juridiques,* 8th ed. (Paris: Dalloz, 1990), pp. 499-500. Detailed discussions of the intracacies of *voie de fait* will be found in Vedel and Delvolvé, *Droit administratif,* vol. 1, pp. 140-48 and in GAJA, pp. 297-304. Brown and Bell, *French Administrative Law,* present a shorter discussion at pages 135-36.

117. Vedel and Delvolvé, *Droit administratif,* vol. 1, p. 141.

118. Ibid., p. 147.

119. Ibid.

120. Ibid., p. 147.

121. *Federalist* 47–51. Publius grounds his discussion of separation of powers in a matter no less important than avoiding tyranny. The relationship in French law between the doctrine of separation of powers, on the one hand, and the separation of the judicial and administrative functions on the other is complicated by the fact that in France the judiciary, strictly speaking, is not a "power" but an "authority." Nevertheless, the separation between the judicial and administrative spheres is often considered to be part of the principle of separation of powers. For an explicit statement to this effect, see Duhamel and Mény, *Dictionnaire constitutionnel,* p. 970. The Constitutional Council addressed the question of the constitutional status of the separation of judicial from administrative functions in its decision of 23 January 1987, which might be generously described as less than a model of clarity. See Louis Favoreu et Loïc Philip, *Les Grandes décisions du Conseil Constitutionnel,* 6th ed. (Paris: Sirey, 1991), pp. 709–23. Americans struggling with the subtleties of the separation of administrative and judicial functions in French law will draw some comfort from French jurists who characterize the question as one marked by "singular complexity and extraordinary confusion" (Duhamel and Mény, *Dictionnaire constitutionnel,* p. 971).

122. *Gravel v. U.S.,* 408 U.S. 606 (1972); *Hutchinson v. Proxmire,* 443 U.S. 111 (1979); *Tenney v. Brandhove,* 341 U.S. 367 (1951). French parliamentarians also enjoy a form of immunity that is in some ways broader than that of their American colleagues. Members of the European Parliament enjoy a similar benefit throughout 1994. Bernard Tapie, the flamboyant entrepreneur turned politician, provided a fascinating example of how an "artful dodger" can manipulate parliamentary immunities to stay one step ahead of the law. See Bruno Abescat et al., "Tapie: l'addition," *L'Express,* 2 June 1994, pp. 8–10; Georges Valence, "L'Argent de Tapie," *L'Express,* 9 June 1994, pp. 28–30; Bruno Abescat et al., "Dans la gueule du Lyonnais"; *L'Express,* 9 June 1944, pp. 31–33; Gilles Gaetner, "Les Intrigues du 'Phocéa,'" *L'Express,* 9 June 1994, pp. 28–35.

123. *Harlow v. Fitzgerald,* 102 S. Ct. 2727 (1982) at 2738. It was no easy task for the Supreme Court to arrive at this sensible formulation. The Court's herculean efforts are recounted in Cooper, *Public Law and Public Administration,* pp. 380–85.

124. *Bradley v. Fisher,* 13 Wallace 335 (1871) at 351. For the immunity of prosecutors, see *Imbler v. Pachtman,* 424 U.S. 409 (1976).

125. 98 S. Ct. 1099 (1978).

126. Ibid. at 1104.

127. The Indiana statute conferring jurisdiction on circuit judges provided that they had "original exclusive jurisdiction in all cases at law and in equity whatsoever." It also conferred jurisdiction on them "over the settlement of estates and over guardianships, appellate jurisdiction as conferred by law, and jurisdiction over 'all other causes, matters and proceedings where exclusive jurisdiction thereof is not conferred by law upon some other court, board or officer.'" *Stump v. Sparkman* at 1105.

128. Ibid. at 1109.

129. Ibid. at 1111. See *Forrester v. White,* 108 S. Ct. 538 (1988), for a unanimous opinion upholding the liability of an Illinois judge under 42 U.S.C. §1983 for sexual discrimination in firing a female probation officer. In her opinion of the Court, Jus-

tice O'Connor drew a sharp distinction between judicial functions (wherein the judge's immunity is absolute) and administrative functions that happen to be performed by a judge (wherein absolute immunity does not apply). O'Connor's opinion emphasizes that the absolute immunity of the judge is *functional* rather than personal. Disciplinary actions taken against probation officers are not judicial acts, even when performed by a judge.

CONCLUSION

1. Brian Chapman, *The Profession of Government* (London: Unwin University Books, 1959), pp. 240–41; L. Neville Brown and J. F. Garner, *French Administrative Law,* 3d ed. (London: Butterworths, 1983), p. 41; Walter Rice Sharp, *The French Civil Service: Bureaucracy in Transition* (New York: Macmillan, 1931; reprinted by AMS Press, New York, 1971), p. 74; Alfred Cobban, *A History of Modern France* (New York: Penguin Books, 1963, 1984), vol. 2, p. 22; Ernest Barker, *The Development of Public Services in Western Europe: 1660–1930* (Oxford: Oxford University Press, 1944; reprinted by Archon Books, Hamden, Conn., 1966) 14; Willam Safran, *The French Polity,* 3d ed. (New York: Longman, 1991), p. 208; Henry W. Ehrmann and Martin A. Schain, *Politics in France,* 5th ed. (New York: Harper-Collins, 1992), p. 358.

2. See also *Federalist* 37 and 63.

3. John Bell, *French Constitutional Law* (Oxford: at the Clarendon Press, 1992), pp. 84–85.

4. See chapter 4, note 122.

5. I have developed this point more fully in *To Run a Constitution: The Legitimacy of the Administrative State* (Lawrence: University Press of Kansas, 1986). See especially chapters 6 and 11.

6. See Preface, note 5.

7. Larry M. Lane, "The Public Administration and the Problem of the Presidency," paper prepared for presentation at the National Training Conference of the American Society for Public Administration (Kansas City, Mo.: July 1994), pp. 14–20 and *passim.*

8. A comprehensive review of the Civil Service Reform Act ten years after its passage will be found in Patricia W. Ingraham and David H. Rosenbloom, eds., *The Promise and Paradox of Civil Service Reform* (Pittsburgh: University of Pittsburgh Press, 1992).

9. *United Public Workers v. Mitchell,* 330 U.S. 75 (1947) and *U.S. Civil Service Commission v. National Association of Letter Carriers, AFL-CIO,* 413 U.S. 548 (1973).

10. Francis de Baecque, "Les fonctionnaires à l'assaut du pouvoir politique," *Pouvoirs* 40 (1987): 73. The remarkable increase in 1981 was due to the substantial increase in the number of teachers in the National Assembly at that time. This was the first Socialist government in the Fifth Republic, and teachers are heavily represented in the Socialist party.

11. Serge Salon and Jean-Charles Savignac, *La Fonction Publique* (Paris: Sirey, 1985), p. 242. For a somewhat different view of the loyalty civil servants should have to the government of the day, see the remarks of Prime Minister Chirac at an ENA conference on 20 October 1975. Salon and Savignac, 243.

12. Jean-Yves Vincent, "L'Obligation de réserve des agents publics," *La Revue Administrative* 26 (March–April 1973): 144.

13. Salon and Savignac, *La Fonction Publique,* p. 243.

14. Ibid., p. 242.

15. Jean Rivero, "Sur L'obligation de réserve," *Actualité Juridique: Droit Administratif* (December 1977): 583.

16. Ibid.

17. Vincent, "L'Obligation de réserve," p. 278. Plenel was not a model civil servant. Earlier he had been recalled to France from Martinique for criticizing the government. His sojourn in Algeria took place without permission from the ministry of education. He was charged with the offense of *abandon de poste.*

18. C.E., 18 May 1956, *Boddaert,* Recueil Lebon, 213. See also the conclusions of M. Heumann, the representative of the government in *Revue Pratique de Droit Administratif* (1956), p. 105. The constitutional mandate appears in the preamble to the Constitution of the Fourth Republic (1946). For a discussion of the important *Obrego* case and other aspects of the obligation of reserve for union officials, see Christine Bréchon-Moulènes, "Obligation de réserve et liberté syndicale: A propos de l'arrêt Demoiselle Obrego." *Actualité Juridique: Droit Administratif* (July–August 1973): 339-52.

19. Vincent, "L'Obligation de réserve," p. 276; citing C.E., 13 March 1953, *Tessier.* This case is reported in GAJA at p. 502. For full reference to GAJA, see chapter 7, note 5.

20. Vincent, "L'Obligation de réserve," pp. 277-78; citing addresses by M. Pleven at *L'Ecole nationale de la magistrature* (reported in *Le Monde,* 14 December 1972) and before the Senate (reported in the *Journal Officiel,* Débats Sénat, 7 December 1972: 2761). See also "Portée de l'obligation de réserve des magistrats" *Actualité Juridique: Droit Administratif* (January 1973): 31-44.

21. Vincent, "L'Obligation de réserve," pp. 278-79.

22. C.E., 28 May 1954, *Barel:* Recueil Lebon, 308. *Barel* is also reported in GAJA at p. 524.

23. Vincent, "L'Obligation de réserve," p. 145; Rivero, "Sur L'obligation de réserve," *passim.*

24. Vincent, "L'Obligation de réserve," p. 145.

25. *Texas v. Johnson,* 109 S. Ct. 2533 (1989). The appellee in this case was not a civil servant, but nothing in the reasoning of the Court would exclude such a person from exercising the constitutional right to burn the flag as a form of symbolic speech, provided, of course, that the civil servant took this action on his own time and did nothing to suggest that he was acting in an official capacity.

26. *Rankin v. McPherson,* 483 U.S. 378 (1987).

27. Rivero, "Sur L'obligation de réserve," *passim.* There is a certain irony in contrasting the rigidity of American law with the flexibility of French law. Ordinarily, the situation is reversed, because equity jurisdiction is much more important in com-

mon law countries than in France. The *Conseil d'Etat,* however, is an administrative court and, as such, escapes many of the rigidities that the French legal tradition imposes upon ordinary courts *(ordre judiciaire).*

28. Ibid., p. 583.

29. Vincent, "L'Obligation de réserve," p. 274, citing C.E., 9 July 1965, *Pouzenc.*

30. Rivero, "Sur L'obligation de réserve," p. 580.

31. Ibid., p. 581.

32. Ibid., p. 583.

33. Ibid.

34. Ibid., p. 581.

35. The document was entitled *"Gouverner autrement"* ("To govern in a different way"), *Journal Officiel,* 27 May 1988.

36. "Le Service public at la déontologie," Institut des Techniques d'Administration (ITAP) No. 49–50 (September 1985), p. 65.

37. Ibid., p. 4.

38. Rivero, "Sur L'obligation de réserve," p. 580.

39. La Modernisation du secteur public et la Relation de Service; Colloque: "A quoi servent les usagers," 16–17–18 January 1991, Paris. RATP, PLAN URBAIN, DRI.

40. Remarks of Daniel Causse at ITAP Round Table cited in note 36, p. 45.

41. Michel Reydellet, "L'Obligation de réserve des agents publics," Thèse pour le Doctorat d'Etat en droit: Université de Droit, d'Economie, et des Sciences d'Aix-Marseille, 1977, part 1: pp. 6 and 26.

42. Vincent, "L'Obligation de réserve," p. 142.

43. Woodrow Wilson, "The Study of Administration," *Political Science Quarterly* 2 (1887); reprinted in J. M. Shafritz and A. C. Hyde, eds., *Classics of Public Administration* (Oak Park, Ill.: Moore, 1978), p. 11.

44. See papers presented at ITAP Round Table cited above (note 36) and at the conference sponsored jointly by RATP, DRI, and PLAN URBAIN also cited above (note 39).

45. Reydellet, "L'Obligation de réserve des agents publics," p. 7, and Vincent, "L'Obligation de réserve," p. 143.

46. Marie-France Toinet, "La morale bureaucratique: Perspectives transatlantiques et Franco-américaines, *Revue Internationale de Science Politique* 9 (July 1988): 196.

47. Michel-Henry Fabre, "Le Serment politique: Etude constitutionnelle, 1789–1941," Ph.D. thesis, Université d'Aix-Marseille: Faculté de droit d'Aix, 1941, pp. 22–23.

48. Maurice Duverger, ed., *Constitutions et documents politiques,* Themis: Textes et documents. (Paris: Presses universitaires de France, n.d.), p. 18. Constitution of 3 September 1791: Title 3, Chap. 2, Sec. 1, Art. 4.

49. Ibid., pp. 21–22. Sec. 4, Art. 3. This article does not actually state the wording of the oath, but it obliges civil servants to take the *serment civique* ("civic oath"), the text of which was given in the decree of 27 April–25 May 1791.

50. Fabre, "Le Serment politique," pp. 200–201. In the United States, the early years of the Revolutionary War brought a flurry of oath-taking in the wake of victo-

rious armies. This prompted Benjamin Franklin to remark, "I have never regarded oaths otherwise than as the last recourse of liars." Leonard W. Levy, Kenneth L. Karst, and Dennis J. Mahoney, eds., *Encyclopedia of the American Constitution* (New York: Macmillan, 1986), vol. 3, p. 1182.

51. The Second Republic fell in 1851 and the reestablishment of oath-taking for civil servants occurred in the following year. The head of state continued to take an oath throughout the short-lived Second Republic. Fabre, "Le Serment politique," pp. 26 and 47.

52. Ibid., pp. 166 and 27-28.

53. Ibid., p. 13. The January 1941 text provides in part: "The secretaries of State, the dignitaries and the high-ranking civil servants of the State, shall take an oath before the head of State. They shall swear fidelity to his person and shall commit themselves to carry out their duties for the good of the State, in accordance with the laws of honor and propriety."

54. An affirmative oath is an oath to uphold the Constitution *in the future*. In contrast a negative oath or "test oath" relates to one's past activities and associations. "McCarthyism" of the 1950s is associated with the latter. Certain forms of test oaths have been declared bills of attainder and therefore unconstitutional. See *Ex parte Garland,* 4 Wallace 333 (1867), and *Cummings v. Missouri,* 4 Wallace 277 (1867).

55. For the text of these laws, see Yves Mény, ed., *Textes constitutionnels et documents politiques* (Paris: Montchrestien, 1989), pp. 218-23. For the fundamental principles of French republicanism, see Jean-Jacques Rousseau, *The Social Contract,* book 2.

56. Fabre, "Le Serment politique," p. 87.

57. American civil servants are free, of course, to call for amendments to the Constitution because the Constitution itself recognizes the legitimacy of amendments. Thus without in any way compromising their oath of office, civil servants could support the Equal Rights Amendment, a presidential line-item veto, English as the official language of the United States, statehood for the District of Columbia, etc.

58. Jean Rivero, *Les Libertés publiques,* 4th ed. (Paris: Presses universitaires de France, 1989), vol. 2, pp. 152-53. For an affirmation in American constitutional law of the absolute character of the right to believe as one wishes, see *Cantwell v. Connecticut,* 310 U.S. 296 (1940).

59. Former presidents of the Republic are also members of the Constitutional Council, but they are not required to take an oath. See "Ordonnance No. 58-1067 du 7 novembre 1958 portant loi organique sur le Conseil constitutionnel," reprinted in Jean-Marie Auby and Jean-Bernard Auby, eds., *Code de droit public* (Paris: Prat/ Europa, 1985), p. 236.

60. There are other historical reasons besides the three mentioned in the text. For example, some French citizens point to the religious background of oaths as being inconsistent with the secular character of contemporary France. They fear that a requirement to take an oath might reopen some painful religious controversies that have been so divisive in France. In addition, the Constitution of the Fifth Republic is a Gaullist document. In 1958, requiring the general's political enemies within the civil service to swear to uphold *his* constitution would have been unfair and unwise.

Today, of course, the general's memory is revered and celebrated. Twenty-five years after his death, he is far less controversial than he was at the height of his power. A required oath today would probably meet little resistance on anti-Gaullist grounds, regardless of what other objections might be raised.

61. Rohr, *To Run a Constitution,* pp. 77–84, 181–86.

62. Auby and Auby, *Code de droit public,* p. 236.

63. For a discussion of the distinction between professional and political oaths, see Fabre, "Le Serment politique," p. 15 and *passim.*

64. Although the Constitutional Council is not really a court, some of its procedures and the format of its decisions are judicial in character. French appellate courts do not issue concurring or dissenting opinions. Hence, secrecy is an important aspect of the judicial process even after a case has been decided. The same is true of the Constitutional Council. The emphasis on secrecy is apparent in the professional oath taken by French magistrates today: "I swear to observe religiously the professional obligation of secrecy and to conduct myself in all circumstances as a worthy and loyal officer of justice." Interestingly, this oath, unlike that of the Constitutional Council, does not even mention the 1958 Constitution. The word "loyal," however, is intriguing: loyal to whom or to what? See *Le Monde,* 8 February 1991, p. 14.

65. *West Virginia State Board of Education v. Barnette,* 319 U.S. 624 (1943).

66. David. H. Rosenbloom, "The Citizen as Public Bureaucrat," in *Public Administration and Law: Bench v. Bureau in the the United States* (New York: Marcel Dekker, 1983), pp. 99–139.

67. *Cole v. Richardson,* 405 U.S. 676 (1972). The severity of the demand to uphold the Constitution is softened by the fact that the Constitution itself expresses principles of government that embody deliberation and, therefore, the possibility of orderly change. This is not to deny that the compulsory oath imposes adherence to political orthodoxy, but the prescribed orthodoxy itself expresses a political order conducive to reflection, deliberation, and prudence.

68. The fact that the French are a people in a way that Americans are not helps to explain the strikingly different attitudes toward immigration in the two countries.

Index